P9-DJK-325

Politics and the Labor Movement in Latin America

Politics and the Labor Movement in Latin America

VICTOR ALBA

ST. JOSEPH'S UNIVERSITY

HD6530.5.A7213   STX
Politics and the labor movement in Latin

3 9353 00087 3990

HD
6530.5
A 7213
LAS

130618

Stanford University Press   Stanford, California   1968

This work originally appeared in Mexico in 1964 under the title *Historia del movimiento obrero en America latina*. In the process of overseeing the translation, which is by Carol de Zapata, the author has considerably revised and reorganized the original material.

Stanford University Press
Stanford, California
© 1968 by the Board of Trustees of the
Leland Stanford Junior University
L.C. 66-15298
Printed in the United States of America

Publication of this book was assisted by a grant from the Rockefeller Foundation and the Latin American Translation Program of the Association of American University Presses.

Author's Note

STUDIES OF THE LABOR MOVEMENT of Latin America are scarce. More-over, the available studies do not deal with Latin American labor in its po-litical context, nor do they analyze the ideological content of the programs and actions of the Latin American unions—yet these unions spring from an essentially ideological base. Without a knowledge of this aspect of Latin American labor, there can be no real understanding of the substantial role labor has played and will continue to play in Latin American politics. This book is an attempt to supply the wherewithal for such an understanding.

In 1953 I wrote a brief history of the Latin American labor movement for Les Editions Ouvrières of Paris. In 1963 I wrote a detailed history of the same movement, emphasizing its political and ideological aspects, for a Mexican publisher. The present book is a completely rewritten, revised, and updated version of the Spanish-language edition.

Because my involvement with the labor movement is so deep, I wish to emphasize the objectivity of the facts I have presented and the exclusively personal character of my interpretation of them. In keeping with these thoughts, I wish to dedicate the book to my wife, whose reasoned skepti-cism has frequently given balance to my enthusiasm and stubborn optimism.

V.A.

October 1967

Contents

PART I

Background

1. Introduction

THE LABOR MOVEMENT, in Latin America as elsewhere, may be considered from either of two standpoints. It can be seen as a simple aggregate of labor organizations, an aggregate concerned with defending the immediate interests of these organizations, and, through them, of the working class. Or it can be seen as the expression, in the age of industrialization, of an ancient tradition of social nonconformism, the refusal to accept society as it is and the desire to transform it. We shall deal in this study with the labor movement in the second sense, and in both of its principal aspects as a movement in this sense: the political aspect (with its anarcho-syndicalist, socialist, Communist, populist, and Social-Christian components), and the trade union aspect.

Only the bare beginnings of a working class exist in Latin America. Out of approximately 226 million people (estimated 1965 population) there are only 25 to 30 million workers or employees, many of them still essentially artisans in mentality and techniques. In rural areas industrial methods of work are little developed and exist alongside genuine serfdom. Even in industry one finds vestiges of the feudal relationships: mines, for example, that employ laborers whose salaries are paid to their "owners."

Tables 1–5, in the Appendix, show various aspects of labor's distribution in recent years, in nine countries that together make up a representative unit. Population growth has been rapid (Table 5), but the working class is growing at a lower rate than the population in general—a rare thing in an industrializing society that is still far from automation. Because industrialization has been so recent, the proletariat in Latin America is still tied to the soil. The workingman is born in the country, and his parents still live in a village. It has been middle-class city dwellers, intellectuals, professional men, students, and a few specialized workers who have fought through the years for a change in Latin American society. The political struggle has affected very few. When great upheavals stir a nation only a handful of those participating are politically motivated, and fewer still have a clear-cut political philosophy.

And there is the racial factor. Negroes, Indians, mestizos (crossbreeds of Indian and white), zambos (crossbreeds of Indians and Negroes), mulattoes, and whites are all legally entitled to the same rights. But subtle social inequalities persist. Precisely because the problem has appeared not in terms of "legal" injustice, but in psychological and economic terms, social progress has been hindered.

The white population is socially in the ascendent, as might be expected. In addition to persons of more or less pure Spanish and Portuguese ancestry, there are several generations of immigrants, chiefly from Europe. From 1850 to 1950, some 17 million immigrants came to Latin America: 7 million to Argentina, 4 million to Brazil, 2 million to Chile, 1.5 million to Cuba, 1 million to Uruguay, and 500,000 to Mexico. They came from Italy (6 million), Spain (4 million), Germany (2 million), Portugal (1 million), the Far East (1 million), Russia (500,000), the Near East (500,000), and a scattering of other countries. Half a million were Jews of various nationalities.

At present, 15 per cent of the Latin American people are Indians, and another 15 per cent or more are mestizos who live like Indians. In some countries the presence of great Indian masses has created important cultural and economic problems. In others there are problems with large Negro, mulatto, or zambo minorities. The importation of Negroes began during the sixteenth century, and by 1888, when slavery was abolished in Brazil, close to 50 million Negroes had been brought to the Spanish and Portuguese New World. At least one-fourth of Brazil's present-day population is Negro and mulatto; the same is true of Cuba and the Dominican Republic. In Haiti the percentage is much higher. At least 10 per cent of the entire population of Latin America is made up of Negroes or mulattoes. Since the percentage of economically active persons in any population is very low (barely 25 per cent), and since Indians and Negroes of both sexes commonly work from the time they are very young until they die, perhaps half the working population is Indian or Negro.

Only one-fourth of Latin America's Indians speak Spanish. The other three-fourths speak thirty-three different languages with more than 3,000 dialects. Only one-third wear shoes. Only 5 per cent enjoy a balanced diet. Coca leaves, marijuana, and alcohol keep many in a state of stupefaction. The Indian's very concept of life differs from that of the Western white man. As may be imagined, the existence of this human mass has greatly influenced the Latin American labor movement, and the problems it poses have fascinated reformers. Efforts at improving the Indians' lot, however, have been impeded by the Indians' inertia, and perhaps even by a fear that once they are mobilized for action, there will be no controlling them.

Any effort at reform must start with the land. Only one-third of Latin America's land mass is arable—the rest is desert, mountains, and jungle— and barely half of this tillable land is being worked. Of this, approximately one-fourth serves as pasture land. Properly and fully cultivated, this much land should satisfy the needs of the continent's entire population, with an enormous surplus for export. Unfortunately, neither proper cultivation nor equitable distribution has been the norm in Latin America.

The difficulty is chiefly the system of land tenure and exploitation. Land- holders fall into three categories: large landholders, called *latifundistas,* most of whom are absentee landlords; ranchers, who live on their property and employ local ranch hands; and rural farmers, to whom fall the most miserable plots, and whose relatives are generally forced to seek employ- ment on the *haciendas* or plantations.* Occasionally one encounters a share- cropper system, in which peasants work a landlord's land in return for a percentage (often half) of the resulting crop. In most Indian areas quasi- feudal customs from the colonial period still survive: personal service (*ya- naconazgo*), lashings (*huasipungo*), and a form of virtual slavery, *pon- gueage,* which obligates the Indian on a hacienda, at the owner's bidding, to work in the owner's house or on public works projects or in the mines. (The owner, of course, collects the wages for any outside work.) If the land is sold, the Indians pass to the next owner.

Very large landholdings are the norm, as a few figures will show. In Chile 1 per cent of the population controls 52 per cent of the land, and there are owners, "the 600 families" as they are called, each of whom claims over 35,000 acres. In Argentina 2,000 families hold one-fifth of the country's land area. One of them alone, in Buenos Aires province, owns 750,000 acres. Four families own 625,000 acres in Tierra del Fuego. In Mexico, before the 1910 Revolution, 1 per cent of the population held 85 per cent of all the arable land. In Brazil 64,000 landholders own 210 million acres, or more than 3,250 acres each. In Bolivia, where much of the land is too mountain- ous to be productive, 516 families owned the richest region, Yangas Valley, before the 1952 Revolution. In Venezuela 85 per cent of the land was di- vided into *hatos,* or large landholdings, of more than 5,000 acres each, be- fore the 1961 agrarian reform. In Paraguay there are reported to be 3,118 haciendas of over 2,000 acres each.

---

* Large landholdings are termed *latifundios* in most of Latin America, but specifi- cally are called *haciendas* in Mexico, *hatos* in Venezuela, and *fazendas* in Brazil.

On these large landholdings, little is produced, usually just enough for the owner's needs. Thus only 2.6 per cent of the tillable soil in Brazil is worked. Of 172.5 million cultivable acres in Venezuela only 1.8 million are worked. In Argentina, of 212.5 million usable acres only 65 million are under cultivation. Everywhere the latifundio is underfarmed.

Even so, Latin America today supplies the world with 90 per cent of all its coffee, 35 per cent of its cacao, 30 per cent of its sugar, 60 per cent of its bananas, 50 per cent of its linseed, 12 per cent of its cotton, and 40 per cent of its meat. Among nonagricultural exports are 18 per cent of the world's petroleum, 45 per cent of its silver, 7 per cent of its gold, 50 per cent of its vanadium, 18 per cent of its tin, 25 per cent of its nitrates, and 45 per cent of its hard woods. The continent exports, above all, raw materials.

But what becomes of this wealth? The Latin American businessman estimates, as normal and legal, that his profits amount to anywhere from 50 to 100 per cent. Industrial investment of national profits is only 11 per cent. Nor does much of it find its way into the public welfare. There are seventeen doctors for every 100,000 inhabitants, and of every 100,000 Latin Americans 230 die of tuberculosis. The average daily food intake amounts to only 2,150 calories.

The average annual per capita income is only $352, and this figure is misleadingly high for the bulk of the population, since the distribution of wealth is anything but even. Archaic tax systems increase the burden on the poor. Indirect taxes (which are hardest on the poor) represent 48 per cent of Argentina's total taxation, 25 per cent of Brazil's, 45 per cent of Colombia's, 28 per cent of Costa Rica's, 56 per cent of Chile's, 39 per cent of Guatemala's. Still worse, the expenses of the military typically absorb from 30 to 70 per cent of the national budget.

Furthermore, the Latin American economy depends almost entirely on the price fluctuations of certain basic export products. In the years previous to 1955 the annual economic growth rate was 2.6 per cent, but dropping prices on export goods have since forced it down to 1.1 per cent. Since the annual population increase rate is 2.6 per cent, even in peak years the economy growth figure never surpassed the population increase. It follows that the standard of living, instead of improving, continues to decline. Rural areas are hardest hit, but the demographic increase is an alarming fact throughout a continent where birth control is generally considered unacceptable.

In 1920 Latin America had a population of 85 million. In 1955 the figure was 155 million, an 82 per cent increase. In 1980 the estimated population will be 316 million. In the next twenty to forty years, nineteen of the world's countries will double their population; of that number, ten will be Latin American. Another strong deterrent to economic development in Latin America is the relative youth of the population. The average life expectancy, though it continues to increase, still holds at forty to fifty years, and 40 per cent of all Latin Americans are under fifteen.

In 1960 it was estimated that $30 billion in additional capital was needed to bring about the take-off of Latin American industrialization, that is, to establish an economic growth rate exceeding the rate of population increase. In the same year banks in Switzerland and elsewhere had close to $11 billion in Latin American deposits. If that amount had been invested at home, it might have greatly accelerated social and economic progress. There is seemingly no valid reason, then, for such overwhelming poverty to exist alongside such great potential wealth.

There have been many explanations of the low growth rate. Some point to the lack of coal (barely 1 per cent of world production), but on the other hand there is an abundance of petroleum and white coal. Others claim that the sources of raw materials are too scattered; but in Brazil, for instance, there are more raw materials than in Japan, Italy, or France. Some claim that effective agriculture is impossible at high altitudes and in dense tropical jungles, yet the Incan civilization was centered over 12,500 feet above sea level and its agricultural production was impressive, probably greater than today's output in the same area. The same is true of the Mayans in the tropical zones. The supposed laziness of Latin Americans, geographic obstacles to communication, and even crossbreeding have been offered as explanations, but all are easily refuted by counterexamples from more economically advanced countries.

It is in Latin America's economic history that we find the true explanation for its backwardness.

2. The Colonial Era

THE FIRST SPANISH CONQUERORS were rewarded generously with titles and lands. Cortez owned twenty-two towns, 115,000 Indians, and 25,000 square miles of territory. Francisco Pizarro was given 100,000 Indians and the title of Marquis of the Conquest. The German bankers Fruger and Welser received, as a guarantee against loans, the right to colonize in Venezuela, a privilege they never chose to pursue. The River Plate country was divided in 1580 among sixty-four Spanish captains. In Brazil the nobles who came after the conquest, the *donatarios,* received 200 miles to the north and south of a fixed point and all the land they could manage toward the interior, up to the line of Papal demarcation between Spanish and Portuguese territory. Some of them owned areas greater than Portugal itself.

More than landowners, these first conquerors were feudal lords who collected taxes, apart from those due the crown, from inhabitants on their lands. When these enormous holdings were later broken up and it became possible to purchase title to South American properties in Lisbon or Valladolid, the large landholdings mentioned earlier, the latifundios, began to appear.

When the Crown decided to impose its laws on these feudal landlords so recently come to power, the first uprisings broke out in Spanish America. Often the settlers of the newly created cities displayed open disregard for the king's envoys. Democracy of a sort appeared: the conquerors, alone against nature and the Indians, decided who should govern them and how. Just as the Spanish nobility had acquired its lands by taking them from the Moors, so the common people and *hidalgos* who sailed to America went convinced that in the New World they would find respect, that the lands they took would be considered their own. They presumed that only through them would their lands be related to the king, and accordingly appointed authorities to administer their great holdings. When the king

chose to appoint his own authorities, trouble came quickly. Defiant conquerors were often sent back to Spain in shackles, or were executed in the
public square. This spirit of rebellion, absent in the Indian, still has its
echoes today in Latin America.

On the other hand, in order to make use of the mines and fields the
conqueror needed hands and strong backs, which meant Indians. In the
beginning no one set out for America intending to work, only to command
and to seek a fortune. When a captain distributed lands among his soldiers,
he doled out Indians as well, without whose labor the fertile valleys would
have been as good as sterile. This was not slavery, only a personal sort of
loan, the classic *corvée* of feudalism. By contrast, the Crown's interest was
in freeing the Indians, in order to make them tax-paying subjects. This conflict of interests over the status of the Indian led to constant friction between
the conquerors and the Crown.

The *encomienda* appeared as a form of compromise. By this arrange-
ment, the settling conqueror to whom Indians were turned over remained
duty-bound to protect them and to instruct them in the Catholic faith; his
grandson, however, no longer had any rights over the Indians so chartered,
or any of their descendants. Thus the Council of the Indies hoped to convert
the Indians in two generations into loyal subjects of the Crown. The scheme
failed absolutely. The Crown's financial needs soon made it necessary to
grant new encomiendas, and the problem, though its acuteness diminished,
continued until 1720, when the system was finally abolished. The *encomendero,* or landowner entrusted with the keeping of his territory's people,
succeeded the conqueror, and continued to oppose all attempts by the
Crown to soften the circumstances of the Indians.

The laws of the Indies required that a permit be obtained from the authorities before land could be bought from the Indians; a Spaniard guilty
of a crime against an Indian was to be punished more severely than if his
action had been against another Spaniard; new distributions of Indians and
the payment of salary in kind were prohibited. All this in Seville. But in the
plantations of Cuba, the valleys of New Spain, the plains of New Granada,
and the mines of Potosí, these laws were simply ignored. The Crown tol-
erated this refusal to recognize its authority because it would otherwise have
been difficult to extract high taxes from the colonies, and the mines would
have produced less. The exploitation of Spanish America began thanks to
serfdom; correcting the situation was possible only by open revolution, a
revolution still unconsummated and still brewing today.

The Spanish rebels wanted two things: recognition of their political authority over the newly discovered lands, and the right to exploit the Indians. In the first objective they failed; the power of the Crown was empha-

sized and reaffirmed, and the royal officials sent from Spain always managed to impose their authority. In the second objective they succeeded; the encomendero, setting aside his ambitions for political power, managed to keep his encomienda in spite of the laws and actually in connivance with royal officials. Two kinds of oligarchy developed at the same time: the economic oligarchy of the landowners and the political oligarchy of the royal officials.

In the beginning there were protests on behalf of the Indians, chiefly from godly ecclesiastics like Friar Bartolomé de las Casas and Friar Vasco de Quiroga. The Church, as an institution, did not uphold them. The religious authorities were frequently at odds with the secular authorities but always sided with them against Indian uprisings. This was perfectly logical, since the Church was one of the chief property holders of the time: one-third of the city of Lima belonged to the missions, and one-fifth of all lands were held in unalienable Church estates (*manos muertas*). The immense majority of clergymen were Spaniards; among the first 400 bishops, only six were creoles and none was Indian.

The piety and zeal of these men as individuals were generally of a high order, and they were responsible for much admirable legislation designed to protect the Indians against exploitation. On balance, however, the weight of the Church was oppressive. In 1644 the inhabitants of Mexico City complained to the viceroy about the excessive numbers of clergymen in the city, in which there were no fewer than fifty-five missions. For some 100,000 Spanish colonists on the entire continent at that time, there were one patriarch, six archbishops, thirty-two bishops, and more than 800 missions. Each mission, as well as each individual ecclesiastical official, owned houses and lands. In the towns, the priests frequently imposed personal tributes and followed their own whims in setting the cost attached to the performance of religious services. In short, to the problems created by the latifundio and the encomienda we may add the problem of the unalienable estates.

THE INDIAN SITUATION

The Indians, under the encomienda system, had to work where their owners sent them. The Indian working in the mines had fixed duties, and he was punished for any failure to meet them. He had to buy food and clothing, *aguardiente,* coca leaves, and the candles for his underground labor, and he had to buy all these things in stores belonging to the mine owners. In addition to his encomienda duties, he was subjected to taxation by the Spanish magistrates—*corregidores*—whose pay consisted of a percentage of the taxes they collected. The corregidores decided how much tax the Indian should pay, and commonly collected far more than they reported to their superiors. Indians of all ages paid this tax, notwithstanding their having to beg in order to get the necessary money together. Those who failed to pay were beaten; those who paid were often given invalid receipts, and in a short time were required to pay again. Weavers were taxed on the legal salary they should have received; since they were in fact paid less, a large part of their salary went into the corregidor's pocket. If the corregidor owned a hacienda, Indians delinquent in their taxes had to work on it. In the event of a lawsuit, a judge might keep an Indian's cow to cover court expenses.

Indians living in settlements under the command of their *caciques* (chiefs or bosses), and therefore living according to their own customs, were privileged, in that they were not subjected to serfdom.* But even in such settlements there was always a civil servant, the "Indian protector," and a *doctrinario* priest, neither of whom, in most cases, either protected or instructed, and both of whom commonly used the Indians to work their own lands.

Thus exploitation was carried out not in a spectacular manner but rather as an everyday matter, directly and indirectly. The Indian's response was resignation. He withdrew into himself, and responded to his masters with silence or lies. He knew, because it was so often told him, which white men wished to defend him, and he knew that the white man's king protected him with his laws; his enemies, therefore, were not the monarch or his viceroy, but the corregidor, the encomendero, and the doctrinario.

When the corregidor set up a monopoly on the sale of merchandise in his district; when an Indian who had failed to pay his taxes was sent to work in a manufactory to work off the debt; when, during the Feast of the Dead, he saw all the inhabitants of the village, one after another, purchase the same bottle of wine—which was offered to the deceased—without even unwrapping it, the Indian said to himself that if the king should find out he would put a stop to such practices. For this reason, all Indian uprisings began with a declaration of loyalty to the king. It was only when the rebellion grew and the king issued orders to suppress it that the Indians' despair became tinged with separatist tones, particularly in areas where the memory of ancient Indian lords was still alive.

In Brazil the situation was different. The white colonists occupied the fringes of territory along the coast, and the Indian tribes, with no national state tradition to unite them, withdrew to the jungle. Adventurers organized expeditions to capture Indians and sell them as slaves, but this enterprise encountered Jesuit opposition and ultimately proved uneconomical.

* The caciques were typically mestizos, but quite often were Indians.

THE NEGRO SITUATION

If the Indian was a serf often treated like a slave, the Negro was a slave often treated like a serf. In the cities, and in private homes, he lived under a patriarchal regime, which to a certain point protected him. It was on the large plantations, where he lived and worked under the eye of the overseer, that his life became hardest and rebellions began sprouting.

The Indian had been subjected to a system of serfdom even before the arrival of the Spaniards, and under them felt no basic change. For the Negro, by contrast, the trip in the holds of the galleons was a break with his past, and he never stopped dreaming of returning. His uprisings were like a waking dream of this return to the African jungle. When the Indians rebelled, they wanted a change of authorities and a reduction of taxes; that is, they did not aspire to any essential reforms. When the Negroes rebelled, they broke with the whites and fled to the forests, where they founded their own societies. The Indian wanted mainly to soften his serfdom. The Negro wanted to erase slavery.

During the struggles for independence in the early nineteenth century, the Indians, for the most part, remained loyal to the king. Indians made up the bulk of the Spanish armies. The monarch was, for them, a protector; the creole, who fought for independence from Spain, was their immediate exploiter. The Negroes, unlike the Indians, saw Spain as the oppressor. The instant Bolívar and the other liberators proclaimed the abolition of slavery (even though it often remained only on paper), Negroes by the thousands joined the rebel armies.

The Portuguese, who even before the discovery of America had kept slave camps in Lagos, were the main Negro importers. The disproportion between the population of Portugal and the size of Brazil spurred the transport of Negroes to the enormous colony, and this traffic kept up unendingly for three centuries. The Negro was an economic factor of great importance in Brazil. His work made possible not only the exploitation of the tropical regions, but also a gold fever of almost half a century, the more remarkable for being centered on areas whose actual gold content was extremely low. The Negro population was also large in the colonies of the Antilles—Martinique, Guadeloupe, Jamaica, and Santo Domingo—and to a certain extent in the Guianas.

Slaves were brought from all corners of Africa, but since each shipment, especially in the beginning, served to populate a city or a region, it happened that Negroes coming from the same area preserved certain customs and traditions in common, which mixed later with the cursory Catholicism they were taught and were adapted to their new reality. Haitian voodoo has an ethnological origin very different from that of Bahia; the Brazilian samba is derived from a Bantu dance, whereas the rhumba has a Congolese origin. In Brazil and the Guianas can be found small groups of Negroes who still speak Arabic and whose religion is a mixture of Mohammedanism and Catholicism; they are called *males,* and are the descendants of the Mandigas, Negroes who had been converted to Islam before being captured. There is a common feature characteristic of all Latin American Negroes: their religious devotion. Among the few saints the continent has had is one Negro, the Peruvian friar Martín de Porres.

INDIAN REBELLIONS

Conditions among the Indians did not persist unprotested or unchallenged by royal or religious officials. But the officials never dared to suggest abolishing the system of rule, contenting themselves rather with offering measures to make the system more bearable: the suppression of corporal punishment among Indians and Negroes; the promotion of Indians to minor positions in the Spanish hierarchy; the punishment of whites who disrupted order in Indian settlements; judicial reforms making for impartiality between Indians and whites. What reforming zeal there was among high officials served, in part, to discourage any sort of group initiative or leadership on the part of the Indians. Of the many Indian uprisings not one was prepared and coordinated, and no secret Indian societies were formed. When the Indians did rebel they could always be subdued, because of the disorganization and spontaneity of their movements. The victim of an injustice commonly took his revenge as an individual and fled to the wilderness, where he became a bandit but not a rebel.

The first rebellion worthy of the name was that of the Indians in the mines of Tepic (Mexico) in 1598, as a protest against the oppressiveness of their labor. The Indians of Tehuantepec (Mexico) rebelled a century later, in 1680, and for eight years were the masters on their land. In Mexico City, in 1692, a famine resulting from a crop failure caused a mutiny of Spaniards, during which an Indian woman was killed; the Indians in the city responded by burning the city hall. This is the only example on record of an urban Indian uprising. In 1761, the Mayans of Yucatan rebelled in protest against excessive taxes and the right of the owners to beat them.

At the other end of the continent, in Chile, a powerful rebellion broke out in 1723, which put an end to some of the abuses of local officials. In 1740 the Calchaquíes of Tucumán (today Argentina) attacked the Spanish governor's forces because of the governor's insulting conduct toward their caciques; a full-scale war ensued, which lasted ten years. The Guaranies of Paraguay revolted in 1752 to protest a treaty transferring jurisdiction over them from Spain to Portugal; the fight lasted for three years, until at last the treaty was nullified. In New Granada, the Indians of the Hacha River region fought from 1761 to 1773 to secure the removal of certain oppressive officials; they were scattered, and their settlements were repopulated with Indians brought in from other regions.

In the areas where the memory of the Incan government was still alive, and where there existed a kind of formless national feeling, the rebellions spread over a wider range. Many of the rebel leaders were genuine descendants of the Inca; for the Spaniards had followed a policy of marrying Incan princesses, and their mestizo offspring provided many settlements with caciques.

The first of these Inca-inspired rebellions broke out in 1655, in Tucumán. Pedro Rodríguez, who was called Inca Hualpa, held out through twelve years of fighting in the Andes against the governor's troops, until he was captured and beheaded. Half a century later, Juan Santos, a mestizo from Oruro (Bolivia) who adopted the name Inca Atahualpa, led an uprising of Indians from the mines. The rebellion lasted from 1736 to 1750, and ended only when Santos was captured and executed. These rebels demanded a change in the local authorities, a reduction of taxes, and lower payments for religious services. Similar demands were made in the most important of all Indian uprisings, that of Tupac Amaru.

The leader of this uprising lived in the province of Tinta, in Peru, and was an authentic descendant of the last Inca, Tupac Amaru, beheaded in 1571. His name was José Gabriel Condorcanqui, and as the cacique of his village of Tungasuca, he had become rich. In 1780 he went to Lima to procure the benevolence of the Lords of the Audiencia for the Indians of the province of Chumbivilicas, who, enraged by the new taxes and the corregidor's brutality, had killed him. José Gabriel also requested that the corregidor in Tinta—one Arriaga, a vicious, arrogant, and implacable man who raised more taxes than any of his colleagues—be removed from his post.

When his request was denied, he kidnapped Arriaga and executed him after a brief trial. José Gabriel then raised a small army, and after a few local victories proclaimed himself Tupac Amaru II. His army grew to 40,000 men, and in time he gave the order to advance on Cuzco. The *cabildo* of the city, in fear, proclaimed that Indians remaining loyal would pay no more excise taxes, and need do no more work in *obrajes*—workshops in which the Indians were obliged to labor. But the obrajes were destroyed by Tupac Amaru's men, and the excise taxes, in any case, were not being paid.

Farther to the south, in Charcas (now in Bolivia), another rebellion flared up, and there were others in Palca, in Oruro, in San Pedro, in Tapacari. From as far away as Buenos Aires reinforcements were sent to hold back the rebels, and these disciplined forces helped turn the tide. Tupac Amaru was captured, seventy-seven of his commanders were executed, and his troops fled to the mountains. In Cuzco, Tupac Amaru endured torture without showing the slightest regret. "The only conspirators," he told the *visitador* sent by the viceroy, "are you and I—you for being an oppressor of the people and I, José Gabriel, for having tried to free them from tyranny." He and his wife and son were hanged the following day, May 18, 1781, in the public square of Cuzco.

NEGRO REBELLIONS

The Negroes were always less submissive than the Indians, and when they rebelled they were more radical in their demands. Some of their rebellions were remarkably successful. A slave uprising near Orizaba, in Mexico, led to the establishment of a free Negro town, San Lorenzo de los Negros, and to the suspension, for many decades afterward, of the importation of slaves. In Central America during the sixteenth century, runaway slaves—*cimarrones*—formed an organized bandit army for the purpose of attacking caravans transporting goods. After a military expedition against them failed, they were permitted to establish a kind of autonomous state of their own, Santiago del Príncipe, and in 1574 the Spaniards granted them their freedom in order to avoid another rebellion. They added to their territory and later began to mix with the local Indians. From that time on the Spaniards never ventured into the Mosquito Coasts.

Often British pirates relied on the slaves' cooperation. When Drake reached the port of Callao, hundreds of Negroes in Lima left the city and headed for the coast to serve him.

Farther to the south, in 1555, in the gold mines of Buria, Venezuela, a Negro miner proclaimed himself king and founded a city and an army, which lasted until his death in battle. The Negro revolt of Coro, Venezuela, in 1795, was inspired by a handful of deported French Jacobins, and the same year Negroes in Uruguay set up a kingdom on an island in the Yi River, using as their slogan that of the French Revolution. Toussaint L'Ouverture, the father of Haiti, was moved by the same two elements: the desire for a Negro "state" and the Jacobin example.

In the other Caribbean islands Negro uprisings were frequent, but were always suppressed. Negroes and mulattoes in Cuba were in the forefront of the island's struggles against Spain in the nineteenth century.

The most important Negro uprisings in Brazil took place during the nineteenth century. Between 1807 and 1835, the *males* (Moslems) in Bahia made seven successive efforts to wipe out Christian whites and establish a state under Allah's protection. The rebellion of Manuel Balaio, in Marañon, in 1839, led to a liberal revolt and ended with the decisive defeat by government forces of Negroes and liberals alike.

An earlier revolt, in the region of Palmares, between the present-day states of Pernambuco and Bahia, lasted sixty-five years, from 1630 to 1695. This was the so-called War of Palmares, or Quilombo War. It was conducted by Negroes who had fled to the great palm forests, where they established *quilombos,* organized settlements, each with a council and a chieftain. Gradually, the congregation of the quilombos constituted a genuine state, with its monarch and its army. Two generations of Negroes lived in this fashion, in freedom from the white man, standing off Dutch expeditions from Pernambuco and Portuguese expeditions from Brazil. The Negroes of the quilombos traded with the whites established closest to Palmares. Indeed, a viable quilombo tradition existed all over Brazil; reinforced by the Palmares example, it lasted (in isolated instances) until the emancipation of the slaves in 1888.

Negroes and mulattoes were the first in Brazil to spread the ideas of the Republic and Independence. In 1789 the mulattoes of Minas Gerais, led by Second Lieutenant Joaquim José da Silva Xavier, known as "Tiradentes," planned an unsuccessful effort to prevent the shipment of Brazilian gold to Portugal. In 1798 Jacobin mulattoes in Bahia conspired to establish "a Republican government, free and independent, with equal opportunities for 'pardos' and Negroes to hold public office." The plot was discovered, and four of the conspirators were drawn and quartered.

Indians thought of separating from the Crown only when the Crown refused to listen to them. Negroes thought of it as soon as they got beyond range of the overseer's whip. But independence came only when these two vital forces were coordinated by the third force, which all the time had been agitating and protesting in the cities of the viceroyship: the creoles.

CREOLE REBELLIONS

The encomenderos' uprisings had barely ended when the creoles began their revolts. Their goal was not to gain privileges in order to exploit the Indians, but rather to maintain municipal privileges inherited from the old Spanish statutory tradition. The creole's enemy was the transitory Spaniard, the officer who would eventually return to Spain. Creole uprisings generally followed a simple pattern. The cabildo received an unwelcome order from Spain, and the formula of "respect but do not comply" was put into effect. If the royal official insisted that the order be complied with, he was ignored, dismissed from office, or even imprisoned. Many times, owing to Spain's distance from the colonies, creole uprisings attained their goals, if not legally, at least in practice. In reality, these uprisings were protests rather than rebellions in the strict sense of the word.

As the years passed, the economic interests of the colonies became increasingly opposed to the interests of Spain and Portugal. Spanish officials saw Latin America as a source of precious metals, rare goods, and taxes, and to a lesser extent as a market for Spanish goods. As trade increased, Latin American merchants sought both a wider market and new sources of supply. Again and again, Spain stubbornly refused to permit trade between her Latin American colonies and other countries. Large-scale smuggling was the consequence, and efforts to suppress it gave rise to further discontent among the creoles. A reform of 1774 authorized the viceroyships to trade among themselves (previously they had been allowed to deal only through Cadiz or Seville), but this solved few problems.

Some Spanish measures were extreme to the point of absurdity: for example, the cultivation of grapevines and olives was prohibited in order to eliminate competition with Spain. Taxes and transportation costs raised the prices on all goods. Everything favored Spain. Latin Americans had to sell cheaply, since only Spain could buy their products and therefore could set the market price; on the other hand, they had to buy at high prices, for only Spain could sell them products and Spain, again, would set the price.

Portugal's stranglehold on Brazil was even worse. Pombal's reforms of 1757 set up government monopolies over the sale of tobacco and salt and the cultivation of sugar; and although they also decreed the freedom of the Indians, they in no way improved existing conditions. María I went a step farther and closed down Brazilian workshops and public works projects to eliminate competition with their equivalents in Portugal.

The first important creole rebellion took place in Mexico in 1624, in protest against a cereal monopoly administered by a friend of a viceroy. Before this, there had been minor disturbances in Buenos Aires, Tucumán, Santa Fe, Asunción, and Santiago, caused by dissatisfaction with officials from Spain. The larger-scale movements were those opposing taxes. Cabildos in Quito opposed tax increases in 1591 and in 1765. In 1630, a commander-general of New Granada who attempted to enforce a new tax decree was forced to flee. In Venezuela in 1749, a serious creole uprising was provoked by the excessive privileges of the Guipuzcoana Company, which monopolized foreign trade. In Cuba the planters rebelled in 1717 against an attempt to set up a tobacco monopoly; the governor was taken prisoner and sent back to Spain.

Another factor making for separation was the organization of defense against attacks from foreign forces. Cabildos organized the defense of southern Chile in the seventeenth century, against the Dutch; of Cartagena in 1740 and of Havana in 1762, against the English; and of Río de la Plata, in 1806 and 1807, against the English. Of course, these were acts of loyalty to the king, but they were also acts in which municipal or regional authority was asserted—occasions to savor the latent power of organization.

In some places the affirmation of this authority went much further, notably in Asunción, which at that time was the capital of the Plata. Almost every time a new governor arrived from Spain, the citizens of Asunción elected one of their own men to the office and sent the Spanish envoy back to Spain. In 1730 Fernando Mompó led a genuine autonomist revolution. "The power of the townspeople is greater than that of the king himself," stated Mompó, and when the new Spanish governor tried to address the people, someone shouted at him: "What does 'Vox populi, vox Dei' mean? Your Grace will answer what he will, but he should know that here are the people." Mompó paid for the revolution with his life, but the city of Asunción continued to protest each new attempt to impose a governor.

The most significant creole rebellion, which coincided with the Tupac Amaru uprising in Peru, was that of the *comuneros* of Socorro—citizens organized to defend their rights against arbitrary encroachment of government in New Granada. In 1781 the Crown raised the taxes; the manner in which they were collected provoked the Tupac Amaru revolt, and the wish to avoid paying them at all provoked the Socorro uprising. On a Sunday morning, at the beginning of mass, the people gathered in front of the mayor's house to protest. A woman, Manuela Beltrán, tore up the edicts in which the new tributes were proclaimed, to the cry of "Long live the King, death to the oppressive government!" Every city in the region followed Socorro's example, all the way to Venezuela and Ecuador, and a comunero army was formed. The army set out toward Bogotá; it was encountered by Archbishop Antonio Caballero y Góngora, who negotiated an agreement with rebel leaders that offered lower taxes and pledges for the future. The comunero army then disbanded; but the Archbishop promptly repudiated the agreement, which he claimed to have signed under duress, and the viceroy's soldiers soon restored the status quo.

In the first place, the fact that this movement had raised an army made it the most important of all. This was something the rest of the creole movements had never dared attempt. Second, it was important because it encompassed Indians and Negroes. One of the movement's leaders, the former seminarist and muleteer José Antonio Galán, freed the Indians from the obrajes through which he passed, and roused to rebellion slaves in the mines of Guarne and Malpaso (the leaders of this revolt, both Negroes, were later drawn and quartered). Galán proclaimed the end of slavery, and opposed the cautious negotiations that ultimately led to the defeat of the movement. He was not a man of great culture, but because he had himself been poor and had witnessed the grinding poverty in his own small village, he could see in the Indians, the Negroes, and the land-less creoles a force of tremendous potential strength, and he believed that such a force could overcome an oppressive government. Young, persuasive, and brave, he became a legendary figure even before his execution.

The antagonism between creole and Spanish interests was the principal force behind the rebellions that led to independence. Napoleon's occupa-tion of the Iberian Peninsula supplied the immediate impulse; a separa-tion of the colonies from Spain was established on the pretext of loyalty to Ferdinand VII, who was being held in Bayonne by the Emperor. The evolution from this posture to actual independence took years, and the ideo-logical evolution led to a peculiar kind of democracy. Indeed, the creoles favored democracy, but only for the creoles. They decided through the ca-bildos, and later through congresses and assemblies, how the regime was to be constituted and who its leaders were to be, and as a class they exer-cised an economic and political dictatorship over all the other classes of society.

Indians and Negroes carried on no struggles of their own during the fight for independence. Their participation in the conflict (the Indians often forming part of the king's armies) seemed to satisfy what political aspirations they had. It was not the fear of being displaced by Indians or Negroes that led the creoles to form an oligarchy, but rather the fact that they alone, of the three groups, possessed nationalistic feeling, a tradition in government, a semblance of education, and economic power.

The first separatist action to surpass simple conspiracy took place in Venezuela in 1797. This was an uprising of urban creoles against an op-pressive aristocratic oligarchy of hacienda owners. The movement was be-trayed and failed, but not before it had printed decrees establishing a Con-gress in Caracas, granting freedom to the Negroes, and distributing land among the Indians. Nine years later another effort to found a Venezuelan republic was made by Francisco Miranda, a colorful figure who had for-merly been a general in the armies of the French Revolution and a lover of Catherine of Russia. Although Miranda had obtained money in London and men and arms in Philadelphia, his invading force was easily repelled and he was forced to flee. Three months later he tried again and occupied the city of Coro, but the indifference of the inhabitants discouraged him and he withdrew.

Up to this point, those who had fought for independence had been en-lightened, intellectual men. They found no response, since their mentality and their methods of action, and even their material means, were not Latin American. But their struggles served to encourage in others the notion that separation from Spain was not impossible. When Napoleon took Ferdinand VII to Bayonne, the Venezuelan oligarchy understood that separation from Spain was inevitable: if the oligarchy failed to take the initiative, it would be taken by the people. Later, this same pattern was repeated in the other colonies. The oligarchy, wealthy and with complex and extensive interests, aspired to rule so that it might put an end, for its personal benefit, to the conflict between its interests and those of Spain. The oligarchy wanted only an economic revolution. It was the people, the common creoles, who transformed the movement into a political revolution. Creole artisans and small landholders saw that their situation would not necessarily improve with economic separation from Spain, and began to feel that they, too, could govern. The fear that this desire might lead to action served to push the oligarchy into the political revolution, which led to the construction of states and to the assertion of independence.

Independence created the preliminary conditions necessary for economic, political, and social change, but independence itself effected no significant change. Landholding continued to be feudal; the Indians remained subjugated by the landowners; and the Negroes, although in many areas nominally free, were in fact slaves of miners and planters. Only the middle class, the small landholder and the artisan, gained something: free trade and a degree of participation in politics. Throughout the nineteenth century the middle class would struggle not only to increase its own power, but also to liberate the Indians and Negroes and to destroy the landholding oligarchy.

3. From Independence to Industrialism

WHEN BOLÍVAR was trying to incorporate Ecuador into Gran Colombia someone asked him, "Why do you want that small country, a jumble of whites, Negroes, Indians, mestizos, and zambos?" Bolívar replied, "Because the combination of all colors produces white." History has not borne out this prediction. As the Mexican pedagogue and politician Justo Sierra wrote half a century ago: "The 'mestizo,' casual product of the dominating and dominated races, was considered by the Spaniard to be capable only of evil, useful only for thievery and murder. But the 'mestizo' became the future master of the country, the future revolutionary, the future creator of nationality."

What happened, in broad terms, was that each race came to make up a social group. The differences in land tenure systems, in cultural levels, in customs, were so great among Indians, Negroes, mestizos, and whites that social and racial categories were essentially one. The incipient proletarian was not only proletarian, but also Negro or mestizo. The peasant was not only a peasant, but also Indian or Negro. The artisan, the intellectual, the tradesman, were all that, but were also mestizos or creoles. The great landholder, the banker, the official in government, were creoles.

CAUDILLISMO

The mestizo was a politician par excellence. His ambiguous situation prepared him for and led him to politics. A dictator when pursuing power, he became democratic in the measure in which he felt incorporated into the life of the country, and as his class replaced the creole class demographically and economically. With a liberal mentality but no deep aversion to despotic methods, he was the typical *caudillo*. Having fought the war for independence with confused aspirations, which, on the whole, asserted an ambition toward human liberty, the mestizo refused to accept the creoles of the landholding oligarchy as his absolute masters. Mestizo leaders were for the most part simply opportunistic. Where the oligarchy was politically liberal, the caudillo was reactionary; where the oligarchs were conservative, the caudillo was liberal. But these were only labels, for with his brutal methods and his perception of the desires of the masses, the caudillo was, up to a point, the interpreter of popular aspirations.

The mestizo politician was driven by personal ambition. If he was successful, he might readily serve the interests of the oligarchy—if the oligarchy, for its part, was yielding enough to accept him into its midst. Nonetheless, every coup d'etat or political revolution, every event that pushed the mestizo up the governmental ladder, undermined the basis of the landholding oligarchy. If the caudillo favored the oligarchy's purposes with his laws, the oligarchy favored the caudillo with its social concessions. In a society that had inherited the complex etiquette and rigid social stratification of Spain, the acceptance of the caudillo in itself constituted an invisible revolution.

The mestizo either remained close to the Indians, living among the peasants or the poor artisans, or turned to urban life, where he acquired western habits and formed the nucleus of a middle class in a period in which industrial capitalism had yet not come into being. Because the mestizo was racially and economically intermediate, he served as a balancing element, and this in spite of the extravagances of mestizo rulers. Nationality, as Justo Sierra said, was forged around the mestizo. The present-day creoles of Mexico and Venezuela have a great deal more in common than the mestizos of the two countries. The oligarch felt like an oligarch everywhere; the caudillo was a caudillo only among his people, whom he understood and served.

The mestizo's role as a creator of nationality was emphasized by the appearance of foreign capital on the scene. In the 1830's and 1840's, when the oligarchy was nearly bankrupt, foreign capitalists began to take an interest in Latin America. They ignored the caudillos, who seemed unstable and offered no security, and dealt directly with the creole oligarchs. It was up to the mestizo, therefore, whether in the government or in opposition, to defend his country from the claims of foreign capital. Similarly, the mestizo opposed the admission of European immigrants, whereas the creole oligarchy favored their admission.

There are four stages in the biography of a caudillo: the people's fascination with his personality, his conquest of power, his administration, and his fall. In order to charm the people the typical caudillo built their longings into his program. To attain power he made use of soldiers and the mob, whom he paid with promises. Few caudillos rose from the opposition to become rulers; many collaborated with the politicians they had over-thrown.

Administer well and avoid making policy, was the motto of the caudillo. The Venezuelan caudillo Antonio Guzmán Blanco (1829–99) remarked, "I have never followed anyone's line of thinking but my own." The caudillo's collaborators were mere executors of his orders, and sometimes reluctant ones: a minister in the administration of the Guatemalan caudillo Manuel Estrada Cabrera (1857–1926) confessed, "I had to choose between jail and this office." The caudillo appointed whomever he wished, even in some cases his heir. Many caudillos occupied themselves with collecting decorations and titles of nobility, some of them absurdly high-sounding: Most Serene Highness, Father of the Country, Supreme Leader, Benefactor, and even Hero of the Desert. Many caudillos were even given papal titles of nobility.

During most of the nineteenth century the struggle of the caudillos was centered around the clerical question (not the religious question, since in their own fashion the majority of Latin Americans are fervent Catholics). The Church, wealthy and confident, had the support of most of the population. The caudillos were the main enemies of the Church, an attitude in which they were supported by groups of liberal intellectuals.

Bolívar had written: "I regard the present state of Latin America as comparable to the state of Europe following the collapse of the Roman Empire, when each dismembered part established a political system according to its interests and situation, or following the personal ambition of some leaders, families, or groups." During the decades following independence, a series of struggles between conservatives and liberals resulted gradually in the decline of the political preponderance of the Church—although the Church continued to exert a great influence. The same struggle led to the abolition of slavery, and to the emergence of minorities bearing no allegiance to caudillismo. Finally, these struggles half-opened the doors to power to mestizos and the middle class generally.

In two countries, Mexico and Ecuador, these changes came about dramatically. There, more than in other countries, both class and economic tensions could be sensed beneath the religious battle. In Mexico the popular caudillo Benito Juárez systematically reformed the entire structure of the state in 1856 and 1857, in order to eliminate the excessive influence of the Church, working with and through the oligarchy. Juárez separated the Church from the state, compelled the clergy to sell its properties, and abolished the *diezmos* (tithing).

Ecuador's first dictator, Juan José Flores, attempted in 1846 to re-establish the colonial regime when the liberals threatened the privileges of the landholding oligarchy. One of his successors, Gabriel García Moreno, a member of the oligarchy and a mystic with political talent, came to power after a long exile in Paris and forthwith consecrated the country to the Sacred Heart of Jesus; in 1862, he signed a concordat giving the papacy full command over education and religious matters in Ecuador. At the same time he had large public works constructed, and succeeded in giving his country a period of peace. He was assassinated, and his liberal successor undid in fifteen weeks very nearly all that García Moreno had done in fifteen years.

By about 1870 caudillismo, at times calling itself conservative and at times liberal, had fulfilled its task. It had weakened the power of the oligarchy by reducing the economic strength of the Church, by abolishing slavery, by fostering certain democratic habits, and by creating an interest in politics among increasingly larger groups—though these were still small. The oligarchy kept its economic power, though no longer to an absolute degree, and had to fight to keep its share of political power.

This ebullient period, during which politics seemed an adventure, has no counterpart in Old World history. Carleton Beals explains this clearly: the cruelest dictatorships in the New World have never stifled the human spirit, or circumscribed opportunities and freedom, to the extent the more infamous European dictatorships have. But the price has been high: Latin American social systems offer the most horrible examples of human injustice to be found anywhere in the world, and great masses of people live in reactionary apathy. The political apathy of the masses was almost unbroken until about 1930. No labor movement and no peasant organizations existed during most of the nineteenth century, and there were no movements of social protest. Protest was expressed by supporting caudillos, or was diverted into foreign wars. All during this period Latin America's social, economic, and human problems were becoming increasingly clear, but no political action was taken to solve them.

THE ABOLITION OF SLAVERY

Although during the wars of independence the liberators declared the freedom of many slaves, the system of slavery as such did not disappear. Abolition was the work of the middle class, and specifically of the caudillos, in their efforts to gain supporters or to diminish the economic power of the oligarchy. Abolition decrees were signed as follows: Chile, 1811; Argentina, 1813; Central America, 1824; Bolivia, 1825; Mexico, 1828; Uruguay, 1842; Paraguay, 1844; Colombia, 1851; Ecuador, 1852; Peru, 1856; Venezuela, 1858; Brazil, 1888. In Cuba, a Spanish colony until 1898, abolition was proclaimed in 1886, and in Puerto Rico, also under Spanish rule, in 1873. Haiti put an end to slavery in 1794. In Britain's Caribbean colonies abolition dated from 1838, although clandestine trading continued until 1865. Denmark outlawed the slave trade in 1795, France in 1815, and Holland in 1863, two years before slavery was abolished in the United States.

Abolition in Brazil was delayed as long as it was by the scarcity of indigenous manpower in the mining regions after the end of the mining boom. The beginnings of industrialism became paralyzed as the mining fever dwindled. Entire cities were abandoned; the *garimperos* (prospectors) returned to their miserable everyday existence; and those who had bought land found themselves faced with the choice of abandoning it or working it with slaves.

In 1871 Peter II of Brazil obtained Parliament's approval of the *ley del vientre libre*—the law of the free womb—which freed the offspring of slaves. In 1885 slaves over sixty years of age were freed, and in 1888 a law abolishing slavery and freeing all slaves was approved after five days of passionate debate in Parliament. The Prime Minister, upon offering the decree to the Regent Isabel for her signature, announced: "Her Highness has won this fight but lost the throne." A year and a half later the Republic was proclaimed.

The abolition of slavery tore apart the system of fazendas, or large landholdings, in Brazil, and left as organized groups only the Army and the Church. The transition from slavery to freedom was often painful for the Negroes: there was no capital on the fazendas to pay them wages, and no market for unskilled manpower. For years ex-slaves scraped a living from small, ownerless plots of land. Later, public works and industrial projects financed by foreign loans created a market for Negro labor.

INDUSTRIALISM

The Industrial Revolution reached Latin America only after it had transformed Europe. There was a delay of some thirty years for the locomotive, forty years for power looms, and still longer for steam navigation and gas lighting. (In the vicinity of the United States, industrialism was imported earlier: in 1823 Cuba had three steamships, and in 1836 a shipping line ran between Havana and New Orleans.) The pressures to industrialize were few: raw material and agricultural exports sufficed to pay for all the imported goods the well-to-do classes wanted, and the lower classes wove their own cloth, cured their own leather, and made their own pottery. For half a century after independence craftsmanship flourished without competition from the machine.

The land was still being cultivated as it had been before the conquest. Indians continued working in obrajes and accepting their pay in goods from the company store. For decades after independence no new technical improvements were introduced in the mines.* Foundries—particularly those turning out cannons—were common, and in 1806 a sawmill was working in Chalco. Flour mills began modernizing relatively early, thanks to the innovations of local mechanics.

Buenos Aires had a water mill in 1590, but the city's first steam-powered mill was not installed until 1845. In 1870 horse-drawn streetcars began circulating in Buenos Aires, and by 1897 electric trolleys were in use. In the last two decades of the century large department stores, breweries, and tobacco factories were established in Argentina and Uruguay, large refrigerating plants were set up to preserve meat for export, and modern methods for the treatment of hides, introduced in 1830 by the Frenchman Cambaceres, were perfected by the use of arsenic. In Argentine cities, workshops were transformed into factories, and new industries came into being where manpower was available. Great industrial fortunes were made, though industry continued to be small, with a maximum of two or three hundred workers in the largest factories. In 1853 there were 1,500 workers among the 76,000 inhabitants of Buenos Aires; by 1887 there were 42,000 workers in a population of half a million; by 1915 there were 146,000 workers in a million and a half inhabitants, and by 1965, 550,000 in four million.

This development, energetic and swift in Argentina, was slower in Mexico, Chile, and Brazil, and virtually nonexistent on the rest of the continent, where the craftsman remained supreme. In 1900, 80 per cent of the active population of Mexico and Venezuela was still engaged in argriculture, whereas in Argentina 47 per cent was in agriculture and 17 per cent in trade. In Peru, 52 per cent was in agriculture. In Chile and Bolivia 11 and 14 per cent, respectively, was in mining, but other industrial work forces were negligible. The industrial proletariat made up barely 10 per cent of the active population of the continent. In Mexico in 1939, before the great impetus given there to industrialization, there were 4 million peasants and 410,000 mining and industrial laborers; in Brazil, out of 13 million *asalariados* (wage earners), 9 million cultivated the land.

* There had been some notable progress in agricultural and mining technology just before independence. In Mexico, for example, José A. Alzate built a cotton gin—twenty-two years before Whitney's—whose production capacity was fifty times greater than a man's. However, salaries were so low it was cheaper to hire fifty ginners than to use one machine, and Alzate's ginner was laid aside. Mining advanced more rapidly, owing to the constant demand by the Spanish Court for precious metals. A school of mines began operating in Mexico in the seventeenth century, and in 1801 a hydraulic machine, built by "monsiú Lachaussée, the inventor from Brabante," was installed in a Mexican mine. Even before this, faster methods for the metallurgical process of removing ore had been put into practice in the silver mines of Taxco and Guanajuato.

FOREIGN CAPITAL

Three periods can be discerned in the penetration of foreign capital into Latin America: the century from independence to World War I, the period of competition between the two World Wars, and the period of development from World War II to the present.

During the semicolonial period European capital predominated, notably (after about 1880) British capital in Argentina and Uruguay. Foreign investment was less concerned with developing Latin American resources than with setting up transportation systems, public utilities, and secondary industries tailored to the needs of primary industries in foreign countries. Although these investments stimulated the appearance of new industries, their essential objective was to obtain profits, in part from low-cost labor, in part by opening new markets. Governments favored these investments, seeing them as indispensable to any future development. The masses showed no mistrust toward European capital, and there was no anti-imperialistic activity.

Between the two World Wars, Great Britain and the United States accounted for 92 per cent of foreign capital invested in Latin America, and almost half of all investments, foreign and national. London and Washington contended over markets, mines, and raw materials. The crisis of 1929 gave a pause to the slow British retreat and the rapid American advance. The masses were aroused to resentment against Wall Street, and specifically against the American intervention policy in Haiti, Santo Domingo, and Nicaragua and the tendency of American companies to interfere in the politics of small countries.

World War II effectively displaced Great Britain and the continental European countries from Latin America's market, leaving the field to the United States. Washington was interested not only in obtaining profits, but above all in securing sources of raw materials for American industries. The United States therefore encouraged mining, oil drilling, and the construction of blast furnaces, and was quick to offer loans and credits to help the Latin American countries free themselves from European capital. Although there were no more cases of open American intervention in Latin American politics until the case of the Dominican Republic, in 1965, anti-imperialism, which had been encouraged by leftists and by the labor movement, during this period became an instrument of agitation used by military groups and Communists. In 1961, President Kennedy's Alliance for Progress offered massive aid to Latin American governments willing to carry out fiscal and agrarian reforms of a democratic nature.

During World War II neither American nor European industries were able to supply Latin American countries, and local industries sprang up to fill the need. When the war ended and competition on the market reappeared, a large number of these makeshift industries faded away. Others were kept alive artificially by protectionist measures that burdened the popular standard of living. The labor movement has thus been confronted from the beginning with a contradiction that remains as yet unresolved: without foreign capital there is no industry, without industry there is no proletariat. Foreign capital is at once the condition of the proletariat's existence, and the enemy of its aspirations. The proletariat must fight against foreign capital even in the knowledge that there is nothing to replace it, and that without it the proletariat would not exist as a class.

THE RIGHT TO UNIONIZE

All Latin American constitutions of the nineteenth century recognized the right to associate and congregate peaceably for legitimate purposes, and to make individual or collective petitions. Those of the twentieth century typically went further and allowed the formation of unions, but in many cases regulated them so sternly as to make their existence meaningless. For example, in Brazil's corporative constitution of 1937 it was established that there could be only one union for each trade in each region. Moreover, the right to form a union was not necessarily the right to strike. Only a handful of constitutions before 1940 acknowledged this right, without which no labor movement is effective: notably Mexico in 1917, Uruguay in 1934, Colombia in 1937, and Cuba in 1940.

Laws regulated the practice of union rights and fixed limits to their application. In Cuba, for example, it was established that union leaders must be Cuban by birth; in Brazil, under Vargas, certain public functions were delegated to the unions; in Chile, in 1946, Communists were forbidden to hold union offices. In every country modern legislation has outlawed direct action, making arbitration compulsory before the declaration of a strike. In some countries, during periods of dictatorship, unions are compelled to present the government with membership lists, and during periods of suspension of constitutional rights—which customarily follow every coup d'etat, until the caudillo issues a new constitution—unions and political workers' parties are suppressed. In many countries unions of agricultural laborers and peasants are forbidden, or, in any case, obstacles are placed in their path.

SOCIAL IDEOLOGIES

For several decades beginning about 1830, Latin American political thinking was concerned primarily with adjusting the new constitutions to legal, social, and economic realities. The first constitutions derived from the liberal ones of Spain, France, and particularly the United States. But imposing the new liberalism on administrative centralization, commercial monopolies, rigid social hierarchies, and political absolutism, all inherited from the Spanish tradition, was difficult.

The political struggles of this period were mainly between liberals and conservatives. The former were backed by the intellectuals and an incipient middle class; the latter found their support in the Army, the Church, and the rural aristocracy. The most important movements were in Argentina and Mexico. In Argentina, the liberal ruler Bernardino Rivadavia did away with ecclesiastical privileges, made it easier for peasants to acquire land, encouraged immigration, and even tried to help Spanish liberals in 1823. Reforms of this sort ceased during Rosas' long dictatorship, but were resumed by Juan Bautista Alberdi, an exponent of economic liberalism and author of the Constitution of 1853. In Mexico, liberals and conservatives fought without interruption from 1824 to 1867, and political power wavered between the two groups. The liberals demanded civil liberties and an end to the privileges of the clergy and the military; their creed had decisive influence on the important Constitution of 1857.

Positivism, notably that of Comte, and to a lesser extent that of Herbert Spencer, was the dominant Latin American political philosophy from 1870 to 1900. The influence of the positivists was very strong, above all in public education. In politics the positivists gave great importance to evolutionary change. In Mexico a group of thinkers of this tendency, known as "the Scientists," furnished the Porfirio Díaz government with its official philosophy, from 1890 to 1910. In Brazil the positivists went so far as to embody their motto, "Order and Progress," in the national flag. But ultimately the positivism of the advanced European countries proved ill-adapted to the social and cultural realities of Latin America, and an anti-positivist reaction set in.

Liberals—and many conservatives also—saw industrialization as a way to social progress and the attainment of political stability. The liberals differed from the conservatives chiefly in insisting on social reforms, whereas the conservatives sought to keep the old social structure intact and to work within it. Liberalism sometimes had self-defeating consequences: in Mexico, for example, reform laws treated the Indians as citizens equal to all others, and thereby left them without defenses against the large hacendados. On the other hand, liberals insisted on the workers' right to dispose of their labor as they wished, and hence generally opposed the anti-strike laws. Certain other attitudes among liberals and positivists, notably anti-clericalism, also influenced the thinking of the labor movement in its early days.

The Mexican Revolution, from 1910 to 1917, combined the economic yearnings of the rural masses and the urban proletariat with the political aspirations of the emerging middle classes. These three elements allied spontaneously, forming a political movement without precedent in the history of Latin America. The Revolution had no ideological program, and no methodological model. Only as the revolution was transformed from a political to a social movement (notably by Emiliano Zapata and the *agraristas*), and still later with the Constitution of 1917, were the bases for the revolutionary ideology established.

In the twentieth century, student political agitation became important. Students began the protest against political oppression, and were the first to offer opposition to the dictatorships. Future politicians received their philosophic indoctrination in the universities, where they were exposed in particular to the liberal ideas of such Spanish thinkers as José Ortega y Gasset and Miguel de Unamuno. Totalitarian ideologies also flourished in the period between the wars, which saw the rise of Vargas in Brazil and Trujillo in the Dominican Republic.

The Latin American labor movement did not emerge from its complete dependence on imported ideas until it came under the ideological influence of the populist movement, known also as the *aprista* movement. The essence of aprista thinking is that "Europe is Europe and America is America.... It is as dangerous to live by imitating [Europe] as to attempt a complete break, a mindless rejection of the past."*

The populist movement did not consider itself strictly a workers' movement; its leaders were not of the working class, and neither were most of its members. Populism attempted and attempts still to unite diverse social groups: middle class, workers, peasants, intellectuals. Beginning in the 1920's the naturalization of imported ideas, and later the forging of new ideas, became more and more clearly the work of a limited number of militant intellectuals, sophisticated politicians, labor leaders, and middle-class leaders, who began working out their doctrines and interpretations according to the demands arising during the struggle. This is of course exactly what had happened in Europe some decades before: social theories were born of action, motivated by action. The kaleidoscopic and protean character of populist thinking makes it one of the most fascinating of Latin American social ideologies. But populist social ideas, for all their concern

---

* The term *aprista* comes from APRA (Alianza Popular Revolucionaria Americana), founded in Mexico in 1924 by the Peruvian Víctor Raúl Haya de la Torre. The aprista movement was populist; it will be mentioned frequently, along with the name of its founder, and will be dealt with specifically in the chapter of this book devoted to the populist movements. The quotation is from Haya de la Torre, *Treinta años de aprismo*, pp. 18–19.

with the labor movement, come from outside the labor movement itself.

Beside the populist influence after World War I must be placed another influence: the preponderant role in labor thinking given to the state, to state action, and even to public ownership. A much tighter bond exists between the labor movement and the state in Latin America than in the Old World or in the United States. In the colonial period, the pressure of circumstances led to a systematic state control of the economy that even the liberalism of the nineteenth century could not eradicate. Today, not only leftists but middle-of-the-road thinkers routinely ask for state intervention in social and economic problems. For one thing, they perceive that their region is backward and wish to make up for lost time by bringing to bear the largest resources potentially at their command. For another, they consider the victorious revolution to be the source of law: revolutionary laws are legal and obligatory. The Latin American concept of property is unusual. In most of the modern constitutions property is defined as a "social function"; it does not represent an absolute right (as in the philosophy of liberalism), but only a privilege granted to the individual as long as he fulfills a useful function in society. Finally, it should be mentioned that the typical Latin American constitution anticipates events: it deals with what should be and not with what is.

Latin American economies were traditionally directed economies, but systematic planning, nationalization, and state ownership did not come until the early twentieth century. The Uruguayan politician José Batlle y Ordóñez (president of Uruguay in 1903–7 and 1911–15) was one of the first to urge the nationalization of certain industries. And a Paraguayan dictator, Higinio Moriñigo, spoke for many others in 1941: "The inertia of the liberal state must give way to the dynamism of the protected and directed state." In almost every Latin American country at least some nationalization has been carried out, much of it by conservative or dictatorial governments. Vargas asked for the socialization of water power, mineral deposits, and transportation. The railroads in Colombia were nationalized decades ago. The Mexican Constitution of 1917 defined the country's underground resources as national property. In 1938, in Mexico, first the railroads and then the oilfields were nationalized; in 1960 the electrical companies were nationalized by purchase. In 1952 the mines of the three largest Bolivian companies were nationalized. In Argentina, Perón nationalized the central bank, the railroads, the merchant marine, civil aviation, the telephones, all port facilities, and even foreign trade. José Figueres nationalized the banks in Costa Rica.

Many populist programs call for the nationalization of land, of certain fundamental industries, or of public services. Similarly, the word "socialist" appears not only in many party programs, but in the very names of reactionary or conservative parties, such as the Bolivian Socialist Falange and the Brazilian Social-Democratic Party. Arévalo, in Guatemala, spoke of his program as "spiritual socialism," and even Vargas called his regime "anti-capitalistic and socialistic."

During the nineteenth century little socialist literature reached Latin America. The main source of socialist ideas was immigrants: political exiles from the revolutions of 1848, from the Commune of Paris, and from Spain, and workers seeking a better life in Buenos Aires, Mexico City, Rio de Janeiro, or Santiago. The Latin American recipients of this verbal propaganda neither discussed nor adapted it, but took it as it came. The adaptation of these ideas to Latin American realities came later, in the course of the struggle itself.

Beginning in the decade preceding World War I, a wave of protest literature, of all political persuasions, reached Latin America in the form of cheap editions published in Barcelona and Valencia. It was in this form that many Latin Americans first read the polemics and doctrines of the anarchists, the socialists, and the rationalists, and later, the first writings of the Bolsheviks. For many, these books and pamphlets were a revelation, a window to a world that their official education had never mentioned, and for which they had not been prepared.

The European socialists had very little concern for Latin America. There are scarcely any references to Latin America in European anarchist literature, and fewer still in Marxist writings. Marx and Engels had only vague ideas on Latin America: Engels defended the annexation of Texas to the United States, and both men approved the annexation of California on the ground that "the energetic Yankees" were more capable than "the lazy Mexicans" of opening the Pacific coast to civilization. (In 1861, however, Marx called a proposed Anglo-Franco-Spanish intervention in Mexico "one of the most monstrous enterprises ever recorded in the annals of history.") Of Bolívar, Marx wrote: "It is infuriating to see this coward, this vile and miserable cur, glorified like a Napoleon."

The influence of the United States among Latin American workers was exerted particularly through the International Workers of the World (IWW) at the beginning of the twentieth century, and later through the American Federation of Labor (AFL). Because of the pragmatic, apolitical nature of United States unions, and their strict concentration on economic matters, their influence on Latin American unions has been at best superficial. On the other hand, the influence of such political concepts as the New Deal and the Alliance for Progress has been significant.

As for Marxism, it has penetrated the thinking of all politicians and intellectuals of the left, and in various adaptations to the Latin American reality continues to exert a considerable influence. It is precisely this Marxism that protects many from Communist seduction, since Marxism as Latin Americans understand the term is incompatible with Communist theory and practice. A strange fusion of Marxism with Keynesianism produces a type of political economist that exerts considerable influence in Latin America, an economist full of strong national resentments but with a total indifference toward social issues.

In Latin America today political liberalism, but not economic liberalism, is accepted as an axiom, as much by conservatives (although they will seldom admit it) as by liberals and by the labor movement. Social ideas remain systematically conservative in terms of ownership of the means of production. The tendency is to preserve the social regime, to adapt it rather than radically transform it. Moreover, there is a constant transposition of social problems to other fields: religious, cultural, economic, and so on.

When these realities become unbearable, the intellectuals are the first to protest, to seek something beyond liberalism; but when the time comes for action it develops along lines unforeseen by the intellectuals, lines foreign to any previous doctrine. Social upheavals of any importance are always followed by a reaction toward realism and a proliferation of technicians. Positivism and the present technocracy of the economists are in effect reactions against the ineffectuality of ideologists' methods. Ideologically speaking, no attention has been paid in Latin America to the production of wealth; the battle is strictly over the distribution of wealth. It is for this reason that Latin American social ideas at times seem utopian when in reality they are only insufficient, incomplete.

In accordance with the principles of classic political liberalism, ideas from abroad are rapidly assimilated, in the sense of being efficiently mined for applicable concepts. Ideas, in this sense, are invariably nationalized. (Communism is the exception to this rule.) Only one foreign influence has increased rather than diminished in the course of this kind of scrutiny: the influence of American labor concepts after the 1929 economic crisis—and not the concepts themselves so much as the methods and procedures. This will be seen in the portion of this book devoted to the union movement.

During the present period of the rapid universalization of problems and ideologies, the Latin American countries still find themselves in the national stage of their evolution. While the forward movement of the world hurls them beyond their borders, the necessity of completing the forging of their own nationality holds them back. This has produced a series of contradictions: how to achieve the synthesis of nationalism and universalism, of liberal optimism and the urgency of utopia, of economic development and democracy, of social justice and freedom. The political and social ideas imported from the Old World, and even the home-grown ideas, do not seem to fill the need. The search goes on for a genuine interpretation of the Latin American reality.

A word of explanation about the organization of the material to follow may be helpful. Since the Communist movement represents an international tendency, its history has been outlined in totality, without a country-by-country breakdown, although individual Communist parties are mentioned in the chapters dealing with the socialist movements in the various countries. The populist movements have been treated only briefly because they are not workers' movements in the strictest sense, despite their influence on the working class and on the union movement. The socialist and anarchist movements are covered by countries because, as opposed to the Communist parties, no bond links the various socialist parties and anarchist groups on the continent. The Social-Christian movement, still at its beginning, is also treated briefly.

PART II

Political Aspects

4. The Anarcho-Syndicalist Movement

ANARCHIST THOUGHT reached Latin America with the immigrants from Europe, particularly with those from Spain and Italy. Its influence was felt most strongly in Argentina, somewhat less in Mexico and Peru. In many countries it became a determining force in the unionist movement and an important element in the ideological evolution that led to the populist movements.

Just as it had in Europe, anarchism in Latin America passed through two periods. The first, which we might call pure anarchism, was individualistic in the extreme, violently impatient, terroristic, and inclined to acts of impractical, almost mystical heroism. The second—militant apolitical or antipolitical trade unionism, or *anarcho-syndicalism*—was collectivistic and propagandistic, impatient but less fanatic, and organized for mass activity. Pure anarchism disappeared before World War I, giving way grudgingly to anarcho-syndicalism, which reached its greatest strength roughly between 1890 and 1930. Anarcho-syndicalism persists today, particularly in Argentina and Uruguay, but its remnants have been reduced to impotence, and its appeal has been minimal since World War II.

Anarchism drew its early strength from the artisan, who valued self-teaching and individual enterprise, and therefore saw in the rise of industry a threat to his way of life. The gradual disappearance of the craftsman, and his replacement by the industrial proletariat, marked the decline of anarchism and anarcho-syndicalism.

Why the proletariat should also for a time have been drawn to the anarchist movement is easily demonstrated. Latin American political life was until recently, and in some countries still is, essentially a fiction. The cult of personality, and the electoral mechanism (whether of the government or of political parties), discouraged confidence in the integrity of the elections. Such tactics as vote buying, threats, and document forgery estranged many workers from politics, and convinced them of the futility of seeking anything through democratic means. The energies of socialist and populist political parties were often drained off in combating these vices, and in trying to pass electoral laws that would guarantee the integrity of the vote. Thus the appeal of anarchism—with its promise of direct action, its extreme ethical severity.

Crises were frequent within the anarchist movement, because of the often violent struggle between individualists and collectivists. And in some cases Communist parties arose from schisms in anarcho-syndicalist groups —which, however, generally proved to be immune to the lures of Bolshevism. The polemics of the anarchists and anarcho-syndicalists, first with the socialists and later with the Communists, constitute much of the history of the Latin American labor movement up to World War II. The battle was everywhere joined—in workers' clubs and study centers, in journals and pamphlets, in public and legislative debates, in strike committees, and in the unions themselves.

What anarcho-syndicalism has meant to the labor movement is difficult to calculate. But if we presume that most of the social victories achieved at the beginning of this century—in Argentina and Chile, for example— were the work of the socialists and the unions, we must also acknowledge that these victories would not have been achieved without prior anarchist and anarcho-syndicalist pressure. Direct action, after a fashion, softened the resistance of governments and of the oligarchy to socialist parliamentary action and nonideological unionism.

Anarchism's brief history in Latin America follows, country by country; its several attempts to affiliate internationally conclude the chapter. Anarchism's intense activity in the development of trade unionism is treated thoroughly in Part III, and is therefore touched upon only briefly in the following.

ARGENTINA

In Latin America, anarchism took its deepest hold in Argentina. Along with the rest of the labor movement, it arrived there in the baggage of the immigrants. Many of the immigrants were active members of the First International, founded in London in 1864, and only when rivalry between Marxists and Bakuninists (i.e., between authoritarians and antiauthoritarians) broke out did these first workers' groups divide.

Some émigrés from the Paris Commune became wealthy industrialists but continued as active militants. One of these, the cigarmaker Eugenio Daumas, founded the French Section of the International in Argentina, which demanded for workers "the right to dictate the laws governing society." In 1872 the French Section founded *El Trabajador,* a newspaper that succeeded in publishing only eight issues but was mentioned in the report of the International's Council General to its congress at The Hague. There were also Spanish and Italian sections of the International, and common issues were dealt with in a federal council made up of two delegates from each section.[1]

In 1874 the Buenos Aires police "surprised" a public meeting (announced in the newspapers) and jailed eleven International members; a court acquitted them a month later. In May of the same year the French-language journal *Le Révolutionnaire* began publication. And in about 1876, a study center was founded by European members of the International who inclined toward Bakunin; in 1879 the center published *Una Idea,* a pamphlet of great influence.[2]

Some fifteen anarchist groups were formed during the 1880's and 1890's, most of them in Buenos Aires and Rosario. For a time, these groups concentrated mainly on propaganda. An Anarchist Confederation was formed and began publishing a monthly bulletin, *La Anarquía.* One anarchist group, La Familia Universal, was actively antimilitarist, and its leaders were often jailed.

Centers for social study, with such names as Los Hambrientos de Barracas, Ravachol, Ne Dio ne Padrone, and Santo Caserio, were among the most effective means of attracting and organizing anarchist support. Important reading in the centers was *El Perseguido,* a newspaper founded in 1890 and published "when possible." Cultural centers, libraries, and free modern schools were also founded, inspired by the Escuela Moderna of Francisco Ferrer Guardia in Catalonia.[3]

Many foreigners, among them the English doctor Juan Creaghe, who published the journal *El Oprimido,* gave the centers a special impetus. Foreigners also led the way in the production of anarchist writings and in the marshaling of anarchist energies. The Spaniards José Prat and Julio Camba contributed important articles to anarchist journals, and Spanish anarchists in Rosario published a journal. The anarchist cause in Argentina was advanced considerably by the efforts, over long periods, of the Italians Enrico Malatesta, from 1885, and Pietro Gori, from 1898. In 1895 Malatesta founded *La Questione Sociale,* a magazine published in Italian and Spanish. Gori gave many lectures and held lively debates with the socialists;* his influence as a theoretician was instrumental in the gradual shift of power from anarchism to anarcho-syndicalism.[4]

* Gori was in fact a close friend of the Argentine socialist José Ingenieros.

Anarchist press material in the early years of the movement was abundant and in some cases excellent. *La Protesta* began appearing in 1897, became a daily, and interrupted its regular publication only in 1933, when the government canceled its postal permit (a permit otherwise granted automatically to every newspaper). Among the contributors to *La Protesta* were Alberto Ghiraldo, Julio Camba, and José Prat. Ghiraldo, who attracted many intellectuals to the anarchist movement, was for a time the editor of *La Protesta,* and also founded the journal *El Sol.* His novel *Humano Ardor,* largely autobiographical, reflected the anarchist mood at the turn of the century.

Thirty different anarchist weeklies and journals were published, among them eight in Italian and three in French. On two occasions, from 1909 to 1910, and from 1919 to 1921, two anarchist daily newspapers appeared in Buenos Aires—the morning *La Protesta* and the evening *La Batalla.* In addition, several publishing houses distributed great quantities of anarchist propaganda literature and educational material.

In 1896 the first controversy between socialists and anarchists, lasting three consecutive days and nights, took place in the cellar of a tavern in Buenos Aires. It was the beginning of a struggle that culminated in the great debates held at the Doria Theater in 1903 and 1904, in which even an Italian socialist congressman took part.[5]

"Debates were arranged among orators from the two groups, but members of the public often joined the debates as well. The anarchists saw the socialists as the traitors of the oppressed class, and direct action as the only suitable means of attaining freedom. Any other means would have meant entering a pact with the bourgeois oppressor. 'Anyone denying that the revolution is an immediate task is in the pay of the enemy, as indeed are anarchists who reject violence.' "[6] For their part the socialists accused the anarchists of squandering their energies in "revolutionary gymnastics" and of forgetting the immediate interests of the proletariat.

The socialists stressed the necessity of organization—and in so doing drove a wedge into the schism of the anarchist camp. "The primitive notion of an anarchism without authority and without organization has been replaced by the concepts of the Italian Pietro Gori," who sought to put anarchist energies to concrete use by directing them toward the establishment of unions. Late in 1900 *La Protesta* published twelve articles in support of Gori, arguing the urgency of an organization "to fight and triumph over the oppressor classes; there is a need for organization and forces superior to those serving the rulers."

In May 1901, delegates from unions in the capital met with delegates from Rosario, Córdoba, and Tucumán. This was the fourth attempt to give the laboring class of the country representation through a union federation. As anarchists and socialists deliberated through eight sessions, Gori found himself deserted by many of his former supporters. He contended that arbitration—anathema to the traditional anarchist—can be useful in resolving "economic conflicts between labor and capital [but that the federation should accept] as arbitrators only those persons who offer reliable guarantees of respect for the interests of the workers." His resolution passed by a small margin, and the Federación Obrera Regional Argentina (FORA) was thus constituted, but socialists and anarchists remained together within its ranks for barely a year.

The anarchists amassed strength in the unions: "In their favor were Argentine socioeconomic conditions and the composition of the Argentine working class. While socialism surged, promoted by the Germans of the *Vorwärts* group and by exiles from the Commune, creating a party in the image of the social-democracy movement of industrial Europe, anarchism spread easily among the rural Italian and Spanish immigrants from agrarian and feudal Europe, and among the *criollo* workers, with their nostalgia for the golden age of Argentine agriculture." Because artisans still constituted most of the Argentine work force, anarchists continued to outnumber socialists.

During FORA's second congress, in 1902, the Socialist Party withdrew from both the congress and the Federation, because of a difference over the accreditation of delegates.[7] In November 1902, the Federation, now led solely by the anarchists, declared a general strike in protest against the antilabor practices of the police. The government promptly declared a state of siege. Union locals and print shops where labor publications were edited were seized. A special session of the national Congress was called, and after a discussion lasting only four hours a law against foreigners— the Law of Residence—was passed, a law empowering the government to deport any alien considered undesirable, and to deny entrance into the country to anyone considered undesirable. The law was invoked frequently and vengefully, and the "undesirables" were usually anarchists. Many anarchist leaders were deported, others went into hiding, and a great number sought refuge in Montevideo.

For years the Argentine labor movement fought the Residence Law. The socialists, although less affected by the law than the anarchists, were no less energetic in opposing it. The law debilitated the unions—some disappeared, others languished—and the anarchists turned to radical protest. The subsequent strikes and May Day marches became occasions for clashes between workers and police. In 1904, 1905, and 1907 the clashes were particularly violent, especially in the anarchist stronghold of Rosario. Many of the protest strikes called out by the anarchists counted on the backing of the socialists; chief among these was the two-day general strike of December 1904 in support of Rosario strikers who had been attacked by the police.

On May Day 1909, police in Buenos Aires broke up an anarchist demonstration. Eight anarchists were killed and forty were injured. Workers blamed the tragedy on the Chief of Police, Col. Ramón L. Falcón, who was present during the attack. The Socialist Party made common cause with the anarchists, and declared a general strike in which 250,000 workers took part.[8]

A strike committee drawn from both groups debated grievances and demands. Anarchist members of the committee announced the strike demands: release of the May Day prisoners and reopening of the labor centers that had been closed. The strike committee thought it pointless, however, "to demand the resignation of the Chief of Police, as the Socialist Party has done...inasmuch as any other police chief would have done the same thing, and equally pointless to demand trial and punishment of those guilty of the May Day massacre...since justice is an organ of the bourgeoisie. The workers would, as always, be found guilty—the cossacks never."

Speaking for the socialists, Dr. Nicolás Repetto answered that "FORA's resolutions would be to the Police Chief's advantage, since they would seem to demonstrate the workers' acceptance of the fact that the police, charged with safeguarding the lives of the people, are led by a man like Falcón, the man directly responsible for the May Day outrage. The Socialist Party's demand for Falcón's resignation should not be taken as in any way asking for the abolishment of the police as an institution, but only as demanding the resignation of one man and his replacement by another who understands his function in an enlightened society.... What is important is what motivated the strike—the inept, reckless behavior of the police in attempting to disperse the defenseless demonstrators. By limiting its demands to the reopening of the centers and the freeing of the prisoners, the strike committee simply reinforces the position of the Chief of Police, who ordered the May Day massacre."[9]

This conflict of opinion reveals the disparate views of the two great political currents of the Argentine labor movement of the period.

In 1910 the anarchists announced that unless the government repealed the Law of Residence and granted full amnesty to those deported or denied entry, a general strike would be called for May 25, the one hundredth anniversary of Argentine independence. On May 13 the government began hunting down anarchist leaders. Within a few hours the directors of *La*

Protesta and *La Batalla,* and members of FORA's executive council, were jailed. On May 14 a state of siege was declared. Members of "patriotic" organizations attacked and destroyed the locals of various unions. The socialist newspaper *La Vanguardia* also fell to their fury. The police did nothing to restrain the vandals.

Understandably, such systematic persecution encouraged the anarchists in their belief that it was impossible to defend the working class by legal means, and that the only effective means of expression lay in terrorism. The memory and example of European anarchist action groups had already inspired their Argentine counterparts. In 1905 Salvador Planas made an attempt on the life of ex-President Manuel Quintana; in 1908 Francisco Solano threw a bomb at President José Figueroa Alcorta, but failed to kill him; and in 1909, after a bomb exploded in Corrientes Street, in Buenos Aires, the police arrested Pablo Karachini as he entered a church carrying another bomb. On November 14, 1909, the young anarchist Simón Rado-witsky (1892–1956) killed Col. Falcón—the Chief of Police responsible for the May Day slaughter—and his secretary, Juan Lartigau, by throwing a bomb against Falcón's carriage.*[10] That same night the government decreed a two-month state of siege throughout the country. The police closed down the labor centers, burned anarchist newspaper buildings, and jailed or deported anarchist leaders in the capital and in the provinces.

Col. Falcón's assassination and the explosion of a bomb in the Colón Theater† led to the enactment of the Social Defense Law. This law went the Law of Residence one better: it forbade anarchists admission to the country and ordered deportation of all anarchists not born on Argentine soil. The congressman Nicolás Calvo contended that the law was directed primarily toward foreign-born anarchists, and that Argentine-born anarchists (he estimated there were some 15,000) were obliged simply to register with the police.[11] But in fact the law prohibited all anarchist activities, including the unfurling of the red flag, and established severe penalties for the manufacture or possession of explosives and for the propagation of subversive ideas—leaving to the police the task of determining which ideas

---

* Radowitzky, born in the Ukraine, was only seventeen when arrested for his successful attempt on Falcón's life. He spent twenty-two years in prison under terrible conditions. After a long and persistent campaign led by the newspaper *Crisol,* he was pardoned. Radowitzky later lived in Uruguay and Brazil, where he was also imprisoned, and fought in the Spanish Civil War.

† The Colón Theater explosion caused no loss of life, although the theater was full. The anarchists insisted that it was the work of the police, seeking to provide the government with an excuse for approving the anti-strike legislation. The police condemned a Russian anarchist to death, but were never able to prove he had set off the explosion.

were and which were not subversive. The law was still in effect during World War II.[12]

The Social Defense Law nevertheless failed to put an end to the anarchist movement. In spite of the arrests and the burning of the print shops that had been turning out anarchist publications, written propaganda was never totally suppressed. *La Protesta* was published secretly for almost two years. In 1913 the harassments declined, and by July *La Protesta* resumed daily publication.

Following World War I the anarchist movement played a major role in several important strikes, including that of January 1919 and the Patagonia strikes of 1920 and 1922. Police forces under the command of Col. Varela harshly repressed the 1922 strike, killing and injuring a number of strikers. Varela was later murdered, and the anarchist Kurt Willikens was accused of his death. Willikens was murdered in jail in 1923 while awaiting trial.[13]

Outbreaks of anarchist terrorism continued into the 1920's and 1930's. Bomb explosions in two United States-owned banks in 1927 were assumed by the police to have been anarchist protests against the Sacco–Vanzetti trial; many arrests were made, particularly among Italians. In 1929 Gualtiero Marinelli fired at President Hipólito Irigoyen, but missed, and was cut down by police bullets. In 1931 two Italian anarchists, Severino di Giovanni and Paolino Scarfó, were condemned to death and executed for placing a bomb in the Italian consulate.[14]

The gradual disappearance of the artisan, and his replacement by the industrial proletariat, led to a steady weakening of the anarchist movement and a strengthening of the Communist movement. If, at its outset, the anarchists defended the Bolshevik Revolution, they soon saw that it was leading toward dictatorship, and began instead to attack it. Nevertheless, the fascination of Soviet revolutionary methods attracted certain anarchist elements to Communism. In Argentina, dissident anarchists constituted one of the bases of the Communist Party, which was formed in 1921. But when, in 1922, both Communists and anarchists joined the newly formed Unión Sindical Argentina, the anarchists managed to sidetrack a proposal to affiliate the Unión with the Profintern.[15]

From that time on, the Communists opposed the anarchist movement. During the period in which the "social fascism" line reigned in the Third International, anarchists were classed as "anarcho-fascists," and antianarchist Communist literature was abundant. In the early 1930's, the Communists accused the anarchists of seeking the end of General Uriburu's dictatorship for its own sake rather than to hasten the social revolution. And a Communist brochure charged that the anarchists' fight for a six-hour workday "is equivalent to the complete abandonment of all revolutionary struggle, in order to fall into the most commonplace reformism—the loss of all revolutionary perspective, precisely on the eve of the great class struggle that will be unleashed in Argentina, as throughout the world."[16] The anarchists, for their part, rejected Communist proposals for a united front. "Any contact that FORA might sustain with those factions opposing it would represent, in theory and in practice, a transgression of principles, a betrayal," stated the anarchist paper *La Voz del Chauffer* in 1931.

Argentine anarchists were at that time aligned with four main groups: the ex-members of the Unión Sindical Argentina, who joined the socialist Confederación General de Trabajadores; the so-called *aliancistas rojos,* who allied themselves with the political parties opposing General Uriburu's dictatorship; the *aliancistas,* whose activity was carried out for the most part on a doctrinal plane; and the *foristas,* or FORA supporters, who represented a hundred unions with 100,000 members. The foristas were in turn embroiled in an internal struggle for the leadership of FORA, between those who supported *La Protesta* and those who backed FORA's Federal Council, a struggle which to a lesser degree reflected the old question of apolitical versus antipolitical action.[17]

But the harsh repressions initiated by the Uriburu government in 1930 marked the decline of the Argentine anarchist movement. The deportation of many Spanish and Italian workers and the changing political, economic, and social conditions "led to the decline of this movement, particularly in its manifestation within the labor movement."[18]

Despite persecution by the Perón government following World War II, the anarcho-syndicalists managed to retain power in some unions, and joined every union protest against Perón. Their influence has been important in several unions since the fall of the Perón government, and they continue to publish several periodicals, among them *La Protesta, Reconstruir,* and *Acción Libertaria.*[19] But anarcho-syndicalism has never regained its leading role in the Argentine labor movement.

URUGUAY

A section of the First International, apparently Bakuninist in tendency, is known to have existed in Montevideo in 1872. Three years later this section proposed the formation of a labor federation, and in 1876 the Federación Obrera Regional del Uruguay (FORU) was organized, to offer "resistance to the monopoly of capital." The union movement in Uruguay was also influenced considerably by the Centro Internacional de Estudios Sociales, organized by anarchists and socialists in 1900.[20]

Propaganda was for many years the chief weapon of the Uruguayan anarchists. Between 1890 and 1904 a dozen anarchist publications appeared, one persisting until 1909.[21] Anarchist propaganda was seldom suppressed, although there were occasions around the turn of the century when, because of strikes, it was confiscated or its distribution made more difficult.

In 1930 union elements from the Unión Sindical del Uruguay created the Ateneo Popular, "the center of popular eclectic culture," which drew support from elements backing Batlle.* The most radical elements, those of FORU, remained aloof from this tendency, but both groups opposed the Confederación General de Trabajadores del Uruguay, which was Communist-dominated.[22]

In 1933, after a surge of strikes, the anarchists were persecuted for a time. Many Spanish workers were deported, and four Italians were returned to Italy, where Mussolini immediately jailed them. The well-known Italian anarchist Luigi Fabbri lived for many years in exile in Uruguay, where he died in 1935.

Today, anarcho-syndicalists preserve a certain amount of strength in the unions. The Federación Anarquista del Uruguay, though small, is very active, and supports a documentation center of great value to historians.[23] Anarcho-syndicalists have also organized several semicooperative food-packing enterprises, as well as a few cooperatives created to keep bankrupt businesses in operation. In 1961, these cooperatives received aid from the Inter-American Development Bank for the purpose of modernizing their equipment and extending their activities. This is the first time in Uruguayan history that a bank—and a public, international bank—has made loans to a genuine labor institution.

CHILE

One faction of Chile's Partido Democrático, founded in 1877, was composed of anarchists. Outside the party, other groups spread anarchist theory and propaganda. A Valparaiso group describing itself as "anarchist-Communist" in 1893 began publishing the newspaper *El Oprimido*. Another anarchist group, the libertarian socialists, originated in the Socialist Party.[24] But in general the anarchists and the socialists remained mutually antagonistic. The socialist leader Recabarren, from exile in Buenos Aires, urged absolute opposition to anarchist initiatives at the unsuccessful congress for union unification held in 1907.[25]

During the 1890's, periodicals published by mutualist groups carried many articles essentially anarchist in character. The works of Kropotkin and Bakunin also appeared in pamphlet form. In 1900 the theorist peri-

---

* José Batlle y Ordóñez (1854–1929), president during 1903–7 and 1911–15. He instituted numerous political reforms.

odical *El Acrata* began publication, to debate with the political labor groups: "Before hoisting a political banner," it said, "we workers must hoist an economic banner."

Among early anarchist newspapers, *La Batalla* survived longest—from 1913 to 1925. During this period an anarchist weekly press existed in half a dozen cities.[26] There were also a few Tolstoyan colonies: one was of artists; another, in Santiago, published *La Protesta Humana,* and boasted among its members several French merchants and a millionaire.

Industry developed late in Chile, and workers immigrated from Europe in small numbers. As a result, unions were not founded until shortly before World War I. Previously, only mutualist organizations had existed, and these were constitutionally opposed to anarchism. Chilean anarchists, unlike anarchists in other Latin American countries, were unable to consolidate the unions they had founded into a single national organization until after World War I. When the time came they followed the example of the IWW, in the United States, even to the extent of using the same name.*

The Chilean "Wobblies," at their first congress in Santiago, in 1919, declared open war against capital, the clergy, and the government, and repudiated political and parliamentary action. But during Ibáñez's regime (1927) the IWW began to lose influence, and its activity was reduced to educational work and to organizing cultural centers, libraries, popular theaters, and so forth.

While the most radical anarchist groups worked in the midst of the IWW, the anarcho-syndicalists in 1925 created a separate union in the north. In 1927, however, it was dissolved by the dictatorship, and its leaders deported.[27]

Chilean anarcho-syndicalist groups tacitly cooperated with political elements opposing Ibáñez's dictatorship.[28] With Ibáñez's fall, these groups regained considerable influence with labor and in 1931 founded the Confederación General de Trabajadores, which, however, soon faded. Anarcho-syndicalist elements remain today in the Confederación Nacional de Trabajadores, a member of the Organización Regional Interamericana de Trabajadores.[29]

BRAZIL

Italian immigrants founded the anarchist movement in Brazil; there were, in fact, more early anarchist publications in Italian than in Portuguese. Between 1890 and 1905 there were fifteen anarchist periodicals in Italian, most of them published in São Paulo; others appeared in Santos

* Industrial Workers of the World.

and in Pôrto Alegre. By 1907 there were two anarchist weeklies in Portuguese.

There was even an anarchist colony: in 1890 a group of two hundred Italian anarchists came to Brazil to install themselves on government land grants. But at the end of four years the colony, called Cecilia, dissolved, torn apart by the squabbling of factions.[30]

The early Brazilian anarchists maintained close contact with their colleagues in Argentina and Peru. As elsewhere, they were also influenced from abroad; in 1909, Edmundo Rossoni, an Italian writer, was deported for attempting to organize an Escuela Moderna, along the lines of those established by Francisco Ferrer in Catalonia.* In September 1911 a public appeal by the anarchist newspaper *La Linterna* raised 95 dollars to help the Mexican anarchists.

The Brazilian positivists tried unsuccessfully to influence the anarchist movement. Raimundo Teixeira Mendes corresponded with Paul Réclus and Kropotkin. In 1911 he defended the "just demands" of Brazilian sailors who rioted in Guanabara Bay under anarchist leadership and were slaughtered by government forces. He called the anarchists "beloved brothers of Humanity" and proposed that the government establish an eight-hour workday and a minimum wage. He also energetically defended the Santos coffee workers, who in 1912 sustained a long strike led by anarcho-syndicalists.[31] Teixeira Mendes was a close friend of the journalist Astrogildo Pereira, then an anarchist sympathizer and later the founder of the Brazilian Communist Party.

The Communist Party in fact emerged in 1921 from a schism in the anarchist groups.[32] Anarchist elements then joined with groups of other political leanings in opposing the Communist influence. They took over the management of the Federação Operário de São Paulo. One important anarchist-led struggle was an extended textile strike in 1931.[33]

Vargas's corporatism, by establishing state control over the unions, precipitated a decline in anarcho-syndicalist influence, but anarchist groups and the anarchist press have persisted, and their propaganda continues. They have organized an archive on social affairs in São Paulo, and a few old anarcho-syndicalists still hold union offices.

PERU

Although Peru's scanty industrial development and very limited European immigration delayed for many years the beginnings of a national labor movement, anarchist groups had already formed at the end of the

---

* Such schools were successfully founded in Argentina (see p. 39).

last century, and succeeded in influencing the first unions. These groups increased their strength in the next few years, and carried on intense propaganda campaigns as well as educational efforts. From 1904 to 1909 anarchists in Lima published the newspaper *Los Parias,* and in 1905 other anarchist periodicals appeared: three more in Lima, three in Trujillo, and one in Arequipa.[34] Anarchist activity continued for several years, and culminated finally in the creation by anarcho-syndicalists of the modern Peruvian union movement.

Latin America produced two important anarchist theorists: one, Ricardo Flores Magón, was a Mexican; the other, Manuel González Prada (1848–1919), was a Peruvian. Both men came to anarchism from franc-tireur liberalism.

Like Flores Magón, González Prada was neither a strict anarchist nor systematically antipolitical.[35] His originality lay in his interpretation of the Peruvian reality, his importance in an instinct for communicating with the masses. His most important writings were published as a series of articles in *Los Parias,* later compiled in a book under the title *La anarquía.* The articles successfully popularized existing anarchist doctrines.

González Prada felt that bourgeois society must be destroyed not in a single attack but "through a series of partial revolutions." He maintained that "if ever there were an area ideally suited to libertarian ideas, that area is South America, and especially Peru. Here there are no deeply rooted traditions of the sort that in older societies offer resistance to all that is new; here the frenzy of military revolutions that stirred our fathers has become a sense of rebellion against all power and all authority; here, where the people have lost faith in public figures and political institutions, not even the restraint of religion remains, and all beliefs are disappearing with astonishing rapidity. Many Peruvians are unwitting anarchists; they exercise the doctrine, but become frightened at the name."

He saw in the clergy and the military the principal enemies of democracy, and charged that Latin American governments build armies not for national defense but to suppress revolutions.[36] He was antagonistic to Hispanicism (in the sense we now give to the word *hispanidad*—the generic character of the nations of Spanish language and culture).[37] He extolled Indian and mestizo values, and built the Unión Nacional and later the Partido Radical mainly with the support of the provinces and youth groups. He sought also to organize Peru's workers, and to associate workers and intellectuals on equal terms.

The question of a form of government, he felt, was secondary, and the social problem remained "the great issue, which the proletariat will solve by the only effective measure: the revolution." If the bourgeoisie continues not to "concede a single inch from the terrain of their convenience," the revolution must be a violent one. "Then it will be said: it is the inundation of the barbarians. But the clamor of countless voices will answer: we are not the inundation of barbarism, but the deluge of justice."

González Prada was among the first to present the Indian question on a social plane. "Schools for the Indians are not enough: there must be schools and bread." Instead of humility and resignation, Indians should be taught pride and rebellion, "since the Indian will be redeemed not by the humanization of his oppressors but by the grace of his own efforts."

He opposed strictly political movements. Socialism was oppressive and regimentarian; anarchists and socialists must share struggles but never form an enduring alliance. He taught that strikes should always evolve from the local to the general, and he criticized the indifference with which one union looked upon the strikes of other unions.[38] After a fashion, he was an evolutionist: "Revolution in the field of ideas precedes revolution in the field of action. One cannot harvest without having sown; by attempting radical reforms without first having preached them one risks lacking supporters, and lacking as well the strength to put down the inevitable strong reaction."[39]

González Prada died in 1919, just as Peruvian anarcho-syndicalist activity was reaching its peak. In 1918 anarchists organized strikes to press for an eight-hour working day. Student groups participated in the strikes. And in 1919 anarchists led Peru's first strike against "hunger."

The anarchists also tried to organize the Indian population. In 1923 they formed the Federación Regional de Obreros Indios. The government banished two of its leaders and persecuted the rest,[40] but the example had been set: the Alianza Popular Revolucionaria Americana later succeeded in politically organizing a large part of the Indian masses.

More recently, anarchist groups in the Confederación General de Trabajadores Peruanos have joined frequently with the apristas* in opposing the Communists.[41] The anarcho-syndicalist influence is still strong among older leaders of the Peruvian unions.

CUBA

During the last years of the colonial period, Spanish workers arriving in Cuba spread libertarian ideas. One of these workers, Saturnino Martínez, founded the Sociedad de Tabaqueros, in 1868, the year in which the first war of independence began. In 1892, anarchists organized the Congreso Regional Obrero, which demanded the island's independence and an eight-hour workday. It was anarchists, again, who led the dock workers' strikes

* See the note on p. 266.

in Havana in 1896. During the second war of independence, the anarchist leader Máximo Gómez drew more support from the workers than from other social groups.

In 1904, with the colonial era at an end, the anarchist periodical *Tierra* appeared in Havana. It pressed an energetic campaign for a boycott of products from Argentina, that "South American Russia," as *Tierra* described it, where anarchists were being persecuted.

Spaniards, especially Catalonians, emigrated to Cuba in large numbers during the 1920's. Anarchism was therefore fed by a constant influx of new elements, in spite of the fact that many of the newcomers let themselves be drawn into regional Hispanic societies, and were quickly distracted from the social struggle. The percentage of Spanish executed during the Machado dictatorship* was considerable. In 1927 the American Federation of Labor sent a mission to Cuba to investigate reports that several dozen Spanish workers who had "committed suicide" had been found one day hanging from trees.[42] The anarchist tradition of direct action found an echo in the other political movements opposing Machado, some of which did not hesitate to resort to terrorism.

Anarcho-syndicalists in 1924 founded the Confederación Nacional de Obreros Cubanos and continued to direct it until 1935. And although they were later driven out of the Confederación de Trabajadores de Cuba by the Communists, the anarcho-syndicalists managed to maintain strength in several unions. Anarchist groups joined forces in the Movimiento Libertario Cubano, or Cuban Anarchist Movement, to oppose the dictator Fulgencio Batista. They pressed for a smaller army, municipal autonomy, agrarian reform, and industrialization through cooperatives.

In June 1960, with Cuba under the Castro regime, the Agrupación Sindicalista Libertaria published a declaration of principles: "We will support, as we always have, all revolutionary measures tending to rout old evils, but we will oppose, with equal determination, any authoritarian tendencies that stir in the midst of the revolution itself." Once in exile, the Movimiento Libertario proved itself ready to cooperate with leftist democratic groups—but for concrete objectives, accepting no compromise, and for the purpose of returning the revolution to its original course rather than destroying it.[43]

The fascination of Castroism led anarchist groups all over the world to dispute violently whether Castro should be supported or attacked. The discussion was pursued even among Spanish libertarians, who knew, from the

---

* The Machado regime, overthrown in 1933, had instituted wide-ranging reforms, but when faced with democratic opposition abandoned its great projects in favor of suppressing opponents.

bitter experience of their own Civil War, how the Communists infiltrate and distort popular movements. But by the end of 1961 the anarchists had no more doubts about the nature of Castroism.

MEXICO

In Mexico, the most prominent anarchist of the Porfirian period (1876–1911) was José María González, a tailor who edited *El Hijo del Trabajo* and *La Internacional*.* González drew most of his recruits from among the artisans, and appears to have been both an anarchist and a cooperativist. In 1876, with evident exaggeration, he wrote, "Can you not see that the International has been more warmly received in [Latin] America than in Europe?" The reaction of the press to his propaganda was of course violent, and was rooted mainly in the argument that the Constitution, in recognizing the equal rights of all Mexicans, had made the class struggle irrelevant. A journalist with the pseudonym Juvenal wrote in *El Monitor Republicano* that "the rich and the poor no longer form the upper and lower classes of former times; rivalry between capital and labor has far less reason for existing now that certain invidious social distinctions are no longer made and our institutions guarantee the freedom of work [from the coercion of craftsman guilds]." To this *El Hijo del Trabajo* replied: "The rich and the flatterer always remind us that 'respect for the rights of others is peace' [a phrase of Benito Juárez], and we ask them, do we *have* rights—as citizens, as workers, as men? For even our natural rights have been taken from us."

The artisan drew closer to the proletariat with the onset of industrialization. González stated in 1877: "We are artisans, we are in continuous contact with the workers. We see their poverty and understand their situation." That same year there were riots in the state of Hidalgo, which official newspapers characterized as "the Communist wave" and "disturbances by overwrought Indians." The periodical *El Socialista* stated that "For them [the Indians] the independence of Mexico only made their situation more terrible, more bitter.... Yesterday they were called slaves and they were free; today they are pompously called free and they are slaves." *El Socialista* demanded the reestablishment of the *ejidos,* and asked that "the sale of lands, of mountains, and of water resources" be declared null and void. For the first time the workers had shown an interest in the agrarian problem, an interest that would only rarely be shown again.[44]

The Partido Liberal Mexicano, created formally in 1906 by Ricardo Flores Magón (1873–1922) and his brothers Jesús and Enrique,[45] was origi-

* The ideas of Proudhon had had a certain influence among Mexican liberals of the nineteenth century, but were seldom reflected in their political attitudes.

nally a liberal party, but its program and the tone of its propaganda soon became more radical. Many came to regard the Flores Magóns as anarchists. Their having been born in an Indian community in the state of Oaxaca no doubt influenced their position on the question of land. But Ricardo's thinking, authentically anarchist only after the 1910 Revolution, was due, more than anything else, to his having allied himself with IWW groups during his exile in the United States.

The "liberal" doctrine can be studied in the newspaper *Regeneración,* which the Flores Magóns founded in 1900, and which was published sporadically, sometimes in Mexico, sometimes in San Antonio, and occasionally in St. Louis. Ricardo's persistence in publishing his newspaper in the United States arose from his conviction that there could be no transformation in Latin America if a powerful anti-interventionist feeling was not first created in the United States.

The Flores Magóns and their Partido Liberal, the sole popular opposition to Porfirio Díaz, were not content simply with propaganda. They organized Liberal Clubs, held congresses, participated in the armed struggles and strikes of 1906 and 1910, and were frequently jailed. They opposed Madero and tried to establish an alliance with Zapata's movement.[46] Ricardo later founded an ephemeral Socialist Republic in Baja California, and died, blind, in the United States penitentiary at Leavenworth, Kansas, in 1922.

Through its first nineteen issues, *Regeneración* limited itself to fighting for improvements in the administration of justice (Jesús was a lawyer and Ricardo had studied law). But beginning with the twentieth issue the paper styled itself as a "periódico independiente de combate." It reproached liberals who contented themselves with being simply anticlerical, who failed to perceive the collusion between the clergy and the Díaz dictatorship. Members of the Partido Liberal proclaimed themselves freethinkers, not enemies of religion; their purpose was to "destroy the clergy's power to influence the government and ... to stupefy the masses."

In 1901, when Díaz was ill, *Regeneración* asked editorially for a candidate from "the productive class, that class which has no vested interest in the present way of doing things." To this end the first Liberal Clubs were founded, in cities across Mexico. In June 1906, in Río Blanco, Veracruz, the Gran Círculo de Obreros Liberales was constituted, an affiliate of the Partido Liberal. With its newspaper, *Revolución Social,* it managed to create eighty more centers throughout the country, particularly in textile factories. The Gran Círculo had help: a group of Catalonian workers encouraged the reading of anarchist brochures among the textile workers, and great quantities of anarchist and socialist literature were obtained from Spain by Camilo Arriaga, founder of the Liberal Club of San Luis Potosí.[47]

The program of the Partido Liberal signed in St. Louis on July 1, 1906, shows how far the ideas of the Flores Magóns had come. A comparison between this program and the Constitution of 1917 demonstrates that the former in fact set the basis for the latter. No government can ever be trusted, no matter how exemplary its appearance, stated the program, and constant vigilance must be exercised. To avoid new tyrannies, this vigilance must be accompanied by reforms: the abolishment of compulsory military service and of military tribunals; and the establishment of military instruction in schools, as a requisite for the organization of a National Guard. Foreigners acquiring property in Mexico were to become naturalized Mexicans, and the immigration of Chinese was to be prohibited, to avoid the competition of cheap manpower. Because the clergy, through third parties, continued to own large properties, they were to be nationalized, and their schools closed down. The conditions of the worker and the agricultural laborer were deplorable. "In fact, and generally, the Mexican worker earns nothing; he performs rough and prolonged tasks, and in return receives just exactly the amount necessary to avoid dying of hunger," declared the party's program, which then demanded a maximum workday of eight hours and a minimum salary of one peso. But, the program added, "the ideal of a man should not be to earn a peso a day; the legislation that determines such a minimum salary should not claim to have led the worker to the goal of freedom."

A labor law was to regulate working conditions, establish Sunday as a day of rest, prohibit child labor and company stores, and set up a system of pensions and compensations. Without all these measures there could be no national prosperity, said the party's program. Neither could there be prosperity without "an equitable distribution of land, with all the facilities to cultivate and profit from it without restriction." Such measures would not only save the peasants, but also accelerate agriculture and industry, which could never develop in a market limited by widespread poverty. The landholder would lose his rights over land he does not work, and the *ejidos* would be reinstated. Land was to be distributed without favoritisms, and to avoid new monopolies was to be withheld from the right of free sale. Land distribution was to be complemented by the creation of an agricultural bank, which would make credit available to the peasants. The program also recommended taxing everything "that is neither a necessity nor a benefit to the people."

The liberals sought many reforms: equality for legitimate and illegitimate children; the transformation of penitentiaries into reform colonies; the establishment of secure bonds of friendship among the Latin American countries, as a guarantee against aggression; and the protection of the Indian race, which, "educated and dignified, will help strengthen our nation."[48] In a letter to Samuel Gompers, the American union leader, Ricardo Flores Magón wrote: "Our brief declaration of principles establishes that we are fighting for the ownership of the land, for shorter working hours, and for higher wages."[49]

The futility of every effort to overthrow Díaz by political methods caused Flores Magón to lean still further toward anarchistic tactics. He sought to abolish all forms of government and law. He felt that the strike, like political action, was "antiquated." He called the supporters of workers' political action the "apostles of pacifism." During the Revolution of 1910 he wrote, "Our brothers of the Partido Liberal fight and die to free the Mexican people from this three-headed monster: government, clergy, capital. For this the rebellious proletariat smashes the law to bits, burns judicial and land-title records, sets fire to the buildings of the bourgeoisie and the authorities, and with the hands that before made the sign of the cross ...takes possession of the land and the instruments of work, declaring it the property of all. It would be necessary also to take possession of the production machinery, and the means of transportation; to organize, by joint planning, work and consumption."[50]

Antilabor persecution had given the anarchists impetus. They formed secret societies, in Tampico, in Aguascalientes, in Guadalajara. Flores Magón later observed of these societies, "It was not the hurricane of 1910 that hurled Porfirio Díaz from Chapultepec to the decks of the *Ipiranga,* but rather the popular awareness awakened in 1906 and 1908 by the bugles of Jiménez and Acayucan, Viesca and Valladolid," sites of popular uprisings.[51]

Flores Magón advised the members of the Partido Liberal to join Madero's followers the moment they rose up in arms, but moreover to attract to the party those others who followed Madero in good faith, to ensure that "the Revolution will benefit the Mexican people and not be the criminal means by which a group of ambitious upstarts climbs to power."[52] Elements of the Partido Liberal and of other anarcho-syndicalist groups formed part of the Casa del Obrero Mundial during the Revolution, and later some joined the Confederación Regional Obrera Mexicana, while others founded the Confederación General de Trabajadores. But in recent years the strength of Mexican anarchism has been scant and has not been increased by the Spanish anarchist exiles who came to Mexico after the Civil War in their own country, for they have played no part in Mexico's labor struggles.

OTHER COUNTRIES

In Paraguay the Spanish anarchist Rafael Barret (1877–1910) carried on
an intense propaganda campaign,[53] and credit for the first attempts at labor
organization (or, rather, artisan organization, for Paraguay had no working class until the twentieth century was well advanced) must go to anarchist groups. But under government persecution, these groups dissolved
quickly or limited themselves to obtaining and distributing Argentine anarchist publications. Later, they collaborated with several of the rebellions
attempted against the country's successive dictatorships.

Anarchists are known to have been active in a union federation in Bolivia around 1918. In 1928 the local federation of La Paz joined the International Association of Workers. And in 1930 the anarcho-syndicalists of
Oruro called a national trade union congress, held jointly with the Communists.[54] Anarcho-syndicalist groups were still active in Bolivia in 1952,
at the time of the revolution. Two organizations founded by them, the Federación Sindical Local and the Federación Agraria Local de La Paz, refused to join the Central Obrera Boliviana (COB) when it was founded,
on grounds that it was linked with the government. To them this seemed
prejudicial to freedom in spite of its being a revolutionary government.
Eventually the COB absorbed both federations.[55]

The Peruvian anarchist González Prada spread his propaganda into
Ecuador, where anarchist groups were formed early in this century. At a
time when Ecuador had barely any proletariat, these anarchist groups led
the country's first strikes: the printers' strike in Quito in 1919, which lasted
twenty-six days; and the general strike in the port city of Guayaquil in
1922. The labor organization in Guayaquil was aided by the Centro de
Estudios Sociales, which had been created by the anarchists in 1910.[56] Although the Ecuadorian union movement later fell under Communist domination and today is divided into factions, the anarcho-syndicalist influence
survives in some unions, particularly in those of the Federación del Guayas.

No legally constituted unions existed in Colombia until 1910. But from
articles sent from Bogotá to anarchist newspapers in other countries, we
know that there were already many union sympathizers in the country,
most of them acquainted with anarchist thought. When unions began
forming, anarchists participated actively in their struggles, and appear in
fact to have been the organizers of a popular demonstration in Bogotá in
1916, which was broken up by the police with an extraordinary number of
deaths and over five hundred arrests. Anarchists were also active in the
dock workers' strike in Cartagena in 1920.[57] Later, their influence de-

clined, but anarcho-syndicalists remained prominent in union life and during the 1920's published the journal *Claridad*.[58]

The dictatorship of Juan Vicente Gómez* in Venezuela was not a fertile period for the development of unions—especially not for unions led by anarchists. The anarcho-syndicalists, although forced to conceal their activities, helped organize the unions that in 1923 made up the Unión Obrera Venezolana.[59] Many anarchists were later active in the union movement.

Anarchist and anarcho-syndicalist publications from Mexico were probably read in Central America and in Haiti and the Dominican Republic. These ideologies doubtless found sympathizers, but no proper documentation on the existence of organized groups can be found. We might suppose that these sympathizers were among those establishing the first unions. In any case, the frequency of dictatorships made all declared anarchist activity, and even the spread of doctrinal propaganda, practically impossible.

INTERNATIONAL AFFILIATIONS

From the outset of their activities, anarchist groups in the various Latin American countries maintained contact with each other, and from time to time sought to establish a continental federation. The Federación Obrera Regional Argentina (FORA) made preparations for a continental convention in 1910, but a state of siege declared by the Argentine government put an end to their plans. The second congress of the Federación Obrera Regional Brasileña (FORB), in which fraternal delegates from Argentina and Uruguay took part, established an international committee charged with preparing a continental congress. The congress finally took place in Buenos Aires in 1919 and was attended by delegates from thirteen countries. The Asociación de Trabajadores del Continente Americano (ATCA), an organization founded by the congress, survived only briefly.

Close contacts, particularly in Chile and Mexico, were also maintained with the American IWW, and the IWW was established in several Latin American countries, notably Chile. Many groups maintained contact with the European anarchist movement. The FORA and FORB were represented in an anarchist congress held in London in 1913. FORA delegates took part in the congress held in Berlin in 1922, during which the Inter·

---

* The Gómez regime, which lasted from 1908 to 1935, was one of total and absolute tyranny, but did manage to force the state into national solvency and material prosperity, largely on the strength of the discovery of oil on Venezuelan soil.

national Association of Workers (AIT) was formed. The Chilean IWW and FORU of Uruguay also sent delegates, but they arrived too late to participate in the debates. In March 1925, delegates from FORA and FORU, and one delegate from the workers' federation of Río Grande do Sul (Brazil), attended the second AIT congress, in Amsterdam.[60]

In 1929 the Asociación Continental de los Trabajadores (ACT) was formed by a congress held in Buenos Aires and Montevideo. The congress was attended by delegates from the following organizations: Federación Obrera Local de La Paz (Bolivia); Confederación General de Trabajadores (Mexico); Comité pro Acción Sindical (Guatemala); Federaciones Obreras de Gabé, Pará, Río de Janeiro, and Pelotas (Brazil); Unión General de Trabajadores Uruguaya; and Federación Obrera Regional Uruguaya. This congress proclaimed anarchical communism to be the best method of promoting the welfare of the working class, and rejected all others. ACT, like the ATCA of 1919, survived only briefly.[61]

An anarchist conference held in Montevideo in April 1957 was attended by delegates from anarchist groups and newspapers in Argentina, Brazil, Cuba, Chile, and Uruguay. Adhesions were received from groups from the United States, Mexico, Panama, and Peru, as well as from individuals from the Dominican Republic, Haiti, Bolivia, and Ecuador. The conference was organized by the Comisión Continental de Relaciones Anarquistas (CCRA), which had been created some years before. The CCRA works closely with the Comisión Internacional de Relaciones Anarquistas (CIRA),[62] and maintains an important international anarchist archive in Montevideo.

The conference concentrated primarily on Latin American problems and adopted all resolutions without vote. These resolutions are interesting as a summary view of recent Latin American anarchist and anarcho-syndicalist thought. Among other things, the conference took these positions:

1. Condemned both capitalistic and Bolshevistic imperialism, and particularly cultural imperialism.

2. Condemned nationalism as "reactionary, jingoistic, and aggressive," and as "antithetical to culture, which is international."

3. Characterized the action of all hemispheric union federations existing at the time as ideological colonialism.

4. Condemned militarism, even when presented in the form of a people's army, in the Soviet fashion, and repudiated all "developments tending to superimpose a military character on the social life of the [Latin] American nations."

5. Opposed religious action on social matters.

6. Demanded the economic integration of Latin America, on grounds

that division into nationalisms facilitates the economic exploitation and cultural disintegration of the continent.

7. Recommended that anarchists work within the labor movement and work toward anarchist leadership of the unions whenever possible.

8. Agreed to back any struggle, whether political, union, or otherwise, seeking to assure "the right to strike and the right of association, and directing its efforts toward anarchistic aims."

9. Reiterated that direct action is useful not only in opposing dictatorships but also in creating conditions unfavorable to their development.

5. The Socialist Movement

IN LATIN AMERICA the socialist movement took root and developed where immigration from Europe was heavy: in Argentina, Chile, and Uruguay. Elsewhere it failed to become an organized movement—or at best, ran to modest careers of brief importance.

But if it has generally been impotent as an organized political force, socialism has had great ideological influence on Latin American politics. Today there is no popular movement, no school of economists, not even an aspiring demagogue, that fails to reveal the influence of socialist thinking. Even the demagogues who have wished to pursue fascism have been unable to divest themselves of socialist thought, however warped they may have presented it.

Such social concepts as government control and state intervention in economy are well entrenched in Latin American tradition. Other aspects, such as the tendency to government planning, suit the aspirations of young technocrats, including the young military. Socialism influences these elements, but its influence does not make of them party militants. Rather, it affords them ideas, concepts, and points of view, as well as methods for analyzing reality.

The phenomenon of nationalization of ideas, which other ideologies had undergone, occurred also in Latin American socialism. Arriving at a time when democracy was a formality, a façade, at a time when elections were won by the candidates who most cleverly faked them, organized socialism found as its first objective the disinfecting of electoral procedures, as its first contest the debate with those—the anarchists—who, disgusted by these procedures, saw in the political processes no more than a scheme for distracting the proletariat from their necessary course.

If today socialism, as an organized movement, finds itself essentially bankrupt, it can nevertheless take pride in having given a decisive impetus to many improvements in the condition of the working class—by stimulating social legislation and the development of the union movement. It is perhaps true that socialism would not have been so effective if the direct action of the anarcho-syndicalists had not driven the oligarchies to concessions. But where socialism was a viable force, these concessions were obtained directly by socialist activity; and where it was not the concessions were extracted by movements whose ideologies were heavily, if subtly, suffused with the influence of socialism. In some countries the founders of the union movements were socialists—in others, anarchists. But there can be no doubt that the socialists' defense of the union movement, in the parliaments and in the press, was effective.

Socialism, then, began its Latin American life struggling for the exercise of political democracy, against electoral fraud and the absolute power of the caudillos and the military. It introduced the practice, unknown to other political parties of the period, of writing and publishing programs of activities and doctrinal definition. It championed the rights of political minorities, and gave direction to student thinking, which led ultimately to the *reforma universitaria* movement. On the social level it pressed for legislation that included an eight-hour working day; the Sunday rest; the protection of the woman worker and of the Indian; the elimination of child labor; and employer responsibility for on-the-job accidents. On the economic level socialists proposed a tax on profits and on inheritance, as well as a land tax to combat *latifundismo,* and demanded agrarian reform, which remains today the objective of broad political sectors.[1]

During World War II socialist parties shared in the fight against Nazi infiltration, and in demanding parliamentary investigation of governments suspected of complicity with the Axis. In Argentina, where the neutrality of President Ramón S. Castillo's government had seemed secure, the socialists forced a parliamentary investigation that revealed unexpected complicity.[2]

As in Europe, Communism in Latin America emerged more often than not from the socialist movement. The Communists first branded the socialists as "social-fascists," then proposed to them the establishment of the popular front.[3]

Latin American socialist parties have also maintained cordial relations with the populist movements, and, at the same time, with parties of the center and the right, and have even allied with them during election campaigns.

The pages that follow examine, country by country, the various careers of socialism in Latin America. The contribution of socialism to the unionist movement, taken up in detail in Part III, are treated briefly here. The chap-

ter concludes with an account of efforts by Latin American socialist parties
to organize internationally.

ARGENTINA

The writings of European socialists began to penetrate Argentina early
in the nineteenth century. Esteban Echeverría (1805–51), a poet, prose
writer, and propagandist who had lived in Paris from 1825 to 1830, was the
chief proponent of their ideas. In 1837, with Juan Batista Alberdi (1810–84),
Juan María Gutiérrez (1809–78), and others, he founded the Asociación
de Mayo, a secret society opposing the dictator Rosas.* The *Dogma socialista,* which Echeverría wrote for the Asociación, bears the influence of
Leroux and of the Saint-Simonians. Leroux also influenced Domingo F.
Sarmiento (1811–88).† But Alberdi‡ and his circle were driven to deny
these leanings when they were declared subversive by the Rosas dictatorship.[4]

In the prologue to his *Dogma,* Echeverría wrote: "Argentine society is
divided into two irreconcilable factions, factions that have for many years
cut each other down on the field of battle: the triumphant federal faction
[the Rosas government], a malevolence supported by the popular masses,
and a genuine expression of their semibarbaric instincts; and the defeated,
unitarian faction, a minority with good intentions but no local bases of
socialist motivation, and somewhat repugnant because of its arrogant attitude of superior political acuity."

He also wrote: "We had hoped that the people could be other than what
they have been until now: an instrument of power and profit for caudillos
and local strongmen, a pretext, a name vainly invoked by all existing parties,
in seeking to conceal, by an honest appearance, their personal ambitions;
but what the people should be is what the May Revolution attempted to
establish, the beginning and the end of everything."

Echeverría sought "democracy in industry and at the root of ownership;
in the distribution and remuneration of work; in the collection and appro-

---

*Juan Manuel de Rosas (1793–1877), governor of Buenos Aires province, then
dictator of all Argentina (1835–52). A ruthless tyrant, he involved the country in
foreign adventures that brought blockades and economic decline. He was finally
routed by combined Argentine, Uruguayan, and Brazilian forces led by Justo José
de Urquiza, a former Rosas lieutenant.

† Statesman, educator, author, and president of the Republic (1868–74). From
exile in Chile, he led the resistance to the Rosas dictatorship, and helped in the
final overthrow. As president, he brought peace, material progress, and numerous
reforms.

‡ Following Rosas' overthrow, the new government adopted a constitution based
on principles enunciated by Alberdi.

priation of taxes; in the organization of the national militia; in a hierarchic order based on capacity; in short, in the totality of the intellectual, moral, and material movement of Argentine society.... An industry that fails to emancipate the masses and to elevate them to equality, but that, rather, concentrates wealth in the hands of a few, is an abomination.... There is no equality in a society ... where the poor class alone suffers the most arduous social burdens, such as service in the militia, ... no freedom where a man ... is restricted in his right to print or utter his opinions." He predicted that "the era of complete emancipation of man is nearing. Despotism by the caste family, and even the caste state, is disappearing, but the property caste still predominates—man, that is, is still enslaved by property."[5]

Frugoni* spoke of the precursor of Argentine socialism in these terms: "Echeverría never surmounted the Utopianist limitations of his European teachers, which in an environment as backward as South America's simply emphasized his remove from the obvious reality. He most assuredly observed the economic causes of the May Revolution, but he failed to perceive the significance of land ownership, which, with its immense latifundios, was and still is demonstrably basic to all national difficulties. In the face of a poor class submerged in the direst ignorance of its own interests and incapable of any initiative, he placed his hopes in the democratic process, and the realization of his humanitarian ideals in a handful of illustrious men and in his Asociación de Mayo."[6]

Alberdi, though a comrade of Echeverría, soon came to renounce his social concepts and declared himself opposed to "the extravagances of the foolishness of socialism." In Latin America, so he said, there was no disproportion between population and resources, and socialism for Latin Americans was therefore "unnecessary and absurd."[7]

Sarmiento considered Fourier's conclusions to be generally "aberrations," but felt that among them were clear and perceptive ideas. Believing that "modern societies tend to equality," he anticipated the moment when the masses who "today revolt for bread will demand that parliaments discuss the number of hours they should work." Politics, then, would be "reduced to a simple issue: how can men agree upon means to provide for their present and future welfare?"[8] Sarmiento in fact saw the solution to social ills in the development of savings institutions: with money in his hands, the worker is drawn immediately to pleasure, "because of the lack of a fixed notion of something he might attain little by little." Something had to be done to avert "the sickness that precipitates revolutions." This something,

---

* Dr. Emilio Frugoni (1880–   ), one of the founders of the Socialist Party of Uruguay. See p. 82.

apparently, was a savings system; Sarmiento at least proposed no other remedy.[9]

In spite of Echeverría, socialist ideas failed to spread. Sarmiento was able to write, in *El Censor:* "Socialism is not even known by its name. People ask themselves what it means, and there are others, held in a curious awe or fear by the word so newly arrived, who answer: 'It is the disintegration of the family,' 'It is free love,' 'It is the worker turned into boss.' The word is pronounced in a voice of alarm. In some homes cautious fathers have forbidden its utterance in their after-dinner conversations."[10]

But awe soon became interest. The French émigrés of 1851 brought republican ideas tinged with socialism. Many of them dedicated themselves to teaching; among these was Alexis Peyret, who later participated in the Paris Congress of 1889 that saw the creation of the Socialist International. Emigrants came also from Spain: Bartolomé Victory, a typographer who in his print shop published a collection of popular works, including those of Cabet, in 1864; and Dr. Serafín Alvarez, an emigrant from the Cartagena rebellion, who in 1873 published several socialist propaganda pamphlets.[11] A new wave of political exiles, those of the Paris Commune, would add organization to propaganda.

Among the founders of Argentina's first socialist group, Les Egaux, were Emile Dumas, who was to become a French socialist congressman, and Achiles Cambier, later an Argentine delegate to the Socialist International.[12] Italian socialist immigrants formed the Fascio de Lavatori. And German emigrants in Buenos Aires founded the Vorwärts Club, on May 1, 1882, to "cooperate in the fulfillment of socialist aims and principles." The Club gave to Wilhelm Liebknecht* its representation at the Paris Congress of 1889.

Argentina's Socialist Party was founded in three stages. The first involved the establishment of the initial nuclei: Les Egaux, Fascio de Lavatori, Vorwärts, and the Agrupación Socialista, founded with thirty members in 1892, which combined Argentinians and Spaniards. In 1894 the Agrupación became the Centro Socialista Obrero, and began publishing the weekly *La Vanguardia,* with a circulation that soon reached 1,500 copies. *La Vanguardia* remains today the voice of mainstream Argentine socialism.

The second stage began in April 1894, when the French and Italian groups, and the Centro, formed the Partido Obrero Internacional. The Germans, convinced that the first goal should be political rights for workers born outside the country, at first declined participation; but by the end of

---

* Liebknecht (1826–1900) was the founder of the German Socialist Party; he opposed the Franco-Prussian War of 1870 and participated in the creation of the Second International.

1895 they had reconsidered, and the Vorwärts Club joined the party. By that time also the Centro Socialista Universitario had been formed and had joined the party. Among its members was José Ingenieros (1877–1925), later secretary of the first Central Committee of the party.

At its congress of October 1895, the Partido Obrero Internacional voted to change its name to Partido Socialista Obrero Argentino. The two terminal adjectives were later seen to be unnecessary and were dropped. The congress also agreed to participate in the elections, and selected Dr. Juan B. Justo as party secretary. At the time the party had 63.93 pesos in its cash box. That year, *El Anuario* said that "socialism is a stain on the sun of our progress."[13]

Juan B. Justo (1865–1928) was Argentine socialism's most important figure. He gave the movement doctrinal personality and an indelible brand. He was a physician, son of a middle-class family, and was just thirty years old when elected party secretary.

The party's first congress, held in 1896, was attended by thirty-three organizations (eighteen socialist centers and fifteen unions). During the congress, Justo explained his view of the party's role: "The Socialist Party is above all the workers' party, the party of the proletariat, of those who have nothing but their capacity for work. The doors of the party are nevertheless open wide to those of other classes, so long as they understand that our interests are those of the proletariat.... We begin thirty years after the European socialist parties, and therefore must begin better, profiting by the experience already accumulated by the international labor movement." After recounting the formation of the socialist labor parties in Germany, England, and Belgium, Justo ended by exhorting: "We must adopt without hesitation all that is science: we will be revolutionary,... but quite unlike those false revolutionaries, the plague of South American countries, whose sole interest is in upsetting what exists, with no capacity for replacing it with something better. The environment in which we operate compels us to ... admit the foreign-born to the party, for the sake of popular impressions, even when the foreign-born have no political rights."[14]

Justo had joined the Agrupación Socialista in 1893 without having read Marx, impelled by reasons of sentiment and by the revulsion he felt toward the policies of the oligarchy. By 1895 he was in Paris, correcting the first Spanish translation of *Das Kapital*. But it was only after returning from a trip to Europe and the United States that he decided to take an active part in political life. His deeper reasons are revealed in a conversation published in *La Vanguardia* in March 1910, in which he recalled his work at the hospital, caring for the workers and the poor: "In preserving those lives condemned to such vile suffering there was something sterile, ... something fanatic and unilateral. Was it not more human to occupy oneself in trying to root out the causes of such suffering and degradation? And could this possibly be attained without illuminating the minds of all the people, without nourishing them with scientific truth, without educating them for the higher possibilities of social life? The task lay before me as an immense germination of customs. ... I soon found in the labor movement the climate for my new aspirations."[15]

After a fashion, Justo applied Marxism to his analysis of the Latin American reality: "In the so-called Latin American countries the mixture of races and the division of classes separate us profoundly from the conditions of U.S. society. The race mixture is to our benefit, the class division to our disadvantage. Only the workers' organization can fuse the productive population of these countries into a common historical awareness. The Central and South American nations will begin to exist only when their working classes achieve enlightenment and spiritual homogeneity. ... Criollo politics have forsaken or submerged our native workers in poverty and ignorance. ... The labor parties, then, have a common doctrine: international organization of the proletariat, for the attainment of political power and the socialization of the means of production." But a heavy admixture of nationalism must also be espoused, he felt, because of the corruption of foreign capital.[16]

Justo had once lived in Junín, a town some 150 miles west of Buenos Aires. About 1905 he began to take an interest in the peasant situation there. He began a campaign under the slogan: "This is how the slaves of the north live." The Ley de conchabos had enslaved the agricultural workers. A conchabado booklet of rules outlined the obligations of the conchabado, and recorded the money advanced to him by his employer. The debt was never liquidated, however, because the worker received his salary in chips or notes negotiable only at the employer's shop, where essential items were sold to him at exorbitant prices. The booklet was also indispensable for obtaining work. The Socialist Party, backed by the press, fought the practice and persuaded Parliament to abolish the conchabo system.

In the Socialist Congress in Copenhagen in 1910, the French delegate Sorge, contemplating Justo's report on the oppression of workers in Argentina, proposed a boycott on Argentine products. Justo opposed the suggestion, on grounds that it would jeopardize the working class not only in Argentina but also in Europe. And during World War I, with those thoughts in mind, Justo urged the party to support neither a break in relations nor a declaration of war by Argentina. He also called for a federation of Europe—at least of Western Europe—and for the establishment of nationalities by plebiscite.[17] In the union conferences in Berne and Amsterdam, in 1919, Justo defended free international trade against the contrary argument of the Belgian delegation. For Argentina, a country with large exports, this freedom was paramount.

During the Congress of the Socialist Party at Bahía Blanca, in 1921, Justo presented a program for international action, which was approved. He proposed that socialism bend its efforts toward securing the equality of races; international labor legislation; the abolishment of customs duties within twenty years; the establishment of an international monetary unit; the obligatory arbitration of secret treaties; and the gradual reduction of military expenses.

Justo's position was also decisive in the elaboration of the party's agrarian program, which favored a method of socialization of the soil compatible with small property. To this end the program adopted Henry George's formula of rescuing for society, by means of taxation, land profits in such a way that the land could remain only in the hands of those who used it as a means of production, rather than as a source of speculation. So that the country's land might be distributed among many free producers, the program sought to socialize land profits rather than land appropriation; thus, by abolishing the privilege of profits for the individual owner, the program reconciled the principle of collective land ownership with private possession of land, as an element of work.[18]

In his *Teoría y práctica de la historia,* Justo attempted once again to give the party a materialistic and dialectical orientation, as seen from the mentality of a biologist with positivist influences. But Marxism provoked firm opposition in party ranks. Many in the party were still addicts of the romantic tradition of the *Dogma socialista* and the Asociación de Mayo; most prominent among these was Alfredo L. Palacios.*

Many Argentine positivists leaned toward socialism, but were comfortable only where the Marxist component had been highly diluted. They considered education to be the cornerstone of social transformation, and encouraged the establishment of secondary and vocational schools for workers. José Ingenieros, a founder of the party and a party leader for many years, and Carlos Octavio Bunge (1874–1918) are the important examples of this evolution. If, in Europe, Darwin and Spencer buttressed the social attitudes of the bourgeoisie, in the Plata they seemed to support the socialists. According to Bunge, a country of immigrants suffers not so much a class struggle as a struggle for individual development, for personal assertion. Justo made use of a historical/biological analogy drawn from his medical past

---

* Argentina's first socialist congressman. See p. 72.

to make bedfellows of Spencer and Marx. He felt that Hegelian dialectic bulked too prominently in Marxism, and that the theory of the plusvalue was "only an allegory." Thus the proletariat should confine itself to practical science, to experience, in seeking an intellectual basis for its struggle. Justo wanted neither a dictatorship nor a sudden revolution, but simply that all people share control of technology, which at that time was concentrated in the hands of a few. He believed that by this means society would gradually eliminate inequality, and he insisted, therefore, that education must precede the revolution. "We should love broad ideals and occupy ourselves with small things. In this fashion we will manage to make them big."[19]

The Italian socialist and criminologist Enrico Ferri visited Buenos Aires in 1919. During his visit, Ferri engaged Justo in an interesting debate. It had been Ferri's contention that because industrial capitalism did not exist in Argentina the Socialist Party had no reason for existing. For answer, Justo described the evolution from feudalism to agrarian capitalism: "The procedure consists in obstructing the workers' immediate access to free lands, by effectively withholding their free-landholder status, so that even should they occupy the land they would find it impossible to pay the assigned sale or rental price. The criollo governing class, guided only by its instinct, its financial needs, and its appetite for easy gain, practices systematic capitalistic colonization. The result of the process, spawned on the fringe of land ownership, is the proletarian mass—both of the city and of the country. Its fate, as an exploited class, demands the presence of socialism." Ferri disagreed: "The proletariat is the product of the steam engine and only with the proletariat is the socialist party born," to which Justo replied: "As an exercise in judicial and political coercion, the relationship between the proletariat and the bourgeoisie was in its beginnings one of violent plunder, of iniquitous laws—not one of technological progress. Only later did the steam engine appear."[20] Justo may have had Ferri in mind a few years later when he suggested that Argentine socialism had reached a stage in its theoretical evolution beyond that of certain European socialist parties, because, in contrast with them, "we try to uphold all that is healthy and viable within the fundamental framework of a capitalistic society."[21]

In 1926, when the party celebrated its thirtieth anniversary, Justo recalled that during the founding meeting, party members had been taken by romantic notions to somewhat radicalize the declaration of principles he had presented to the meeting; but the lesson of "the enormous Slav tragedy [the U.S.S.R. was living the final period of the NEP, Lenin having already died] has shown us that the working class will have reached maturity only when it is capable of modifying relationships of property by law or decree —and, while so doing, raising, or at least not depressing, the techno-economic level of the country."[22] This had been his objective, and it remained the objective of Argentina's Socialist Party.

The platform of the Socialist Party at the time of its first bid for electoral offices illustrates the problems that faced the Argentine labor movement in 1896, and the solutions socialism offered. The political demands of the platform were:

1. Universal suffrage, in both national and municipal elections, for both men and women.

2. Permanent electoral registration.

3. Revocability of elected candidates, should they fail to fulfil the obligations of office.

4. Municipal autonomy.

5. Suppression of the privileges accorded the clergy, and confiscation of their properties.

6. Suppression of the permanent armies and general armament of the people.

7. Abolishment of the legal precept that ignorance of the law does not constitute an extenuating circumstance.

Economic and social demands were for:

1. Working day of eight hours for adults and six hours for minors from fourteen to eighteen years of age, and the abolishment of work for minors under fourteen.

2. Establishment of rules and regulations governing women's work, and the prohibition of anti-hygienic and immoral work.

3. Equality of remuneration, where production is equal, for workers of both sexes.

4. Creation of supervisory commissions for the inspection of factories and workers' dwellings.

5. Allotting to employers the responsibility for on-the-job accidents.

6. Creation of tribunals, appointed ad hoc by both employers and workers, to arbitrate differences.

7. Abolishment of indirect taxes.

8. Establishment of both direct and progressive taxes on profits.

The manifesto directed to the voters read: "The Partido Socialista Obrero, unlike other parties, makes no claim to pursue its goals out of sheer patriotism, but for its legitimate interests; makes no claim to represent the interests of everyone, but rather those of the working people against the oppressive and parasitic capitalist class; would not have the people imagining they might achieve well-being and freedom from one day to the next, but would assure them of inevitable success if they will submit to a protracted struggle, with tenacity and determination, expecting nothing from fraud or violence, but drawing rather upon education, intelligence, and courage."[23] The program received 134 votes, and in 1898, 104 votes.

With scanty resources, but great energy, the party pursued cultural activity and the indoctrination of party militants. Socialist activities were backed by several prominent figures, including José Ingenieros and the poet Leopoldo Lugones (1874–1939). Lugones was later an independent socialist, then a conservative, still later a Communist, and finally a fascist.

Competition with the anarchists for labor support led also to the establishment of socialist libraries, schools, and study centers. In 1896 the Centro Socialista de Estudios was founded. A labor library was formed the following year.* The Escuela Libre para Trabajadores and the Sociedad Luz were formed in 1899, the latter to give instruction by means of "magic lantern" projections. The same year *El Diario del Pueblo* was created, but survived only two months, for lack of funds. The party would have to wait six more years before elevating the weekly *La Vanguardia* to daily publication. In 1904 the Universidad Popular was constituted, and Dr. Enrique del Valle Iberlucea, later the first socialist elected to the Senate, created the Ateneo Popular, which for ten years published its own journal. In 1913, the wife of Dr. Nicolás Repetto (Dr. Repetto was a party leader for many years) founded the Asociación de Bibliotecas y Recreos Infantiles, with sections in many socialist centers. In each of these, of course, there was a library. *La Vanguardia* expanded into publishing, and produced many popular books, in general carelessly put together, but very cheap. Choirs and dramatic art groups completed the socialist cultural repertoire. The net effect of all these efforts on the uncommitted was considerable.[24]

Socialists also lent assistance to the cooperatives and mutualities, much to the disgust of the anarchists. Groups of workers, principally sandal-makers and woodcarvers, who were involved in disputes with their employers, on several occasions consulted Dr. Justo on ways and means of establishing workers' production cooperatives. In 1898 ten workers proposed the creation of a consumers' cooperative; within a month, they attracted thirty-four stockholders and seventy-seven pesos in cash capital. During that same year the Asociación Obrera de Socorros Mutuos was founded, the first cosmopolitan society to accept members of both sexes, without distinction of creed or nationality. The Cooperativa de Crédito y Edificación, which later became El Hogar Obrero, was created in 1907 with the help of nineteen socialists, including four party leaders: Juan B. Justo,

---

* In 1928, when Dr. Justo left to the library his own collection, it became the Justo Library, as a memorial to the party's founder. Perónist mobs set fire to the library in 1954, during an attack on *La Vanguardia*'s building.

Nicolás Repetto (1871–1965), Angel M. Jiménez, and Enrique Dickmann (1874–1955).

Differences within the party began with its founding. The Centro Socialista Revolucionario of Barracas was made up of Spanish workers for whom naturalization as Argentine citizens represented renunciation of internationalism. Francisco Cúneo and the poet Leopoldo Lugones shared this viewpoint, and presumed the party to be obligated to demand political rights for immigrants. Finding the party's response less than satisfactory, the Barracas Centro left the party in August 1898, and founded, with six other centers, the Federación Socialista Obrera Argentina, which was to rejoin the Socialist Party during the third party congress in 1900.[25] In 1898 the party met another difficult test, when the chronic conflict with Chile once again broke out. Rallies and the daily press agitated for war against Chile, but *La Vanguardia* made its own stand: "The working class feels no hatred toward the Chilean people."[26]

Nevertheless, socialism still had not taken root among the masses. Years later the French socialist Jean Longuet had this to say of the party's failure to attract popular support: "The party may point with pride to its eminent educators and scholars ... but it displays the frequent defect of the socialist movements in the Latin American countries of being not preëminently a labor movement. It is not, in the main, led by men emerged from the working class. The result of, and at the same time an excuse for, this defect is the inorganic and chaotic state of the Argentine union movement."[27]

The nature of socialist thought during the period of the great socialist-anarchist debates* is reflected in the later remarks of José Ingenieros at a conference in 1910: "The Marxist concept of the labor dictatorship is a sociological error; no society can be abruptly changed; there are no sudden transformations; these are the dreams of the fanatic and the deluded.... This theory is one of the great delusions propagated by the socialists of the past, a delusion tenaciously upheld by socialist and anarchist rhetoricians." On the other hand, "to all socialist sociologists it is clear that capitalism's transformation into a socialist regime, which implies collective ownership of the means of production as its basis, is a slow and progressive process operating ... sometimes in spite of the proletariat, though ultimately to their benefit. Indeed, all institutions—economic, political, judicial, moral —evolve gradually in a direction favoring the proletariat. I believe these Latin American countries must pass through more advanced phases of capitalistic economic evolution before a regime based on socialized ownership of the productive forces can be expected to take form.... Socialists

---

* These debates are described on p. 41.

must stand firm in this belief, without fear of being labeled conservatives, retrogrades, renegades, or somnambulants. In the Argentine Republic the Junín socialists have adopted a modest communal reform program, following the inspiration of Dr. Justo, who precedes us all in the clear comprehension of these questions: the Junín program makes no mention of the social revolution, nor does it seek to socialize production sources; rather, it tries simply to achieve those reforms that are at once advantageous to the working people and compatible with the present circumstances of Junín's municipality."[28]

To other parties, the socialist motives did not seem so humanitarian. Immediately after the 1902 elections, for example, a violent attack against the Socialist Party took place in the Chamber of Deputies, at the instigation of Deputy Eliseo Cantón, who said: "I believe we should not give the arguments of socialist philanthropy more importance than they deserve. I am the first to applaud immigration, but only when it consists of men who come to this land to enrich it with their labor, seeking bread for their children and well-being for themselves; I detest an immigration that arrives proclaiming false principles and waving banners repudiated even in old Europe, attempting to convince the sensible and educated mass of this country that the socialist banner of regeneration is the one to wave on the beaches of the Plata, bringing, to persuade us, for lack of more convincing devices, a bomb in one hand and a stiletto in the other." This same Eliseo Cantón, in 1905, supported the dismissal of Justo and Repetto from their professorships in the School of Medicine at Buenos Aires University.

In 1904 the Argentine Socialist Party included 1,700 members and one congressman—the first socialist congressman in the country—Alfredo Palacios (1880–1965), then twenty-four years old, elected by the workers of the Boca dock area, in Buenos Aires, by 840 votes. He refused to take the oath "For God and the Gospels," and instead solemnly swore "For Honor and My Country." Palacios, a lawyer and an elegant, mustachioed bon vivant, was the principal figure in half a dozen duels. He managed, in time, to achieve the approval of, among other measures, the Sunday rest and the law protecting women's and children's work.[29]

Within the party, discussion of tactics raged. Soon, two currents became apparent: one progressive, typically socialistic, the other revolutionary, syndicalistic. In the 1904 party congress the strength of the syndicalist trend was felt: the Congress resolved that every socialist group patronize a free public school in its area; that propaganda be launched at the hearts of workers' organizations; and that positions favoring cooperatives for both production and consumption also be supported. The proposed National Labor Law was discussed during the congress, and the party instructed Palacios to vote against it.

The Seventh Party Congress met in April 1906. Internal struggles, which had lasted three years, led to a crisis. After five days of debate, Dr. Repetto announced that "The congress will be pleased to hear that the group of members calling themselves syndicalists now constitute an autonomous party, to put to experimental verification their doctrine and tactic." The congress approved the declaration, and the syndicalists withdrew.[30]

In the early years of the century the Argentine anarchist movement was subjected to constant persecution. The Residence Law,* which the Socialist Party also emphatically opposed, was particularly crippling. On occasion, in the face of these repressions, socialists and anarchists made common cause for a demonstration or a strike.† When the centennial of Independence was celebrated the Socialist Party reiterated its position in a manifesto: "The Argentine labor movement is the work of men born here and elsewhere, as any healthy collective activity must be, in a cosmopolitan country.... The labor movement carries on the task of assimilation, freeing natives and foreigners from racial prejudice, and encouraging them to work together in the development of a stronger Argentine people. Feelings and ideas circulate in the world now with the same freedom as men and merchandise.... If Europe's art and science have been copied, if seeds and breeding stock to refine our crops and our herds have been brought from the Old World, why is it not also considered a blessing for concepts and practices to be imported, especially as these imports are to lead us out of the swamp of criollo politics?"[31]

The persecution inciting these reactions came to a head in 1910. The socialists were to hold their Ninth National Congress in May; despite the announcement of a general anarchist strike, the Chief of Police assured the socialists, on May 14, that they would be permitted to hold their Congress. That same night, nationalist gangs, supported by the police, destroyed *La Vanguardia*'s print shop. The staff managed to escape, but Justo, the editor, was arrested. The same group also attacked the anarchist daily, *La Protesta*,‡ and several workers' centers. The attacks had been prepared in the Municipal Administration and in the Secretary of the Presidency offices, not at police headquarters. The same night the government declared a state of siege that lasted three months. *La Vanguardia*'s print shop was rebuilt a year later, with 25,000 pesos collected through popular donation.

An extraordinary congress called by the Executive Committee for January 1911 was held in Montevideo because Argentina was once again in a state of siege, but the political climate soon improved. The new President,

---

* A law sanctioning deportation of aliens, enacted in 1904 following the assassination of the Chief of Police by anarchists. See p. 41.

† See p. 41, for example.

‡ See pp. 42–43.

Roque Saenz Peña (1851–1914), echoed popular pressure and obtained the approval, in 1911, of the law named after him, which guarantees the freedom and validity of the universal secret ballot.

Socialism could now aspire to effective parliamentary action. Its election platform for 1912 called for:

1. Opposition to the armed peace.
2. Repeal of obligatory military service.
3. Reduction of indirect taxes that raise the price of consumer goods.
4. Proportional representation.
5. A municipal system based on universal suffrage.
6. Political rights for foreigners with more than two years' residence, and their registration on electoral records.
7. Employers' responsibility for accidents on the job.
8. Repeal of the Residence Law.
9. An absolute divorce law.
10. Labor inspection.
11. Separation of Church and state.[32]

Justo was elected congressman for the city of Buenos Aires; he was reelected successively as congressman and senator until his death in 1928.

Socialist candidates drew increasingly greater numbers of votes in Buenos Aires: in 1896, 134; 1898, 104; 1900, 135; 1902, 165; 1904, 1,257 votes and one congressman; 1906, 3,495 votes and one congressman; 1908, 5,178 votes and one congressman; 1910, 7,006 votes and one congressman; 1912, 32,000 votes and two congressmen. Manuel Ugarte (1878–1932) received 14,000 votes, but not victory, as a senatorial candidate in 1912.

The Socialist Party in 1912 had fifty-two sections and 4,000 dues-paying members, a daily newspaper, La Vanguardia, with a circulation of 75,000 copies (it had become a daily in 1905), a bimonthly journal, Vida Nueva, publishing 3,000 copies, and several weeklies, including, among others, El Trabajo in Junín, La Palanca, in Pergamino, and Antorcha Socialista.[33]

In September 1911, the French socialist Jean Jaurès visited Buenos Aires. The philosopher Alejandro Korn (1860–1936) commented on his visit: "Jaurès' apparent success in Buenos Aires is enormous; his real influence is much slighter. The great public and the bourgeois press showed their admiration for the orator, pondered his eloquence, and praised his leadership of the political struggle in his own country. They did not, however, appreciate the great wealth of his ideas; they did not probe the depths of his thinking; nor were they able to comprehend the importance of his stature within the socialist movement."[34]

The work of Justo and Palacios in the Chamber of Deputies brought the Socialist Party victory in the elections of 1914: elected congressmen were

Dr. Nicolás Repetto and Mario Bravo (1882–1944); and as senator, Dr. Enrique del Valle Iberlucea (1877–1921), who had founded the Ateneo Popular in 1904.

Del Valle Iberlucea, a man of arresting personality, began distinguishing himself not only in the party but outside it as well. He joined the Socialist Party as a young lawyer in 1902, and while teaching at the University was elected senator. His legal background was to set the tone for most of his speeches. Like another party leader, Enrique Dickmann, he was foreign-born, and felt compelled to express ardent nationalism in the Chamber. The abundance of immigrants within socialist ranks laid the party open to chauvinistic criticism, and the necessity of appearing eloquently patriotic was a chronic irritation to party leaders.

Del Valle presented a bill to Congress for a law establishing an eight-hour working day, as a measure to reduce unemployment. It was not approved, and such a law was in fact not ratified until 1929. During World War I he sided with the Allies, and opposed Argentina's neutrality. The Russian Revolution modified many of his concepts, and he found himself favoring the Third International. In 1920 he began, in fact, to wonder if the party should abandon the electoral struggle and take the course of direct action; he felt that socialism, all over the world, had entered into a "catastrophic period of revolution," and that it had lost faith in the bourgeois democracy. The thesis of the proletarian dictatorship, he said, must be adopted by each country as suits her needs.

Frugoni contrasted the political positions of the three prime movers of the party in this manner: "Justo supported neo-Marxist theoretical tendencies bordering on Bernsteinism, with not a few departures from the hypothesis and logical method of Marx; del Valle Iberlucea, also a man of vigorous intellect and vast erudition, maintained an almost absolute adherence to orthodox Marxism, as well as a deep affinity for Soviet Communism; whereas Palacios, who had always rejected the narrow interpretations of the materialist concepts of history ... drew his strength from a fervent adherence to nationality and homeland.... In a country where currents of the narrowest nationalism exploit patriotic sentiments for their own purposes, and exalt the fanaticism of the homeland, he was determined not to relinquish to them a monopoly on national love and the cult of patriotism."[35]

Palacios had often been accused of party insubordination. When his socialist colleagues in Congress were attacked for their foreign birth, in 1914, he defended them with a passion that led finally to his challenging Congressman Oyhanarte to a duel. During the Party's Constitutional Congress of 1896 a clause had been voted into the statutes requiring that: "No Party member can accept the judgment of arms in order to solve personal differences of any kind, on pain of separation from the Party." Invoking this regulation the socialist parliamentarian group "separated" Palacios, and the executive committee declared him excluded from the Party. Palacios appealed the judgment before a special congress in 1915, but was denied reinstatement. Some days later he resigned his office as congressman. Palacios' friends formed a new party, and in their statutes guaranteed the right of dissent: criticism of party leaders could in no way cause a member's expulsion. But the group was unable to amass influence, and failed to endure; in 1931 Palacios rejoined the Socialist Party.[36]

Manuel Ugarte's "separation" came about on more doctrinal grounds. In 1912 he had attracted a large socialist vote in his unsuccessful bid for the Senate. But in 1913 he opposed the strictly proletarian concept of anti-imperialism sustained by the party; he believed that anti-imperialism should be a continental and national issue, above and beyond class considerations. After a debate in *La Vanguardia* Ugarte withdrew from socialism, and although he tried to form his own party, his followers soon dispersed.

But the gravest schism resulted from the question of Argentina's neutrality in World War I. The majority of the executive committee declared in 1917 that it was imperative to adopt a "position in defense of ... our international commerce, without which the economy of the country would be paralyzed; of freedom of the seas; and of the political ideals pursued by socialist democracy." *La Vanguardia* said: "Neither the parliamentary group nor the executive committee have suggested the country intervene in the war. They wish only to assure the effectiveness of the Republic's commerce, for the purpose of avoiding greater economic isolation, national ruin, and poverty among the workers." During the party's extraordinary congress of April 1917, spokesmen for the majority in the executive committee, and for the parliamentary group, reiterated the necessity of keeping the routes of sea communication open. Only the most strictly conservative line, they said, could suppose the country to be self-sufficient during those war years. Minority spokesmen charged that the war was a capitalist conspiracy to create markets for industry—for production that in every country was confiscated from the proletariat by capitalism. The line taken by the executive committee won 3,500 votes, and that of the internationalist minority, more than 4,000.

But the debates persisted. When the question of breaking relations with the Central Powers was put to a vote in the national Chamber, the socialist congressmen voted in the affirmative. Justo understood that these relations had already been broken by circumstances, and that the vote in favor of the rupture was of little importance. The internationalists, however, chose to interpret this action of the parliamentary group as a direct betrayal of the line approved in the recent party congress, and through their press—the newspaper *La Internacional*—persisted in presenting the war as an inter-imperialist conflict. The parliamentary group resigned: "We do not believe the World War to be the simple and fatal consequence of private ownership and mercantile production," said the text of the resignation written by Justo.

The internationalists constituted a committee of the defense for the resolutions adopted by the congress. The executive committee submitted to general membership vote the question of whether to accept or reject the resignation of the members of the parliamentary group. The resignation was rejected. The executive committee invited the committee of defense to dissolve itself. Its members refused to do so, and the executive committee then proceeded to bar all its members from the party, as well as members and groups who had preserved solidarity with the internationalists, such as the Socialist Youth group.

During early January 1918, delegates from all the expelled groups met and constituted the Partido Socialista Internacional. Its manifesto announced that it would "fight to defend workers' interests. But we seek not simply to *achieve* our minimum program, but to *saturate* it—in a manner of speaking—in the revolutionary yeast of the maximum program of collective ownership, for which we shall fight ceaselessly and tirelessly."

The Russian Revolution broke out. The war ended. In the press and in party platforms, discussion concentrated on a critical question: had the moment come to acknowledge the uselessness of democratic institutions, the inadequacy of the parliamentary method, and the imminence of great social changes, and therefore to heed the advantages of insurrectional measures? Del Valle Iberlucea had already presented to the Senate a bill for the creation of a National Economic Council, which proposed a socialist-type organization of Argentine society and production.

Justo warned: "Dictatorship, even in the hands of the noblest and most intelligent men, is always a recourse of exception. Whatever the immediate effects might be on the measurable well-being of the people, dictatorship negates the development and exercise of popular aptitudes. The subjects of a dictatorship may live better, or perhaps worse, but they will remain passive and possibly unconscious instruments."

The party's next congress, in 1920, precipitated the confrontation of the two tendencies. The two camps concurred in hailing the Russian Revolution inasmuch as it had destroyed Czarism and opened new prospects for social transformation; but the current defined by del Valle Iberlucea sought adherence to the Third International. Antonio de Tomasso challenged del Valle, maintaining the evolutionist position. The voting produced 3,651 votes for Moscow, 5,013 against. The schism: the supporters of the pro-Moscow position left the party; del Valle did not. Soon afterward, because of his speech before the party's congress, and at the request of the Federal Judge of Bahía Blanca, the Senate authorized Senator del Valle's indictment; but the indictment never took place, as the accused died two months later.[37]

The period of persecutions seemed definitely to have passed. Socialists debated with the Communists and applied themselves to parliamentary tasks and to propaganda. By now they had a daily newspaper and ten weeklies in seven languages, and in 1918 drew 60,000 votes—but party members totaled less than 8,000. They continued their work in the unions, hoping to counteract Communist and anarcho-syndicalist gains, and to increase their electoral influence—101,000 votes and eighteen congressmen in 1925. Socialists attained the majority of Chamber seats in the federal capital, and two Senate seats. They also obtained representation in several provincial legislatures, and in many municipalities.[38]

But a new schism appeared, the fifth in the history of Argentine socialism. This split, of the so-called "independent" socialists, was led by the Party's Secretary General, Congressman Antonio de Tomasso, who had earlier championed the traditional evolutionist position. In 1927 the socialist parliamentary group proposed a bill for federal intervention in Buenos Aires province, as a protest against the establishment there of race tracks and gambling casinos, which violated a provincial law forbidding games of chance. When the provincial legislature suppressed the law, the group felt there was no recourse but to withdraw its bill. Several socialist congressmen opposed the withdrawal of the demand, and eleven congressmen, two councilmen, and 109 members were accordingly expelled from the party. The expelled group formed the Partido Socialista Independiente, which in the 1930 elections attracted 109,000 votes (with ten congressmen), against 83,000 votes (and one congressman) for the old party.

Hipólito Yrigoyen (1852–1933), leader of the radicals,* governed at the time. Since 1911, when universal suffrage had been restored, the radicals had expressed the most popular current opinion. Yrigoyen sought to limit the privileges of the oligarchy, and to restrain foreign capital, but the worldwide economic crisis fomented tensions, and Yrigoyen allowed himself to be drawn into suppressing certain strikes. In August of 1930 the Socialist

---

* A moderate, left-of-center party, similar to the French party of the same misleading name.

Party (of the old camp), warned of a military coup. And in September Generals Agustín P. Justo (1876–1943, no relation to Juan) and José Félix Uriburu (1868–1932) forced Yrigoyen to resign, and jailed him—he was then seventy-eight. Confronted with the military takeover the Socialist Party published a vague manifesto, which concluded with the statement: "The Socialist Party urges the working class and the people of the Republic to cooperate in the quick restoration of democratic institutions, suggesting that in the immense perspective of its historic evolution, this episode of democracy is an experience to be avoided in the future."

The Independent Socialists immediately inclined toward the military, to whom they accorded a demogogic image. But it took Uriburu only until December to unmask his fascist tendency: he denounced the democratic regime as the "evil of evils," launched a tirade against universal suffrage, proclaimed the need of a government by a select minority, favored corporative representation, denounced the "corruption of the minimum wage," and announced a constitutional reform and modifications to the electoral law.

The General's Minister of the Interior quickly met with socialist leaders in hopes of reaching an agreement with the Party, to facilitate the acceptance of these positions. Mario Bravo and Nicolás Repetto expressed the party's willingness to cooperate, but only insofar as cooperation would hasten the return to constitutional normalcy. Of course there was no agreement. When a military coup was attempted in Corrientes the government took severe measures. On July 22, 1931, *La Vanguardia* was closed down and the principal socialist leaders—Américo Ghioldi (1899–   ), Mario Bravo, Enrique Dickmann, and others—were arrested.[39]

In the 1931 elections the Independent Socialist Party backed General Justo for president. The old party, on the other hand, allied with the Partido Demócrata Progresista, proposed a democrat (Lisandro de la Torre) for president and a socialist (Nicolás Repetto) for vice-president. The democratic-socialist candidate received 126,370 votes in Buenos Aires, against General Justo's 166,358. With help from the radicals, the Socialist Party seated forty-four congressmen; the radicals had offered no candidates, preferring to support those offered by the socialists. At the time of the election the Socialist Party could count about 21,000 members, with 423 local organizations. The independents participated in the General's government, but finally dispersed.[40]

After the expulsion of the independent socialists, Communist groups began to infiltrate into the ranks of the Socialist Party, upsetting its internal life. During the 22nd Party Congress in 1934, a proposal made by Communist sympathizers was rejected, and a new schism was produced, to decimate the ranks of the young socialists. The expelled members formed the ineffectual and short-lived Partido Socialista Obrero, a simple arm of the Communist Party.

With the return of the radicals to the political struggle, the socialist vote began to decline. In the 1936 election the socialist parliamentary minority dropped from forty-six to seven.

Opposition to Nazi activities in Argentina allowed the Party to hold the line briefly. In 1938, socialist Congressman Dickmann was one of the first to denounce the Nazi activities, and the socialist Juan Antonio Solari (1899–   ) was elected secretary of the Comisión Investigadora de Actividades Antiargentinas of the Chamber of Deputies. The socialists also shared in the organization of Acción Argentina, a group made up of democratic elements of different political creeds, with the purpose of resisting the Axis influence. In 1940 the Socialist Party drew 135,000 votes, enough to elect five congressmen and one senator.[41]

General Justo's government stimulated the organization of armed nationalist groups, and paved the way for a second military overthrow, after a brief period of conservative civilian government. Dr. Ramón S. Castillo (1873–1944) took the presidency because of the illness of President Roberto M. Ortiz, and maintained the country's neutrality during World War II. In an interview granted by Castillo to a commission from the Socialist Party's executive committee, Dr. Dickmann predicted a coup. The President refused to be convinced, but on June 4, 1943, the military came to power. Some supported the takeover, believing it would reestablish democratic institutions; others considered it a fascist movement. But the struggle for power among the military factions, and the anti-democratic speeches of the new government officials, soon exposed the totalitarian nature of the new regime.

On June 7, 1943, the socialist executive committee stated: "It is indispensable and imperative that political, civil, and democratic organizations be heard concerning measures for assuring national recuperation and the restoration of the constitutional government ... and the new direction of foreign policy. ... Only through the democratic reconciliation of all Argentinians can the country face the grave political crisis."[42]

The dictatorship at first had no social program. It did not, for example, persecute socialism. But Colonel Juan Domingo Perón (1895–   ), Minister of Labor, began developing a mechanism of union control. In 1945 he organized the Partido Laborista with his friends from the unions, who backed him in his electoral campaign the following year, and helped him gain the presidency.[43]

Under Perón the Socialist Party maintained a policy of active resistance, and collaborated extensively with democratic and conservative elements in opposing Peronist demagoguery. Socialist leaders were persecuted, although the Party was never actually outlawed. Repetto, Ghioldi, and other Party leaders were jailed or forced into exile, and socialists holding union posts suffered the same fate. If it accomplished nothing else by this resistance, socialism seemed to have assured itself a prominent role in the post-Perón reorganization.

But it was not to be. Perón's fall, in September 1955, was engineered by a faction of the armed forces and the Catholic Church—the working class had taken no part in intervening against a dictator who had himself known how to attract the workers. An ironic circumstance had left the Socialist Party isolated and politically impoverished, to become, oddly enough, a middle-class movement. Even with its legality restored, the party was by internal dissensions prevented from becoming a viable force in the country.*

In 1958 many friends of the Communist Party, finding support among youth groups, infiltrated into the Socialist Party. Failing to attain the majority in the party congress at Rosario that year, the leftists dissolved the congress by violence. Then, constituting themselves an executive committee, this minority took party headquarters by surprise, and in a meeting at Palacios' home expelled the old leaders without permitting them even a word. Under the leadership of Ramón A. Muñiz (1906–65), Dr. Alicia Moreau de Justo, and Alfredo L. Palacios, the leftist group seized the party name and was quickly recognized by the Socialist International. When the deposed group confirmed that it had assembled the support of two-thirds of the party members, a judge ordered the leftists to return the party premises to the legitimate socialists. The deposed socialists had in the meantime constituted the Partido Socialista Democrático, under the leadership of Repetto, Américo Ghioldi, Luis Pan, and other old and very active socialists, and were publishing the weekly *Afirmación,* and later, again, *La Vanguardia.*

By 1961 the Argentine Socialist Party's political identity had collapsed. Four fragments remained: one led by Muñiz and Palacios, which in May created a second fragment by expelling David Tieffenberg's group (each with its own party congress and its own edition of *La Vanguardia*); the Partido Socialista Popular, a pro-Perón splinter from the Muñiz group with a firm hold on Buenos Aires province; and the Movimiento Socialista Principista, composed of old militants. The four groups ran an ideological

* On Peronism see the chapter on Argentina in Part III; see also Lux-Würm, *Le Peronisme.*

gamut from nationalism to Marx-tinted Perónism to Trotskyism. The splits had been stimulated by the fractionalism of the nuclei of impatient young militants, and were exploited and encouraged by Communists seeking to use the Party as a façade for their own activities. These were the Communists who, in 1961, carried the full weight of Palacios' electoral campaign, and managed to install him in the Senate with a pro-Castro program.[44]

After the military coup of July 1966, the leftist socialist groups accepted General Juan Carlos Ongania's takeover; only the Partido Socialista Democrático opposed it. But all of them—as the remaining political parties— were suppressed and all their buildings and assets expropriated by the military regime.

URUGUAY

During the first half of the nineteenth century a Frenchman named Eugène Taudonnet, living in Montevideo, edited and published socialist materials. Among these were *Le Messager Français,* a commercial, literary, and political daily that appeared from 1840 to 1842, several works by Víctor Considerant, and a biography of Fourier. On returning to Europe in 1847 he met, aboard ship during the crossing, Domingo Sarmiento, who later wrote of him: "He was a disciple of Fourier's. . . . He had closed his eyelids, and had kept in his possession a few precious relics—the pen Fourier had used during the last moments of his life, a lock of his hair, and his shoes." Later, in Paris, Taudonnet edited the *Chronique du Mouvement Social.*[45]

But it was only toward the end of the century that these first seeds bore fruit, under the heat of socialist literature from across the Plata. By 1896 several socialist groups had formed in Montevideo, and some years later the Centro Obrero Socialista was created. One of its members, Dr. Emilio Frugoni (1880–   ), describes the beginnings of the Uruguayan Socialist Party: "With the Centro Obrero Socialista as its nucleus, and with the union activities of several of the Centro's components ensuring its local appeal, a Unión de Trabajadores was constituted. The Unión grouped together a few labor organizations, but never effectively consolidated itself. After publishing a journal, *El Espíritu Nuevo,* for six or seven months, this primitive amalgam was reorganized by a group of students and young intellectuals as the Centro Carlos Marx. The new Centro—its general secretariat was entrusted to me—was intensely active: frequently it was involved in the organization of important public functions; it published manifestos; and it took part in workers' rallies, often in the form of speeches by the secretary general. In effect, the Centro was the training ground for the Socialist Party. Another center, the Centro Emilio Zola, was formed later, and on the eve of the 1910 elections a congress to constitute a political party was held, so that the new Party might take part in the electoral struggle precisely when a withdrawal by one of the traditional political parties afforded us the chance to capture a seat in Parliament. (The law at that time enfranchised only the two parties with the most votes; at the time of the congress these were the Colorado and the Blanco, or Nacional.) During the congress, the Socialist Party was born. An electoral coalition with a nucleus of freethinkers from the Centro Liberal defeated the Catholic Party* in the contest for minority seats in the department of Montevideo. Thus the Socialist Party had its first congressman, Emilio Frugoni, who served in the legislature from 1911 to 1914."[46]

Many felt that the Socialist Party had been born stripped of its purpose by the reforms proclaimed by President José Batlle y Ordónez (1854–1929).† Batlle's reforms did in fact relegate the Uruguayan Socialist Party to a mission unlike those of other Latin American socialist parties: opposition to a genuine reform government, but opposition to force Batlle's special brand of capitalism, a mixed economy, to respect the interests of the working class.

The new Socialist Party directed its energies toward driving the anarchists out of the union administrations, and to discouraging workers and middle-class elements from favoring Batlle and his reform program. To this end the party raised the agrarian question, which Batlle had consistently avoided. In its declaration of principles, the Socialist Party placed the land problem among its chief concerns—it was, in fact, the first Uruguayan party to make of the land problem a key issue of politics. But the party never succeeded in organizing the peasants, a fundamental weakness never subsequently overcome.[47]

Frugoni himself had this to say of the party's tactics: "A gradualist tendency can be observed in its behavior, which suggests a concept of the socialist struggle at once revolutionary, in the extent of the social transformation it seeks, and evolutionary, in the methods of action it chooses to use."[48]

The single tax theory proposed by Henry George became popular in this period. In 1915, in his book *Los impuestos desde el punto de vista sociológico,* Frugoni discounted the George theory, insisting that the emancipation of the workers could not be achieved simply through a reform in the fiscal system, however radical it might be.

In the 1916 elections the socialists captured 1,635 votes in the capital, and returned Frugoni to his seat, this time in an assembly charged with writing

* The Unión Cívica; like the Socialist Party it was, at the time, in its infancy.
† Batlle's politics and reforms are discussed on pp. 241–43.

a new constitution. At the time of the elections the party had 500 members and two weekly publications. Frugoni declared in the assembly that his party's essence lay in a program of action, that "we form a party of ideals, not of illusions." The party had elevated its official organ, *El Socialista,* into a daily, called *Justicia,* and had increased its influence among the unions.

But a party congress held early in 1921 produced a schism; the majority at the congress broke away to join the Third International, accepted Lenin's twenty-one conditions, and formed the Uruguayan Communist Party. The minority hewed to the program of the Socialist Party, and retained the party name. With the daily, *Justicia,* now in the hands of the Communists, the minority socialists founded a new weekly, *Germinal,* and later, *El Sol.* The party recovered, slowly, after the Communist schism and even managed to gain three seats in the Chamber of Deputies, as against one for the Communists.[49]

In 1925 the party won 1,794 votes in all of Uruguay, barely more than it had won in the capital alone nine years before. In 1928 it attracted 2,931 votes, enough to reelect Frugoni to the Congress. Internal reorganization took up much of 1930, and the party presented no candidates. But in 1931, with its popularity again increasing, the party once more elevated its weekly journal to daily publication, and joined the Socialist International.

When the dictatorship of Gabriel Terra (1873–1942) emerged, in 1933, the unions and students immediately declared a general strike. In February 1933, when the executive committee of the Socialist Party brought pressure on Parliament to impeach Terra, the dictator reacted quickly. The party came under heavy attack, and Frugoni was forced to flee to Argentina, where, from exile, he accused Terra of defending foreign petroleum interests.

Terra's grip on the country relaxed somewhat as time passed. The exiles came home. And during the first elections under his new constitution, in 1934, the socialists elected two congressmen, the Communists one. In the 1938 elections, in spite of election fraud and government pressure, the dictator's choice for president was defeated, by General Alfredo Baldomir (1884–   ). Frugoni, candidate of the Socialist Party, received 26,057 votes, as against 121,000 for Baldomir. In the same election the socialists won three seats in Parliament, the Communists only one.

Under Baldomir's government, the Socialist Party supported the hemispheric solidarity policy and cooperation with the United States, and actively opposed the maneuverings of the Nazis in Uruguay. A young socialist, Hugo Fernández Artucio, built an impressive case against the Nazis and brought suit in the courts, asking that immediate punitive action be taken. So ardent was the anti-Nazi feeling generated by the socialists that a congressman in the conservative Herrera party tried to assassinate Frugoni in the Chamber of Deputies.[50]

Through all this period Frugoni worked diligently to promote the socialist doctrine. For years he published theoretical books, including *Génesis, esencia y fundamentos del socialismo,* and *La esfinge roja*—the latter a product of his stay in Moscow as an Ambassador, during World War II. Written under the full euphoria of the alliance with Stalin, *La esfinge roja* is one of the first objective analyses of the Soviet reality. But in the postwar period the Socialist Party made no progress.

Toward 1960, young elements of the Socialist Party launched an offensive against the party's old-guard leaders. The result was to weaken democratic leadership and to put the party at the service of Castroism, or at the least to divide and cripple it, leaving the field open for the Communist Party. Ricardo Durán Cano, chief target of the young leftists, opposed within the party "the majority that accidentally dominates the national executive committee, because of its lack of capacity for judgment and leadership, its abdication of partisan responsibility, its notorious inclination to tolerate and facilitate militant Communist doctrine, and its penchant for ideological–intellectual subversion of the principles and methods of action of democratic socialism." Vivián Trías and Dr. José Pedro Cardoso, old-socialist members of the national executive committee, worked inside the party with the Communizing majority. This strange Castroist–Trotskyist alliance later dissolved, once it had attained its objective. By 1961 four groups had become chief rivals for the control of the party: the Trotskyist Vanguardia Socialista; the Grupo Leninista, which scattered in June 1961 when most of its members turned to the Communist Party; the group called Nuestro Tiempo, whose journal of that name demanded the union of socialists and Communists; and the group known as Socialismo Auténtico, made up of the few old democratic militants who had not been expelled by the executive committee on one or another trivial pretext. Frugoni remained on the fringes of party activity.

This fragmentation was the product, as it had been in Argentina, of the impatient fractionalism of a few young people, and of the machinations of the Communist Party, eager to crush a rival and absorb its followers.[51] In the 1964 election, what remained of the Socialist Party allied with extreme right-wing groups—Frugoni resigned from the party at this point —and won not a single parliamentary office.

PARAGUAY

A group of Australians, adherents of Robert Owen's social philosophy, in 1893 obtained deed to 94 square leagues of land in the department of

Ajos, in Paraguay, where they established the colony of New Australia. *La Vanguardia,* the Buenos Aires socialist daily, predicted the colony's failure, on grounds that a group of this sort would inevitably bend to the influence of its radically different milieu. The colony's 263 members cultivated 613 acres, but disbanded within two years.

William Lane, the journalist who had led the Owenists, created another colony, called Cosme, in 1898, on the site of what had previously been a Jesuit mission. The colony consisted of several villages, each with its own council, and a central council elected democratically from among all the villages. Lane toured England and collected many donations. The colony published a newspaper and enjoyed a relatively active cultural life. There were internal difficulties and the population never exceeded 100 persons, and toward 1903 Cosme ceased to be a colony as such.[52]

The winds of Argentine socialism barely penetrated the isolation of Paraguay. But toward the second quarter of the present century, socialist ideas, more or less altered, influenced the political concepts of several militant and civil groups. From these groups arose the *febrerista,* a movement of some importance. The movement is more populistic than socialistic, and is accordingly discussed in Chapter 7.

CHILE

The influx of European workers into Chile fell far short of that into Argentina, but was nonetheless considerable. And many of the immigrants were among the founders of the first proletarian organizations.

In 1849 a translation of Louis Blanc's *Organization du Travail* was published (it was not translated into English until 1911). Curiously enough, many Santiago newspapers reproduced it intact. And during the ensuing ten years Santiago bookstores sold, in French editions, the works of several other European socialists.[53]

The origin of the Chilean socialist movement is often placed in the Sociedad de la Igualdad, and in its prime movers, Francisco Bilbao and Santiago Arcos. But much of the groundwork was laid by others who, though not themselves socialists but rather liberals tinged with positivism, nevertheless sustained some ideas that were later developed by socialist theorizers: of these others the most influential were Genaro Abasolo (1833–84), a disciple of Bilbao and the author of *La religión de un Americano* and other works of a philosophic nature; Alejandro Venegas Carús (Julio Valdés Cango), author of *Sinceridad,* a courageous denunciation of the country's social reality; José Victoriano Lastarria (1817–88), liberal politician and positivist philosopher; Valentín Letelier (1852–1919), sociologist and educator; and Roberto Espinoza (1869–1931), author of financial studies. Such diversity of viewpoint reflects the nature of Chilean socialism, a movement perhaps lacking in solid theoretical bases, but one well disposed toward immediate political action.

The Sociedad de la Igualdad, founded in January 1850, was secret and conspiratorial in character—not unlike the Masonic lodges, but lacking their ritual. The conservative government, in a move to oppose it, ordered that its meetings be opened to the public.[54] The picture that emerged was, according to a Communist historian, that of the "typical petty bourgeois organization." But the exposure had unforeseen results: for the first time in Chile, people demonstrated in the streets, held meetings to discuss politics and candidates, and organized public debates. Hundreds of workers attended the classes on elementary education held at the Sociedad's headquarters, and the society grew to 4,000 members during the seven months the authorities recognized its public existence.

In November 1850, taking advantage of a declared state of siege, the government outlawed the Sociedad. But its influence was enduring; similar societies, founded by its members, turned up in cities around the country: the Club de la Opinión in Valparaiso; the Unión Republicana del Pueblo in Santiago; the Escuelas Republicanas in several cities; the Sociedad de la Igualdad in Valparaiso; the Sociedad Republicana Francisco Bilbao, also in Valparaiso; and another of the same name in Coronel. The Igualitaristas were pre-Marxist liberals with socialist overtones, and among them were many who could be called anarchists.

Francisco Bilbao (1823–60) was a leader of the Sociedad and its chief theorist. His *Sociabilidad chilena,* an attack against the oligarchy, was written when he was very young. Its appearance led to his excommunication and his expulsion from the Chilean University. For a time, he traveled in Europe and fought beside Edgar Quinet at the barricades of 1848. On returning to Chile he founded, with Arcos, the Sociedad, with the motto "The sovereignty of reason as the authority of authorities. The sovereignty of the people as the basis of politics. Universal fraternity as moral life." When the Sociedad was outlawed, Bilbao fled to Peru and finally found refuge in Paris. There, he made one of the first continentalist proposals on record, during a conference which he called "A proposal for a federal congress to conciliate universal citizenship, the abolishment of inter-American border customs, and the establishment of international courts."

Again in Buenos Aires, he founded the *Revista de Ambos Mundos.* When the French invaded Mexico he wrote *América en peligro,* a polemic containing such violent attacks against the Church that the book appeared in the Index. Nevertheless, the influence of Lamennais on his thought was apparent from his youth, and his writings seem actually to be more the work of a mystic than of a politician. In his *Mensajes del proscrito* he perhaps best summarized his concepts. For him, "Credit is an obligation of ownership permitting every being to come to own property." He favored free trade, unified industries, and a land tax calculated in relation to the land's area and its distance from an urban center. He argued for colonization and for the industrial armies conceived by Fourier that would be dedicated to the building of roads and canals, to reforestation, and to vocational training. Also apparent in Bilbao was the influence of Rousseau and of the pre-Marxist socialists, and a great admiration for the French Revolution. He can be considered fundamentally a libertarian. His goal was the rule of freedom, which "in its purest form is direct government by the people." In the existing society, he felt, there was neither harmony nor the possibility of freedom, for both were negated by inequality. The people, "image of the infinite," were unaware of their own power, and toiled mindlessly for the wealthy, the priests, and the state. The reigning feudalism of Chile obstructed "the rise of a middle class, such as the bourgeoisie of Europe, as a prelude to freedom." He asked for a revolution that would establish "the liberty of man, the equality of the citizen."

But Bilbao was not of the turn of mind that could lay precise plans for the overthrow of feudalism; he never cited, for example, the need to destroy *latifundismo*. His close colleague in the Sociedad, Santiago Arcos Arlegui (1822–74) was more specific. In his *Carta a Bilbao,* published in 1852 by a Masonic print shop, Arcos, who had just arrived from Europe, described his amazement at what he found in Chile. For him the desperate condition of Chilean society was sustained by the profound differences between peasants and landowners: there could be no progress, then, "while inquilinaje [the tenant system] persists in the haciendas ... while the owners continue to suborn the authorities with their omnipotent influence—an influence that punishes poverty with slavery ... while 1,400,000 Chileans live in poverty, ignorance, and degradation in a country of only 1,500,000 people." He sought the formation of a democratic republican party that would welcome the poor and the partyless. Once a seat had been won in the government, the new party would proclaim a declaration of rights and duties. To the traditional lists of rights Arcos made five remarkable additions: the rights to education, to work, to protection (for orphans and the aged), to retirement, and to rehabilitation of the delinquent. These, in the middle of the nineteenth century, and in Chile, were audacious suggestions. But Arcos had an even more stunning proposal: "to bestow humanity on those wretched beings now serving as instruments for cultivation ... it is necessary to take lands from the rich and distribute them among the poor"—with compensation. His program, in short, was to "enrich the poor without ruining the rich," with the motto "Bread and Liberty." During the same period certain Chilean bourgeois groups and newspapers had, in fact, begun considering the necessity of land reform.[55]

Arcos' family had emigrated to France and from there had returned to Chile in 1848, when Santiago was twenty-six years old. When the Sociedad was dissolved, Arcos was exiled to Peru. He returned to Chile in 1852, and after being jailed was expelled from the country. He lived for some years in Argentina and later in France, where he committed suicide at the age of fifty-two. His father had grown wealthy through dealings with politicians and smugglers, and Santiago seems to have derived from this fact a compulsion to erase by his actions the guilt of his father.

Chile also had a utopian socialist in the early years—Martín Palma (1821–84), who in 1858 published *El crisianismo político o reflexiones sobre el hombre y las sociedades*. He was the author of several serialized novels and was on the staff of the daily *El Mercurio*. Inequality, which frustrates all revolutions, had its origin, he said, in the fact that men work in the service of other men. Ownership was "an ominous institution," he insisted, and in the Chile of that period it was more truly a "negation of ownership," since for a very few to have possessions the majority did without them. The universal desires for freedom and the pursuit of happiness would be the fulcrum, he claimed, in any effort to overturn the condition of inequality maintained so assiduously by the governments and the Church. He was confident society could be transformed, not with bloodshed, but through persuasion, to establish a regime of social providence and absolute democracy, the abolishment of borders, and the union of all nations into one.

In Chile, as in other Latin American countries, there were utopian experiments. In 1866 Ramón Picarte Mújica, an engineer and mathematician who had lived in France and had a professorship in the Chilean University, created a Fourierist community, or phalanstery, in Chillán. He pursued an intense cooperativist propaganda campaign, and organized cooperatives among tailors and shoemakers, as well as a consumers' and producers' cooperative, the Sociedad Trabajo Para Todos. But neither his phalanstery nor his cooperatives survived long.

Socialism in Chile was not violently suppressed, as it often was in other countries, but was constantly under fire from conservative elements and from the Church. In 1893 the Archbishop of Santiago, Mariano Casanova, issued a pastoral denouncing socialism, in which he stated that "poverty is a treasure for the future life, a fertile seed for the harvest of eternity," and the workers should take heart from the thought that "they have nothing in this world; but they can encounter the treasures of heaven in the other if they will but bear with Christian resignation the privations of their poverty."[56]

Within the Partido Radical was a group of essentially socialist bent. It was led by Malaquías Concha (1859–1921), who in 1885 founded the newspaper *La Igualdad*. An editorial in *La Igualdad* asserted that "radicalism, to flourish, must descend to the people and assume the character of German democratic socialism."[57] Finding no acceptance for their ideas among the radicals, these socialist elements withdrew to found a new Sociedad de la Igualdad, in 1886. The following year, the new Sociedad became the Partido Democrático, the party that, according to Concha, was to be "the working people's party." Its charter framed its objective as "the political, economic, and social emancipation of the people." Because the party comprised extremely heterogeneous elements, its program was one of moderate reforms; it would have been impossible to gain broad party acceptance of radical measures. The Partido Democrático was an excellent training ground for labor militants and it achieved considerable popularity. Within the party were socialist, liberal, and anarchist groups, all, of course, competing for control of the party.[58]

At its first congress, held on Bastille Day, 1889, the Partido Democrático adopted a program and structure similar to those of European socialist parties of the period. Its baptism by fire followed quickly, in a successful protest against a proposed fare raise in the Santiago urban transportation system.

The party's first election triumph came in 1894—Angel Guarello, a Valparaiso lawyer, was placed in the Chamber of Deputies. In 1897 Artemio Gutiérrez was elected congressman and Guarello was reelected. The same election placed five democrats in the Valparaiso Municipal Council. Shortly afterward, however, party dissidence caused the most radical elements to break away: they founded the Partido Proteccionista, in 1891, and the Partido Proteccionista Obrero, in 1899.

In 1896, elements from the Partido Democrático, along with politically unaligned workers, created the Centro Social Obrero, in Santiago, which quickly established branches in districts throughout the capital and began publishing *El Grito del Pueblo*. The Centro intended educating the proletariat, and giving "national representation to citizens belonging to the working class." Santiago was also the base for the Organización Fraternal Obrera, a group with tendencies somewhere between socialism and anarchism. In October 1897, the two factions merged to form the Unión Socialista, an organization of predominantly anarchist character that was soon outlawed by the police, although it continued to publish a newspaper, *El Proletario.*

In December 1897, the same elements created the Partido Socialista de Chile, with a membership of 148 persons. The new Socialist Party soon split, this time between anarchists and authoritarians. The former left the party, primarily to take part in union activities. The latter, in 1898, created the Partido Socialista Obrero Francisco Bilbao, with elements that had separated from the Partido Democrático, and in 1900 came once again to be called simply the Partido Socialista. The party published several newspapers, among them *El Socialista,* but in spite of its doctrinal propaganda it faded, and the majority of its members returned to the Partido Democrático in 1902.[59]

Perhaps the most colorful character in the Partido Democrático was Juan Rafael Allende (1850–1905), often called the Voltaire of Chile. He was an impetuous, rousing orator, famous for his caustic humor and his penetrating anticlericalism. But Malaquías Concha was the soul of the party. As a young lawyer he had become famous defending the poor. He was the party's theorist, and the author of the party's program. In other respects similar to the socialist platforms of contemporary Europe, his program was artfully adapted to Chilean conditions.[60]

In 1912 the weekly *El Despertar de los Trabajadores* appeared in Iquique, edited by a picturesque and impassioned personality, the typographer Luis Emilio Recabarren (1876–1924). In the 1906 elections, Recabarren, a member of the Partido Democrático, had been elected to the Chamber of Deputies, but was denied office. The election was repeated, Recabarren won again, and the Chamber again gave victory to the defeated candidate.

Recabarren was a socialist, with socialist convictions. After an honest and arduous effort to establish a dialogue between the Partido Democrático and the working class, and in the process to promote socialist doctrine, he became convinced of the impossibility of the Partido's becoming a party of the proletariat, and founded the Partido Socialista Obrero, in June 1912. The new party, an immediate success, was joined by elements from the Partido Democrático, as well as dispersed survivors of the series of socialist parties spawned around the turn of the century. Recabarren was elected congressman for Tarapacá in 1912, but again failed to occupy his office. In 1913 the party won several posts in city councils in the nitrate regions, and published two papers. In 1915, during its first congress, it elected a shoemaker, Ramón Sepúlveda Leal, from Viña del Mar, as secretary general.[61] All this time Recabarren was also committed to strengthening the Federación Obrera de Chile, created in 1909 by the unification of the mutualities, in which he had been an active member. As a political refugee in Argentina, Recabarren joined the fight to oust the anarchists from the union movement, as he had done in Chile. And during a later, unexplained visit to Argentina, in 1918, he contributed to the founding of the Partido Socialista Internacionalista.[62]

Most of the more notable personalities in the Partido Democrático remained with the party after the schism of 1912, and with Recabarren's following no longer goading them toward socialist reform, the party pursued a moderate tendency, which culminated in 1917 with Angel Guarello accepting an office in the conservative cabinet of President Juan Luis Sanfuentes. In 1918 Artemio Gutiérrez also became a cabinet minister, for a a brief period. In 1910 a law for obligatory retirement was enacted by the national legislature; in 1916 the first law for workers' compensation was approved; and in 1919 a retirement system was initiated for the railroad workers.

In 1921, after he and Luis Cruz had been elected to congress, Recabarren forced two dramatic changes: under his influence, the Socialist Party became the Communist Party, and the Federación Obrera de Chile affiliated with the Profintern. Recabarren then visited Russia. Shortly after his return, in 1924, he committed suicide, for reasons that have never been made clear. In the 1924 elections the Communist Party placed not a single congressman in the Chamber. Sepúlveda continued as the party's secretary general, until his expulsion during the Bolshevization campaign.

The military junta that emerged from a coup d'état in September 1924 sought to attract the working class, even to the extent of sending representatives to lecture in workers' centers. And the congress was forced to approve sixteen laws in a single session, in such areas as insurance, labor contracts, and union regulations.

The Communist Party, though delighted to extol Recabarren's virtues and to exploit his prestige, nevertheless resisted the influence of his thinking. The Party's national conference in 1933 declared that "Recabarren's ideology is a heritage the party must rapidly overcome. Recabarren is ours, but his concepts of patriotism, revolution, and the building of the party are at this moment a serious obstacle to the fulfillment of our mission."[63]

Opposing the Communists was a proliferation of small, more or less socialistic political fragments. In 1926 the Unión Social Republicana de los Asalariados de Chile was constituted. It sought to create a "new society founded in justice, cooperation, and solidarity," as well as the socialization of the means of production and distribution. The Unión Social backed the candidacy of Dr. José Santos Salas, a military doctor and author of the laws on workers' housing. Santos won 74,000 votes—but not victory—and the

Unión Social dispersed.[64] In 1930, encouraged by reforms in the electoral law, the Congreso Social Obrero and the Unión de Empleados de Chile created the Confederación Republicana de Acción Cívica de Obreros y Empleados de Chile. The Confederación supported the dictatorship of Carlos Ibáñez del Campo from 1927 to 1931, but vanished completely shortly after the dictatorship fell.[65]

After 1931, the labor movement revived. Paramount in the revival was the formation of a group led by Col. Marmaduke Grove (1878–1961), and supported by numerous small socialist factions. Grove, a man with advanced political and social ideas, became restless when the aristocracy returned to power in 1931. A Mason and a liberal, he had been one of the instigators of the military revolts of September 1924 and January 1925. During the first period of Ibáñez' regime he organized the Chilean Air Force, and later became attaché to the embassy in London. Disgusted with Ibáñez' dictatorial methods, he went into exile, and in the fall of 1930 he returned from Argentina with a plan for raising a revolt in the Concepción garrison. To be assured of successfully overthrowing the oligarchic president Juan Esteban Montero, who had succeeded Ibáñez, Grove was forced to cooperate with elements in Ibáñez' dictatorship, particularly with Carlos Dávila (1887–1955), ex-Ambassador to the United States.

The revolt, on June 4, 1932, was successful. The new Junta proclaimed a socialist republic. In its program the new government promised to summon a Constitutional Assembly, which would proceed to write a socialist constitution; create a government organization of industries dealing with food products; establish government monopolies of petroleum, matches, tobacco, and other products; plan the division of the large haciendas; effect the reorganization and reduction of the armed forces; socialize credit. The government took swift measures to control the price of food, to distribute aid to the 250,000 unemployed, and to make restitution of objects held in official pawnshops. In addition, it created a Consejo Económico Socialista Nacional, with representatives from the unions. Finally, it nationalized the Banco Nacional.

The government junta was made up of Carlos Dávila, General Arturo Puga, Col. Marmaduke Grove, and Eugenio Matte. Matte, a militant socialist, was the political head of the group.

Communists and democrats opposed the new regime. The Communists considered it "an instrument of British capital." The democrats were among Montero's supporters at the time of his overthrow, and were quick to back Dávila when he broke with Grove. The Communists and democrats, supported by the recently organized radical socialists (a faction from the Partido Radical) and other groups, overthrew Grove's twelve-day-old regime on June 17. A new government, headed by Dávila, was installed. It lasted but 100 days, still under the name of "socialist republic," but managed to nullify many of Grove's reforms. The workers, violently opposed to the Dávila administration, revolted on June 22, but were suppressed. Harsh laws against "the agitation of the masses" were approved, and Grove and his leading supporters were jailed. But another coup d'état ended Dávila's regime, after the radical socialists and half the democrats had withdrawn their support. Elections were called for November. Grove was named candidate for the Alianza Revolucionaria Social, an amalgam of several groups that had supported the socialist republic. Arturo Alessandri (1868–1950)* won 183,744 votes, against Grove's 60,261. The Communists also presented a candidate.

Alessandri's role during this period has been widely discussed. Later he claimed that he had acted as mediator between President Montero and the rebels. Grove conceded that Alessandri had indeed known of the conspirators' plans, but denied that he had taken a part in establishing the socialist republic itself, neither in Grove's twelve-day regime, nor in the hundred days of the Dávila administration.

The June 4 revolt was more than the inspiration of a handful of men. It was the culmination of a long process that had brought about, during the preceding months, a marine rebellion, violent strikes leading to the "Tragic Easter" in the north, and a general strike in January. The world economic crisis, which had strong repercussions in Chile, had created the conditions for a rebellion attempt. But there was no party to lead it, and the unions, decimated by Ibáñez and confused by the Communists, lacked strength.

A fifty-point plan, prepared by the revolution's civil leader, Matte,† can be summed up in the watchword of the movement: "Bread, roof, and clothing." His *Programa de acción económica inmediata* suggested measures that tended not toward the creation of a socialist state but toward the diminution of power of the oligarchy and the foreign interests. The program can be said to have proposed the creation of a controlled national capitalism. In this sense the socialist revolution of Chile intended doing what today the populist movements seek. No mention was made of socializing either land or industry, nor of confiscating great fortunes. But there was such popular enthusiasm for the program that many capitalists has-

---

* Alessandri served two terms as president, 1920–25, 1932–38. During his first term and much of his second term he sought to better working conditions and to institute a sort of state capitalism, but he later turned to repressive measures.

† Matte, deported to Easter Island during Alessandri's government, after he had been elected to the senate, died there in 1935.

tened to adopt measures that seemed to them socialistic; for example, the owner of *El Mercurio* decreed the "socialization" of his newspaper.

Confronted by the June 4 movement the Communists adopted two different tactics: the official group, led by Elías Lafertte (1886–1961), attacked the government junta, while a dissenting group, headed by Manuel Hidalgo (1882–1961) who had succeeded Recabarren and later became a Trotskyite, supported it, on the condition that it arm the workers and hand over municipal power to them. The Lafertte Communists took control of the University, and there proclaimed soviets of workers and peasants. The junta attempted to divert the Communists from their penchant for creating incidents and unrest, but their efforts were in vain.[66]

The year 1933 saw the founding of a new Socialist Party, concocted of various groups: Nueva Acción Pública, Alianza Revolucionaria Socialista, Partido Socialista Marxista, Orden Socialista, the Partido Socialista Unificado, and the Izquierda Communista (Trotskyists). The new party grew rapidly, winning 46,000 votes and nineteen seats in Parliament in 1937, and served as the base for the Popular Front and the Bloque Parlamentario de Izquierda. But in 1939 the party split into democratic-socialist and doctrinaire-Marxist factions. The latter, in 1940, created the Partido Socialista de Trabajadores. Two new Trotskyist groups also appeared: the Partido Obrero Revolucionario and the Partido Obrero Internacionalista. The Socialist Party responded to the announcement of the Hitler–Stalin pact with an energetic campaign against the Communist Party.[67]

Oscar Schnake (1899–   ), general secretary of the new Socialist Party, explained the reasons for its rapid growth: "The lack of an effective political instrument to express the people's hopes and faith implied the need for a party that by its organization, its leaders, and its forcefulness of action could guarantee a new political destiny." The declaration of principles stated: "The socialist doctrine is of international character, and demands a solidarity and coordination of action from the workers of the world. Toward the realization of this postulate the Socialist Party will work for the economic and political unity of the Latin American peoples, so as to arrive at a federation of the socialist republics of this hemisphere, and the creation of an anti-imperialistic economy." Other steps were to be taken: stimulation of modern social and economic policy, by means of integrated planning; transformation of the structural bases of the national economy; and direction and control of private enterprise.

One of the socialists elected in the capital, Ricardo Latcham (1903–65), soon withdrew from the party to found the Unión Socialista, which began working for Ibáñez' return and formed the Alianza Popular Libertadora to support his candidacy.

The downfall of the ephemeral socialist republic, the consequences of the world economic crisis, and the advance of fascism could have produced grave dangers in Chile, where a Nazi party had already been organized. The dangers were averted primarily by the counterattack against fascism carried on by the Bloque de Izquierdas. This group had been created at the initiative of the Socialist Party, and included as well the Partido Radical Socialista, the Partido Democrático, and the Izquierda Comunista. The Bloque, which functioned during 1934 and 1935, preceded by two years the Popular Front later encouraged by the Communists, and it was established while the Communists were still talking of "social-fascism."[68]

In the 1937 elections the Communists allied with the radicals, presented themselves as national democrats, and won six seats in the congress and one in the senate, with 17,162 votes. In the following elections, calling themselves national progressives, they obtained 54,114 votes, good for fifteen seats in congress and three in the senate. When the Popular Front was organized in 1937 (its activities are detailed in the next chapter), the Communists tipped the balance in favor of Pedro Aguirre Cerda (1871–1941), a radical landowner, as candidate for the presidency, opposing Grove, who was supported by the socialists.[69]

Following the victory of the Popular Front in the election of October 1938, the Socialist Party took part in the government of Aguirre Cerda. In a declaration delivered on September 20, 1939, at the outset of World War II, the Socialist Party explained its thinking in the following terms: "We condemn the bloody provocations of Hitler's fascism, for such policies establish the brutal principle that imperialistic nations can take possession of weaker countries through the simple expedient of force; we repudiate the Nazi–Soviet pact, and denounce Stalin's attitude as a betrayal of the international policy of defense of the democratic countries in the fight against fascism; we condemn the policy of distribution of small countries, adopted by the imperialistic nations, and reaffirm the principle of self-determination for all peoples; we condemn the invasion and division of Poland, verified in mutual agreement between Hitler and Stalin; we reaffirm our position in the fight against fascism, both on national and international levels; we call upon all the socialistic and democratic forces of the Americas to join in the anti-fascist struggle."

The illness and subsequent death of Aguirre Cerda coincided, in Chile, with the Stalinist turnabout of 1941 inspired by the Nazi attack on Russia, and under Aguirre's successor the Popular Front was reconstituted, using the name "Alianza Democrática." In 1943 the Communists proposed to the Socialist Party that they create a single party. Conversations were held, and linking committees with the Communists were established, but without result.[70] In 1946 the Socialist Party offered Bernardo Ibáñez (1902–) for the presidency, but Ibáñez attracted only 12,000 votes against Gabriel González Videla, who had the support of the Communists and the radicals.

Shortly afterward, during the next party congress, the majority elected Raúl Ampuero (1917–) as general secretary, to replace Dr. Salvador Allende (1908–), whereupon Allende withdrew, taking the party's name with him. The majority then adopted the name Partido Socialista Popular. Later, Allende, who all this time had been a vehement anti-Communist (he supported the outlawing of the Communist Party), would accept an alliance with the Communists, to serve as their candidate against Ibáñez del Campo, in 1952 (Allende won 50,000 votes, the ex-dictator 450,000). Ibáñez, because he carried the endorsement of the masses, was supported by the Partido Socialista Popular; on the strength of his victory, the socialists drew 70,000 votes in the election, and four socialist senators and nineteen congressmen won office. But when it was apparent that Ibáñez had forgotten his campaign promises, the socialists withdrew their support.[71]

This socialist-Communist alliance, which persisted for several years, illustrates the short political memory of Chilean socialism, accustomed as it has been to frequent schisms and fusions. It failed even to recall that three Communist ministers had formed part of Gabriel González Videla's cabinet in 1946,* and that the Stalinist leader, Carlos Contreras Labarca (1899–), from his office as Minister of Public Works, immediately began the persecution of the "brother" party, expelling Raúl Ampuero and other socialist officials of the ministry.

Among the documents most characteristic of Communist activities during that period, a letter from the Communist governor of San Vicente, Bello Oliva, is particularly impressive. The letter was intercepted and made known to the public in 1946. In it he informed the party's central committee of his activities in the area, and among other considerations declared that the presence of the provincial secretary of the interior and police, a man of socialist leanings, was an obstacle to his plans—he had been unable to eliminate him because the secretary was an official of great prestige, highly esteemed by the local population. Accordingly, said the governor, the "comrades" would provoke a "casual accident" so that they might be relieved of his "annoying presence."

This letter caused considerable alarm and a strong anti-Communist reaction, but not so strong that it would be remembered some years later, when socialist leaders sought their climb to power with Communist votes. They failed even to recall the Communists' fervent defense of a planned treaty

* See pp. 139–40.

with Perón, which would have put sources of Chilean wealth as well as the Pacific markets at the disposal of Argentina. Perón had coveted access to Chilean raw materials (iron, coal, copper, manganese, electrical energy, timber), in order to fulfill his five-year plan for heavy industry, on which he had founded his economic and military strength; the addition of Chile's raw materials to Argentina's rich agricultural and livestock economy would ensure the success of the plan. Censure from Chilean political parties and public opinion put an end to the projected treaty, which the Communists had defended because Perón was then actively anti-U.S.

Notwithstanding, the Partido Socialista Popular resolved to create an alliance with the Communists and the dissenting socialist groups. Later all these elements united in a new Socialist Party controlled by Ampuero and with Allende as figurehead. The alliance, realized in February 1956, was called the Frente Revolucionario de Acción Popular (FRAP).[72] Among other things FRAP demanded the nationalization of the copper mines, and in 1958 won 356,000 votes for its candidate, Allende, against the conservative Jorge Alessandri, who drew 382,000. Soon after the election, differences arose between the Communists and the socialists, when the latter evinced a strong tendency to favor Tito.[73] In the following years the Socialist Party became more and more a nationalist, Titoist party, to the great annoyance of the Communists.

In September 1964, FRAP's Dr. Allende lost the elections to the Christian-Democrat candidate Eduardo Frei, who had been backed also by the Partido Socialista del Pueblo. This socialist group had been organized shortly before the elections by elements that had fallen out with the Communists. After the election, the conviction grew, among the socialists who had remained in the alliance, that the Communists had sabotaged the campaign to assure the defeat of FRAP's candidate, whose victory could have placed Moscow in the embarrassing situation of having a new Cuba in the southern tip of the hemisphere.

Shortly after the parliamentary elections of May 1965, which gave the majority to the Christian-Democrats, a defeated Communist senator, Jaime Barros, was expelled from the Communist Party because of his criticism of its leadership. Barros formed a new, pro-Chinese party, to which several dissident Communist, Trotskyist, and small socialist groups fused.

BRAZIL

Brazilian socialism dates from 1840, when a group formed in Rio and began publishing O Socialista. The same year a society was founded in Paris to create a phalanstery in Brazil. The colony was established at Oliveira, in Santa Catarina province, under the leadership of Dr. Benoit Mure. A second group established a phalanstery at Palmetar. Within a few years both colonies disbanded, and by 1846 Mure was in Rio, promoting Fourierism.

European immigrants found themselves in a society dominated by positivism—Brazil was one of the few countries in which Comte's cult caught hold and endured. The social concepts of the Brazilian positivists are illustrated by their favoring the abolition of slavery—not utterly, to be sure, but to the extent that the slave might be transformed into a kind of serf of the soil. In some politicians and writers, such as Lima Barreto (1881–1922), Joaquin Nabuco (1849–1910), and Euclides da Cunha (1866–1909), the influence of European socialism is evident in their penchant for quoting Marx.[74]

Various socialist, anarchist, and leftist republican groups flourished in Brazil around the turn of the century. One of the more interesting of these was the Uniaó Sociocrática, in Rio, which published a weekly newspaper, *O Libertarista,* dated by the number of years that had passed since the French Revolution. By 1916 *Avanti!,* a socialist daily in Italian, and *Vorwärts,* a weekly in German, were being published. A Socialist Party had appeared fleetingly in Rio in 1906; in 1916, several groups merged and recreated the party with sections in Rio, São Paulo, Bahia, and four other cities. In less than two years it had attracted 2,750 members. In 1917 the party was threatened with schism; its Portuguese-speaking members favored immediate entrance into the war, but the Italian and German members felt the country should remain neutral. Then, when the Communist Party was created from groups that had broken away from the anarcho-syndicalist movement, most of the socialists decided to join its ranks.

In 1925 the Socialist Party formed once again, and managed to elect two members to the municipal assembly in Rio. By 1930 local socialist groups had sprung up in São Paulo, Rio Grande do Sul, Rio de Janeiro, Santos, and Paraña. Intense state-level political activity absorbed the interests of these groups and left them without impetus or inclination to organize nationally.

Meanwhile, a Partido Trabalhista had been formed, in 1929. At the time of its second congress, in 1930, it claimed 175,192 members in 112 groups. Taking as their model the British Labour Party, the Brazilian laborites regrouped and applied for admission to the Socialist International. It was agreed that the unions would seat eight representatives in the party's central committee. During the same period a Partido Socialista Independente had been operating in São Paulo. Both socialist groups joined the Aliança Nacional Libertadora, which developed in 1934 and 1935. In its ranks were workers' groups, socialist parties, peasant organizations, and several liberal politicians. The Aliança undertook campaigns against the *integralistas* (fascists), cooperated with the unions in protest strikes that had been inspired by police brutality and government repression, and supported the peasants of Minas Gerais against tenant-eviction policies. The Communists, who had encouraged the Aliança, directed its fortunes secretly.

In July 1935 the Aliança published a program demanding suspension of foreign debt payments, control of public services, distribution of the latifundios among the peasants, separation of Church and state, an eight-hour working day and a minimum wage, and social security. A week later President Getulio Vargas (1882–1954) dissolved the Aliança, but it continued to function until November 1935. In October there were strikes in the north and northeast of the country and the troops refused to attack the strikers. Leaders of the Aliança proclaimed a government, with Luis Carlos Prestes as president, and its militants attacked the Rio de Janeiro garrison. The attempt failed; the rebels surrendered after nine hours of fighting. And the labor movement, driven by this pathetic failure into a twilight that would last for several years, could look to itself for blame, for having embraced Communist leadership in the Aliança. Some time afterward the followers of dictator Vargas organized their own Partido Trabalhista Brasileiro.

The present Socialist Party emerged with the founding of Esquerda Democrática, in August 1945. When the Vargas dictatorship was overthrown in 1946, Esquerda Democrática registered as a political party, and in 1949, under the leadership of João Mangabeira, became the Partido Socialista Brasileiro. At its 1953 congress the party drew up a program and declaration of principles espousing no single philosophical school, but favoring the socialization of land and other means of production, with the motto "Socialism and Liberty." No single class was to be represented by the party.

The party found the working class's political tastes running to poles, but to poles opposite only in appearance: Vargas, the former dictator of the *Estado Novo,* and Prestes, the Communist leader. Although crippled in its development by these forces, socialism nevertheless exerted certain pressures in São Paulo, where the party's efforts helped to elect Janio Quadros as Governor.[75] In the elections of 1960, the Party supported Marshal Texeira Lott, while its São Paulo section, Açao Socialista, supported Quadros.

The Partido Trabalhista, organized by Vargas and left by him to João Goulart's leadership, is a strange mixture of extremists from both right and left, seasoned with opportunists. Its program is vague, and it is sustained more by the prestige of some of its leaders than by a solid political position. Fernando Ferrari, a party leader with clearly populist leanings, was expelled in 1959, and created his own group, the Movimiento Trabalhista Renovador.[76] When Ferrari was killed in an accident, in 1962, the new group disbanded.

In spite of the rapid industrial growth of some regions of Brazil, notably São Paulo, a strong socialist movement has never emerged, and such movement as has existed has been composed, above all, of intellectuals and middle-class elements.* The failure of Brazilian socialism can be traced to the working class's attraction to the social demagoguery of Getulio Vargas, who fashioned a semipopulist program into a fascist state. Vargas, with his Partido Trabalhista and his social legislation, exerted almost total control of the working masses, through unions controlled in turn by the Ministry of Labor.

In his second, constitutional, period of power (he was elected in 1950), Vargas installed João Goulart as labor secretary. Goulart was forced to resign, however, when confronted with proof of his plotting with Peronists. Later, the Partido Trabalhista, under Goulart, twice achieved his election to the vice-presidency. In his second term he passed from that office to the presidency, when President Janio Quadros resigned in August 1962. Goulart was at first opposed by the Communists, but soon brought them into the fold with the offer of choice government positions. But more than Communistic, his administration was one of simple social demagoguery. Confronted with Goulart, the socialists were divided: some opposed him, others supported him, and a few allowed themselves to be put in government harness. Goulart's fall, brought about in 1964 by concerted action of the military and the country's conservative groups, should have been all the opening the socialists needed to emerge as the voice of the workers and peasants, who had seen themselves abandoned by their demagogic leader, but no viable socialist movement could be pieced together out of its ancient remnants. A handful of small, pseudo-Marxist groups (Trotskyists, Titoists, pro-Chinese Communists, etc.) was thus afforded the opportunity to don the mantle of sole opposition in the labor field. Once its old leaders had been exiled, the Partido Trabalhista rapidly expanded, and the cult of personality that had long been the plague of Brazilian politics continued to obstruct the political labor movements.

BOLIVIA

An early step toward the formation of workers' and socialist organizations in Bolivia was the importation of several works on socialism, in

---

* The Partido Social Democrático of former President Juscelino Kubitschek is not socialist but rather of progressive capitalistic leanings.

Spanish editions. These prompted the foundation, in 1913, of a short-lived Socialist Party, and of several unions, principally in the city of Oruro.

But more than twenty years were to pass before the influence of socialism would again be felt. In May 1936, a group of army officers overthrew the government, with Col. David Toro (1898–   ) taking power. The instigator of the movement was Toro's chief of staff, Col. Germán Busch (1904–39). In its manifesto the new government declared that the Chaco War with Paraguay had revealed Bolivia's pervasive weakness and the necessity "of organizing a new nation, conceived on the foundations of social justice, equity and equality, in harmony with our times." Toro headed a new Socialist Party, which had been reorganized at the close of the Chaco War. Under fire from the traditional civil parties and influenced by the corporative tendencies of the period, Toro attempted to bring the unions under state control. The situation became untenable when it was made clear that Toro was bringing about none of the promised reforms. Busch drove him from the government in July 1937, and formed a civilian government, but faced with the massive effort of overhauling the country's social structure, a task made impossible by the opposition of many interests, he committed suicide.

The works of Ingenieros, Haya de la Torre, and Mariátegui, as well as the brief presence, in 1927, of the *aprista,* Manuel Seoane (1900–1963), exerted considerable influence in Bolivia. Marxism was imported by Tristán Maroff (Gustavo Navarro), who came upon it during a stay in Paris as consul. Among Marxist theoreticians were José Antonio Arze, in sociology; Ricardo Anaya, on nationalizing of the mines; and Arturo Urquidi, on the agrarian and Indian questions. The Marxism of these theorists was rather schematic, in the Stalinized manner—lacking subtlety, and above all lacking roots in the Latin American reality. Thus, their political ventures bore no relation to their doctrine.

The power of the left was neutralized by a profusion of Marxist parties and groups all calling themselves socialistic. In 1947 a Marxist writer commented: "After twenty years of orthodox propaganda, astonishingly well organized and efficient, in the manner of the Russian Revolution, the confusion and ideological disorientation of the Bolivian labor movement remains as it had been before World War I. The movement consists of intellectual coteries, rather than of organized masses with the strength necessary to assume power as the proletarian dictatorship, and embark on the socialist revolution."

The history of the Partido de Izquierda Revolucionaria (PIR) illustrates this view.[77] In 1940, at a meeting in Oruro, the PIR was founded. Its program made no demands for the economic independence of the country or for an antifeudal and anti-imperialistic struggle, and on the agrarian question it asked only for "an intensive plan of irrigation and modernization." Socialists, Communists, and leftist liberals united in the PIR, but the Communists, little by little, rose to dominance in its leadership. From the beginning, the party aroused great sympathy. The Communists, who until then had never managed to establish a solid organization, had found their instrument of penetration.

When, in 1942, General Peñaranda's soldiers slaughtered the Catavi miners, the PIR permitted itself to upbraid two ministers in Parliament, but not the oligarchic regime—pursuing, in this hands-off fashion, the Communist policy of avoiding internal rifts while the war continued. When Col. Gualberto Villarroel (1908–46) came to power in 1943, supported by the Radepa military lodge and the Movimiento Nacionalista Revolucionario (MNR), the PIR offered its support. Its offer rejected, the PIR joined the opposition, aligning itself with the oligarchic parties in a Frente Democrático Antifascista, under the pretext that no steps should be taken that might weaken the efforts on behalf of aid for Russia. The PIR contented itself with encouraging a teachers' and students' strike.

After Villarroel's hanging, in 1946, the PIR supported the new oligarchic government, even in the face of another mass killing of Catavi miners and a subsequent "white massacre" (the discharge of 5,000 miners) approved by the Labor Minister, who was one of the two Communist ministers in Enrique Hertzog's cabinet. Soon after this, the PIR was dumped from the government.

In 1952, following the MNR revolution, PIR leaders declared the party's official dissolution, and party factions went their separate ways. One group joined the MNR, and another formed the Communist Party. At the same time, PIR youth groups organized a second Communist Party, but by the end of the year the two parties had merged. In 1955 a few members of the old PIR, mainly intellectuals, reorganized the party, but in the 1956 elections the several candidates presented jointly by the PIR and the Communists met with complete defeat.

Bolivia is the only Western nation (and Ceylon the only nation elsewhere) in which the Trotskyists gained notable strength. Their Partido Obrero Revolucionario (POR), in fact—which came to dominate the Federación Obrera de Cochabamba and to wield influence in the Central Obrera Boliviana—was for a time the MNR's leftist opposition, after the 1952 revolution, demanding permanent revolution and a labor-peasant government. The POR, led by Guillermo Lora, saw in Paz Estenssoro a kind of latter-day Kerensky, in the MNR a Bonapartist party, and in the Confederación Obrera Boliviana a burgeoning opportunity to make of

Bolivia a Soviet state. Union leaders, members of the POR, differed with these party positions. And within the party, other differences arose, when "Pablo," secretary of the Fourth International, averred, after Stalin's death, the possibility of reconciliation between Trotskyists and "genuine" Communists. Because the workers in the POR opposed this position, and observed that the intellectuals favored it, many POR union leaders bolted the party and joined the MNR. Most recently, the POR divided into two factions, each claiming to be the genuine party.[78]

PERU

The fighting tradition of the anarcho-syndicalists and of the youth that would later constitute APRA made the emergence of a socialist party in Peru unnecessary.[79]

José Carlos Mariátegui (1895–1930), who in 1928 created a socialist party, was one of the few Latin American Marxists to attempt adaptation of Marxism to the reality and the necessities of the South American continent. Mariátegui had formed an almost mystic concept of the revolution: "A revolution is religion; and in this sense the word religion is for me something more than the designation of a rite or a church. Nor am I dissuaded by the Soviets' proclaiming from their propaganda placards that 'religion is the opiate of the masses'..." Mariátegui departed from the well-trodden paths in analyzing his country's problems. For example, "The Indian problem ... must be stated in its social and economic terms—must be identified, above all, with the problem of the land. Each day, evidence mounts to support the conviction that this problem cannot find solution in a humanitarian formula. And each day it becomes clearer that teaching people to read and write does not educate them."[80] In spite of his sympathy for the Russian Revolution he had no wish to imitate it: "In Latin America we are not interested in carbon-copy socialism. Our socialism must be a heroic creation. We must give life, with our own reality, in our own language, to Indo-American socialism," he wrote in his review *Amauta*.

Accordingly, when Mariátegui founded his Socialist Party, he refused to call it Communistic, and by his refusal invited a running conflict with Moscow. Moreover, during the period of Bolshevization of the Third International, Mariátegui welcomed alliances with petty-bourgeois groups, declining to limit the party, as Moscow had wished, to an exclusively proletarian base. After Mariátegui's death, in 1930, Peruvian Communists founded the Communist Party, and though the party exploited the appeal of Mariátegui's name, party leaders sought to suppress the ideological influence of his writings among their militants.[81]

His Marxism was not one of sterile dogma: "It is not possible to seize in a theory the entire panorama of the contemporary world...it is not possible to confine a movement to its theory. We must explore it and expand it, episode by episode and facet by facet." Like all those of his generation he believed that "Politics is today the only great creative activity. It is the realization of an immense human ideal. Politics is ennobled, dignified, and elevated, when it is revolutionary. And the truth of our time is the revolution. Politics," he concluded, "is my philosophy and my religion." The revolution, for him had to be "the conquest not only of bread, but also of beauty, of art, of thought, and of all the pleasures of the spirit."[82]

The Latin American Communist Conference, held in 1929, criticized Mariátegui's Socialist Party, to which it imputed "a confusing character." Mariátegui proposed that his party group together elements from both labor and the middle classes, and that it not officially affiliate with the Third International, although he would accept a secret alliance with it.[83]

One who has studied him well has remarked: "Mariátegui, though a brilliant leftist, was not the founder of the Communist Party in Peru. He was essentially a socialist, a Marxist confirmed and confessed, but never a Communist toeing the party line. Though it is true that his socialism accommodated the praxis of the Red International, it is slanderous to assert that Mariátegui was, for tactical benefit, a clandestine Communist."[84]

Dr. Luciano Castillo, president of a small Socialist Party locally influential in Talara, founded in 1930, was one of the several candidates who, with no possibility of winning, nevertheless opposed the dictator, Manuel Odría, in the 1950 election, and was of course defeated.[85]

ECUADOR

The Partido Socialista Ecuatoriano was organized in 1926 along the lines of the British Labour Party; i.e., it was built up from both political elements and union elements. But it soon came to be dominated by the Communists, and in 1928 joined the Third International. At the time it numbered about 10,000 members. The Socialist Party was the only party in the country to recognize in the Indians a political entity, and established in its statutes that among the forty-eight members of its congress there should be two Indian representatives, though they need not themselves be Indians.

Early in 1930 a new Socialist Party was organized, this time with no Communists. This group, led by Senator Luis Maldonado (1902–   ), held a position of some importance in national affairs—advancing, above all, in the coastal provinces, where, on occasion, in alliance with the radicals, they attracted more votes than any other party. The socialists frequently entered these electoral coalitions with other parties. In 1938 a Socialist-Communist coalition won the majority in congress, but failed to reach agreement on a presidential candidate, thus forfeiting the office to the liberal Aurelio Mosquera, to the latter's great amazement. Later the socialists, with Vanguardia Socialista Revolucionaria, the Communists, and several democratic organizations formed the Alianza Democrática Ecuatoriana, and carried José María Velasco Ibarra (1893–   ) to power in 1944. The socialists considerably influenced the writing of the 1945 Constitution, which Velasco Ibarra repudiated in 1946. Once again among the opposition, the socialists allied with the radicals, and took 16 per cent of the parliamentary posts in the 1948 election.[86]

In the Socialist Congress of 1955, Juan Isaac Lovato's following, which favored the development of a Frente Democrático Nacional, defeated the class-front tendency.

The "revolutionary socialists" (whose leader, D. Agustín Aguirre, received the Stalin Award), in alliance with the Communists, supported Velasco Ibarra in his electoral campaigns of 1952 and 1960. The democratic socialists, on the other hand, opposed him, and when he fell, in November 1961, formed part of Carlos Julio Arosemena's first government. Among Arosemena's liberals, social-Christians, and independents were two socialists;[87] they were, as one would suppose, in opposition to the military junta that overthrew Arosemena in 1963, and supported the alliance of traditional parties that toppled the junta in 1966. More and more, the Ecuadorian socialists are losing, it seems, their ideological identity.

COLOMBIA

During Colombia's liberal administration of 1849–53, socialist clubs were organized and were looked upon apparently with favor by José Hilario Lopez (1798–1869), the president in whose administration slavery was abolished. A "socialist influence" was spoken of in Colombian politics as early as 1890, but no socialist political organization developed.[88]

Following World War I the writings of Luis Tejada and Luis Vidales (1904–   ), generally protests against convention, influenced the intellectual youth—the "new ones," as they were called—often nurturing the socialist thought that had reached them through the inexpensive printings from Barcelona. The writings of these two young men were described as "lofty and convulsive, written with the sting of challenge."[89]

Toward the end of 1920 the Partido Social Revolucionario was created, and drawn quickly into the Communist International as a sympathizing member. In the 1930 elections, Alberto Castrillón, who had led the famous banana workers' strike of 1928, was proposed for the presidency. He took third in the balloting. And in June 1930, a new, semisocialistic organization, the Partido Laborista Colombiano, was founded. This group, led by union elements, attracted only a few votes in the election, and dispersed.

During Alfonso López' regime, the Popular Front was organized. López' liberals, the Communists, the socialists, and labor-union leaders all joined in the Front. The Communist leader Gilberto Vieria reviewed the troops with President López during a May Day parade in the capital in 1936. But as their comrades in Mexico had done during the Cárdenas regime, the Colombian Communists had at first assailed the López government as one in which "the young industrial bourgeoisie and the old landholding aristocracy jointly play their roles, in spite of certain differences in economic interests."[90]

For many the Communist Party's decision in 1946 to adopt the name Partido Socialista Democrático was simply confusing. When Earl Browder's theses, which had inspired the 1946 decision, were repudiated by Moscow, the party split, one group becoming Partido Socialista Popular, and the other openly Communist. One group was led by Gilberto Vieria, the other by Augusto Durán; the latter was expelled when the two parties settled their differences and were once again the Communist Party.

Immediately following World War II there was great social agitation. Jorge Eliecer Gaitán (1904–48), a liberal leader with broad popular support, demanded sweeping reforms. The conservatives had won the 1948 presidential election when the liberals divided, some favoring Gabriel Turbay (1901–), a right-wing liberal supported by the Communists, and others backing Gaitán, a left-wing liberal opposed by the Communists. Realizing their error, the Communists tried to regain Gaitán's good graces, and managed to enter a collaborative agreement with Gaitán and the Federación Colombiana de Trabajadores. But the parliamentary elections soon revealed that the Communists commanded less support than they pretended, and Gaitán broke the pact, which from his point of view had been of no value. Using his new influence, he hoped to see his friends take over the administration of the union movement. But in 1948, while the Inter–American Conference was convening in Bogotá, Gaitán was murdered. The masses, among whom he had been very popular, immediately began rioting in the streets.

The Communists are said to have provoked the Bogotá riots; it is more probable that they did what they could to channel them, once they had broken out, for the purpose not of seizing control of the country but of assuring the failure of the Inter–American Conference. Their efforts floundered. (A sidelight to the rioting was the presence in Bogotá of Fidel Castro; that he had been in the city during the rioting has led to claims that he had already become a militant Communist.)

A new Partido Socialista Popular of Colombia (non–Communist) was founded in 1950. Under the leadership of Antonio García (1902–), the party began to amass strength in the Universities. But the group made the mistake of taking the dictator, General Gustavo Rojas Pinilla, at his word on promises of social reform, and allowed itself to be swept into a "third force" maneuver, which in 1955 failed. When Rojas fell, in 1957, the Colombian socialists found themselves in an untenable position. Some members simply withdrew, but others created, in 1960, with Luis Emiro Valencia and his wife, Gloria Gaitán (daughter of the liberal leader assassinated in 1948), the Castro-inclined Gaitán Movement,[91] of no real influence.

CENTRAL AMERICA

Central American social thinking is reformist. Those who have dealt with social issues have done so on an intellectual plane and without pursuing a close analysis of the Central American reality. Among these the following are most notable: Rafael Cardona, Julián Pérez Pineda, Antonio Zelaya, Luis Demetrio Castro, and Alfonso Guillén Zelaya; more recently there have been Juan José Arévalo (1904–   ), expounding spiritual socialism, José Figueres (1906–   ), and Monsignor Víctor Sanabria (1899–1952), the archbishop of San José. The groundwork for their thinking had been laid by a few sociologists, notably Ramón Zelaya (1873–   ) and Jorge García Granados (1900–   ). But despite these urgings, the union movement and labor's participation in politics were late to develop in these countries. All but Costa Rica endured long periods of dictatorship.

Central America's most interesting figure was the Salvadorian Alberto Masferrer (1868–1932). Consul in Antwerp, traveler, teacher, and journalist, he first aroused attention with his theory of the vital minimum, a theory that struck at the roots of one of Latin America's most vexing problems. The doctrine of the vital minimum is "an appeal to the basic goodness of man, to his spirit of self-preservation. It asks not so much for an ideal state as for a tolerable one, for an upper limit for the man who dominates and treasures wealth, and a lower limit for the man who works for bread." For Masferrer, anything above this vital minimum should be conquered by personal effort, but the minimum was something to which one had a right by the simple fact of existing.[92]

But toward the end of his life the brutal reality of his country had driven Masferrer to a more radical position. His dealings abroad with socialists and anarchists, especially in Chile, probably encouraged this shift. He saw himself as an anticapitalist, an enemy of land monopoly who urged "free land, as well as free use of everything necessary to work it." Workers could look only to themselves, he felt, for the means to realize emancipation, and could take "as a right their intervention, as a class, in the management of the community. A life spent in work can be neither recovered nor compensated."

Although Masferrer took no part in the peasant uprising of 1932, he was accused of inspiring it with his writings, and was forced to leave his country—to die in exile. He was neither a leader nor an organizer, but his writings, and the legend that formed around his memory, exerted an enduring influence in all of Central America.[93]

Juan Pablo Wainwright, an American native of Honduras who first introduced Communist literature into Guatemala, also laid the foundations for the Communist movement in El Salvador, before 1930. The Guatemalan dictator General Jorge Ubico (1878–1946) had him arrested and executed in 1931. In 1932 the group Wainwright had founded in El Salvador organized a peasant uprising, though it is not known if this was done on the group's own initiative or at Moscow's instructions. The revolt cost thousands of lives. Taking advantage of rural discontent, a Comité Militar Revolucionario had been organized, and even a Red Army, and the workers and peasants had been asked to form Soviets. Of course, all this remained on paper; meanwhile, the countryside was strewn with dead, victims of the ferocious repression brought down by the dictator Maximiliano Hernández Martínez (died 1966).[94]

Shortly after World War II, the Nicaraguan dictator, General Anastasio Somoza, paved the way for certain Communist elements to form a Socialist Party. Vicente Lombardo Toledano, head of the Communist-dominated Confederación de Trabajadores de la América Latina, mediated the negotiations. Somoza turned over to the new party the leadership of a recently organized union movement. But when, during the 1947 election campaign, the Socialist Party rejected an alliance with Somoza's own Partido Liberal (because of the first maneuvers of the Cold War), Somoza declared the party illegal, and once again assumed the role of the anti-Communist. The Communists, not publicly extant, pursued their influence in the unions and among the students, and were abetted in their efforts by the dictatorship's obstruction of the domocratic movements.[95]

The first evidences of a socioideologic struggle in Panama are found in the *inquilinato* movements of 1925 and 1932—movements organized by prominent intellectuals and middle-class elements to force rent prices down.

In 1933 the Socialist Party was founded, and Demetrio Porras, leader of the party, was elected to the Chamber of Deputies the following year. In 1936 the socialists supported Domingo Díaz as presidential candidate for the Popular Front. Following a period of persecution during the regime of President Arnulfo Arias, the party was given a seat in the cabinet of Ricardo Adolfo de la Guardia's government. Two socialists, Diógenes de la Rosa (who had led the rent protests) and José A. Brewer, won seats as representatives to the 1946 Constituent Assembly. The two defended the right to organize union activities, a right the projected Constitution had barely touched upon. And when the Assembly assumed legislative power, de la Rosa and Brewer were instrumental in obtaining passage of a Labor Code and of laws regarding education and university autonomy.

Panamanian socialists played a decisive role in the organization of the unions and in the formation of peasants' associations. But composed as it was primarily of intellectuals and middle-class elements, the party never exerted decisive influence on national life.[96]

Before 1950 a Partido del Pueblo, in reality a Communist front, engaged in activities directed chiefly toward agitation.[97] Col. José Remón (a chief of police who became President and was murdered in 1955) suppressed the party, but it later reappeared. Today the party publishes *El Mazo*, successor to *El Patriota*. Although illegal, the party acts openly.[98]

CUBA

Protest literature printed in Spain reached Cuba when the island was still a colony, and found an echo in popular sentiment. But not until after the War of Independence did the first socialist nucleus form. In 1901 the poet Diego Vicente Tejera (1848–1903) created the Club de Propaganda Socialista. A genuinely socialistic party was founded the same year. Its founder, Carlos Baliño, a Marxist, believed the party would find greater acceptance if it were given a name not reflective of its socialist character —thus, it was born the Partido Popular, but in 1905 became the Partido Obrero Socialista. In 1911 an admittedly socialist party, the Partido Socialista Cubano, was formed. Composed mainly of union militants, the party published *El Socialista,* and joined the Second International.[99] But it was the Partido Popular that in 1925 was reorganized to become the Communist Party, with Baliño and Julio Antonio Mella (1903–29) as its leaders.[100]

Though there have been no socialist organizations per se in Cuba, apart from a few small groups of little consequence, socialist ideas exerted considerable influence on national thought—especially among the elements who wrested power from the dictator Gerardo Machado in 1933, and later still among those who supported Fidel Castro but drifted away after his submission to Communism. The government of Grau San Martín, in 1933, enacted important social legislation: obligatory unionism, the creation of a labor ministry, peasant housing, the reduction of tariffs on public services, anti-usury statutes, on-the-job-accident benefits, and land-distribution measures representing, no doubt, a generalized response to socialist influence.[101]

HAITI

Socialist parties have appeared and reappeared in Haiti; some were suppressed, others vanished for lack of a suitable ambient. A socialist movement of sorts, inspired by the vague notions of the poet Jacques Roumain, appeared before World War II. The successive dictatorships have effectively blocked progress toward legally constituted socialism, but the Communist Party managed to obtain legal sanction in 1946, under the leadership of a fanatic Episcopalian named Félix Dorleans Just Constant. Moscow's distrust of Constant led them to send Max L. Hudicourt to Haiti to create the (Communist) Parti Socialiste Populaire. When Moscow certified the authenticity of the PSP, Constant's party dissolved.

Daniel Fignolé, who in 1946 was President Dumarsais Estimé's minister, organized a Mouvement Ouvrier et Paysan, more populistic than socialistic. This movement and the unions it inspired developed during Fignolé's short presidential tenure, in 1957, and languished when Duvalier systematically purged the opposition, later in 1957. Fignolé was the only congressman to oppose the previous dictatorship of Paul E. Magloire.[102]

MEXICO

In 1861 a Greek tailor and Fourierist, Polonio C. Rhodakanaty, went to Mexico. During the same year he wrote a *Cartilla socialista, o sea el catecismo elemental de la escuela de Carlos Fourier,* and the following year wrote *El neopanteísmo: consideraciones sobre el hombre y la naturaleza.* In 1863 he tried to found a school, but managed to attract only a small group of students. Two of these, Hermenegildo Villavicencio and Francisco Zalacosta, and a hatmaker, Santiago Villanueva, were his closest disciples. While Zalacosta spread socialist thought, Rhodakanaty and Villanueva extolled mutualism. After participating in the 1865 strikes—they demanded a fourteen-hour working day and the closing of company stores —they tried to found a Fourierist colony, or phalanstery, in Chalco, but abandoned the project, establishing instead an Escuela Moderna y Libre. Meanwhile, Zalacosta organized a Club Socialista de Estudiantes and a journal, *La Internacional.* Mata Rivera, another of Rhodakanaty's disciples, founded *El Socialista.*

The Gran Círculo de Obreros de México was founded by Villanueva and a group of Rhodakanaty's disciples in 1870, with President Benito Juárez' sanction.[103] And in 1871, Zalacosta, Rhodakanaty, and others created La Social, an organization proposing to bring together "all persevering elements of the socialist class ... who will help the poor and the oppressed as if it concerned themselves." On July 4, 1878, the Partido Socialista Mexicano was constituted in Puebla. The party published *La Revolución Social,* a newspaper in which we read: "The Mexican socialists, on constituting a party, resolve to organize all elements sympathetic to the goal of seizing, as rapidly as legal processes allow, the political power of the Republic, and of establishing, thereupon, the Law of the People, either by party action or by declarations forced from the Federal Government." Party members came to speak of themselves as Communists, so as to be distinguished from "those who refuse to agree that the proletariat constitutes a class party." Four months later the party had established seventeen centers throughout the country, but its leader, Alberto Santa Fe, was jailed the following year. The party included several minor poets of utopian socialist orientation, among them Pantaleón Tovar (1828–76) and Juan Díaz Covarrubias (1837–59).

Only after the 1910–17 Revolution was socialism again discussed. In 1917, immediately after ratification of the Mexican Constitution, a Partido Socialista Obrero was founded. The new party was quickly recognized by organized labor as their entrée into government activities. Although in its congresses and through its press the Confederación Regional Obrero Mexicana (CROM) advocated direct action, its leaders in fact engaged heavily in political labor action, which Luis N. Morones disguised under the name "multiple action." CROM in fact transformed the Partido Socialista into the Partido Laborista, in December 1919, so as to use it as its political arm. The participation of organized labor in government activity continued under the regime of Plutarco Elías Calles (1877–1945), who appointed Morones to a post in his cabinet. Still, in 1931, the CROM National Council agreed that CROM members could support candidates only from the Partido Laborista, for "although unionism has an important historic role ... it is not sufficient for the transformation of the capitalistic regime; so long as the government is not in the hands of the workers it is useless to await the creation of a new social order, and the only manner of attaining public power is through political action."[104]

Meanwhile, a Grupo Marxista Rojo was created in 1918, and in December 1920, the Federación Comunista del Proletariado Nacional was founded. These groups, their names notwithstanding, were more anarcho-syndicalistic than socialistic. They joined the Confederación General de Trabajadores (CGT) when it came into being in 1921, after a Gran Convención Radical Roja called together by José C. Valadés (1902–   ). In October 1923, Rosendo Salazar (1888–   ) and others formed the Partido Socialista Mayoritario Rojo; their purpose was to oppose the Laborista, but the party survived only briefly.

The Partido Socialista del Sureste, another political labor party, was founded by General Salvador Alvarado (1880–1924). In 1915, as governor of Yucatan, Alvarado had approved a labor law that declared, in its preamble, "Exercise of the freedom of work is the best hope for the liberation of the proletariat." The right to strike was recognized by the law, but was to be exercised only in extreme instances. Alvarado distributed lands on which sisal was to be cultivated among the *ejidos,* and favored union activity. Shortly afterward, Felipe Carrillo Puerto (1874–1924), aided by the American Robert Haberman, introduced important reforms to the Yucatan Peninsula, through the Ligas de Resistencia—reforms that were considered socialistic, but whose doctrinal basis was very vague. However, Alvarado's Partido Socialista del Sureste and Carrillo Puerto's Liga Central de Resistencia remained linked with power in the people's view, and therefore failed to sustain their effectiveness. Carrillo Puerto's death—he was executed by followers of Adolfo de la Huerta's uprising in 1924—made him a hero of the labor movement. A man more of action than of theory, and a member of CROM, perhaps his only long-range programmatic affirmation was the statement: "The sisal industry must be conceived as public wealth, and as such is entitled to government protection," a claim running counter to the traditional thesis that this industry belonged exclusively to its legal owners.

A project to institute social security, initiated by President General Alvaro Obregón (1880–1928), became a reality during the administration of General Manuel Ávila Camacho (1940 to 1946). Obregón's principal support in this campaign came from the Partido Socialista Radical. This party, organized by Tomás Garrido Canabal (1890–1943), of Tabasco, was socialistic in name only, and its program was both anticlerical and Jacobin.

Under Lázaro Cárdenas (1895–   ), who governed Mexico from 1934 to 1940, organized labor made the same decision its North American counterparts had made during Roosevelt's New Deal: the majority of the leaders of labor adhered to the governing party, confident that it would satisfy at least their immediate aspirations. As a result there are no labor parties in Mexico today, discounting the Communist Party, the Partido Obrero y Campesino (formed by expelled members of the Communist Party), and the anti-Communist Grupos Socialistas de la República Mexicana, all of scant influence.[105] A Partido Popular was founded in 1948 by Vicente Lombardo Toledano (1894–   ); although in 1961 the party added the word "Socialista," to its name, it remains, in fact, not socialist but pro-Communist.

OTHER COUNTRIES

Socialist literature was no doubt read all over Latin America, and it is reasonable to believe that study groups or informal conversational gatherings formed frequently among these readers. But such groups developed into socialist political organizations per se only in the countries already mentioned. For example, when the death of Juan Vicente Gómez (1854–

1935) encouraged political exiles to return to Venezuela, a proliferation of parties arose, all of them more or less socialistic: the Organización Venezolana (from which emerged, later, the founders of Acción Democrática), the Partido Republicano Progresista (which later produced the founders of the Venezuelan Communist Party, although since 1931 a clandestine Communist nucleus has existed), the Frente Obrero, the Frente Nacional de Trabajadores, and others.[106]

In the same fashion, in Costa Rica, the Movimiento de Liberación Nacional grew out of the small Partido Social-Democrático, which was formed almost entirely of students and intellectuals.

In some countries, what might have been a socialist party has been contorted by force of local circumstances into a liberal party or a populist party. But in the programs of these parties there is an evident reflection of democratic socialist concepts, and lately, some of these parties have joined the Socialist International.

INTERNATIONAL AFFILIATIONS

Only two Latin American socialist parties—Argentina's and Uruguay's —affiliated with the Socialist International before and after World War I, and again after World War II. The Chilean Socialist Party affiliated with the Second International between the wars but not after World War II. The Uruguayan party withdrew from the International in 1962, when pro-Communist elements took over its leadership. And several parties, on various occasions, sent observers or delegates to congresses of the International.*

On the continental level there were several attempts, all unsuccessful, to establish a coordinating mechanism for the Latin American socialist parties. In 1919 the Primera Conferencia Socialista y Obrera Panamericana met, attended by delegates from Paraguay, Bolivia, Peru, Chile, Uruguay, and Argentina. The conference had been called at the initiative of the

---

* The Socialist International, or Second International, was created during a congress in Paris in 1889. It disappeared with World War I, but after the war was reconstructed in a conference held in Hamburg in 1923, under the name Socialist Worker International. World War II dissolved it. In Antwerp, in 1947, the COMISCO was created, or International Socialist Conference Committee, which became the Socialist International at a conference in Frankfurt in 1951. Forming part of the First International, which lasted from 1864 until 1876, were all the socialist parties existing at that time, as well as many unions and anarchist groups, though the latter withdrew later. All the socialist parties in Europe and the United States, and those of Argentina, Chile, and Uruguay, made up the Second International. All the socialist parties in the world— but in the Latin American countries only Argentina and, until 1962, Uruguay—took part in the Socialist International. See *Yearbook of the International Socialist Labour Movement,* pp. 25–36.

Argentine Socialist Party. U.S. delegates were denied passports to attend, and Chile and Peru were at the time involved in a dispute, verging on war over the Tacna–Arica region. The conference unanimously resolved to propose arbitration of this conflict. It also resolved to favor free exchange, and to send expressions of support to the workers in Russia, Hungary, and Germany, who were at that time in the midst of revolution. The 44-hour work week, compulsory education, and other social measures were called for. It was agreed, finally to hold another conference two years later, but local political climates following the war drove the unionist and leftist movements everywhere into such inflamed debate concerning methods and objectives that any thought of calling a second conference was out of the question.[107]

The next important continental congress in which socialists took part, the Congreso Internacional para la Democracia, took place in Montevideo, in the spring of 1939. The Congress, actually a colloquium of liberal parties and socialist and labor organizations, resolved to oppose fascist penetration of the Western Hemisphere, and to undertake a campaign to remove power from the hands of fascist elements and the landholding aristocracy.*

A year later, in October 1940, the Congreso de Partidos Democráticos de América Latina was held in Santiago, Chile, attended by delegates from the Socialist Parties of Chile, Ecuador, Uruguay, Panama, and Argentina, and from the Partido Socialista Independiente de Bolivia, the Partido Democrático Nacional de Venezuela, the Partido de la Revolución Mexicana, and the Movimiento Aprista Peruano. The delegates discussed problems raised by the war, and methods by which parties could achieve and maintain a democratic society.[108]

In 1946 a Congreso de Partidos Socialistas y Populares was held, again in Santiago, to study Latin American problems in the light of the world situation presented by the war's end. A declaration of principles was adopted and a coordinating committee was created. Representatives of Acción Democrática and of APRA contributed outstandingly to the work of the coordinating committee, but it functioned only a short time because of military overthrows that forced the two parties underground.

The Latin American Secretariat of the Socialist International was created in November 1955, by a resolution of the International Socialist bureau. The Socialist Parties of Argentina and Uruguay, both members of the International, had conducted the preliminary negotiations; their purpose had

---

* The Uruguayan government had warned the Congress that delegates could mention no specific country by name. When the governments of the United States and Mexico were praised and Franco's regime in Spain condemned, Uruguayan authorities threatened to close the meeting.

been to create a center for the exchange of information. The financing of the center went poorly, particularly because the Argentine Socialist Party was at that time operating illegally, under Perón's regime. Both parties sought moral and political support from the worldwide socialist organization, which included forty affiliate parties with some 11 million members, more than 60 million voters, a daily press with 7 million circulation, and weeklies with a print run of 6.5 million copies. The International, agreeing to the suggestion, created the Latin American Secretariat, with regulations establishing that affiliation with the International was not prerequisite to joining the Secretariat, which included a consulting committee made up of all member parties.

With the Secretariat now expanded to include the Partido Socialista Popular of Chile, the first conference was held in Montevideo in May 1956. An ordinance called "Purposes and Standards for the Activities of the Consulting Committee" was adopted. It established (1) that the consulting committee is an organization for all Latin America, and that its prime function is to promote the exchange of information; (2) that belonging to the consulting committee in no way implies affiliation with the Socialist International; (3) that matters placed on the agenda must previously be submitted in the form of reports; (4) that only Latin American problems shall be considered; (5) that resolutions shall be unanimously adopted; (6) that members are enjoined not to interfere in matters of a national nature in the countries of the other member parties; and (7) that members remain at liberty to carry out their own national policies, in keeping with what they consider most expedient.

The second meeting of the consulting committee was held in Buenos Aires in December 1956, the third in Santiago in April 1958. A conference of economists was also held in 1958, on the subject "Socialist paths for economic development in Latin America." It was agreed that socioeconomic development using Latin American resources was possible, by means of economic planning, and that foreign capital may be a complement to this development, but not its basis.[109]

In 1961, after a visit to Latin America by Morgan Philip, from the British Labour Party and the Socialist International, the Bulletin of the Latin American Secretariat of the Socialist International ceased publication, and no further meetings were held; the Secretariat had admitted parties (the Partido Socialista Popular of Chile, for one) that had broken with the principles of the International by signing agreements with the Communists.[110]

In 1964, a delegation from the International toured Latin America. The visit encouraged Acción Democrática, of Venezuela, to join the International in the category of observing party, and two other parties—APRA of Peru and Liberación Nacional of Costa Rica, and even the Partido Radical, of Chile—to join also as observing parties. Moreover, the Montevideo office, which had been all but defunct, began to function again with the title of Buró Coordinador de la Internacional Socialista en América Latina. Humberto Máiztegui is its secretary and the editor of its Bulletin; he had already performed these duties in the Latin American Secretariat.

6. The Communist Movement

A HISTORY of the labor movement in Latin America could perhaps be written with no more than passing reference to Communism. Communism is not a modern expression of social nonconformism, as we have defined it, and it has not, except in two or three countries, drawn significant support from the working masses. It is true, however, that Communism has influenced students, intellectuals, and some members of the middle classes, who have in turn helped determine the direction of the labor movement; and since many persons have simply assumed, without studying the matter, that Communism must have been a major force in the labor movement, it may be worthwhile to trace briefly its history in Latin America.[1]

Communist parties were formed in Latin America much as they were throughout the rest of the world: some were produced by schisms in socialist parties or anarchist groups; others—usually where socialist parties or anarchist movements did not exist, or where they proved impervious to Communist influence—grew out of the activities of groups that sympathized with the Russian Revolution.

In Argentina in 1921, the Congress of the Partido Socialista rejected by a two-thirds vote a proposal that it affiliate with the Third International; members of the defeated group then separated and formed the Communist Party, which almost immediately absorbed the Partido Socialista Internacional, a splinter party formed in 1917. The Communists claimed a party membership of 3,500, and struggled with the socialists for leadership of the Unión General de Trabajadores, though with little success.[2]

In Chile, the Communist Party was founded on January 1, 1922, when the Congress of the Partido Socialista Obrero voted to affiliate with the Third International and to change the party's name. It claimed some 2,000 militants, including the labor leader Luis Emilio Recabarren, who visited the U.S.S.R. for six months in 1924.[3]

In Brazil in 1921, a majority of the members of the anarcho-syndicalist movement, led by Astrogildo Pereyra, decided to form a Communist party, which they officially founded in March 1922, during a congress attended by delegations from Rio, Niteroi, São Paulo, Cruzeiro, Juiz, Recife, and Porto Alegre. Though this Communist party was destined to become the most powerful on the continent, it began with only 500 members, most of them intellectuals who lacked contact with the masses.

In Peru the Communists, led by José Carlos Mariátegui, formed the Partido Socialista in 1926, and directed almost all of their activity to fighting against the populist APRA movement; in 1930, on orders from the Comintern, the party changed its name to Communist Party of Peru.

In Colombia, the Partido Socialista Revolucionario, under the leadership of Alberto Castrillón, had voted to affiliate with the Third International in 1922; but it took a schism within this party in 1930 to create the Communist Party. In Uruguay the Partido Socialista voted in 1920 to change its name and join the Third International; the socialist minority quickly reconstituted its party, leaving the Communists some 2,000 members. The Partido Socialista of Ecuador was organized in 1926, and in 1928, when Communists gained a majority in its congress, affiliated itself with the Third International; at this time, under party secretary Ricardo Paredes, it claimed 10,000 members.[4]

Communist parties were established in Bolivia in 1920, in Cuba in 1925, in Costa Rica in 1930, in Venezuela in 1931, in the Dominican Republic in 1945, and in Haiti by 1946. Parties were legally formed in Paraguay in 1945 and in Guatemala in 1950, though in both countries Communists had been active in other parties for many years.

It is only superficially remarkable that by 1923, a mere four years after the founding of the Communist International, Communist parties should be functioning in every major Latin American country. The same proliferation of parties occurred throughout the Old World, and for essentially the same reasons. Many socialists, and others who had long dreamed of a radical transformation of society but had achieved only piecemeal change through minor victories, were dazzled by the Russian Revolution. Suddenly, at the end of a great war that had confused and demoralized the socialists of Europe, a radical socialist group in Russia (the Bolsheviks called themselves socialists before 1919), seized power—and not only seized it, but maintained it, through a civil war that could hardly fail to inspire men who had for years fought the "lost causes" of the underdog. The Russian Communists had great plans for improving the lot of the worker, and had the ability—or so it seemed, at first—to implement them. Given the demonstrable failure of many unions and socialist parties in

Latin America to solve any labor problems at all—and the problems were more acute than in Europe—it is not surprising that Communism spread rapidly. It flourished, however, only among certain sectors of the middle class, chiefly students, intellectuals, and socialist militants who were capable of discussing politics in terms of ideology. For several years workers remained indifferent to the movement, peasants unmoved by its propaganda.

Until the mid-nineteen-twenties, Latin American Communism remained an indigenous movement, inspired by propaganda from Moscow but not bound by organizational ties to either the Kremlin or the Communist International (Comintern). Until 1920, with the civil war still raging and the International lacking funds, Moscow could make little contact with the outside world. Lenin's famous twenty-one conditions, adopted at the Second Congress of the Comintern in 1920, set forth tactics to be employed by Communist sympathizers throughout the world—the use of schisms to create Communist parties, the promotion of civil war, the creation of secret and extralegal organizations, to name a few—but these ideas were freely interpreted by Communist groups in Latin America, who geared their activities and propaganda to local circumstances.

For those Latin Americans who tried to become Marxist theoreticians, the virtual absence of Marxist writings on Latin America was at best a mixed blessing.* It left them free to theorize at their pleasure, without fear of contradicting statements made by the founders or authorized interpreters of Marxism. But it also meant that they could not support their ideas by quoting from accepted doctrinal writ. They were thus confronted with the task of constructing, without guidance, an original Marxist interpretation of Latin American reality, and then promoting its acceptance in countries where very few men were well-versed in philosophy, sociology, or economics—to say nothing of dialectical materialism. Given ten or twenty years of relative freedom, a school of truly Latin American revolutionary thinkers might have developed. This did not happen, in large part because the Communist parties of Latin America fell under an increasing degree of control from Moscow; but it may be useful to describe briefly at this point the careers of two notable Marxist intellectuals—José Carlos Mariátegui and Vicente Lombardo Toledano.

Mariátegui was born in Peru in 1895. He began earning his living as a printer's apprentice, and by the age of thirty had made a reputation for

---

* Only a handful of references to Latin America exist in all the works of Marx, Engels, Lenin, Kautsky, Plekhanov, and Bebel. Most of these refer to Mexico, but even the Mexican Revolution was not studied seriously by any Marxist theoretician during the twenties.

himself as a journalist and poet. His interest in social problems grew in the years following the Russian Revolution, and in 1926 he organized a Partido Socialista with Leninist leanings. In his journal *Amauta* and in his chief theoretical works—*Seven Critical Essays on Peruvian Life* and *The Contemporary Scene*—he eschewed mechanical applications of dialectic and offered some original interpretations. For instance, at a time when even Communists were offering idyllic solutions for the Indian problem, he wrote: "We must not content ourselves with vindicating the rights of the Indian to education, culture, progress, and love. We must begin by categorically vindicating his right to the land." Nor did he, like so many others, overestimate the modern potential of Indian communal traditions. "Modern communism," he said, "is very different from the communism of the Inca period. Each is the product of a different human experience, the expression of a different civilization. The Inca civilization was agrarian; the civilization of Marx and Sorel was industrial."[5] His assertion that "the future of Latin America depends on the fate of the peasantry" was condemned as Trotskyite, and statements such as "the revolutionary is a man of order" were viewed with deep suspicion in Moscow.

Mariátegui died in 1930, the year the Comintern ordered the Partido Socialista, which he had founded, to change its name to Communist Party of Peru. The party has made a ritual of praising Mariátegui's name, but it has never followed any of his teachings.

Vicente Lombardo Toledano, the most influential Marxist in Mexico, was born in 1894. In 1910 he attended Antonio Caso's lectures, which though critical of dialectical materialism nonetheless served to inspire most of the country's first Marxists. He became a successful lawyer, entered politics, and in 1920 was made governor of the state of Puebla. In 1921 he joined the Confederación Regional Obrera Mexicana (CROM); in 1932 he organized a short-lived confederation of workers and peasants; and in 1936 he helped found the Confederación de Trabajadores de México (CTM), in which he played a leading role until 1945, when he became vice-president of the Communist-dominated World Federation of Trade Unions. Since 1938 he has also been president of the Confederación de Trabajadores de América Latina (CTAL). In the area of domestic politics Lombardo's Marxism has strayed somewhat from orthodox party lines.[6] His ideas in this realm may be suggested by the following summary.

Throughout its history Mexico has faced three major problems: a relative lack of natural resources, the survival of colonial forms of social organization, and the intervention of foreign capitalists and imperialists. By the time the Revolution began in 1910, domestic markets had grown large enough to make industrial development possible, and a true bourgeoisie had emerged. The working class in 1910 was very weak, so the peasants had to carry the burden of armed struggle; and since the majority of peasants were illiterate, they could not prevent leadership of the Revolution from falling into the hands of the petty bourgeoisie—who have since maintained social fossils of the colonial period and allowed foreign imperialists to remain powerful. Thus what is needed is a return to, or rather a new development of, the ideals of the Mexican Revolution. The new revolution, however, should be a peaceful one, accomplished by an alliance of workers, peasants, middle-class elements, and "patriotic businessmen"—a thesis that was attacked on several occasions by Mexican Communists before the Popular Front period.

In matters of international politics, however, Lombardo has been a Latin American Zhdanov, a man committed to twisting facts and theories to bring them into apparent harmony with Moscow's latest party line. While devoting his efforts to this sterile role, Lombardo has written no political or economic studies of value or originality.[7]

THE BOLSHEVIZATION OF THE PARTIES

Until 1924, under the leadership of Zinoviev, the Comintern made no concerted effort to control the activities of Communist parties outside Russia. It began rather by trying to inspire them, and for this work it sent out agents or "advisers." Perhaps the best-known agents to work in Latin America were Manabendra Nath Roy (1893–1954) and Sen Katayama (1859–1933). Roy, an Indian socialist, went to Mexico in 1918 and became convinced that the course of the Mexican Revolution could be turned further to the left. He joined the Comintern in 1919, and in 1922 was sent to Mexico, where he managed to unite as one party the several Communist groups that had sprung up during the previous year. He also visited other Central American countries, and though he was not able to set up Communist parties in any of them, he did leave behind groups of sympathizers.[8] Katayama, a socialist leader who left Japan in 1913 (for the United States, where he remained until after the war), became a member of the Comintern's Executive Committee in 1921. In 1924 he spent eight or nine months traveling in Latin America, along with Luis Fraina, a Communist from the United States. (It should be mentioned in passing that the U.S. Communists participated actively, often as leaders, in the formation of Latin American Communist parties.)[9] Where Communist parties existed, Katayama worked to strengthen them; where they did not, he ably promoted schisms in existing organizations.[10]

In 1924 the Fifth Congress of the Comintern passed a resolution calling for the "bolshevization" of Communist parties throughout the world. As implemented over the next several years, bolshevization meant that national parties were to obey orders issued by the Comintern. In the realm of policy, leaders were to adhere to the "social fascism" line—the claim that socialist parties were abetting the victory of "fascism," and that all socialist, anarchist, and unionist militants (except their leaders) should be absorbed by Communist parties. Leaders who were unwilling to accept this—and they included the founders of some Latin American Communist parties—were replaced with leaders approved by Moscow.

But the Latin American parties, in contrast to their European counterparts, were not yet completely controlled by the Comintern. One reason for this was that their various sections or "aparats" (for example, their political police and espionage sections) were never integrated into the parties, but acted autonomously on orders from Moscow—which reflected the scant confidence the aparatchiks had in the discipline of the rank-and-file membership. Another reason was the flexibility with which Comintern orders were applied by a Lithuanian named Guralsky, chief of the Comintern's Latin American Bureau or Secretariat, which was transferred in 1928 from Moscow to Buenos Aires.* A third reason for the partial failure of the bolshevization policy in Latin America is, quite simply, that the Comintern was never deeply concerned about events on the continent. The situation in 1928 may be understood by considering some of the proceedings of the Sixth Comintern Congress of that year.

Bukharin stated at the Congress that "Latin America now enters, for the first time, into the sphere of the Comintern's influence." Echoing him, though doubtless for different reasons, the Brazilian leader Fernando Lacerda declared that although the Communist movement had existed in Latin America since 1920, it was not until now, in 1928, that "the Communist International has shown interest in the Latin American Communist movement." Kuusinen's theses on the colonial question, which were approved by the Congress, are also revealing.[11] Kuusinen wrote at some length on China, to justify Comintern policy there, but he mentioned Latin America only in passing, as one of many "colonial" and "semicolonial" regions.

* In Buenos Aires, Guralsky was known as "Rústico," in Chile as "Juan de Díos." Other members of the Bureau deserve passing mention: a Russian called "Pierre," apparently a representative of the Soviet secret police trying to pass as a Frenchman; a Tunisian called "Nemo"; an Italian called "Orestes"; another Italian by the name of Marcucci; and a Czech, Frederick Glaufbauf. (Many of these names were doubtless false, but they appeared on their holders' passports.) Members added later included the Argentine Communist leader Victorio Codovilla, and a Bulgarian named Stepanov, who had been the head of the Third International's Latin American section.

The Latin American delegates to the Congress, who met several times, must have given highly exaggerated reports. Kuusinen claimed that "the leading role in the struggle against imperialism in Latin America is retained by the Communist parties." At this time, the total membership in Communist parties throughout the entire hemisphere was between twenty and twenty-five thousand. Kuusinen said that "the working masses and the peasants of Latin America have learned in recent years how to overthrow their governments by force." It is doubtful in the extreme whether they had "learned how"; in any case, there was no country in Latin America in which the workers and peasants had overthrown a government—except in Mexico, whose revolution preceded Russia's. As proof of what he called "the growth of Latin American Communist parties," Kuusinen offered only the fact that the Sixth Congress was attended by representatives from eight Latin American parties.

The Sixth Congress, however, appointed a commission, on which all the Latin American delegates were seated, to prepare special theses on Latin America. The commission's report, while admitting that there existed no reliable statistics on the size of the industrial proletariat of Latin America, added hopefully that "the political history of [our] countries, in recent years, has offered a series of examples which have come to demonstrate that the proletariat has already affirmed its hegemony in the revolutionary movement." This thesis maintained that Latin American countries were on the eve of bourgeois-democratic revolutions. But in contrast to the bourgeois-democratic revolutions of Europe in the nineteenth century, the revolutions in Latin America would be characterized by the following distinctive features:

1. The existence of Communist parties, in constant contact with the Comintern leadership.

2. The existence of revolutionary union organizations maintaining close relations with the Profintern.

3. The decisive role of agricultural workers in the countryside; the existence in the countryside of a tradition of armed struggle to overthrow governments; and the existence, in some countries, of strong peasant organizations under the influence of Communist parties.

4. The enormous popularity of the Russian Revolution.

5. The weakness of every national bourgeoisie, which (except in Argentina) is always simply an appendage of British and U.S. imperialism.

6. The existence of acute antagonisms between the British and U.S. imperialists.

The same sort of schematicism may be seen in another Congress resolution, which, after stating that the eventual mission of Latin American Communists would be to transform the coming bourgeois-democratic revolutions into socialist revolutions, set forth immediate objectives for them. These were to be:

1. The creation of Communist parties in the countries which still lacked them.

2. The strengthening of existing Communist parties.

3. The strengthening to be carried out by the following means: (a) creating strong local organizations; (b) increasing the number of workers in large factories, and throughout the agricultural proletariat; (c) founding and giving maximum support to Communist factions in mass organizations, especially unions and peasants' organizations; (d) intensifying ideological work and breaking completely with petty bourgeois revolutionaries; (e) establishing or strengthening official periodicals of the Communist parties; and (f) enforcing severe and harsh discipline within the parties.

During the period in which these theses were in effect not a single bourgeois-democratic revolution took place in Latin America; when the outbreaks did occur, during and after World War II, the Communist position was completely different, and the objectives suggested in 1928 were not pursued. It does not, for that matter, appear that they were strenuously pursued even to begin with. In 1929 a Latin American delegate to the Tenth Plenary Meeting of the Communist International's Executive Committee declared: "I believe Latin America has been discovered by now, and that it is no longer enough to content oneself with declarations and highflown resolutions. . . . The Communist International must give constant attention to our small parties in Latin America; it must make a more tenacious effort to organize them, and lend them more effective political support."[12]

THE TACTIC OF THE BACKWARD POLICY

In December 1927, when several Latin American Communists were in Moscow to celebrate the tenth anniversary of the Russian Revolution, the Comintern called together a Latin American Conference. Among the Latin American representatives were Eudocio Ravines of Peru, Victorio Codovilla of Argentina, the Mexican poet Germán Liszt Arzubide, the Brazilians Karracick and Astrogildo Pereyra, the Venezuelan Ricardo Martínez, and the Peruvians Julio Portocarrero and Fernando Bazán. Jules Humbert-Droz from Switzerland and Alexander Losovsky of the Soviet Union represented the Comintern.[13] The Latin American delegates agreed, no doubt at Losovsky's suggestion, to make every effort to unite "all union and class organizations" in a struggle against the United States, the Pan American Federation of Labor, and the bourgeois offensive; and on December 11, 1927, in the presence of Losovsky and other Communist leaders from France, Italy, and the United States, they signed a document which committed them to organize a Latin American Labor Conference in 1928.[14]

When the 1927 conference discussed the situation in Peru, Losovsky favored seeking an alliance with Haya de la Torre's populist APRA—a tactic apparently in violation of the "social fascism" line, which decreed radical intransigence toward socialist and populist parties, whose members were to be wooed but whose leaders were to be opposed. But Losovsky explained that "in backward countries, a backward policy is needed." "Fascism," he said, "is impossible in backward countries, which are unable to support the complicated economic, political, and social machinery necessary to a fascist regime." Of the proposed alliance, he said: "I find nothing particularly revolutionary in Haya's Alliance [the APRA], nor anything popular nor even very [Latin] American about it. But while I do not believe Haya is capable of organizing an effective political party, I think he will create a very important movement. He is brave, ambitious, and tenacious. Our alliance with him will fill a need, and when one supplies something that would otherwise be lacking, one is successful." The proposed alliance was never made, however; Haya rejected it. Losovsky's statements in his pamphlet *El movimiento sindical latinoamericano* are also revealing: "Actually, we have in Latin America," he wrote, "a young movement, a movement that embraces hundreds of thousands of workers, but which is, from the ideological point of view, very confused, and from the organizational point of view, very weak. The revolution is not brought about through proclamations, strikes cannot be declared every twenty-four hours; and to fight against the bourgeoisie more is needed than a weekly publication and a hundred militants. Far more necessary is an organization sufficiently strong to fight and defeat the capitalistic state.... In Latin America too much is being said about the social revolution. Every Latin American letter ends with 'Long live the social revolution!' This is all very well. In no way am I opposed to it. But there are some comrades with too primitive a notion of the social revolution. They think that if the socialist revolution failed to come about yesterday, it will surely be a reality tomorrow.... In Latin America there are too many small guild unions, too many phantom unions."

A few examples will confirm this description of the state of Latin American Communism during the period from 1926 to 1930. In Mexico a Swiss "adviser" named Alfred Stirner, sent by Moscow, managed to expel the most highly qualified labor leaders and to initiate several strikes, all of which were failures. He pushed the Sindicato de Inquilinos del Distrito Federal to resort to violence, which brought about the dissolution of that organization. The same thing happened, over a longer period of time, to the Communist-led Confederación Sindical Unitaria.[15] In Argentina, the Communist-led Comité Clasista of the metallurgical industry managed to foment half a dozen strikes in as many steel factories. The strikes were not an expression of popular feeling but only of obedience to party orders, and they were lost, one after another, at great cost to the workers.[16]

The most significant example of Communist failure comes from Colombia. In November 1928 workers on the Santa Marta banana plantations declared a strike. Months before, workers on other plantations had staged successful strikes, without leadership from Communist elements. There was at the time no Communist party in Colombia, but individual Communists, led by a Frenchman known as "Austine," had infiltrated the Partido Socialista Revolucionario. When the Santa Marta strikes broke out the Partido Socialista Revolucionario came to the defense of the strikers. Among the Communists opinion was divided. Some felt it was just another strike. Others believed that a walkout of 40,000 laborers should be transformed into an insurrectional movement, which would bring on the revolution. Raúl Mahecha—a leader of this second group—organized the strikers, divided the plantations into sixty districts, each with its strike committee, and collected almost $40,000 for the cause. The Partido Revolucionario's Executive Committee sent an order to Mahecha: "Do not confuse the strike with an insurrection." He paid no attention. On December 6 the government suspended constitutional guarantees throughout Magdalena Department, where the plantations affected by the strike were located. When four thousand strikers held a demonstration in the Ciénega railroad station, troops opened fire with machine guns, killing 200 and wounding 400 more. Twelve thousand strikers then formed action groups, took the guns of several military detachments, and engaged in open fighting. Hundreds more died, including the socialist leader Erasmo Coronel. The strike eventually failed, at a terrible cost: 1,004 dead, 3,680 wounded, 500 arrested, and hundreds of years of prison sentences pronounced by the courts. By making the strike appear to be an insurrection, the Communists isolated it from liberal and socialist support, without which it was doomed from the beginning. But the Colombian Communists and the Frenchman "Austine" were at least able to report their "heroic activity" to Moscow.[17] Months later, at the Communist Conference of Montevideo and Buenos Aires, Mahecha reported on the strike and said: "If we do not make the revolution, it is certain, absolutely certain, that the liberals will." For this Communist fear of competition the Santa Marta strikers paid with their lives.

From June 1 to June 12, 1929, the first Latin American Communist Conference was held in Buenos Aires. Twenty-eight delegates from the Communist parties in Argentina, Brazil, Bolivia, Colombia, Cuba, Ecuador, El Salvador, Guatemala, Mexico, Paraguay, Peru, Uruguay, Panama, and Venezuela attended. Chilean delegates were prevented from attending by the authorities then ruling the country.[18] In addition, representatives from the Communist International, the International Communist Youth, the American Communist Party, and the Comintern's Latin American Bureau also participated: that is, Guralsky, "Pierre," the Argentinian Codovilla, and the Bulgarian Stepanov, who was head of the Latin American section of the Comintern and called himself "Luis."

All the delegates presented reports. Stepanov, in his report on the anti-imperialist struggle, pointed out that bourgeois elements were playing an important role in it, and that "class against class" tactics were inappropriate. He was supported in this view by many others, including the Colombian Mahecha, who reminded the conference that middle-class elements had lent financial support to the banana strikes in his country. The fact is that the middle class had carried on most of the anti-imperialist activity in Latin America for years, without orders from Moscow. For Communists, the problem was how to lead instead of simply follow. Stepanov proposed that one tactic for wrenching the coming revolution "from the hands of the ca-pitulationist petty bourgeoisie" was the organization of workers' and peas-ants' blocs, in which an otherwise non-affiliated mass would be led by Com-munist party members of the bloc; the bloc would be, in effect, a front or-ganization of the Communist Party. It was necessary to prevent these blocs from becoming parties, each with its own political line, as Stepanov claimed was about to occur in Brazil and also in Mexico, where the Liga Agraria exerted a greater influence in the bloc than did the Communist Party. In reality, those two worker-peasant blocs were the only ones Latin American Communists ever managed to create, and both of them failed.

Conference delegates also admitted failure to act successfully on the peas-ant question. "Suárez" (the Mexican painter David A. Siqueiros) con-fessed: "Our parties have occupied themselves very little with the peasant issue," and suggested that all parties begin studies of the land problem. This recommendation, made to parties founded eight or nine years earlier in overwhelmingly agricultural countries, amounted to a confession of in-difference toward the condition of millions of Latin Americans. The Guate-malan delegate, Villalba, read a letter addressed to him by a group of peas-ants, in which they said: "You insist on not understanding that we lack schools, that we are dying, abandoned in the mountains for lack of hy-giene, electricity, or food. You close your eyes to the truth, pretending not to see that work is imposed on us as a punishment." There was some dis-cussion about what should be done when peasants from other countries (Mexican braceros in the United States, for example, or Jamaicans in Cuba) drove down the wages of native workers, but no decision was reached.

The race problem was another vital matter that was left unresolved. Saco, a Peruvian, argued in his report that the Communist International should combat "Negro Zionism" and oppose any attempts to found American Negro states in Africa. In the same vein he added that the establishment of an autonomous Indian state "would not be conducive at this time to the formation of an Indian proletarian dictatorship, and much less to the formation of a classless Indian state, as some have stated, but rather to the creation of an Indian bourgeois state." He therefore opposed supporting nationalistic tendencies among the Indians, since this could lead "to a massacre of whites, workers included." "Peters," the Comintern's youth representative, protested that this stand would be an implicit criticism of the policy of nationalities, which (on paper at least) was followed by the Russian Communist Party. When Ricardo Martínez, from Venezuela, spoke of defending Indian culture against white depredations, "Peters" supported him: "Our slogan must be the right of the free development of each culture." Guralsky felt compelled to try to justify the Comintern's failure to adopt theses on the race problem at its Sixth Congress, saying that (in 1926) "Latin American comrades had been insisting that such a problem did not exist." He proposed adopting no resolutions, and added that "it is understood that the Latin American Secretariat will take charge of indicating appropriate projects for practical work in each country." Not a single delegate mentioned Mariátegui's essays on the Indian problem. Once again, obsession with party orders and formulas prevented a close examination of Latin American realities.

The rest of the reports also pointed out weaknesses in the Communist movement. Unions knew too little about how to enlist the support of non-union workers, Communist-led groups were not successful in grasping union leadership. Codovilla of the Secretariat was criticized for not paying much attention to countries of the north, especially Cuba and Mexico; to which he replied that the Mexican Communist Party had not answered any of the Secretariat's letters for several months. He concluded, predictably, that the Latin American Secretariat "should become more and more the leading organization of the Latin American Communist movement, and the parties should link themselves more closely to it"—which meant, in effect, that parties should take more orders from agents Guralsky, Codovilla, and "Pierre."

The weaknesses mentioned by delegates to the Buenos Aires conference barely suggest the gap between reality and party statements. In Mexico City, for example, the Communist Party claimed 2,000 members; but according to reliable witnesses, no more than 400 Communists marched in the May Day parade in 1930, in which 70,000 men and women took part. In Ecuador the party officially claimed 2,000 members, but confessed that only 200 had paid dues. From Cuba came vague references to a membership of "several thousand"; only 300 persons were registered with the party. In Paraguay, according to that country's delegate at Buenos Aires, "a bare handful of urban workers makes up the party." To this Codovilla could only lament, "And we thought we had formed a solid party in Paraguay"— which suggests the scarcity of information at the disposal of the Latin American Secretariat. Communist parliamentary strength, which Lenin had considered so important, was also negligible: in Argentina, a country with relatively honest electoral practices, the Communists had only one congressman; Mexico had three, Chile two, Colombia one. About all that can be said for the boasts of Communist strength in this period is that Communism was in fact the only truly revolutionary force at work in Latin America, since the socialist and anarchist movements were in decline and the populist movement was just beginning.

ANTI-IMPERIALISM AND ADVENTURISM

In the decade before the tactic of the Popular Front was proclaimed in 1936, Latin American Communists channeled most of their efforts into anti-imperialist activities. If this work seemed to serve Latin American aspirations, it was in fact intended by the Comintern to serve the interests of Soviet diplomacy. Few militants realized that this explained why Communists were occasionally ordered to oppose strikes against national enterprises, on the grounds that foreign companies, even when they paid higher wages, were to be attacked first; or that a damper was put on anti-imperialist campaigning for several months in 1928 because Russia was then making an effort to increase trade with the United States.[19] Moscow's purpose was to weaken England, France, and the United States wherever it could. But since the United States was considered less dangerous than England and France, the Comintern reserved most of its aid for anti-imperialist efforts in North Africa and Asia, to the neglect of Latin America.

The first congress of the League Against Imperialism—an assemblage of delegates representing pacifists, labor unions, writers, and so forth, all brought together by the Comintern's master organizer, Willy Münzenberg —met in Brussels in February of 1927. (Münzenberg concealed the Comintern's hand quite effectively; Nehru wrote in his memoirs that he believed the congress had been called by the Chinese Kuomintang.)[20] Among the Latin American delegates were Carlos Quiljano from Uruguay, Julio Antonio Mella from Cuba, Eudocio Ravines and Víctor Raúl Haya de la Torre from Peru, and the Mexican José Vasconcelos. Haya opposed the congress resolution on Latin America and the formation of national anti-imperialist leagues. He argued that the anti-imperialist struggle should be carried on not by an avowed one-class party, such as the Communist Party, but rather by parties in which various classes were integrated; these parties realized that imperialism was an economic phenomenon which offered opportunities for progress as well as threats of further exploitation, and they would not attack it according to Communist tactics originated in industrial countries, where imperialism, in Lenin's formula, was the last phase of capitalism. As Haya put it, "in Indian America imperialism is the first phase of capitalism." Haya's APRA delegation maintained complete independence, and was the only delegation at the congress to openly express reserve about the decisions reached by it.[21] The congress formally established the League Against Imperialism, with an executive committee that usually found itself divided: the relatively moderate English and American members, along with Nehru, against the French, Russian, and Latin American members, who were much more dogmatic. (In fact, Nehru was expelled from the League in 1931 for having accepted a truce in the fight for India's independence.)

In 1929 the League held its second congress in Frankfurt, Germany. Haya de la Torre took no part in the Frankfurt congress, nor did many other labor leaders and liberals who had been in Brussels. Nehru wrote that both congresses were riddled with spies from every nation. An American delegate, in Paris after the Frankfurt meetings, was questioned by an agent from the Sureté Nationale. The two had met in Brussels, where the police agent, hands and face blacked, had posed as a delegate from an African colony.[22]

In Brussels all sorts of nationalist movements had been accepted; the Communists had tried to influence them but had not openly criticized their tactics. In Frankfurt, however, it was stated that the League should be backed not so much by petty bourgeois nationalistic parties as by the working and peasant masses. From that moment on the League became, for the Communists, a means of grasping the leadership of unions and peasant organizations, by directing them in protests against imperialism.

In Latin America the League's Continental Committee, led by Julio Antonio Mella, maintained headquarters in Mexico City and published a magazine, *El Libertador*. In 1929 national leagues existed in Argentina, Brazil, Uruguay, and Cuba, and local leagues had been set up in Panama, Quito, Guatemala, San Salvador, and Bogotá. But the League was never strong. "Simons," the American delegate to the Communist Conference of Buenos Aires, reported that in 1930, three years after its foundation, "The League is not a united front, and does not even bring the masses under party influence; it is an organization without masses." "The party," he added, "must take over control of the League."[23] The World Committee of the League in Berlin said that the Continental Committee in Mexico was not maintaining the necessary contact, and added that it "lacked a solid organization."

Perhaps the League's decisive failure was the Sandino case in Nicaragua. Nicaragua had been occupied four times by U.S. Marines, attempting to enforce the Byran-Chamorro treaty. During the last occupation a former lieutenant, Augusto C. Sandino (1893–1934), first an oil man in Mexico and later a miner in his own country, organized a small guerrilla army in the Sierra de Segovia. For six years, from 1927 to 1933, using weapons captured from the enemy, and grenades made from tin cans, he fought the Marines and the National Guard, as the Nicaraguan army was called. Sandino awakened nationalist enthusiasm all over the Americas, and in 1933 the Marines were withdrawn from Nicaragua by President Roosevelt. Sandino requested lands for his men and was received by the Nicaraguan president; on leaving the presidential palace a platoon of National Guards murdered him.

Latin American Communists had supported Sandino at first, but when he continued to insist that the anti-imperialist struggle should be carried on by intellectuals and the middle class, as well as by workers, the Communists began slandering him. The early Communist attempts to claim Sandino's struggle as their own resulted in a terrible waste of funds collected for the Nicaraguan cause, hindered the help which several nations (such as Mexico) were ready to offer, and alienated many sympathizers. A few details will suggest the nature of the Communist failure. Sandino had authorized only Dr. Pedro José Zepeda, provisional president in exile of Nicaragua, to collect funds for him. The Mexican Communist newspaper, *El Machete,* however, repeatedly stated that only a Communist-founded committee called "Mafuenic" was authorized to collect funds, and it frequently claimed credit for funds collected by others. Of the first $1,000 actually collected by Communists, Sandino received only $250; a Venezuelan named Guntaro Machado (later the leader of the Communist Party of his country), who was to deliver the sum, claimed the rest for "travel expenses." When Sandino dismissed his private secretary, a Salvadorian Communist named Farabundo, the Communists angrily claimed that Sandino had collected $60,000 from the United States and used it to buy a hacienda in Mexico—an accusation so clumsy that even the League Against Imperialism had to deny it.

Sandino broke off correspondence with the Communists in 1929, and with this break the Communists lost their best chance to gain influence by leading the anti-imperialist movement. They continued to try, but their efforts were feeble and ineffective. Until the Popular Front tactic was presented to them in 1935, they suffered through a period of adventurism, trying to cover up defeats in hopes of remaining on good terms with Moscow. A few examples of this adventurism are worth considering.

In Mexico in March of 1929, the Communists, on orders from Moscow, attempted to utilize a military uprising in Durango to create soviets in the northern parts of the country; they feared that if they supported the Mexican government, if only temporarily and in order to quell reactionary elements, they would incur the wrath of Moscow—as had happened in 1927.[24] Diego Rivera, in a pamphlet published in 1935, wrote that the Mexican party's Central Committee "had agreed to print in *El Machete* instructions to the peasants for insurrection, even though the Mexican government had been confiscating all copies of *El Machete* for three weeks— a maneuver that led to the imprisonment and execution by firing squad of many comrades, especially peasants."

In Chile in 1925, the Communists tried to convert a copper miners' strike into a revolt against the government of Arturo Alessandri, a liberal president who had managed to enact laws providing for social security, compensation for discharged employees, and tribunals of arbitration. The Communists failed, but their leaders avoided censure from the Comintern, which had previously condemned them as "counter-revolutionary" for having supported Alessandri's social reforms. In September of 1931 there was also a navy rebellion in Chile, and though the Chilean Communists had not organized it, *International Press Correspondence* stated that it was "the first attempt in the history of Latin America to raise the flag of power by workers' and peasants' soviets."[25]

In 1932 the peasants of El Salvador, who lived under a feudal landholding regime and a brutal dictatorship, rebelled at the instigation of the Communist Party. The repression of the revolt was ferocious, and thousands of lives were lost. Nevertheless, *International Press Correspondence* praised the action of the Communists of El Salvador, thanks to which, it said, during the next stage of the fight, with a more powerful Communist party, Peasant Leagues and Workers' Unions would be created.[26]

In Cuba, when Machado was overthrown in 1933 by a general strike which the Communists had opposed, the Communist leader J. Gómez stated that the Communist Party had been "the only revolutionary party, the militant vanguard of the Cuban proletariat"; and while he admitted that non-Communist groups had also played a certain role in the anti-Machado movement, he claimed that "in the final analysis, it was through Communist efforts that the tryant was toppled."[27]

The Communist Party of Brazil began acquiring strength when it was joined by several members of a military group known as *os tenentes*. One of its best-known members was Luis Carlos Prestes, who had gained popularity for leading a band of guerrilla fighters in a revolt in 1926, which had forced him into exile. The tenentes helped bring Getulio Vargas to power in 1930, but many of them wanted more democracy in politics and more social legislation than Vargas was willing to promise.[28] Prestes joined the Communist Party in Moscow in 1934, and in 1935 returned to Brazil to organize—with the help of two other Communists, the German Ernst Ewer (alias Harry Berger) and the Argentinian Rodolfo Ghioldi—the Aliança Libertadora Nacional.

At a congress attended by representatives of unions which had remained free of Vargas' control, and by many of the old group of tenentes, the Aliança proposed suspension of payments on the foreign debt, an eight-hour working day, a minimum wage law, redistribution of land, and a social security system. Vargas declared the Aliança illegal in July, but it went on to stage a military insurrection on November 23, in Rio de Janeiro and two northern cities. The revolt was quickly suppressed, and the Aliança leaders, including Prestes, were imprisoned for several years.

International Press Correspondence, after admitting that "Communists and non-Communists fought shoulder to shoulder" in the Aliança, claimed as usual that the Communist Party had played the leading role in the revolt. This was not strictly true, but it was a relatively plausible argument, and helped make the Brazilian Communist Party the strongest on the continent.*

During this period of adventurism, not a single Communist party escaped schisms and expulsions. The most important results, by virtue of the personalities involved or the number of those expelled, were as follows. (1) After 1927, in most Communist parties the militants and local leaders who supported Trotsky and the Russian opposition to Stalin were expelled or left voluntarily. Only in Bolivia (where they formed the Partido Obrero Revolucionario), Argentina, Mexico, and Chile did the Trotskyites gain any strength. The most important adherents to Trotskyism were the Mexican G. Munis, the Argentinian J. A. Ramos, the Chilean Manuel Hidalgo, and the Bolivians Guillermo Lora and "Tristán Maroff" (Gustavo Navarro). (2) In Argentina, the leaders Cayetano Oriolo, Juan Greco, and José F. Penelón split and founded another Communist party in 1929. (3) Party crises were frequent in Mexico, where the most notable expulsion was that of Diego Rivera, in 1929, on the grounds that he was a Trotskyite.

---

* In the postwar elections of 1946, the Brazilian party won a higher percentage of votes than any other national Communist party; Prestes was elected a senator. (Alexander, *Communism,* pp. 109 and following.)

In the mid-thirties, Rafael Ramos Pedrueza was also expelled. Rivera tried to rejoin the Communist Party several times, but only managed to do so, officially, shortly before his death in 1957. (4) The elimination of Codovilla, for a period of ten years, from the Latin American scene. In 1930, when General José F. Uriburu overthrew President Irigoyen in Argentina, Codovilla gave his list of party leaders to several comrades for safekeeping and then fled the country. Guralsky called him a "charlatan and a coward," and criticized him so harshly that Codovilla asked to be sent to Moscow, from whence he went to Spain as a representative of the Comintern.

THE POPULAR FRONT AND THE SECOND WORLD WAR

Since 1922 at least, Communist parties throughout the world had attacked socialists, and had accused all other leftist parties of complicity with imperialism, fascism, and "capitalist reaction." In Germany, it was said, "The best way of defeating Hitler lies in destroying German Social Democracy."[29] Although this line helped assure Hitler's victory in 1933, attacks against socialists and other leftists continued for two more years.

The leadership of the Comintern was at this time deeply divided, or at least as deeply as Stalin permitted; and as a result the Seventh Congress, scheduled to take place in 1934, was postponed. But the delegates from the Latin American parties who were supposed to attend were nevertheless called, by Manuilsky and Dimitrov, to a Latin American Conference in Moscow. Dimitrov, doubtless aware that a change in Comintern strategy was on the horizon, proclaimed: "The Latin American question is one of the utmost interest, for the policy we adopt there will serve as a global precedent." Delegates from Argentina, Brazil, Cuba, Mexico, Colombia, and Uruguay were joined, for the last sessions, by such eminent European Communist leaders as Kuusinen of Finland, Pieck of Germany, and Togliatti of Italy. The most significant result of the conference, for the Latin Americans, was a reorganization of the Comintern's Latin American Bureau. Guralsky and G. Sinani were purged, and new members appointed: the German who called himself Manuel Cazón, a Russian named Kazanov (nicknamed "Casanova"), the Italian Marcucci, the Venezuelan Martínez (who was in charge of union affairs), and the Peruvian Eudocio Ravines. Santiago, Chile, was picked as the Bureau's new headquarters, and after the Popular Front tactic was announced at the Seventh Comintern Congress in July 1935, Dimitrov picked Ravines to experiment with the new tactic in Chile.[30]

The maneuver in Chile began with the intellectuals. Some of them were invited to visit the U.S.S.R.; several of them, upon returning, wanted nothing further to do with the Communists, but others became good propagandists. Chilean socialism and unionism had suffered from chronic divisions, and the Communists had always opposed attempts at unification. But in December 1936 the two union federations drew together, forming the Confederación de Trabajadores de Chile (CTCH). A long battle for its leadership posts raged between socialists and Communists, with the socialists finally winning a majority. Alessandri's government had been leaning to the right, and in 1936 the Partido Radical pulled away from him. A year before a leftist bloc had been formed by the socialists, the Partido Demócrata, the Trotskyite Izquierda Comunista, and the Partido Radical Socialista. When the Communists, along with the Partido Radical and the CTCH, joined the bloc, they claimed credit for creating it because they managed to get its name changed to Popular Front, which the Third International's Seventh Congress had popularized.

The Chilean Popular Front demonstrates that Ravines and his comrades knew perfectly well how to apply Moscow's advice. They flattered those who were inclined to support them, and cast suspicion on others; they offered financial aid to their chosen candidates, and slandered their adversaries. Each party belonging to the Popular Front soon had a pro-Communist and an anti-Communist wing. The Communists tried to bring Carlos Ibáñez, an ex-dictator friendly to the Nazi Party of Chile, into the Popular Front, justifying this maneuver by saying that it might help to draw Ibáñez away from the Nazis. In the congressional elections of April 1937, the Popular Front won 10 out of 25 senatorial seats and 66 of the 146 seats in the Chamber of Deputies. The Communists elected only one senator and seven congressmen; the socialists placed fifteen congressmen.

The socialists wanted Marmaduke Grove as their presidential candidate in the 1938 elections. Grove was the leader of the short-lived Socialist Republic of 1932, which the Communists had fought. The radicals wanted one of their own men. The Communists supported the radical Pedro Aguirre Cerda, a great hacienda-owner and Alessandri's Minister of the Interior, who had been accused of having been responsible for a slaughter of the strikers in San Gregorio. He was finally the Popular Front candidate. The Communists managed to win for Aguirre the votes of several fascist groups, who hated Alessandri because he had suppressed their activities. Aguirre won the election with 229,982 votes, against 213,000 for Gustavo Rosas, a conservative.

When Aguirre formed his government the Communist Party declared that it had no ambition for power, and aspired to no ministerial posts. This is what the Communists had done in France, and in Spain before the Civil War: stay out of the government, criticize it if it failed to apply the entire Popular Front program, and take credit for any of its actions that seemed effective and well received by the masses.

Communist parties in the rest of Latin America never managed to establish truly organized Popular Fronts. In Argentina and Uruguay the socialists and the leftist parties reacted coldly to Communist proposals for an alliance. In Peru the APRA always rejected Communist flattery without hesitation, even when Romain Rolland personally wrote to Haya asking him to accept the Popular Front's proposition. In Cuba, when the Partido Auténtico, headed by Dr. Ramón Grau San Martín, refused to accept the alliance, the Communists turned toward Colonel Fulgencio Batista. In Venezuela they tried to form a leftist bloc, and when they failed they shifted their support to the dictatorial Isaías Medina Angarita. In Colombia they collaborated for a time, although not officially, with the Partido Liberal.

As in Europe, where Communists collaborated with fascists and Catholics, in Latin America they showed themselves willing to reach understandings with the extreme right. In Cuba, for example, they allied with Batista, who supported their unions and legalized their party when he came to power as a result of a military coup. In Brazil they offered to collaborate with Getulio Vargas, who had their leaders in jail, but they never convinced the dictator that he should listen to them. In Peru they made a deal with another dictator, Marshal Oscar Benavides; by supporting his candidate, Manuel Prado, they gained a congressional seat (for Juan P. Luna) and were given great influence over the union movement.[31] These alliances with dictators reflected a schematic application of orders to extend the anti-Nazi front, even through local fascists. This tactic alienated several local party groups, especially in Peru (in Arequipa and Cuzco), and Brazil (in São Paulo); and in July 1939, General Francisco Múgica withdrew as the candidate supported by the Communists for the Mexican presidency, accusing the Communists of "abandoning the historic mission of a vanguard party, and giving in to the vital interests of groups with disguised reactionary tendencies."

The Popular Fronts in Latin America began to break down when Hitler signed his pact with Stalin on August 23, 1939. After the shock wore off, Latin American Communists dutifully stated, as their colleagues all over the world were doing, that the Allies were imperialists. In March 1940, during the Thirteenth Communist Party Congress in Uruguay, the party's secretary general, Eugenio Gómez, asked for a "united front among all peace-loving, progressive forces, in order to fight against the imperialist war, and for the defense of the Soviet Union, socialism's homeland." But it was not easy, as the invasion of Europe continued, to offer wholehearted support to the Nazis. In August 1940, Blas Roca, the secretary general of the Cuban Communist Party, maintained that Cuba should be kept out of the war. Leaders in other countries felt the same, and so they argued that since Communists in Latin America could not collaborate directly with the Nazis, as was possible in Europe, the correct Communist position was "socialist neutrality." This position tended to isolate the Communist movement from the masses, and particularly from the democratic groups.[32] Miguel Angel Velasco, from the Communist Party's Central Committee in Mexico, said on June 21, 1941: "This war is totally foreign to the interests of the Mexican people, because two groups are contesting for the power to dominate and exploit the world."[33] That night the Nazis attacked Russia. A few days later, Velasco demanded that all parties, all legislators, and the entire Mexican populace support the U.S.S.R. and the Allied forces. The same turnabout occurred in other countries, with minor variations.

Just as their opposition to helping the Allied Powers had isolated the Communists, their new position, of advocating everything that could be useful to Russia in the war, won them considerable popularity: to the masses, at least, they could now appear as the most active group supporting the Allied cause. On balance, however, this was not enough.* The Communist tolerance of dictators, and their failure to support strikes and workers' protests during the war, isolated them still further from democratic forces. It may be said that by 1942 the Communist movement in Latin America had entered a ten-year period of decline, which would end by leaving the national Communist parties (except in Chile and Brazil) as skeleton organizations with almost no influence. After World War II Latin America entered a period of profound transformations—first political, then social and economic; but the Communist movement found itself unable to assume a leading role in them because of its anti-democratic attitude during the Soviet-Western alliance.

POSTWAR DEVELOPMENTS AND THE POLICY
OF "CRITICAL SUPPORT"

For a while after the war, Moscow encouraged Communist parties not to oppose existing governments but rather to strengthen themselves. During this period Communist parties offered extreme expressions of national patriotism, appeared moderate in their programs, and avoided attacking anyone who might possibly become an ally, reactionary as he might be. In this way they managed to infiltrate many apolitical or non-Communist organizations and conquer the leadership of many unions; they achieved considerable influence among students and intellectuals, created organizations of friendly journalists and politicians, and even gained some favor with the military. Open collaboration with a government was rare. The

* For further details on the position of the Communists during World War II, see the discussion of the CTAL in Chapter 18, pp. 325–28.

Communist Juan Marinello served in Batista's government in Cuba in 1943, and in Ecuador in 1944 a Communist served briefly in the provisional government headed by José Maria Velasco Ibarra. But the only significant example of overt collaboration occurred in Chile, whose case merits special attention.[34]

Just as in 1938 Chile had been the only Latin American country with a Popular Front movement and government, so in 1946 it was the only Latin American country with Communist ministers in its cabinet. During the war the Chilean Communists managed to participate with the socialists in the leadership of the Confederación de Trabajadores de Chile (CTCH), and widened, through their maneuvering, the division already opening up within socialist ranks. In January 1946 they won a majority of administrative posts in the CTCH, thanks to help from the radicals, the liberals, and the falangists (Christian democrats). Immediately, they organized two general strikes against the government of their former ally, President Ríos, Aguirre Cerda's successor. As their price for calling off the strike the Communists asked to be admitted to the government, which produced a schism in the CTCH.

In September 1946 the Partido Radical candidate, Gabriel González Videla, was elected president of Chile, with Communist backing. Along with three radicals and three liberals, three Communists took part in his government: Carlos Contreras Labarca became Minister of Communications, Miguel Concha became Minister of Agriculture, and Víctor Contreras was named Minister of Lands and Colonization. The Communists, then, had in their hands the instruments for trying to resolve one of the country's fundamental problems: the agrarian question. During its five months of participation in the government the party grew considerably, and asserted its domination in the unions; but it did nothing about the land question, except to organize many peasants' groups. In general, the Communist ministers acted as if they held supreme power, and used government intervention against non-Communist unions attempting to declare strikes. In attacks in the streets, members of socialist and anarcho-syndicalist organizations were murdered by Communists.

During the municipal elections of April 1947, the Communists gained votes, as did the socialist and conservative opposition; the Communists' allies, the radicals and liberals, suffered severe losses, which led them to consider breaking their alliance with the Communists, which was costing them dearly. They asked the president to dismiss the Communist ministers or to accept their own resignations. The Communists refused to resign from their posts, and González Videla dismissed them to organize a radical government. At the end of a month the Communists began to attack González Videla, slandering him and fomenting strikes. In October 1947 the government broke diplomatic relations with Czechoslovakia, Yugoslavia, and the Soviet Union (because from their embassies help had been given to the strikers) and arrested several Communist leaders. In September 1948 González Videla secured passage of a Law in Defense of Democracy, which outlawed the Communist Party, although in practice the law was only used to keep Communists from running for office.

The Communist Party was weakened, but the frontist tactic permitted it to pull itself together, and in 1952 it formed the Frente del Pueblo, with dissenting factions from the socialist, democratic, and radical parties; the Frente then supported, unsuccessfully, the candidacy of the socialist Salvador Allende. In 1956 the Communists joined in a new front, the Frente Revolucionario de Acción Popular (FRAP), and participated in yet another one in 1958, when the Law in Defense of Democracy was revoked. This last front again supported Allende in the elections of September 1958. FRAP failed to win, and the socialists (among whom there is a strong Titoist tendency) criticized their Communist allies for wanting to establish an unviable front for national liberation, and for presenting, in their congress, a report that was "biased, loaded with Soviet material, and inexact."[35]

Meanwhile, Moscow's policy had changed considerably; the Comintern had been abolished in 1943 and replaced by the Cominform in 1947, and the Cold War was rapidly developing. This new policy was characterized by three features: pledges by Communists that they would refuse to defend their own countries against any attack by the U.S.S.R. (Togliatti and Thorez made declarations to that effect in 1948); a campaign against the United States and against democratic governments; and the campaign of "peace partisans" in favor of the Stockholm manifesto of 1950.

In Latin America the new policy was translated into the following tactical movements by Communists and their allies—chiefly groups of intellectuals and students, but also nationalist movements that still had not suffered the consequences of contact with the Stalinists. (1) Campaigns by Lombardo Toledano and the Confederación de Trabajadores de América Latina (CTAL) against the Clayton Plan in favor of free trade and for trade with the Soviet bloc. (2) Campaigns "for peace," with Congresses in Mexico (September 1949) and Montevideo (March 1952). Signatures in favor of the Stockholm manifesto collected.* Stalin Awards given to the Mexican

---

* According to the Communist World Peace Congress, in a report dated January 1952, when all the signatures for the Stockholm manifesto had been collected, the results in Latin America were as follows (countries under dictatorships in italics): *Argentina,* 3,000,000 signatures; *Bolivia,* 8,500; Brazil, 3,000,000; Chile, 500,000; *Colombia,* 25,000; Costa Rica, 34,000; Cuba, 850,000; Mexico, 300,000; *Paraguay,* 16,000; *Peru,* 5,578; Uruguay, 216,000; *Venezuela,* 45,000.

General Heriberto Jara, to the Brazilian Jorge Amado, and later to the former President of Mexico, General Lázaro Cárdenas. Trips for Latin American delegates to the Soviet party congresses at Warsaw, Moscow, Vienna, and Peking. (3) Utilization of unions for these campaigns, as a means of disguising their Communist origin. The employment of unions for strikes which could damage regimes refusing to "play the game" or which could jeopardize U.S. interests. (4) Student agitation used to harass regimes unfriendly toward the U.S.S.R. or friendly to the United States, especially in Mexico, under Miguel Alemán's government, and in Chile, under González Videla. (5) Utilization of the embassies of the East European "peoples' democracies" (rarely those of the Soviet Union) to introduce propaganda, transmit orders, and so on. (In 1947 this led Chile to break relations with Yugoslavia, Czechoslovakia, and Russia, and Brazil to break with the U.S.S.R.; in 1959 Mexico expelled two Soviet diplomats, and Argentina another two, for the same reason.) (6) Completely changed propaganda techniques. Works by Marx and Lenin, for example, played down in favor of works by Stalin, and of novels and works of art dealing with "socialist construction." Propaganda directed not toward encouraging the study of Marxism but toward arousing enthusiasm for and loyalty to Russia.

Since the period of the Popular Front the Communists in Latin America, even more than in the rest of the world, have tried to act through agents or intermediaries, in order to appear inoffensive and without great influence. Only in those countries in which they have had considerable strength—Chile, Brazil, and Cuba—have they published newspapers confessing their affiliation.* In the rest of the countries they have concealed the party name and orientation.

The phrase "critical support," though coined not by orthodox Communists but by Trotskyites, serves well to describe the tactic adopted by the Communists in Latin America after World War II. "Critical support" is supposed to mean giving support to all governments or movements claiming to be anti-imperialistic and desirous of bringing about reforms in their countries, but criticizing those same governments or movements whenever they exhibit weaknesses or fall into error. This had no relation to the concept of loyal opposition. In practice, the support has been given exclusively to governments or movements, whatever their principles and their deeds,

---

* In 1954 the Communists could rely for support on the following papers: *El Diario Popular* in Montevideo; a weekly in Panama called *La Opinión*; the daily *El Siglo* in Chile; the daily *Hoy* in Cuba; the weekly *Trabajo* in Costa Rica; the *Diario Popular* in Colombia; *Tribuna Popular* and *Hoja* in Argentina. Furthermore, *El Diario de Centroamérica* in Guatemala was sympathetic, and many other union weeklies, supposedly technical, or designed for students, followed a more or less Communist line.

that can prove harmful to the policies of the United States and the non-Communist world; the criticism has been reserved exclusively for governments or movements that refuse to act in ways that will support Soviet diplomacy. Here are a few interesting examples of "critical support."

Perón, in Argentina, always counted on the advice of the Communist Rodolfo Puiggrós, and on the support of his Movimiento Obrero Comunista and its youth section. It had been the Communists who had collaborated most closely with Peronist leaders in driving socialists and anarcho-syndicalists out of the unions. The Communists were not attacked in 1953, when Perón launched his partisans against the socialist headquarters in the Casa del Pueblo, which the crowd burned. On the other hand, the opposition Communist group led by Ghioldi and Codovilla was never very aggressive, and in exchange for this Perón never refused a passport or a visa to Communists who wanted to attend international congresses. Two months before Perón's fall, in September 1955, the first Soviet industrial exposition to be held in Latin America opened in Buenos Aires. Since the fall of Perón, Peronists and Communists have collaborated in a constant effort to sabotage the stability of the democratic regime.[36]

In Colombia the Communist party, the Partido Socialista Popular, has called the struggle of the liberal guerrilla plains fighters—first against the police forces of extreme conservatives, and later against the forces of the dictator General Gustavo Rojas Pinilla—a "reactionary maneuver."[37]

In Cuba the Communist party, the Partido Socialista Popular, after having opposed the governments of Ramón Grau San Martín and Carlos Prío Socarrás, placed several high officials in General Batista's government following the 1952 military coup. These Communists formed a group that was apparently at odds with the official party, which though illegal was benevolently allowed to survive. When Fidel Castro called for a general strike in April 1958, the leaders of the Partido Socialista Popular announced that the strike was "destined to fail." In August 1958 the Partido tried to separate from Batista, and proposed the unification of all opposition groups, a suggestion severely censured by Castro's July 26 Movement.[38] At the same time, the Communist Carlos Rafael Rodríguez joined Castro in the Sierra.

In Venezuela the "black" Communists collaborated with a military junta that overthrew Rómulo Gallegos and the Acción Democrática government in 1948, and later supported Colonel Marcos Pérez Jiménez; their "red" colleagues worked from the outside, in exile. Both parties, however, made fierce attacks against the most active force in the resistance opposing the dictatorship—Acción Democrática and its militants. When Pérez Jiménez came to power, "black" Communists replaced democratic elements at the heads of unions. When Pérez Jiménez fell, in January 1958, "red" Communists were accepted on every democratic committee, and the "black" Communists were conveniently forgotten. The "red" Communists, however, did not manage to take over the union movement, nor did they secure victory for their chosen standard-bearer, Rear Admiral Wolfgang Larrazábal —the candidate with the least political experience, and therefore the one that would be easiest to influence.[39]

The Communists in Peru, led by Juan P. Luna (who had been a senator under the dictatorship of General Manuel Odría), collaborated actively with the dictatorial government, especially in replacing, with the help of the police, APRA elements in union administrations. Some of these unions, particularly in the southern part of the country, continued under Communist domination after Odría's retirement. The Communists backed the most inexpert candidate aspiring to succeed the dictator, and when Manuel Prado won the Communists organized several strikes — the bargaining power of which turned out to be nil — hoping to create an atmosphere propitious for a new military coup.

In Brazil the Communists supported Getulio Vargas—who had persecuted them—and maintained considerable influence over the voters. In the elections of October 1958 the Communists allied with two parties of unquestionably demagogic character: the Trabalhista of João Goulart and the Social Progresista, headed by Adhemar de Barros, the mayor of São Paulo. Prestes declared that the alliance was "unconditional and permanent." Nevertheless, it failed, and the Communists lost a great many votes. In the 1960 elections, they backed Marshal Teixeira Lott against Janio Quadros. After the 1964 military overthrow of João Goulart's government, Prestes fled, leaving behind all his files, which contained many compromising facts. As a consequence, Prestes was replaced in the party high command, but a year later he was again the leading public figure, in the party, which by now was seriously divided between pro-Russian and pro-Chinese factions. The latter formed the Communist Party of Brazil (the pro-Russia group was called the Brazilian Communist Party), and accused Prestes of having left his files in return for safe conduct from the country.[40]

In addition to these examples, it may be pointed out that the Communists were in no way involved in the fight against the dictators Trujillo of the Dominican Republic, Somoza of Nicaragua, and Stroessner of Paraguay. On the other hand, in 1955, when Costa Rica was ruled by the democrat José Figueres, the Communists collaborated with their old ally, Calderón Guardia, and with other elements, in an attempted invasion of Costa Rican territory from Nicaragua, in which they were actively aided by Somoza and Pérez Jiménez.[41]

From a dictator's point of view, Communists can be useful. By allowing them to operate in the open, he can claim that under his regime no political persecution exists. They will destroy, frequently with the help of his dictatorial police, the democratic leadership of the unions. (There have been no Communist-led strikes under the dictators.) They can supply advisers of unquestionable political training (which military men usually lack). And by pretending to oppose the Communists, perhaps by sending a few of them into exile, the dictator can appeal for aid and support from Washington. For the Communists, too, this political concubinage has its uses. In addition to taking advantage of the dictator's strength to destroy their democratic adversaries, they can create political and union organizations which, when the dictator falls, can be taken over by other Communists, often those in exile.

The "critical support" tactic was not planned, but emerged naturally from the desire of Communists to persecute democratic forces by making use of the virtual monopoly on propaganda which had been given them by dictators. It also reflected the Communist need to maintain good relations with dictators, in order to serve the interests of Soviet diplomacy. This led to splits in many Communist parties in Latin America: one group would side with the dictator and the other would form an almost harmless opposition.[42] There were three Communist parties in Mexico, two in Colombia, two in Venezuela, two in Brazil, two in Argentina, two in Bolivia, and two in Peru. In all cases, the schisms were provoked by a disagreement over local tactics, or by rivalry for leadership within the national party. In each case, furthermore, no single party was recognized by the Cominform as its "official" organization. In all cases, both groups remained orthodox on international matters, and retained their loyalty to the Soviet Union.

The first schism came in Mexico. In 1940 the principal leaders of the official Communist Party—Campa and Laborde—were expelled, and they organized the Partido Obrero y Campesino. In 1947 Lombardo Toledano formed his own party, the Partido Popular, which in 1964 became the Popular Socialista; it attracted several notable ex-members of the Communist Party and well-known Communist sympathizers. Lombardo's party maintained friendlier relations with the government than either of the other two groups.

The schism in Venezuela dated from the time of World War II and reflected different attitudes of the various party leaders toward General Medina Angarita's government. Some of them, called the "black" Communists, wanted to support Medina, while others, the "red" faction, wanted to remain neutral. This divergence in internal matters continued during the Acción Democrática's regime (1945–48), and under the military dictatorship. Although the "reds" were the "official" party, it was significant that the Federación de Trabajadores del Distrito Federal, controlled by the "blacks" under Pérez Jiménez, was affiliated with the WTUF and CTAL, and that Rodolfo Quintero, the "black" leader, attended the WTUF's Milan Congress, and was later invited to visit Hungary by the Labor Federation of that country.

In Colombia the party's split dated from 1948, and the struggle for power between Augusto Durán and Gilberto Vieira within the Partido Socialista Popular; Durán lost, was expelled from the party (which again adopted the name Communist Party), and organized his own group.

In Argentina a group led by Rodolfo Puiggrós separated from the party in 1946, after violently criticizing the election-year union between the "official" party and Perón's opposition; Puiggrós organized his own Movimiento Obrero Comunista, which openly supported Perón. In Peru in 1949, Juan P. Luna, a leading Communist and a senator, placed a few comrades in the Odría administration, whereupon the party split and its secretary general, Jorge del Prado, went into exile.

In Bolivia the Communists were for a time divided into three groups. For many years no Communist party existed, although the Partido de Izquierda Revolucionaria (PIR) had more or less followed the international Communist line. In 1951 the PIR youth group separated from the party that supported the dictatorship, declared itself a Communist Party, and was recognized by the Cominform. After the 1952 revolution the PIR dissolved and was reorganized as the Communist Party—which meant that there were two parties operating under the same name. However, a group of PIR leaders—among them José Antonio Arce and Ricardo Anaya—opposed this decision; they stated their intention of remaining neutral and of attempting to organize a unified party. These maneuvers had two chief results. First, they established one party that supported, and one that opposed, the existing government of the Movimiento Nacionalista Revolucionario (MNR). Second, the name PIR was buried, the party having been discredited in the eyes of many Bolivians for its cooperation with oligarchic regimes. In 1953 the three groups fused into one Communist Party.

THE COMMUNISTS IN POWER: GUATEMALA

Guatemala affords an interesting example of frontist tactics applied with success in Latin America.[43] Within three-quarters of a century Guatemala had four dictators: Carrera, Barrios, Estrada Cabrera, and Jorge Ubico. In 1944 Ubico, facing growing opposition to his terrorist regime, left the country and entrusted affairs to his friend General Federico Ponce. Ponce organized elections, and the exiled Juan José Arévalo came to power. During the six years of his presidential administration, Arévalo put down twenty-three uprisings and attempted military takeovers. He built schools and enacted some modern labor legislation. The first unions were organized, and half a dozen political parties came into being.

The men who came to power in 1944, after Ubico's fall, had virtually no political experience, having lived under one of the most rigid dictatorships in Latin America. Thus when Col. Francisco Javier Arana, whom all had looked upon as Arévalo's successor, was murdered in June of 1949, the Communists found themselves in an excellent position. Ubico's practice of calling his opponents Communists (when few in fact were), and executing many of them, had long since persuaded many Guatemalans that the Communists were staunch opponents of dictatorship. The death of Arana eliminated an energetic adversary who had enjoyed great popularity. There was no unity among the revolutionary parties, and within the general conglomerate of parties, where doctrinal differences were minimal, only the Communists had a coherent program and solid experience. The Communists thus had no difficulty securing the election of Colonel Jacobo Arbenz, a weak and politically inexperienced officer whom they hoped to control.

It is interesting to trace the growth of Communist infiltration into the government. In 1944 Carlos Manuel Pellecer, a twenty-four-year-old teacher, had distinguished himself as a peasant organizer and become a congressman for the Frente Popular de Liberación. In 1945 he was sent as a secretary to the Guatemalan Embassy in Moscow, to keep him out of the country. At about the same time José Manuel Fortuny, a teacher and an employee in the British Embassy press section during the war, formed part of the Partido de Acción Revolucionaria (PAR), along with Víctor Manuel Gutiérrez (another teacher). Pellecer, apparently converted to Marxism in Moscow, returned to Guatemala in 1948, and ingratiated himself with Fortuny and Gutiérrez. In 1949 Gutiérrez broke with the PAR, because it had refused to participate in a Peace Conference held in Mexico, and founded the Partido Revolucionario Obrero Guatemalteco (PROG). In 1950, the three teachers and several of their friends formed the Comité Político Nacional de los Trabajadores, in order to support the candidacy of Arbenz. In 1951 the PAR, under the influence of Pellecer and Fortuny, who had come back into the fold, agreed to join in a front with the Communist Party and PROG. In 1949 another group of Communists had held its first congress and had adopted the name Communist Party of Guatemala; in October of 1952 it fused with the Vanguardia Democrática to create the Partido Guatemalteco de Trabajadores (PGT), a thoroughly Communist organization.

The Communist organization in Guatemala, then, sprang from the efforts of small Communist groups working within other parties, leading them into organized fronts, and drawing reinforcement from several experienced Communists, who had lived for long periods of time in Moscow.*

The first acts of the original groups were to create study groups (such as the schools called "Claridad" and "Jacobo Sánchez"), and to try to place their members in high offices, using the parties to which they supposedly belonged. Communists gained access to congressional seats, and to such posts as Undersecretary of Education, presidential press secretary, and labor federation secretary general. The Communists Pinto Usaga and José Alberto Cardoza managed to gain control of the Federación Sindical Guatemalteca (FSG), and to restore its alliance with the CTG. Communists founded a series of mass organizations—youth groups, women's organizations, and the Peace Partisans. They penetrated the University, and proselytized among the teachers; the high posts held by Communists in the Ministry of Education enabled them to offer appointments to friends and discriminate against adversaries. They gained domination of the unions partly by using the tribunals for arbitration, and also the Instituto de Seguridad Social, in which little-known Communists held influential posts; and partly by rigging union elections, often with the help of the police (as they did in the case of the Railroad Workers Union).

In a country just beginning its political development, any party can attract the masses if it knows what the masses want and can gain access to official posts. The political inexperience of Guatemalan leaders allowed administrative immorality to spread, and the Communists covertly encouraged it, for by occasionally exposing it they could discredit their adversaries and by tolerating it they could gain allies. It also permitted them to penetrate many government agencies, through which they could give the masses something—provided, of course, that the masses would formally adhere to Communist front organizations. In a period when the Communist movement all over the world was breaking its alliances with democratic parties, in Guatemala such alliances were being strengthened and increased in number.

Personal friendships, most of them formed when Communists worked only within other parties, as well as the support of President Arbenz, proved extremely useful in securing strategic posts. Fortuny was secretary to the Congress and later held a position in the presidential press office. Gutiérrez, Humberto Ortiz, Pinto Usaga, and Carlos René Valle were members of the board of the Instituto de Seguridad Social. Alfredo Guerra

---

* Communists from all over Latin America visited Guatemala; and between 1945 and 1952 seventy-five Guatemalan Communist leaders visited Moscow.

Borges was the presidential press secretary and later edited the *Diario de Centroamérica*. Mario Alfredo Silva was Undersecretary of Education. De Buen was an instructor of the Guardia Civil (police). Raúl Leyva was director of a broadcasting station. Hugo Barrios Klee was Inspector General of Labor. The list of names is short, but the posts were numerous—many men held three or four jobs. Through reports, proposals, and suggestions from those posts it was easy enough to influence government decisions, to favor friends, and to frustrate the opposition. This can be seen most clearly in the field of agrarian reform.

Agrarian reform was a fundamental issue for the country. The need to reform the system of land tenure was being discussed as early as 1944, but it was not until 1952 that a law was proposed, and by that time the Communists were entrenched in key administrative positions. Gutiérrez wrote the proposal for the reform law and presided over the Congressional Commission that studied it. Communists sat on commissions which were charged by the law with distributing uncultivated or state-owned lands (which were the only lands affected by the reform). And the Communists in enforcing the law made sure that the Instituto de Reforma Agraria, which they succeeded in controlling, gave only usufruct, and not title, in the land. As a result, the peasants found themselves at the mercy of agrarian inspectors who could take their land from them on almost any pretext. These inspectors—two-thirds of them Communists—thus transformed the peasants into servants of the Communist Party, either as members, as propagandists, or as voters. Furthermore, the Communists organized groups of peasants who proceeded to attach cultivated lands for themselves, in violation of the law, leaving only abandoned lands open for expropriation by the state. Since possession of these cultivated lands depended on Communist strength, the peasants who occupied them had to support the Communists in order to continue enjoying their new properties. The Communist Party had in fact become, through intermediary agents, the largest latifundista in the country.

If the Communists could exercise decisive political influence in Guatemala in 1952, we may ask why they chose not to place ministers in the president's cabinet or become formally part of the government. The answer was not—as many militants believed—that refusal to participate in the government was necessary to defend the liberties gained in 1944 (which were not threatened), or to work more effectively to increase the well-being of the people (whose welfare was not being significantly increased). In reality the primary Communist goal was to lead an ostensibly non-Communist regime into taking positions that would provoke hostile reactions from Washington, which would then serve as an invaluable basis for anti-U.S. propaganda; and for this a certain amount of concealment was necessary.

The tactic for achieving this goal, we have already seen: gaining control of the masses through various front organizations, which the government could even be forced to subsidize and which could issue statements and manifestos that non-Communist leaders would support. Among the more notable successes of the tactic were the position taken by the government at the Conference of Caracas in 1954, at which the Guatemalan delegation opposed any condemnation of Communist interference in the Western Hemisphere;* withdrawal from the Organization of Central American States; and several pro-Soviet votes in the United Nations. More trivial, but nonetheless suggestive, examples abound. During the Korean war, government-owned buses equipped with loudspeakers bounced through village streets protesting alleged bacteriological warfare by the United States. When Stalin died, the Guatemalan Congress observed a minute of silence. The government once sent no fewer than four ministers to meet Lombardo Toledano at the airport in Guatemala City.

Attempts were made to limit Communist influence, and especially to guarantee the independence of the unions, but these failed; Arbenz stubbornly resisted many of them, and the PGT was growing rapidly. (Fortuny claimed in 1954, at the party's Second Congress, that in two years the number of party members "had multiplied by fourteen.") It took the military coup of 1954, led by Col. Castillo Armas and backed by the United States, to bring an end to the Arbenz regime, which the Communists had wanted and had supported. The frontist regime had done little to solve the country's problems, and in the end brought in a reactionary government—to the great loss of the people of Guatemala and the former liberal allies of the Communists, who were forced into exile.

THE COMMUNISTS IN POWER: CUBA

The nature of the Cuban revolution has by now been widely discussed in print,[44] and for the purposes of this volume it should suffice for me to provide a very brief outline of my own interpretation, giving particular attention to matters that relate to the labor movement.

The Cuban Communist Party was founded in 1924, and from the beginning Communists were active in Cuban unions. In 1933, however, they opposed the general strike that overthrew Machado, claiming that an armed struggle would simply provoke "imperialistic intervention." They then attacked the successor government of Grau San Martín, which proposed

---

* In May of 1954, Fortuny boasted that Guatemala's position at Caracas had not really been adopted by the government, but had been decided upon at a meeting between Arbenz and the delegates of the Frente Democrático—among whom the Communists, by virtue of their front organizations, formed a majority.

land reforms and nationalization measures, on the grounds that a more radical "workers' and peasants' government" was needed immediately— an error, according to the Comintern. When Col. Fulgencio Batista, who had been one of Grau's allies, seized power in January of 1934 and installed Colonel Carlos Mendieta as president, the Communists continued to attack Grau. In 1937 Batista allowed the Communist writer Juan Marinello to organize a frontist party called the Partido de Unión Revolucionaria (PUR), which was joined by many intellectuals and a small socialist group. A little later Batista permitted the Communist Party—which he had out-lawed—to publish a daily newspaper, *Hoy*; and in July of 1938 the party's plenary session resolved to adopt "a more positive attitude toward Col. Batista," saying that he was "no longer the focal point of reaction but the defender of democracy." This, of course, was an expression of the Popular Front Tactic in Cuba. The party's secretary general, Blas Roca (whose real name was Manuel Caldeiro), then met with Batista, who restored the party's legal status; in September 1938 the PUR was dissolved. The Communists intensified their campaign against Grau and the parties who op-posed Batista, and helped elect Batista president in 1940, after a new constitution had been adopted. Juan Marinello served briefly as a cabinet minister under Batista in 1944, when the Communists again backed Batista. Grau won in 1944, but the Communists managed to elect nine congressmen and three senators, and continued to oppose Grau, and later Prío Socarrás. In 1952 the Communists, whose party was now called the Partido Socialista Popular (PSP), did nothing to impede the coup that brought Batista to power again. Batista outlawed the PSP shortly afterward, no doubt as an obliging nod toward Washington, but the party continued to operate under the eyes of a benevolent police, and many well-known Communists entered Batista's party (the Partido de Acción Unitaria) and assumed influential posts.

On July 26, 1953, a group of boys led by Fidel Castro attacked the Moncada barracks in Santiago. Several of them, including Castro, were captured, sentenced to prison, and later released. Castro went to Mexico, where he organized an expedition that landed in Oriente Province in 1956; for the next three years he and his group of guerrilla fighters remained in the Sierra Maestra, where their numbers multiplied. They received supplies from the governments of José Figueres in Costa Rica and Rómulo Betancourt in Venezuela, and financial support from ex-President Prío Socarrás and many urban industrialists in Cuba. They were also supported by liberal groups in the United States.

In 1952, the Confederación de Trabajadores de Cuba (CTC), from whose leadership the Communists had been expelled in 1947, had abandoned its plan for a general strike against the military when the deposed ministers and president went into exile; after that it had not taken part in any opposition to Batista's regime. And when Fidel Castro, writing from the Sierra Maestra in April of 1958, ordered a general strike against the dictator, the unions of Cuba did not respond. The Communist PSP did not oppose the strike, but said that the objective conditions needed for its success were not present and ordered its members not to support it.

Communist officials in Batista's government refused to resign, despite the deadline Castro had given everybody for breaking with the military regime. In August the July 26 Movement condemned the Communist attitude and commented ironically that it was interesting to see Communist leaders still living peacefully in Havana, unmolested by Batista's police. It is not surprising that after Batista's fall the revolutionary government reorganized the management of the CTC, and that the nine directors appointed on January 24, 1959, did not include a single Communist.

The most acute social struggles in Cuba had always developed in rural areas, among sugar workers; and because agrarian reform presented one of the greatest challenges to the revolutionary government, we should describe briefly the economic and social situation created by Cuba's dependence on sugar.

In 1861 there were 1,368 sugar plantations in Cuba; in 1894 there were only 450. In that period sugar production more than doubled (from 540,000 tons to one million tons yearly) and allowed Cuba to compete with beet sugar from France and Germany. The island's economy became dependent on one export crop destined for a single market—the United States. When Cuba gained independence from Spain in 1898 and from the United States in 1902, sugar accounted for 80 per cent of its exports, and half of all its cultivated lands were dedicated to sugar. Holdings of less than fifty acres accounted for 70 per cent of total ownership but covered only 11 per cent of the tillable lands. Firms owning more than 1,250 acres each occupied 47 per cent of the canefields and 56 per cent of the total land cultivated. Cuba, then, had a plantation economy.[45] Agriculture was not intensive. Only 27 per cent of the workable land was plowed; the large sugar companies let great areas remain fallow for future crops, because cane quickly depletes the soil. Only 40 to 45 per cent of pasture lands was used. Barely one per cent of sugar's possible derivatives was utilized. In 1930 an agricultural worker earned 25 cents for a twelve-hour working day. In 1958 he earned approximately four dollars for an eight-hour day. But he received that salary only during the two-month harvest season, and often could earn nothing else to support his family for the rest of the year.[46]

Cuban peasants had traditionally looked upon Batista's "rural guards," who practiced terror and extortion in the villages, with implacable hatred. The simple fact that the guards opposed Castro was enough to account for much of the loyalty shown toward him by the peasants of the Sierra, who gave the guerrillas men, shelter, information, and constant aid. It should be added that sugar workers, who numbered more than 400,000, made up the CTC's strongest union.

It was logical that Castro—by temperament an impassioned man, according to those who know him—should have felt committed to improving the lot of the peasants, who had been his allies when the union movement, the Communists, and the urban population had professed little faith in his cause or in his chances of victory. When he finally promulgated a comprehensive political program for the July 26 Movement—which was in August of 1958, after the failure of the general strike—he gave considerable attention to agrarian reform. The Movement's program described the land problem in these terms: the best cultivated lands were under foreign ownership; three hundred thousand *caballerías* (10,000,000 acres) remained uncultivated while 200,000 peasant families were without land; 80 per cent of all small farmers paid rent for their lands and lived under the constant threat of eviction. The essence of the proposed solution was as follows.

The revolutionary government, after granting ownership of land parcels to 100,000 small farmers now paying rent, would proceed to solve the land problem once and for all, by the following means. First, by prescribing as ordered in the Constitution [of 1940], a maximum amount of land that may be owned by a single agricultural enterprise, expropriating remaining lands for the state, and gaining additional land by draining tidelands and swamps. Second, by distributing the land thus made available among peasant families, giving preference to the largest ones; by setting up peasants' cooperatives for the common use of costly equipment; by providing technical guidance in matters of land cultivation and animal husbandry; and in general, by making available all the knowledge, resources, equipment, and legal protection that would be useful to the peasant community. A measure to be put into effect immediately was "the granting of ownership to peasants who had long tilled land they did not own, and to those who paid half a year's crop as rent, in holdings of five *caballerías* (166 acres) or less, with the state to compensate the previous owners by paying them a yearly rent equivalent to the average rent collected over a ten-year period." On October 10, 1958, Castro wrote that the maximum area to be held by one owner was thirty *caballerías* (1,000 acres). In December of 1958, when the revolution was close to success, Castro's men began distributing land, according to this pronouncement, in the Sierra de Escambray.*

* It should be pointed out that Castro's proposals for agrarian reform, at this time, were not supported by Cuban Communists, and were in fact in the spirit of recom-

Lenin wrote that in any revolutionary situation a second power would replace the traditional power of the state. In Cuba, where Batista's sudden flight brought about the collapse of the country's political structure, not one but three powers appeared, and the struggles between them dominated Cuba's political life in 1959.

The first of these powers, Castro's army, was officially still termed "rebel," and during 1959 it functioned as a small state within a state, publishing pamphlets, building homes, organizing schools, and so forth. Its high command was staffed by politically oriented men who had been with Castro in the Sierra Maestra since 1956. Its lower-ranking officers and a large portion of its troops were men who had joined the movement only in 1958 and had very little political background. It also harbored several Communists, who had joined in 1958, when the Communist Party had become interested in cooperating with Castro, and these men quickly worked their way into the middle ranks.* Of the three power groups, the rebel army possessed the least political training and functioned on the lowest intellectual level, and it was therefore the group most susceptible to Communist influence. It was precisely because of this influence that the most notable early defectors from Castro were rebel army officers—men like Pedro Díaz Lanz and Hubert Matos, who had joined the guerrilla forces with the single aim of overthrowing Batista, and whose ideological background kept them hostile to Communism. As veterans of the revolutionary struggle, they believed that they could state their objections and receive a fair hearing; they were wrong, and found themselves put in prison or sent into exile.

The second group was the Instituto Nacional de Reforma Agraria (INRA), created in May 1959 and led by a Communist army captain, Antonio Núñez. Like the army, it founded schools, edited publications, and engaged in various public works; and as the only governmental organization formed by Castro, its members came to fill most of the vacant posts in the government.

---

mendations made earlier in the U.S. In 1950 the International Reconstruction and Development Bank suggested "a moderate renovation of the agricultural structure of the country, in favor of the small farmer." And as early as 1935 the U.S. Foreign Policy Association's Commission on Cuban Affairs advised the undertaking of a program of rural colonization, by means of voluntary transfer of lands and state repossession of illegally held lands, to establish small ownership; it also recommended crop diversification, and said that sugar plantations should be legally required to parcel out lands among their workers for the growing of food crops. (Foreign Policy Association, *Problemas de la nueva Cuba,* pp. 501 and following.)

* Although not all of them called themselves Communists, they were communists in the organic sense; some, who called themselves Titoists and Trotskyites, paid less attention to the party line, but most of them agreed on matters of immediate concern.

The third group was what remained of the government bureaucracy, which was placed under new leadership by Castro's movement. Its principal weakness was that its new and inexperienced leaders (mostly civilians and returned exiles) were bound to make mistakes, and that these leaders—except for Castro and a few of his ministers—were men who had little influence over public opinion and were intensely disliked by officers of the rebel army.

Within the July 26 Movement—which was composed of the three power structures just mentioned—there were two other groups, besides the army, who were struggling to influence the political development of the new regime. The first, and the smaller, of these groups might be called the urban guerrillas—citizens and student leaders who had opposed Batista. The Communists exerted little influence over this group; and in fact the students within it were the only revolutionary element that dared to expose its differences with the July 26 Movement. City dwellers sympathized with the students, who had fought hard and bloody battles with Batista's police. The urban opposition had no concrete political position. It simply wanted a rapid return to political normalcy, with the state free to act as the one true power in the country.

The second group, those who had been in exile, was larger but less influential, despite the fact that it contained men with the best technical and administrative skills (some of these acquired abroad). The influence they could exert from government posts was small, because the common people distrusted them and the "rebel" army regarded them with open hostility. As a group they hoped for a quick return to normal political life because they were somewhat apprehensive about the growth of a new dictatorship.

The rebel army, the urban guerrillas, and the former exiles had one thing in common, besides belonging to the July 26 Movement: they all lacked, in varying degrees, political experience and background. Members of the younger generation were no exception—and this was most unfortunate, for young people were gaining control everywhere; the age of leaders in most political and governmental organizations was seldom over thirty-five. Thus when Castro came to power many of his partisans were influenced by old Communist propaganda of the Popular Front period and adopted a frontist position, believing in good faith that they were taking a democratic stand. Few knew of the real consequences of frontism in Latin America, or remembered the Communist support of Batista. Many who were not Communists ended by thinking like Communists, and collaborated in organizing the masses and in applying policies that could only provoke unnecessary hostility from the United States.[47]

In Cuba's case the bare facts are sufficient for understanding, once the background has been examined. Here, then, is a chronology of principal events during the first three years of Castro's government.[48]

1959

January 1. Fulgencio Batista flees to the Dominican Republic.

January 2. Castro appoints Dr. Manuel Urrutia provisional president.

January 3. Urrutia places Fidel Castro at the head of the armed forces. Castro announces the quick restoration of constitutional guarantees suspended by Batista.

January 5. Urrutia appoints José Miró Cardona head of the government.

January 6. Urrutia dissolves the Congress made up of political parties, and with his cabinet assumes legislative powers. He announces he will govern by decree for eighteen months and then hold elections.

January 7. The United States recognizes the provisional government.

January 10. Castro expresses resentment against U.S. military missions that trained Batista's forces. He authorizes the return to legal status of the Communist Party.

January 13. Castro states that military trials and executions must continue.

January 15. Castro says that Cuba desires strong bonds of friendship with the United States, and that he does not believe the U.S. will intervene in Cuban affairs.

January 22. Popular demonstrations in favor of the executions; a public trial held in Havana stadium. Promulgation of a labor law.

January 30. The government suspends several articles of the Constitution of 1940.

February 3. Castro announces agrarian reform plans.

February 10. A law lowers to thirty years the minimum age required for the presidency and allows the naturalization of Ernesto Guevara (an Argentinian).

February 13. José Miró Cardona resigns, stating that Castro should preside over the government.

February 16. Castro is appointed Prime Minister.

February 28. Castro states that two years must pass before elections are held. He accuses the United States of having intervened in Cuba's affairs for half a century.

April 16–27. Castro visits the United States. He denies Communist influences in his government, and prohibits the ministers accompanying him to negotiate or to accept loans or credits.

May 17. The agrarian reform law is proclaimed. The Minister of Agriculture, Humberto Sori Marín, who had drafted the agrarian reform proposed in the Sierra Maestra, resigns because Castro would not submit the

new law to his ministers for discussion. (In March 1961 Sori was executed.) This agrarian reform law was replaced on June 3 by a new law,
which declared government ownership of all the land and created the
Instituto Nacional de Reforma Agraria (INRA), which was placed
under the leadership of Captain Antonio Núñez, a member of the Communist Party.

June 10. The U.S. government expresses its "concern" over compensation
for confiscated lands. Raúl Roa, the Minister of Foreign Relations, states
in Montevideo that Cuba has decided to "break the structure of its commercial relations with the United States."

June 26. Cuba breaks diplomatic relations with the Dominican Republic.
(In 1960, when Trujillo was condemned by a meeting of the Ministers
of Foreign Affairs, in the OAS, Cuban attacks on Trujillo ceased.) This
permits a Castroite movement, led by Máximo López Molina, to operate
in the Dominican Republic.

June 30. Major Pedro Díaz Lanz, the head of the Cuban Air Force, resigns
and takes refuge in the United States, where he declares that Castro's
government is Communist-infiltrated.

July 17. During a television address Castro accuses President Urrutia of
defaming the Revolution, and forces him to resign. (The day before, Urrutia had said that a Communist danger existed in Cuba. In 1961 he went
into exile.) Urrutia is succeeded by Dr. Osvaldo Dórticos Torrado.

October 16. Creation of the workers' militias.

October 20. Hubert Matos, one of Castro's old collaborators, resigns in
protest against Communist influence; he is jailed and later sentenced to
twenty years imprisonment. Camilo Cienfuegos, one of Castro's old guerrilla comrades, mysteriously disappears.

October 21. Flights of unidentified aircraft release a rain of anti-Castro
(in fact, anti-Communist) manifestos over Havana. Castro accuses the
U.S. of permitting these flights.

October 28. President Eisenhower states that his government is making
every effort to stop illegal flights over Cuba originating from U.S. bases.

November 18–21. Tenth Congress of the CTC. Castro asserts his support
of the Communists.

December 10. Foreign Relations Minister Roa, in an interview with U.S.
Secretary of State Christian Herter, announces that his government is
prepared to negotiate the sums to be paid in compensation for confiscated
lands.

December 12. Passage of the "Dagger Law," which suppresses the right
to strike and authorizes the Labor Ministry to appoint union leaders.

1960

January 11. United States Ambassador Bonsal protests measures that "deny the fundamental right of ownership in Cuba."

January 22. The "Law of the Labor Census" establishes a system of control over workers.

February 13. Soviet minister Mikoyan, on a visit to Cuba, concludes an agreement by which the U.S.S.R. will purchase five million tons of sugar over five years and will grant Cuba a credit equivalent to 100 million dollars at an interest rate of 2.5 per cent.

February 18–21. Planes bomb sugar plantations. President Eisenhower authorizes the confiscation of all planes and weapons whose unlawful destination is Cuba. Castro denounces these flights as originating in the United States. The government in Washington admits this and offers its apologies.

February 27. Guevara announces that a cooperative system will be used for Cuba's economic development, claiming that it is the only form of modern production which permits capitalistic use of production sources and the equitable distribution of profits.

March 4. Explosion on board the French ship *La Coubre* is attributed by Castro to U.S. sabotage.

March 21. A law is passed allowing the unions to order salary deductions: for industrialization, agrarian reform, armament, etc. All in all, the deductions amount to approximately 15 per cent of salaries.

April 5. Troops of the "rebel army" occupy CTC headquarters. Communists take control of the unions. David Salvador disappears. (Months later he is arrested for trying to escape into exile.)

April 10. Appearance of the first clandestine manifesto of the Movimiento de Recuperación Revolucionaria, made up of some of Castro's former companions.

May 1. Castro states in an address that he has no intention of holding elections.

May 8. The Soviet Embassy reopens in Havana.

May 27. The U.S. government announces that it will put an end to technical and military aid to Cuba in six months.

June 3. Khrushchev accepts Castro's invitation to visit Cuba.

June 10. Czechoslovakia offers Cuba technical assistance and credits worth 20 million dollars.

June 11. Castro announces that British and U.S. refineries in Cuba must refine Soviet petroleum or accept the consequences of their refusal.

June 23. Castro threatens to seize all U.S. property in Cuba if the United States reduces the Cuba sugar quota.

June 29. The Cuban government takes over U.S. refineries (which had refused to refine Soviet petroleum).

July 6. President Eisenhower, as authorized by Congress, reduces the Cuban sugar quota in retaliation for what he calls Castro's "policy of deliberate hostility toward the United States."

July 6. U.S. firms and Cuban plantations and refineries are expropriated.

July 9. Eisenhower warns that the United States will never permit the establishment in the Western Hemisphere of a regime dominated by international Communism. Khrushchev promises to aid Cuba in case of "American aggression" and offers to buy 700,000 tons of Cuban sugar.

July 11. Cuba complains before the United Nations Security Council of "aggressive acts on the part of the United States."

July 13. Peru proposes that the foreign ministers of all Latin American countries meet in order to study the Cuban threat to the security and democracy of the Western Hemisphere.

July 22. The Frente Democrático Revolucionario is formed by groups of Cuban exiles.

July 23. The People's Republic of China announces that it will buy 500,000 tons of Cuban sugar per year, for a period of five years.

August 11. Castro attacks the Catholic hierarchy for its "systematic provocations."

August 14-28. A Foreign Ministers' meeting in San José, Costa Rica, condemns attempts at intervention in the Americas from outside the Western Hemisphere.

September 2. The Government of Cuba recognizes the People's Republic of China.

September 10. Blas Roca, a Communist, speaks of the necessity of uniting all revolutionary forces into "a single movement."

September 13. A new wave of repressions and executions begins.

October 19. The United States places an embargo on exports to Cuba.

October-December. Guevara, President of the Banco Nacional, visits Russia and Eastern Europe. He announces in Moscow, "We will support with all our hearts the declaration adopted by this conference" (the Conference of Eighty-one Communist Parties).

December 21. Dismissal of Supreme Court magistrates and several judges.

1961

January 2. A parade of Soviet arms is held in Havana. Castro asks that the U.S. Embassy retain only eleven employees; Washington breaks diplomatic relations with Cuba.

January 6. Guevara, in a speech, speaks of "our friend Trujillo."

January 21. The arrival of a thousand Soviet experts is announced; they are to help organize "people's farms" of the Soviet type, which are gradually to replace the agricultural cooperatives organized at the outset of the agrarian reform.

February 1. Castro, interviewed by *L'Unità,* the organ of the Italian Communist Party, says: "The Communists mistrusted me and the rest of the rebels...Later we were able to meet, mutually understand each other, and begin to collaborate."

February 24. Guevara, previously the director of the Banco Nacional, is appointed Minister of Industry.

March 13. Cuba's Ambassador to Moscow, Faure Chomon, says in a speech: "Tomorrow's students will tell of how the Cuban people became Communistic, and we will see how all the peoples of Latin America will turn to Communism."

March 15. Importation of Boris Pasternak's novel *Dr. Zhivago* is forbidden.

March 22. Formation of the Consejo Revolucionario Cubano, made up of the Frente Revolucionario Democrático and the Movimiento Revolucionario del Pueblo and led by José Miró Cardona. Its program states: "During the immediate post-revolutionary period, some of the people's ideals were fulfilled....It will be necessary to incorporate them in the Constitution. There must be no turning back, either to the past, to which we were all opposed, or to Communism, or to reaction." In March the Junta Revolucionaria de Liberación Nacional, made up of right-wing exiles, is also formed.

April 17. Cuban exiles, backed by the United States, land at the Bay of Pigs. After two days of fighting the expedition fails. Castro later proposes exchanging prisoners for tractors, but finally rejects tractors paid for by a U.S. popular subscription. (The prisoners were sentenced and Castro offered to free them in exchange for 62 million dollars worth of products; the exchange took place in December of 1962.)

May 1. Castro announces in a speech that the Cuban Revolution is socialistic, and all political parties will be united in one party, the Organizaciones Revolucionarias Integradas (ORI). (In fact, the only party really functioning at this time was the Communist PSP; the July 26 Movement had ceased to exist months before.) Later the ORI became the Partido Unido de la Revolución Socialista (PURS), which in turn became the Partido Communista de Cuba in 1965.

May 19. Castro receives the Lenin Peace Prize.

August 13. Substitution of new bank notes for the old ones and exercise of control over current bank accounts.

August 16. Deterioration of the Cuban economy, owing to insufficient foreign aid, induces Guevara, at the Punta del Este Conference, to suggest negotiating with the United States.

October 18. In the United Nations, Cuba votes with the Soviet bloc opposing a discussion on the question of Russia's resuming atomic tests. Executions begin again in Cuba; since January 1959 some 995 persons have been executed.

December 2. Castro declares that he was already a "Marxist-Leninist" in 1953.

A reading of this chronology leaves no room for doubt: the Cuba regime in 1961 bore little resemblance to the one promised by Fidel Castro in 1953 and 1958, or to the one the Sierra Maestra fighters had envisioned, or to the one desired by the middle-class and peasant groups that had backed Castro. The regime, as we know it today, is a "people's democracy" (or "direct democracy," as Castro calls it). It has a "socialistic" economy—collective ownership by a privileged social group which retains control of all production sources—which can be sustained only by the underconsumption and overwork of peasants and laborers. This does not mean that the regime has not accomplished anything; it has in fact achieved much. But how are we to evaluate the changes brought about?

In 1958 Cuba had the highest standard of living in Latin America, and the most prosperous international trade. This should have permitted the transformation of its social structure without great economic risks. The Castro regime brought about the transformation, but without taking advantage of the favorable conditions, and has reduced the country to a standard of living inferior to what it had enjoyed in 1952 or 1958. It will not do to attribute this simply to inexpertness or improvisation; the same sort of economic decline has occurred in every country in which Communists have come to power.

In the Cuban agrarian reform the land was not given to the peasants but to the state, and the state granted it in usufruct; the peasants are therefore unable to resist state pressure of any sort. The cooperatives organized by the INRA in 1959 were replaced, in 1960 and 1961, by "people's farms," and their owners, individual or corporate, were replaced by INRA bureaucrats. The peasants' condition has been improved in some areas, notably housing and education; but in general it has worsened, because crops have been smaller and because nothing is left to individual initiative, the peasant having been militarized and subjected to systematic political control.

The working class, once the unions had been taken over by the Communists, was rendered defenseless. As in the "people's democracies," the right to strike was declared counter-revolutionary, and wages were cut—through deductions—as much as fifteen per cent. The working day was increased through "voluntary" renunciation of vacations, sick leave, and overtime pay; the scarcity of many consumer goods nullified any material advantage the workers might have attained.

Cultural life is completely state-directed because the press, radio, and television are in the hands of the state. There exist no information media of any sort that are not controlled by Castro's government—that is, in the final analysis, by the Communist Party. But there is little or no artistic censorship, and intellectuals can therefore experience at least an illusion of freedom.

Naturally, all this has diminished Castro's popularity. One result has been periodic outbursts of anti-American propaganda, designed to galvanize declining public solidarity. Castro has been constantly plagued by a series of new enemies—first Urrutia, then judges, professors, doctors, priests, and union leaders from his own July 26 Movement. He has therefore created one organization after another to hold the population in check: there are state-sponsored groups for women, young people, teachers, peasants, artisans, writers and artists; there are Vigilance Committees for every street and block, and labor militias everywhere.

A revolution, in Latin America, must have two objectives: to assure political freedom and to attain social justice. In 1959 Castro had an opportunity to lead all of Latin America toward the realization of these objectives. With his tremendous prestige, he could have given decisive support to the destruction of oligarchic power and to continental planning for agrarian reform, economic integration, and the democratization of Latin American life. In the beginning, he did support guerrilla expeditions against several dictatorships in small countries. But by 1960 he was devoting his efforts abroad almost exclusively to financing movements that were rhetorically leftist, but whose activities were directed toward the destruction of democratic movements and governments of the left. The most patent example was his backing of the insurrectional movement against Betancourt's government in Venezuela, beginning in 1960, in which Castroites, Communists, and supporters of the dictator Pérez Jiménez all joined forces. He needed the failure of the Venezuelan experiment with democratic social reform in order to be able to maintain his claim that the only road to social change in Latin America is the Cuban road. Castro, then, did more than abandon the original, and praiseworthy, goals of the Cuban Revolution; he set back the cause of true revolution everywhere in Latin America.

7. The Populist Movements

THE POPULIST MOVEMENTS of Latin America—which we might call revolutionary nationalistic or revolutionary democratic movements—have exerted a definite influence on the union movement, and thus deserve some mention in this history. Despite national differences in their programs, the populist movements have certain features in common. All have formed parties whose support has come from groups within the peasantry, the workers, and the middle class. All have made an effort to develop a specifically Latin American approach to political problems, in theory and in practice; and in so doing they have all drawn to some extent on concepts formulated by Peru's Víctor Raúl Haya de la Torre, the founder of APRA. Finally, although they cannot be described as middle-class movements, their principal leaders have been produced by the middle class. For this reason, it may be well to begin with a brief sketch of the middle classes in Latin America.

Until after World War I, Latin American society was strongly polarized, with the submerged classes at one extreme and the oligarchies at the other; between them lay only a thin layer of professionals—doctors, lawyers, teachers, intellectuals, minor clergymen, bureaucrats, small merchants, and artisans. But beginning in 1919 a new middle class, no longer professional, began to arise. It was directly dependent upon economic progress, and was composed chiefly of industrialists, merchants, technicians, and bureaucrats of a more technical orientation. The economic condition of this new middle class, which we can call wealthy, improved. Along with it the traditional middle class developed and grew in numerical volume; we could call it well-to-do, whereas in the past it was decidedly poor. Specialized workers began entering its ranks, artisans became semi-technicians, and moderate-scale agricultural landholders, merchants, and provincial industrialists added their numbers. The wealthy middle class exerted a considerable political influence, and in a certain fashion the older well-to-do class served as its maneuvering mass.[1]

In Latin America the middle class was not being towed in the wake of other forces, such as the fascist movements. It took the political initiative, in the democratic and nationalistic sense, and exerted growing economic pressure. The movements we can call revolutionary nationalist—using both words in their Latin American context—were the result of this rise of the middle class, and produced the political parties that held power from 1944 to 1948 and again from 1955 to 1959: Acción Democrática in Venezuela, the APRA in Peru, Liberación Nacional in Costa Rica, Auténticos y Ortodoxos in Cuba, the MNR in Bolivia, the PRI in Mexico (in power since 1917 under different names), the Colorados in Uruguay, the Febreristas in Paraguay, some sectors of the radical parties of Chile and Argentina, the liberals in Honduras, and the PDR in the Dominican Republic.

What gives the middle class cohesion, more than anything else, is its cultural and ideological unity, which derives from the following characteristics. (1) It is essentially an urban class, although in some countries a rural middle class is beginning to develop. (2) It believes in industrialization as the fundamental means of solving great national problems. (3) Although it favors public education, it increasingly insists on promoting higher-level culture and professional education, in preference to measures aimed at elementary education. (This is not an unwise attitude in view of the failure of many literacy campaigns, which, though spectacular for the numbers involved, are often handled inefficiently and produce few short-term benefits.) (4) It is nationalistic, frequently favoring protectionist policies and at times anti-American positions. (5) It recognizes the beneficial role of labor unions and social legislation in national development. (6) It generally favors agrarian reforms as means of strengthening the political basis of democracy and opening up larger domestic markets for industrialization. (7) It looks with greater favor on international investments of a public nature than on those of a private type, toward which it displays a systematic mistrust. (8) It does not oppose nationalization or state ownership of large industries, sources of mineral products, or public utilities. (9) It tends to favor state intervention (by which it usually profits), and would look with pleasure toward even greater emphasis on a directed economy. (10) It firmly favors public investment in industrialization. (11) It distrusts the army and is congenitally fearful of a military take-over, even though middle-class elements form part of the new generation of military men. (12) It is deeply interested in Soviet methods of development, which sometimes explains a certain receptivity to Communist propaganda, especially on international issues. (13) It has in recent years developed a strong "continentalist" feeling, which impels it toward accepting such projects as a common market, the Inter-American Bank, and the Latin American Parliament. (14) Politically it is liberal, democratic, to a large extent Catholic (important in view of the Church's increasingly liberal attitude in many countries), and socializing. (15) It contains a great number of immigrants, who have generally adopted the most radically nationalistic notions of the class.

There arose during the first three decades of the twentieth century a series of political parties of the bourgeoisie, in which part of the middle class participated: the radicals in Argentina and Chile, the Colorados in Uruguay, the liberals in several other countries. When these parties managed to come to power they proclaimed social laws for which the labor movement had laid the groundwork. But in many cases they ended by leaning toward the right, realizing that the movement for social advancement was drawing them beyond their original goals. The failure of these parties—as agents of real reform—was that they had no interest in transforming the structure of society; they wanted only to mitigate the most obvious injustices. This failure created a political vacuum, which was filled in certain areas by demagogic and fascist regimes (Perón in Argentina, Vargas in Brazil), and was filled in others by the populist parties, who had no wish to preserve social fossils. Rather, they hoped to create something new, to represent not the bourgeoisie but a larger conglomerate made up of middle-class elements, workers, and peasants.

Like almost all leftist democratic politicians in Latin America, the populist leaders began with Marxism (not Marxism-Leninism) or at least studied it in depth. And they ended by finding that Marxism, as a doctrine, failed to offer them a theory of economic development. This was to be expected, for Marx believed that socialism is the logical outgrowth of capitalism, and capitalism had barely taken root in Latin America. Precisely because Latin American socialists failed to create a theory of development that was socialist (or Marxist), they never managed to play a decisive role in Latin American politics. The populists, confronted by this failure, were led to create their own theory of development. In general, the populist movements may be characterized as follows. (1) They are "native" movements, whose ideology began to take shape after World War II and is based chiefly on the theses of Haya de la Torre. (2) They acknowledge the influence of the early advocates of Latin American federalism and Latin American anti-imperialism; of the labor union movement; of the movement for university reform; and of the Mexican Revolution, the Russian Revolution, and the *ejidos,* or *comunidades indígenas.* (3) They are mass parties of a united-front or class-alliance type, embracing the peasants, the proletariat, and the middle class. (4) They are autonomous parties, independent of other international parties and their extracontinental party lines; they are anti-Communist, but they do not maintain the reactionary "anti-Communism" stance simply to maintain privileges. (5) They are democratic, and uphold the principle of free political expression for all people through suffrage. (6) They are revolutionary; they conceive of the revolution as an accelerated evolution, destined to transform the socioeconomic structure of the countries in which anachronistic and imperialistic structures predominate. (7) They are anti-imperialist but refuse to have their anti-imperialist actions linked with "anti-Yankeeism" or "anti-Russianism." (8) They favor Latin American federation, believing that political and economic coordination of the Latin American countries is the best basis for the defense of common sovereignty and the planned development of the continent. (9) They are nationalist, but patriotically concerned with the development of the entire Latin American continent. (10) They are decentralists, eager to develop national regions through the decentralization of public power and the creation of effective forms of municipal government.[2]

The Communist movement, though it has never become a powerful influence on the workers and peasants, has acquired considerable influence among the middle classes, particularly among students and intellectuals. The Communist attitude toward the middle classes is well expressed in the following statement by Ramón López, of the Communist Party of Colombia:

"The petty bourgeoisie is an intermediate class, standing between the bourgeoisie and the proletariat. Its ideology is not, nor can it ever be, clearly differentiated from the bourgeois ideology. Its economic situation is undergoing a complete transformation: while one part becomes poorer and begins to fill the ranks of the workers, another part, though smaller, prospers economically and incorporates itself into the bourgeoisie. Its attitude in relation to social and economic conditions will inevitably waver between the two classes, which represent, for it, the two extremes.... The petty bourgeoisie tends, oddly enough, to be more radical in the semicolonial and dependent countries, because there, in addition to bourgeois exploitation, it carries on its shoulders the burden of exploitation by landholding monopolists and imperialists. This explains its desperation, its impatience to see the economic structure transformed. But it cannot be said that this is a developing class, a class on the rise. On the contrary, it is politically unstable, because of its ideological proximity to the bourgeoisie.... For this reason it is not the petty bourgeoisie that is called upon to be the leading force in the revolution. The petty bourgeoisie should drink from the ideological fountain of the proletariat if it wishes to assume an important role in the revolutionary transformation of society; and the proletariat must not 'nourish' itself at the ideological fountain of the petty bourgeoisie and 'other popular sectors,' as the modifiers of Marxist theory insinuate."

The Communists seek to deny initiative to the middle class because they want to use it to climb to power, and then to eliminate it altogether by proletarianizing it. To make use of the middle class, they offer it, in the words of Cuba's Blas Roca, "a popular revolution, advanced, patriotic, and democratic, anti-imperialistic and agrarian."[3] The populist parties also seek this revolution but are nevertheless systematically attacked by the Communists: they have, for their part, made it very difficult for the Communists to influence the masses, and have reduced many Communist parties to the status of travel and publishing agencies for intellectuals.

After World War II, from 1944 to 1948, populism flourished. In the words of Mario Monteforte Toledo, the Guatemalan political scientist, "All parties incorporated in their programs the objectives of agrarian reform, industrialization, social justice, and unified economic development. Their organizations became more permanent and more effective, both inside and outside the government. Their members were drawn from all social classes, to form entities of truly national character. More or less progressive tendencies dominated; they were of the reformist and evolutionary type, and emphasized a constitutional order that would permit free play among all parties. Totalitarian practices (Communist or fascist) were categorically rejected, and contacts were initiated with foreign organizations."[4]

The populist parties never formed a permanent international organization, but they did meet at times to exchange points of view and adopt common positions. The first meeting of this sort was the Congress of Partidos Democráticos y Populares de América, held in Santiago in October 1940; the next was the first conference of the Inter-American Association for Democracy and Freedom, held in Havana in 1950. In August 1960, representatives of MNR of Bolivia, Liberación Nacional of Costa Rica, Partido Revolucionario Febrerista of Paraguay, Partido Aprista Peruano, and Acción Democrática of Venezuela met in Lima with the object of formulating a continental policy. The Lima Declaration, formulated during the 1960 meeting, is important because it set forth the populist position on a series of problems, among them the problem of Cuba (which had provoked debates and even schisms in some of the parties signing the declaration). The following are quotations from the Declaration:

"The parties here assembled believe that in Latin America historical experience has demonstrated that the people's parties—that is, the nationalist and revolutionary movements, formed by a front of exploited classes, with a doctrine and a program genuinely Latin American and with a firm basis of support among the majority of citizens—are the most effective instruments for achieving economic independence and establishing social justice in our countries.

"We believe that the problems of each Latin American country, though they differ in particular details ... nevertheless constitute variations of an integral continental problem, the solution of which requires close coordination on the economic, political, and cultural levels, and the creation of a federation of peoples dedicated to justice and freedom.

"There are two clearly defined zones in the Western Hemisphere, the industrialized north (the United States and Canada) and the economically underdeveloped south. The virtually uncontrolled exploitation of the south by the north, which has predominated until now, has brought injustice and international imbalance to the American continent; it is a source of legitimate discontent among our peoples, who, in their desire to accelerate their economic development, could choose totalitarian forms of political organization analogous to those existing on other continents.

"We believe that the industrial and economic development of our countries, which implies a raising of the standard of living, must be accompanied by the eradication of illiteracy on the continent and the elimination of rural oligarchies through agrarian reform.

"We reiterate our firm opposition to Communist penetration in Latin America. Our parties have always resisted Communism, not only because of hopeless differences in social and political philosophy but also because of Communist cooperation with dictatorships and reactionary forces, which has been frequent in Latin America. Communist intervention, characterized by a servile dependence on Soviet imperialism, has obstructed the search for a realistic and Latin American solution to our problems, and has exposed Latin America to grave danger of devastation in a nuclear war." The document concluded by asking that the Cuban Revolution follow a democratic course.[5]

In March 1964, on the occasion of Raúl Leoni's inauguration as president of Venezuela, a new meeting of the populist parties was held. A coordinating committee was created, with headquarters in Caracas; after the meeting, several of the attending parties decided to join the Socialist International.

PERU AND APRA

Although its history is intimately linked to the biography of its founder, Víctor Raúl Haya de la Torre, the Alianza Popular Revolucionaria Americana (APRA) was the first nonsocialist group in Latin America that can really be considered a party; that is, it was not simply a group following a charismatic leader but a politically coherent organism, with a distinct ideology, program, organization, and set of methods.[6]

Víctor Raúl Haya de la Torre was born in Trujillo, Peru, in 1895. As a student he fought against the Leguía dictatorship and founded the Popular Universities. Exiled, he traveled throughout Europe and the Americas, visited the Soviet Union, discovered Marxism, and studied Spengler and later Toynbee. Haya founded APRA in Mexico in 1924, and hoped to see it spread throughout Latin America. At the peak of the anti-imperialist struggle, APRA movements existed in Cuba, Mexico, Chile, Costa Rica, Haiti, and Argentina; APRA even had sections in Paris, Berlin, and London. In 1931, APRA became the Partido Aprista Peruano.

APRA was attacked very early by the Communists, who reproached Haya for seeking to base the revolution on an alliance of the middle class, the peasants, and the workers, and not on the proletariat alone. Later, when the Communist Party proposed to APRA the formation of a popular front, APRA simply replied that it already was, in fact, the Popular Front in Peru.

APRA insisted on discipline and political training of its militants. APRA groups, legally or secretly, extended all over Peru. APRA's maximum program set forth five goals: action against imperialism; political unity for "Indo-America" (Haya de la Torre's word for Latin America); nationalization of lands and industries; internationalization of the Panama Canal; and solidarity of all peoples and oppressed classes of the world.

Haya wrote: "Our peoples must emancipate themselves from all forms of imperialism. They must unite, transforming their present borders into mere administrative limits. They must progressively nationalize their riches under a new type of state. The three classes oppressed by imperialism—our young industrial proletariat, our vast and ignorant peasant class, and our impoverished middle class—will constitute the normative social forces of this state."

"It would be futile," said Haya, "to argue that the Indo-American working classes have not directed their movements of social protest against imperialism, as the middle classes have, for lack of fighting spirit. We have a long history of rebellions of workers and peasants in Indo-America. But these protests were directed, for many years, only against the visible exploiter. Now, when imperialist exploitation is felt in all its implacable force, our working classes understand the danger and have discovered the real economic enemy. Now the oppression of imperialism can be seen as a form of national oppression, and this has demonstrated to the working classes the necessity of joining forces with the middle classes." For this reason, "APRA maintains that before the socialist revolution, which would bring the proletariat to power, our peoples must pass through preliminary periods of economic and political transformation, and perhaps through a social revolution that brings about national emancipation from the imperialist yoke, and the political and economic unification of Indo-America. The proletarian revolution will follow." "It is impossible," Haya said, "to separate the fight against foreign imperialism from the fight again national feudalism."

APRA's definition of imperialism is realistic. "In the industrialized nations, imperialism is the last stage of capitalism. But in our nations it is the first stage. Our capitalisms were born with the advent of modern imperialism; they were born dependent, and as a result of the culmination of imperialism." A reflection of this concept may be found in APRA's proposal to create an Inter-American Federation, with a customs union, two monetary units (one for the United States and the other for Latin America), a congress, and a common guarantee of support for democratic national institutions.

In his books *El antiimperialismo y el APRA, Teoría y Táctica,* and *Por la emancipación de América Latina,* Haya offers an interpretation of Latin American history. Aprismo, he says, "formulates a new interpretation of Marxism for Indo-America, and applies Einstein's concept of space-time to the sociohistorical field." According to Haya, "By the juxtaposition of different states of human evolution in the same space, time varies. Europe is living in a homogeneous time, in which all its countries are in the twentieth century. In Latin America, the twentieth century exists in Buenos Aires ... but as we travel from the coast to the Peruvian jungle we pass from the twentieth into the sixteenth or seventeenth century, into the time of feudal and semibarbaric Andean agriculture, until we stumble on naked and hostile tribes in the tropical forests."

Haya claims that just as for modern physics no absolute space or absolute time exists, for modern history no single historical process exists—the processes are many. "Each special-temporal area has its peculiar rhythm of development, and consequently its own sociological characteristics."[7]

Aprismo was the first movement to urge the political and economic unification of Latin America, and the bringing of problems of imperialism, democracy, nationalization, and industrialization into a specifically Latin American context. In 1942, though still without legal status, APRA supported plans for the United Nations and proposed a twelve-point Plan for the Assertion of Democracy in Latin America.

Aprismo has differed from Communism since its inception. For Haya, Indo-American life exhibits "the disparity in the historical evolution of Europe and Indo-America, and, consequently, the differences in European and Indo-American socioeconomic problems. ... If the socioeconomic problems of Europe and Indo-America are different, the solutions must also be different." Communism, as a specifically European phenomenon, is by this reasoning useless in Indo-America. APRA did not want to be a single-class party because "the proletariat of the advanced capitalistic countries, who make the machinery, cannot be equated with the proletariat of countries with only incipient industrialism, based on raw or semifinished materials, who do not make machinery."

APRA has maintained over the years a persistent and often bloody struggle for survival. On several occasions it was cheated out of election victories. When the dictator Augusto B. Leguía fell in 1930, Haya returned to Peru, and in 1931, as APRA's candidate, he outpolled Col. Luis Sánchez Cerro for the office of president. But the results were falsified and the colonel took power. He persecuted APRA members and kept Haya incommunicado for sixteen months, but failed to head off two uprisings, several strikes, and a navy rebellion. Sánchez Cerro was assassinated by a student in 1933 and Haya regained his freedom, but the new dictator, General Oscar Benavides, again persecuted the APRA. The next election was held in 1936, after four postponements. When the government ruled that APRA could not participate in the election, because of its illegal status, APRA gave its support to Luis Antonio Eguiguren, the candidate of the Partido Social Demócrata. When the government learned that Eguiguren had won 75,000 of the first 125,000 votes cast, it suspended the ballot tally and announced that Eguiguren had been disqualified because of his APRA support. Congress then elected the dictator for another three years.[8]

Until 1939 Aprismo operated illegally. During the war, it was shown a certain tolerance, and in the elections of 1946 APRA votes helped elect a moderate candidate, Nicolás Bustamante Rivero. APRA gained three ministers, but they had little time to accomplish anything. Within a year Bustamante had broken with APRA, and in October of 1948 a group of military men, led by General Manuel Odría and supported by the Communists, came to power. They fiercely persecuted APRA, opened concentration camps in the Amazon region, and established a state monopoly on cocoa leaves in order to secure more revenue for the military. Haya was given asylum for five years in the Colombian Embassy in Lima, and was the object of litigation between Peru and Colombia before the International Court at The Hague, which finally ordered that safe conduct be given to the APRA leader.

Odría held new elections in 1956. Without legal status, APRA at the last minute ordered a vote for Manuel Prado, who had also persecuted APRA during a previous presidency. This election alliance, which was criticized by both friends and enemies of APRA, was the result of the democratic-coexistence line favored by the party's secretary general, Ramiro Prialó; the line was intended to impede further military take-overs. APRA regained its legal standing, and prepared to campaign actively in the 1962 elections. But when Haya won the election that year the military took over, and deposed Prado, and once again nullified APRA's victory. In the 1963 election, APRA, although it improved its parliamentary position and increased its votes, failed to win a victory for Haya. It did, however, play an important role in preparing the Agrarian Reform Law of 1964.

During its thirty years of existence as a party, APRA has enjoyed only about fourteen of legal life: 1931, part of 1934, from 1946 to 1948—when Aprismo supported Bustamante at the polls—in 1956, under Prado's government, and since. Between 1931 and 1963 eight general elections were held in Peru. Aprismo was able to participate directly in only three of them.

Here are a few dates from the history of the APRA struggle. In May 1932, a rebellion in Callao left many dead, and eight were executed; in July of the same year, 6,000 died in Trujillo and 120 in Huaraz. In the Cajamarca combats of 1933, there were 200 casualties, and many civil and military Apristas shot by firing squads. From December 1934 to February 1945, there were serious fights in Lima, Huancayo, Cajamarca, Ayacucho, and Huancavelica. Between 1935 and 1945, Apristas attempted sixteen times to set off the revolution. From 1948 to 1956, three new insurrections were bloodily repressed. During that period secretary-general Luis Negreiros and more than a hundred local leaders were murdered.[9]

Though APRA never came to power, its legislators did manage to get certain measures in its program adopted and to propose others of considerable importance. When Leguía had barely fallen, APRA, recently formed in Peru, asked that the secret ballot be established. The daily *La Tribuna,* with a capital investment of one hundred *soles,* was founded. A new census was demanded (the last one had been taken in 1876), as well as the creation of a General Statistical Department. Both demands—for the secret ballot and the new census—were successful. During the constitutional assembly of 1931, APRA's twenty-two representatives asked, unsuccessfully, for the establishment of a National Economic Congress, in which labor, capital, and the state would be represented; for a new territorial division made on the basis of economic criteria; for administrative decentralization; for free public schooling; for social security; for women's suffrage; for the creation of ministries of labor, agriculture, education, and health and welfare, which did not exist. They defended the weekly day of rest, and paid vacations.

During the nineteen months in which the Aprista minority acted in parliament, from 1945 to 1947, it achieved the approval of a municipal law and women's suffrage; it sustained a program of subsidies to reduce the cost of living, which was administered by Aprista Manuel Vázquez Díaz in the Department of the Treasury (the subsidies were drawn from a special tax on tobacco); and it proposed the creation of a new state census service, the establishment of a credit system, the holding of an economic congress, and the establishment of a national bank, a finance corporation, a public petroleum corporation, and a public works fund. The majority of these projects were not approved by Congress; those that were were never proclaimed by the president or were nullified by Odría's coup.

APRA managed to see a law passed that would make obligatory the formation of consumer cooperatives in every enterprise with more than fifty employees. The paid Sunday day of rest was approved as a law, and insurance for white-collar workers was established. A law providing for free secondary education was proclaimed, but Odría annulled it. The same fate befell the approved University Statute, prepared by Luis Alberto Sánchez (born 1900), which gave legal form to the principles of the old university reform. Finally, a law was approved that created a housing corporation.

The changes that swept the continent after World War II have been taken account of in APRA policy. Here is a statement by Vázquez Díaz: "Imperialist capital is predominantly extractive, drawing colonial resources into the metropolitan market, disregarding the development of an internal market and public investment in the colony. Nevertheless, it helps make the economic relations of the colony more and more money-oriented, and also creates a minor commerce in native hands. From these native commercial sectors and from others there arise small industries serving the national market. . . . If imperialist capitalism allies with the feudal interests of the colony, national capitalism, which arises from the periphery of the interests of imperialist capitalism, soon begins to ask for protection and privileges for its nascent industrial enterprises. As a result, local industrial interests begin to confront the alliance of imperialist and feudal capital. The growth of national capital, and its final triumph over imperialism and feudalism, depends on the strength at its disposal, and this, as is well known, depends on the markets fed by national industries. . . . The economic integration of Indo-America widens in an extraordinary fashion the scope of the markets served by the national industries of each country. The strengthening of these markets will promote the modernization of the socioeconomic structures of the various countries and will invigorate the forces of national industrial capitalism. Supporting the interests of national capitalism, and directing them toward the international integration of Indo-America, promotes the foremost ideals of Indo-American integration: by defeudalizing the region, diminishing the strength of imperialism, raising the rate of capital formation through a scaled economy, and finally raising the standard of living." These views have led to a slogan: "It is not a matter of taking wealth from those who have it, but of creating it for those who do not."[10]

APRA sees "national sovereignty" and "continental sovereignty" as necessarily linked, since both aim for "the solidarity of all oppressed peoples and classes of the world." It holds that the progressive nationalization of lands and industry will be necessary; this will require the defeudalization of the peasant—whether peón, serf, comunero, ejidatario, sharecropper, or small landholder—and the organization of a new state economic system on a cooperative basis, a system that will control industry, destroy imperialist monopolies, and assure national control of wealth. "We are not after bread without freedom, or freedom without bread; we want bread and freedom both," Haya has said in summing up APRA's objectives.[11]

The Communist struggle against Aprismo has been systematic, and Communists have never hesitated to ally themselves with dictators in order to replace APRA members in the union movement, or in student or peasant organizations. In 1960 they managed to promote the defection of a small group of young people (APRA Rebelde), which first declared itself Castroite and then came to follow the Communists. They have attacked the Popular Universities in Peru, as they have in Argentina, accusing them of wanting to estrange workers from the political struggle.[12] The Communists have always feared an organized, disciplined party with a coherent program of reforms, for such a party suggests the practical possibility of democratic revolutions, and therefore the uselessness of Communist methods. The Communists fear Aprismo most of all because it is "a political theory directed toward redeeming Latin America from underdevelopment through the acceptance of foreign capitalism, and through democratic planning, and as such tends toward the creation of mixed forms of economy."[13]

VENEZUELA AND ACCIÓN DEMOCRÁTICA

Venezuela's Acción Democrática, though not founded until 1941, was the first populist movement in Latin America to rise to power and hold it democratically. Its political history begins in the late nineteen-twenties.

Juan Vicente Gómez, who governed the nation from 1908 until his death in 1935, reigned by terror, crushing rebellions and attempts by exiles to land again in the country. Gómez's huge family—he had dozens of children, hundreds of grandchildren—owned the best ranches and held the most lucrative sinecures. The discovery of oil in Maracaibo in 1922, and soon after in other places, brought great changes to the country. Until this time Venezuela had been poor indeed. But by 1930 it had liquidated its entire foreign debt and had very few state taxes. The workers and an urban middle class were rising, and in 1928 the Gómez regime was shaken by strikes from students and oil workers, a military rebellion, and two attempted landings by exiles. Those who took part in, and were deeply influenced by, these events came to be known as "the generation of '28."

When Gómez died in 1935 he was succeeded by his war minister, Eleazar López Contreras, who was in turn followed by General Isaías Medina Angarita. Agitation was constant, strikes were frequent, and the police systematically fired on demonstrators. Popular pressure was such that the government was obliged to confiscate Gómez's properties, and to establish an agreement with the oil companies in 1943 by virtue of which they accepted an increase in the percentage of their income that was to go to the state.

Meanwhile, in September 1941, the Partido de Acción Democrática had been formed by Rómulo Betancourt (born 1908), a member of the generation of '28 who had been imprisoned and exiled. His party was made up of workers (especially union leaders), students, several young military men, and middle-class elements; most members were drawn from several small socialistic and nationalistic parties that had been formed at the time of Gómez's death. The party defined itself as a national revolutionary party, democratic, anti-imperialist and anti-feudal, and as a front of exploited classes (workers, peasants, and the middle class).[14]

Caracas, nourished by the dollars—oil dollars, as they were called—brought in by the new taxes on the oil companies, became a luxurious city, where life cost more than in New York; everyone's concern was with finding some means of investing oil dollars in a country that imported 40 per cent of its food and 90 per cent of its manufactured goods. For the approaching elections of 1946, the Communist Unión Popular backed Medina Angarita's candidate and attacked Acción Democrática. The promotion to general of two illiterate colonels exasperated the young military men; two of them—Delgado Chalbaud and Mario Vargas—organized an uprising, by agreement with Acción Democrática. From October 17 to 19, 1945, there were fights in the streets, and on October 20 Rómulo Betancourt established a Revolutionary Junta, which expropriated the properties of the two previous presidents, raised taxes on the oil companies to exactly half their profits—which covered 50 per cent of the national budget—and disarmed the Communists, who had fought alongside the police in defending the defeated regime. For two years the Revolutionary Junta carried out a program of moderate but essential reforms. In December 1947 a new Constitution was proclaimed, and Rómulo Gallegos was elected president against a Christian-socialist candidate, Rafael Caldera, and one Communist. The losers admitted that the elections had been the fairest in the country's history. The unions, for the most part led by elements from Acción Democrática, developed and thrived. The Confederación de Trabajadores de Venezuela (CTV) came to exert a real influence on the country's economy.

On November 24, 1948, when an agrarian reform law was about to be applied, the military staged a coup. Gallegos did not resign from the presidency and was expelled from the country by force. After that a military junta, made up of three colonels, governed. One of them, Delgado, was murdered in 1950 (apparently because he wanted to hold elections), and was succeeded by Colonel Marcos Pérez Jiménez.

Neither the dissolution of the CTV, in February 1949, nor the closing down of the University of Caracas, in February 1952, nor the imprisonment and murder of hundreds of local leaders and the exile of many others, could suppress popular resistance. Newspapers, radio stations, and even a university, operated secretly. The Communists, out of hatred for Acción Democrática, courted the colonels, in whose service they organized phantom unions.

In January 1958, public action and a navy rebellion overthrew Pérez Jiménez. A junta, presided over by Rear-Admiral Wolfgango Larrazábal, was established, and parties were organized. At the end of the year, Rómulo Betancourt, Acción Democrática's candidate, was elected president against Caldera of the Christian-socialist COPEI and Larrazábal, who was supported by the Unión Democrática and the Communists.

In 1960, the Cuban problem provoked a schism in Acción Democrática. The withdrawing group founded the Movimiento de Izquierda Revolucionaria (MIR), led by Luis Alberto Rangel; it ended as a simple Communist appendage. At the end of 1961, Acción Democrática was divided between the old guard, who favored continued collaboration with the COPEI in the government, and more bourgeois elements, called *arsistas,* who opposed this and withdrew from the party.

Let us examine the policy followed by Acción Democrática after it came to power. In 1946, AD's government created the Corporación Venezolana de Fomento, which took charge of what was called "the sowing of petroleum"—investing profits from oil company taxes, and also advising workers on consumer purchases. The following is Betancourt, on the concepts behind the creation of the Corporación: "The state instrument was created to stimulate production. We Venezuelan government officials of 1946 were —and are still—convinced that our country cannot leap over the capitalistic stage of its economic development. The stage we find ourselves passing through is more related to the bourgeois-democratic revolution than to the socialist revolution. The problem is not one of socializing wealth but of producing it, permanently and nationally, because the country's current wealth is, to a substantial degree, perishable and manipulated by foreign consortia. The state, rich in fiscal resources, ought to accelerate the pace of nonpetroleum production, which is weighted down with feudal remains, toward production with modern industrial features; but it must control, direct, and condition this process so that it will not grow anarchistically and create an overpowering business oligarchy dissociated from the country's needs and obstinately opposed to sharing benefits with workers and consumers.

"We never conceived of the economic revolution in Venezuela as a historical necessity.... In Venezuela this 'leap,' in the Hegelian sense, from the colonial to the modern in the economic structure of society, was to be planned and regulated by a government loyal to the social conscience of our time, and in agreement with the interests and aspirations of those who have offered the most solid support: the professional, technical, and middle classes and workers, artisans, peasants, and modern-minded industrial groups. More concretely stated: we have not simply said 'get rich,' as Guizot did to the French bourgeoisie, but have wanted to direct production in three ways: (1) by studying the characteristics of the economy and guiding its development in line with these technical investigations; (2) by assuming the administration of those programs which, because of their magnitude or their unattractiveness to private investors, would absolutely require state management; and (3) by actively encouraging, through credits and technology, enterprising and dynamic businessmen, provided they channel their industrial efforts in the direction of the country's production needs, adjust their costs to what consumers can reasonably pay, and accept the necessity for maintaining the social benefits already being received by Venezuelan workers."[15]

The government stimulated irrigation, diversification, and mechanization in agriculture; it proposed an agrarian reform law (which the military overthrow kept from being applied); it participated in the creation of the Flota Grancolombiana; it reformed education; it outlined a plan for industrialization; it initiated a housing and social security policy; it tried to plan immigration; and it began an administrative reform. It did all this without infringing on political freedom and without having to put down many attempted military coups.

In 1959—during its second period in power—Acción Democrática collaborated in the government with the Christian-democratic COPEI and with the bourgeois party URD—until in 1960 the URD withdrew to ally itself with the MIR and the Communists. Acción Democrática had to face not only attempted military takeovers but also frequent harassment from Castroite and Communist terrorists and guerrillas. In 1960 an agrarian reform law was approved, and gradual application of it was begun immediately. Betancourt managed to avoid the intervention of the army in politics, and in spite of the mistrust of certain wealthy sectors he maintained the population's standard of living and political freedoms. The party had always given top priority to nationalization of the petroleum industry. Its negotiational formula in 1961 was to readjust the proportion of royalties and taxes, by which the national treasury received 69 per cent of oil-company profits, and to organize a great national enterprise which would assume the operation of the oil industry as soon as foreign concessions lapsed.[16] In 1963, Acción Democrática again won the presidential elections and put Dr. Raúl Leoni in the Palacio de Miraflores. The following year AD joined the Socialist International.

Betancourt has considered it essential to demonstrate with facts that a stable democratic and reforming regime can survive in Latin America. He has written: "An important sector of our intellectual minority has traditionally upheld the thesis that our people are by nature ill-suited to perform the great civilizing functions. This thesis derives from the theories of European sociologists of the nineteenth century, whose most characteristic spokesman was Gobineau. In our own time this thesis has been upheld by the apostles of Nazi Aryanism. According to Gobineau, the mestizo peoples are incapable of creating a solid and stable culture. His theory was transplanted in Latin America, and not even a thinker like José Ingenieros, who in many respects prefigured the modern movements toward the social and national liberation of our peoples, could escape the influence of it. Ingenieros maintained, in some of his works, that [for reasons of climate] the Nordic white races were the only ones fit for constructing stable institutional systems, and that the political destiny of mestizo countries was to waver between two extremes—the imperious dictatorship of a man or a group of men, or anarchy. This thesis was accepted by most Latin American sociologists of the nineteenth century. They were entirely mistaken.... Venezuela, like all the other Latin American nations, is perfectly capable of creating economic, political, and social order. We are a people disposed to being governed legally and democratically. We are determined to find our own way, to make our own history; we no longer wish to maintain a contemplative gaze backwards, burning incense before the portraits of our liberators and behaving like their unworthy grandchildren. We are a people carrying out a labor that will be the pride of the new Latin America."[17]

Betancourt sees the future as follows: "Latin America has 'entered the revolution,' as Martí put it. From one end of the continent to the other a great popular upsurge can be observed. As in the African and Asian countries—and in all other areas suffering from the prolonged domination of antinational oligarchies and the subjugating influence of the great powers—in the region extending from the Mexican border to Cape Horn a powerful redeeming movement has come into being. Its goal is the creation of an organic Latin American front, which, without diminishing the essential sovereign attributes of each of the nations comprising it, will affirm and establish in each one of them a representative and democratic system of government; it will promote cooperative development of its national economies, permitting them to overcome their depressing secondary position in the field of international relations. A front thus conceived will have the solid support of Latin American public opinion and will be sympathetically looked upon by those in the United States who profess liberal and democratic beliefs. The relations between the two Americas will become more normal, less plagued by resentments and misgivings, when a more equal balance of power exists between the two different portions of the continent.

"To Venezuela falls the responsibility of playing an important role in the process of Latin America's regional integration. Its territory was blessed by nature with great reserves of mineral wealth, some of them—such as oil—of elevated and stable value, and of uses as diverse as they are essential. This circumstance permits Venezuela not only to develop its own economy, but also to contribute to the development of the economies of those peoples with whom it shares a common destiny. This is feasible because it responds to a tradition deeply rooted in the national collectivity, originating at the time of the Independence—that of cooperating with neighboring countries, without harboring expansionist intentions or assuming jealously self-protective attitudes."[18]

BOLIVIA AND THE MNR

Twice the size of France, yet with only 4 million inhabitants, Bolivia is "like a beggar sitting on a pot of gold." Its mountains contain gold, lead, silver, and, above all, tin. Seventy thousand miners produce 90 per cent of the country's exports. Peasants' and miners' revolts have occurred frequently in the country's contemporary history.

The proletariat formed in the mines in 1923 demanded a wage increase in Uncia, one of Antenor Patiño's mines. President Saavedra stifled these first social demands with a slaughter of miners, but he dictated the first social laws—compensation for accidents on the job and for occupational illnesses. (A miner's work is exhausting; a miner's life rarely extended beyond twenty-seven years, the last of them racked by tuberculosis or pneumonoconiosis.)[19]

In July 1938, Col. Germán Busch (1904-1938), who took power with a program of reforms, dictated a decree that arranged for the delivery to the state of all foreign currency originating from the export of minerals. A month and a half later he was found dead of a bullet wound.

The disillusionment resulting from the Chaco War (1933–35), and the failure of reformist attempts by colonels Busch and David Toro (born 1898), inspired the formation of the Movimiento Nacionalista Revolucionario (MNR); it was founded in 1941 by Víctor Paz Estenssoro (born 1917), an attorney who had fought in the Chaco War. Paz said: "This is a movement and not a party ... because it represents all the oppressed classes of Bolivia (and will represent no one of them exclusively), united by a common anti-imperialist and antifeudal interest. It is nationalist because it favors the recovery of national wealth for the benefit of Bolivians. And it is revolutionary because it understands that to do this it is necessary to liquidate a social and economic system, at its roots, and replace it with something else."

When striking miners were slaughtered in Catavi in 1942, MNR's small parliamentary minority accused not specific ministers but the system itself. Paz stated in Parliament that the entire country, with its 3.5 million inhabitants, was being "exploited by only three men [the owners of the three tin companies] and their cohorts." And he added: "It has been said that, owing to international agreements required by World War II, Bolivia must maintain its production uninterrupted, and that workers cannot legally declare themselves on strike. Why not apply the same argument to the Patiño Company [owner of the Catavi mine]? Its refusal to reach an agreement with the workers also represents an interruption in production."

Later, in 1943, MNR participated in a plot with the military lodge Radepa, which led to a coup and to a new government presided over by Major Gualberto Villarroel (1908–46). MNR at first formed part of the government, then withdrew to calm the military's misgivings, though it continued to support Villarroel, who adopted several reform measures. The MNR won a substantial majority in the parliamentary elections of July 1944. At that time several MNR leaders suggested going beyond moderate reform— organizing the masses and nationalizing the mines, for example. Paz opposed them with this argument: "The major points in a program such as nationalization of the mines cannot be used for political ends; they are stated because the process of economic development absolutely requires them ... but at present there does not exist the collective support that would make them possible." Members of the MNR were frequently accused during this period of having Nazi sympathies, and it is possible that there were some members who saw in a totalitarian dictatorship the only means of solving national problems.

Villarroel once said, in a sentence that revealed his temperament and also pointed toward the limitations in his government, "I am not an enemy of the wealthy; I am more a friend of the poor." His main objective was minimal: a return to Busch's decrees, cast in a much more practical form, which would refute the contention of the tin companies that because Busch had dictated the decrees they were not binding. The companies were obliged by one decree to build 5,000 dwellings for their workers, and a Peasant Congress was called at which Indian delegates could explain their needs. According to another decree, the personal service to which peasants had been obligated since the colonial period was suppressed. Another decree established the obligation of paying a wage to agricultural workers; previously, the owner of a large property had given the peasant only a small parcel to cultivate for himself, in exchange for the duty of working five days every month at no pay.

Villarroel's regime achieved much. It gained approval, with the help of MNR, which held a majority in both houses, of a labor-union statute, a law allowing voluntary retirement, and a law for the protection of tenants. It restored to the public domain more than 250,000 acres of gold-bearing lands being exploited by the Aramayo Company. The Federación Sindical de Trabajadores Mineros was founded. New vigor was injected into Busch's decree that the state should control all currency originating from the exportation of minerals; this produced a reserve fund of 36 million dollars, which was intended for use in a plan for the diversification of production. A new constitution, approved in 1945, recognized workers' rights and abolished the feudal duties with which the peasants were burdened. MNR, which had left the government in June 1944, returned at the beginning of 1945. During this period the number of unions increased six-fold, and payments by big companies for social benefits increased a thousand-fold. More than 2.5 million acres of fallow lands reverted to the state.

Villarroel's regime had to face defection of a few of the military groups that had at first supported it, opposition from the PIR (already Communist-dominated), attacks by the oligarchy, and several attempts at military takeover. Finally, on July 21, 1946, a coup succeeded, and Villaroel was hanged from a lamp post in Murillo Plaza in La Paz. The oligarchy again controlled the government, with the support of the PIR Communists.

In Potosí, in February 1947, a new slaughter of striking miners gave MNR an opportunity to regain political influence. As the government, backed by the PIR Communists, bloodily repressed peasant uprisings and miners' strikes, MNR gained almost complete control of the mining union's leadership and the leadership of several other union groups just beginning to develop. In May of 1950 the Communists proposed an alliance with MNR. Another rebellion was organized, and a general strike was staged.

The strike was well received by the people, but the Communists reneged on their promised support, and their leader, Ricardo Anaya, took refuge in the Interior minister's own house.

A year later, in May 1951, MNR won the presidential election, with Paz Estenssoro winning more votes than all his opponents combined. To keep him from coming to power, President Mamerto Urriolagoitia organized a military coup and stepped down in favor of General Hugo Balivían. But in April 1952 a military group (which included General Antonio Seleme, one of Balivían's own ministers who had secretly joined MNR) rebelled and gave arms to MNR militants. After three days of fighting, the miners took Oruro, and the military forces fled La Paz. On April 11, Hernán Siles Suazo (elected vice-president in 1951) formed an MNR government that could function until Paz could return from exile in Buenos Aires. The Bolivian revolution had entered its period of fulfillment.[20]

Once in power, MNR dissolved the army (it later organized another smaller one, which carried out useful tasks) and created a Ministry of Indian and Peasant Affairs. In October 1952 the three large tin companies were nationalized. (In 1958 compensations of approximately 12 million dollars were paid to these companies.) Agrarian reform was decreed in August 1953. For lack of funds, inflation could not be contained, living conditions improved, or much land distributed. Nevertheless, the workers and peasants continued to support the regime (MNR's government held power longer than any previous one in Bolivia), and all attempts at takeover failed until 1964. The revolution in Bolivia was not free from corruption, violence, and dissension, but its positive achievements were considerable, and it did find a genuinely Latin American way of resolving Latin American problems. MNR's great achievement was, basically, to lift Bolivia's submerged classes to a level at which they could participate in the government.

The revolution was terminated in the following manner. MNR had, before and after coming to power, two wings: the left, or Vanguardia Obrera Movimientista, headed by union leaders Juan Lechín and Nuflo Chávez; and the right, or Acción de Defensa del MNR, led by Walter Guevara Arza and Hernán Siles Suazo. Paz Estenssoro was a sort of arbiter between the two wings. Siles, elected president in 1956 with Chávez as vice-president, was confronted with the leftist tendency, which opposed a stabilization plan suggested by the World Bank and the International Monetary Fund; and Paz, as a candidate and later as president after 1960 (with Lechín as vice-president) was faced with the right, which opposed him with Guevara's candidacy. On occasion these differences led to violence, as in 1957, when the unions fought Siles's anti-inflationary measures.

Later, as the 1964 elections approached, a rivalry between Paz and Lechín developed. Lechín moved to the opposition, with the backing of the miners, who constituted a privileged minority; but the peasant masses supported Paz and returned him to the Presidency in 1964, after the Constitution had been amended to allow his reelection. Then Lechín, Guevara, the Falange Socialista (an extreme right-wing party), the Communists, and even Siles Suazo formed an alliance with General René Barrientos (Paz's own vice-president) and overthrew Paz. The miners were the basic force in this coalition. They opposed the army's plan to reduce the privileges they had been given in return for their support of the 1952 revolution, though the reduction was necessary in view of the high cost of tin production. When Barrientos took power he exiled Lechín and Siles and imposed restrictions on the miners far more drastic than those suggested by Paz. The revolution had come to a halt.

MNR then sought to draw upon the experience of other revolutions, especially Mexico's. The agrarian reform, though it encouraged cooperative ventures, avoided the Mexican error of establishing a priori standards for the possession and use of the land, and left the peasants themselves to find those that best served their purposes. The revolution found most of its difficulties in the mines: the Bolivian Mining Corporation (COMIBOL), which administered them, had never managed to check increases in personnel and falling production, and the unions did very little to help solve this economic problem.

Paz Estenssoro has explained the MNR's policy as follows: "The measures we took were brought on by the facts of Bolivian life. We had to nationalize the mines; we had to carry out the agrarian reform. Nationalization of the mines carried obvious risks, but these were inescapable in a backward and exploited country. We had neither capital nor technicians, but if we had waited until such time as we did, we would never have been able to nationalize the mines...; we had to take the essential step and overcome obstacles as they presented themselves, because obtaining capital and technicians is possible only in an independent and sovereign country.

"Agrarian reform also carried with it the dangers that have faced all countries adopting similar measures. A fundamental change in the system of land ownership always brings on, at first, a decline in production. In Bolivia the upset has been minimal, because the peasant had been indoctrinated and was aware of his responsibilities.

"That the agrarian reform brought dislocations in the rural areas is evident. But if one takes into account the depth of the transformation, and compares it with the disorders caused by the Mexican Revolution or the Civil War in the United States, our problems have been minimal. In Bolivia we have done away with servitude; we have leapt from the Middle Ages to modern times....

"A people seeking to emerge from poverty creates the conditions for achieving democracy, because only when there is an economy of abundance does democracy function well. But if that people, in the exploitation of its riches, also takes into account the possibilities of interchange with neighboring peoples, it is working as well for another still more distant objective, one that will be possible only for our children's children, but one which should be kept constantly in view—the integration of all the nations of Latin America.

"In this direction the Bolivian Republic also has plans. There is the case of oil, for instance. We have exploited it first for ourselves; but we now seek the possibility of using this oil to serve neighboring countries ... as part of the process of Latin American integration, which is so vital for our countries. In this age of industrial civilization, only within the borders of our whole continent is it possible to find a framework large enough to permit our full collective development."[21]

By about 1950, MNR had managed to allay the suspicion its measures had awakened in the United States, and began to receive considerable economic aid from the U.S. It was symptomatic that when the United States showed an understanding attitude toward the Bolivian revolution, the support lent to it by Communists and fellow-travelers on the continent vanished. Bolivia, for them, was only a pretext for attacking the United States; as soon as the pretext vanished, the revolution no longer interested them.

MNR's program can be summed up as follows. If profits from mining were to be retained for use in Bolivia, state intervention in matters of foreign currency, and control of wages and salaries, would be necessary. To protect the national economy against the effects of a possible world economic crisis, in which the price of minerals would fall almost vertically, it would be necessary to diversify Bolivian production. Other goals were these: (1) to destroy feudal production relations, dissolve latifundio and labor servitude, offer arable land to dispossessed peasants, adopt capitalist techniques for agricultural production, and promote cooperative and collective ownership by means of agrarian reform laws; (2) to achieve national control over sources of raw materials and to create a diversified manufacturing industry; (3) to develop an internal market by raising the minimum standard of living for all, through the efforts of all productive and progressive classes; (4) to work for a more diversified foreign market, principally through cooperation with other Latin American countries; (5) to bring the masses into the institutional and political life of the country by means of universal suffrage; (6) to perpetuate and support a lawful regime that would permit free action by classes and political parties, with the understanding that MNR embodied the spirit of the revolution and should continue in the government as the representative of the workers and the poor middle class; and (7) to resist imperialism, the chief support of local oligarchies, and to resist regressive forces in general.[22]

COSTA RICA AND LIBERACIÓN NACIONAL

Coffee made Costa Rica's prosperity, and the unions achieved for the workers a standard of living that was, if not high, at least higher than that of neighboring countries. But Costa Rica's recent history demonstrates that a stable democracy, based on a comfortable middle class and an agriculture without latifundios, can degenerate until it has become unworkable if it fails to rejuvenate itself with needed social reforms.

From 1940 to 1948 the government of Costa Rica was headed by Rafael Calderón Guardia and his Partido Nacional Republicano; the party was principally interested in keeping itself in power, but in pursuit of this interest it gave the workers the first civil rights laws. The government, based on nepotism, was inefficient and corrupt; as it became progressively more dictatorial, Calderón Guardia sought support against popular resentment by giving several important posts to the Communists, who changed their party's name to Vanguardia Popular.

In 1944, after a violent election campaign, Teodoro Picado, Calderón Guardia's friend, assumed the presidency. The opposition alleged fraud in the vote count. Calderón Guardia was supported by personal backers, the country's coffee exporters, and the Communist party; each of these three groups had its own objectives, but they managed to maintain electoral cooperation. The opposition came from students and the majority of their teachers, the middle class, the small farmers, and the peasants.[23]

Shortly before the war, professors and university students had created two formal organizations—the Center for the Study of National Problems and Acción Demócrata. Both organizations thought the creation of parties with well-defined ideologies was a necessity for strengthening democratic government, and both were concerned with reorganizing and modernizing the country's economy. In 1943, José Figueres (born 1906) published a book entitled *Palabras gastadas,* in which he argued for democracy, socialism, and freedom. The book put him in contact with a group of young people who had formed the Institute of Political Studies, and whose purpose was the formation of a genuinely ideological party. In March 1945 this group merged with Acción Demócrata and created the Partido Social Demócrata, which became the government's formal opposition. During the 1948 presidential election the Partido Nacional Republicano nominated ex-president Calderón Guardia and the other parties nominated Otilio Ulate. Ulate won, but in March 1948 the legislature voided the election and had Ulate arrested. José Figueres and his friends rose up in arms. A short but bloody civil war was fought against Picado's government, the army, Calderón Guardia, and the Communist party. Many citizens joined the ranks of the revolution. The dictatorial governments of Nicaragua and Honduras aided the Picado coalition, but the Guatemalan government supported the revolutionaries. The civilian army defeated the government's forces in a few weeks. Figueres was appointed president of the government junta, and proclaimed Founder of the Second Republic of Costa Rica on May 8, 1948. The army was dissolved, the Communist party was outlawed, and all the country's banks were nationalized. A small contribution drawn from the wealthy was used to repay the damages caused by the war. Administrative systems were readjusted, and promotion on the basis of merit and seniority was provided for.

After the army was dissolved, three hundred armed men from Nicaragua invaded the country in December 1948. In two weeks the country without an army defeated the invaders. In November 1949, Figueres, the people's idol, with power in his hands, delivered the presidency to Ulate. Figueres said: "The health of democracy in Latin America demands that the men who have taken power by force go home when normalcy is reestablished. We have restored normalcy and we are going to our homes." But Figueres remained in politics.

It was soon seen that the alliance between Partido Social Demócrata and Ulate could not survive. The Partido Social Demócrata wanted a moderate revolution, while Ulate and his friends sought only an electoral system that would permit them to gain power. On the other hand, some of the forces backing Figueres in his opposition to the corruption in previous governments refused to support his program of social reforms. In December 1949, elections for the constitutional assembly were held. The junta's partisans fell short of the majority, and the Assembly approved a Constitution hardly different from the former one.

The Partido Social Demócrata was dissolved and a new organization was created, the Partido Liberación Nacional. José Figueres was elected president of Costa Rica in 1953, and his party won thirty of the forty-five seats in the legislative Assembly. Figueres wanted to diversify his country's agricultural production, encourage industrialization, improve and extend social security, improve housing, and increase public works without resorting to foreign loans. He also wanted to adjust the governmental structure so that democracy could continue to function even should his own party lose power. Although he was unable to accomplish all the things he proposed, autonomous organizations were created to place a few nonpolitical activities under government control; these activities included the operations of the banking system and the insurance companies, the construction of dwellings and electrical production plants, and the building of the railroad to the Pacific.

In spite of the improvements in the country's economic system the opposition to Figueres continued, and culminated in a new invasion from Nicaragua in January 1955. The forces this time were made up of Communist groups, and the movement was well-organized and well-financed. The money apparently had been supplied by the Venezuelan dictator, and the movement's handling was left to two ex-presidents, Calderón Guardia and Picado. Groups of Liberación Nacional volunteers, supported by the OAS and Washington, had no difficulty in repelling the invasion.

As the presidential elections of February 1958 approached, Liberación Nacional found itself divided, for although Figueres and the party's majority believed that Costa Rica needed more reforms, businessmen felt that no more innovations should be introduced and they formed the Partido Independiente. Mario Echandi, the right-wing business candidate, was elected by a bare plurality—104,500 to 98,400 for his Liberación opponent, Francisco Orlich. The result was unexpected, as far as Liberación was concerned; it had been certain of victory. In Congress, however, it made up the most numerous minority.[24] In 1962, Liberación brought Orlich to victory against Calderón Guardia and came to power for a second time, but was defeated in the 1964 elections.*

In recent years several political theorists have risen from Liberación ranks—Daniel Oduber, Benjamín Núñez, and Luis Alberto Monge, to name the best-known. And although the party's youngest elements tend to consider Figueres a conservative, Liberación Nacional's program remains based on concepts expounded by him. At the conference of the Inter-American Association for Democracy and Freedom in 1950, Figueres summarized his thinking as follows: the Latin American political system is filled with imperfections; economic inequalities are excessive, and the same is true in cultural matters; these deficiencies are causally related, and reinforce each other.[25]

Liberación Nacional has wanted to study economic facts in order to increase production, and, at the same time, to place the distribution of wealth

---

* Orlich's government had failed to attack the basic cause of social unrest—the control of the coffee export trade by a small group of businessmen, who in their way control the economy of the country. Orlich himself is a coffee exporter.

on a criterion of social justice, as much in a direct way (through salaries) as in an indirect fashion (through social security, schools, and so forth). It believes that the best economic system for attaining these objectives is a mixed one balancing socialism and capitalist private initiative, and one subjected to controls and planning.[26] In 1964, Liberación Nacional joined the Socialist International.

OTHER POPULIST MOVEMENTS

The influence of APRA concepts and of populism in general has extended to practically all leftist parties in Latin America, and even to a few middle-of-the-road parties. In addition to those examined above, there were and are other populist movements: the Fernando Ferrari Movimiento Trabalhista Renovador in Brazil; the Partido Revolucionario of Guatemala; the Partido Liberal of Honduras; the Partido Revolucionario Institucional of Mexico; the Partido Conservador and the Partido Liberal Independiente of Nicaragua; the Partido Revolucionario Dominicano, which after Trujillo's death in May 1961 came to be the most powerful party in the Dominican Republic, under the leadership of Juan Bosch (born 1900). Also worth mentioning are *socialismo espiritualista* and *febrerismo*.

Socialismo espiritualista is a concept propounded by Guatemala's ex-president Juan José Arévalo (born 1904). Arévalo's "spiritual socialism" is concerned with establishing a just relationship between the collective and the individual factors in politics. Democracy must be "the organization of all the social classes of a country, made harmonious by generous laws that give to each its appropriate value and its appropriate place in economic and cultural development." The Marxist class struggle would theoretically lead to the extinction of minorities, something that will never happen; democracy is therefore superior to Communism. Materialistic socialism of all sorts (Communism, fascism, Nazism) has been unable to satisfy true human aspirations. For Latin America, which "until now has debated with itself over conservatism, liberalism, and Marxism, spiritual socialism represents a true doctrinal innovation," which aims at freeing man "by returning to him the psychological and spiritual integrity denied him by conservatism and liberalism." Government must represent the legitimate economic interests of all social classes; therefore, the right of private ownership and private capital, if these are subordinate to the country's interests, should be respected. Social reforms should be gradual: "our feudal vestiges will be softened by discreet measures in defense of workers, by a more beautiful distribution of lands ... by a prudent raise in wages, by the improvement of the miserable dwellings of the Indians, by the socialization of primary education, by the socialization of hospital services."[27]

At the other end of the continent, in Paraguay, in February 1936, military officers trained during the Chaco War overthrew the government and called Col. Rafael Franco, a popular hero of the war, to power. His regime lasted until August 1937, when another coup replaced him with a dictatorship. Franco's government, in its first few months, stripped itself of both extreme right-wing and left-wing elements and was formed almost entirely of intellectual components of the Liga Nacional Independiente. It proclaimed an agrarian reform law, created a labor department, and established an eight-hour working day and a forty-eight-hour work week, Sunday rest, and the payment of wages in cash. These measures—and especially the outlawing of chits, or "plata blanca"—constituted almost a social revolution. Since 1937 Paraguay has had no single period of democracy, or even of relative freedom, except for a parenthesis of seven months during 1946, during which a Colorado-Febrerista government proclaimed measures complementary to Franco's social laws.

During the 1936 revolution the Unión Nacional Revolucionaria and a student club called Pedro P. Samaniego were created. These merged in 1945 as the Concentración Revolucionaria Febrerista and in 1951 became the Partido Revolucionario Febrerista, a movement with a populist ideology.[28]

THE CHRISTIAN-DEMOCRAT MOVEMENT

The Christian-democrat movement is a relatively recent development in Latin America, though it has some distant antecedents. Its relationship with the labor movement as such has adopted different forms. In a few areas the Christian-democrats have tried to form their own unions. Elsewhere they have joined existing unions. In certain countries, furthermore, social-Christian, Christian-democrat, and Catholic parties exist side by side, and with diverse ideologies. In Mexico, for example, Acción Nacional can be considered a right-wing party, but in Chile the Christian-democrats are reformist. Likewise, in certain countries the Christian unionists adopt positions that could be qualified as leftist, whereas in others they are conservative.

A Christian union leader, Emilio Maspero, states that Christian unionists have not always been able to count on support from either the ecclesiastical authorities or the Catholic bourgeoisie. He writes, for example: "In 1910 a Christian Labor Federation was organized in Argentina, but it was soon suppressed by those Catholics too compromised with the existing regime and with the conservative and bourgeois oligarchies.... The same thing happened in Chile, and the Jesuit who had inspired the movement (Vives del Solar) was forced to leave the country. This does not mean that everywhere it was the same. We are aware of generous and admirable exceptions, but they do no more than confirm the general rule." Prior to 1954, attempts were made at organization in many countries, "but the wavering of the great majority of Catholics on the one hand, and political conditions peculiar to Latin America on the other, were obstacles to these initiatives."

Maspero points out as an element favorable to the organization of Catholic unionists the fact that "the young generation of priests who studied in Europe has been a source of inspiration and of action in support of Christian unionism; frequently, in spite of the hierarchy and in opposition to Church authorities, the militants exerted the natural right of association and of organization, which cannot go unrecognized by any responsible and democratic organization."

The Juventud Obrera Católica (JOC) played a decisive role in the foundation of groups of Christian unionists. In Argentina, under Perón, the Asociación Sindical Argentina (ASA) was created. Similar organizations were created elsewhere: Movimiento Sindicalista Paraguayo, the Federation Haitienne de Syndicalistes Chrétiens, Acción Sindicalista Panameña, the Acción Sindical of Uruguay, the Frente Auténtico del Trabajo of Mexico, the Frente Cristiano de Trabajadores in Guatemala, the Unión de Obreros Católicos in El Salvador, the CEDOC of Ecuador, the CUSIX of Venezuela, the ASECH of Chile, the CNCO of Brazil, the MOSSICP of Cuba (whose members have been persecuted by Castro's regime since 1960). In the Dominican Republic the Confederación Autónoma de Sindicatos Cristianos was created in 1962.

All these organizations created the Confederación Latino Americana de Sindicalistas Cristianos (CLASC) during a congress held in 1954 in Santiago, where the Christian-democrat movement counted on a certain tradition. Caracas is headquarters of the CLASC. According to Maspero, CLASC tries to act as the third force between CTAL, or Communist-controlled unions, and ORIT, but appears disposed "to collaborate with any other union organization . . . born of the free determination of the workers themselves, in a climate of union freedom." As its name indicates, the confederation is not really made up of unions; for though Christian unionists lead some unions, there are Christian union federations in only a few countries, notably Colombia, Ecuador, and the Dominican Republic. CLASC claims 1,200,000 members. In addition to unionist action groups, the Escuela Padre Hurtado was organized in Santiago to train militants, and unionist schools were created in Argentina, Brazil, Venezuela (the Instituto Nacional de Estudios Sindicales), and Guatemala. CLASC has prepared seminars on labor and peasant questions and has eighty-three officials stationed throughout the continent.[29] In recent years, unionist priests and a few ecclesiastical organizations with Christian-democrat leanings have carried on intense activity in support of ideological education and the training of members for their movement.

The Christian-democrat movement has had varying success in Latin

America. In Argentina the Catholic movement, led by Monsignor de Andrea, has had a certain influence among white-collar workers. It now claims 25,000 to 30,000 members.[30]

In Chile in 1844 a translation of Lamennais's *Le livre du peuple* was published in Concepción. When the mutualist and cooperativist movement took hold around 1870, societies were created by Catholic groups; these included the Sociedad Católica de Obreros de la Parroquia de Santa Ana, the Asociación Fraterna de la Unión del Progreso, and the Asociación Católica de Obreros, the last one established by the conservative politician Abdón Cifuentes and the priest Rafael Angel Jara. These lasted only a short time; the workers were indifferent. In 1883 the Unión Católica de Chile was created, and later a Sociedad de Obreras Católicas, as well as two workers' educational units, La Ilustración and the Institución León XIII.

In 1893, after a sermon by the Archbishop of Santiago, the Orden y Trabajo society was founded by Monsignor Mariano Casanova, an opponent of socialism. In Chillán two workers' clubs were created, to keep workers from taking part in "the current of socialism." These soon failed.

In this century the so-called white unions, with social-Christian tendencies, have attained a certain importance. But they have never acted as obstacles to the development of nonconfessional unionism.[31] In 1910 a Congreso Social Católico took place, and in 1913 an Agricultural Social Week was held; at the latter meeting the rural–urban exodus was deplored, but nothing was said of Latifundismo. At the end of World War I there existed a few Catholic unions, one cooperative, and a social secretariat, all founded by the Jesuit Ignacio Vives del Solar. At the fringe of this movement, progressing very slowly, young Catholics with liberal tendencies successively founded a Partido Social Sindicalista, a Partido Cooperativo Popular, and a Liga Social.[32]

Among other unions the Unión Chilena Ferroviaria was formed in 1926, but it survived only a few years and never managed to command much importance. A year later, during a convention of Catholic unions, the Confederación de Sindicatos Blancos was created. In a 1940 interview the Archbishop of Santiago, Monsignor José María Caro, said that the employer reaping huge profits who gave his workers "less than an adequate salary ... should without doubt be energetically denied the sacraments." And he added that he was in favor, "without qualification," of unionism. "The worker has the natural, God-given right to associate and to unionize. And there is no good law nor management consideration to support a contrary assertion. I say the same of peasant unionism. I will say that the agricultural worker not only can but should unionize."[33]

In 1947, Father Hurtado created the Acción Sindical y Económica Chilena (ASECH), which, without being a union, is considered by the ecclesiastical hierarchy as an institution through which Catholics can exercise "their union activities," and which joined the International Confederation of Christian Workers.

Eduardo Frei, founder of the Chilean Falange (which should not be confused with the Spanish fascist group, with which it has nothing in common, and which later became the Partido Demócrata Cristiano), has maintained that life has been governed more by formulas than by living facts. The facts, furthermore, indicate that a just government cannot be controlled either by capitalists and landholders or by workers, and that a democratic path must be followed. It must not involve repetition of the old electoral and demagogic procedures, but must be the expression of a program in which human groups may join together no matter how varied their origins. On the other hand, he feels it cannot be denied that classic individualism has ceased to operate and that it is incompatible with reality. Capitalism's particular function has been replaced by state capitalism, which tries to satisfy collective objectives, and which would theoretically be more justifiable; but in practice, state capitalism tends toward dictatorship. To prevent this tendency, democratic counterbalances should be built into the economy. To preserve democracy it is necessary to bring all the people into democratic parties. The democracy must be a social and constructive one, one in which authority imposes responsibility, and through that responsibility incorporates the people in its effort, and brings them the dignity and the benefits of power. It is necessary to alter Latin America's fate, and the essential responsibility for so doing falls to Latin Americans. Latin America must integrate, and for this it is necessary that a widespread constructive democratic regime to reign, with no exceptions permitted.[34] Frei was elected President of Chile in September 1964, against the socialist candidate of the Communist-socialist alliance, Dr. Salvador Allende.

In Brazil the Confederação de Obreros Católicos, founded in 1912, was replaced by the corporative union movement organized by the Estado Novo in 1935, which confined Catholic activity to workers' clubs.[35]

In Peru, during the thirties, there were many attempts among the Indians to organize by religious groups. The Centro Católico Obrero, in Cuzco, was one of the few results of this effort, which for the most part failed.

In Ecuador, during the twenties, Catholic unions were formed, with such names as Sociedad Cultural del Obrero and Sociedad del Señor de la Buena Esperanza. A Confederación Ecuatoriana de Obreros Católicos exists today.[36]

In Colombia there is a Catholic union movement headed by the Unión de Trabajadores Colombianos (UTC). Begun in 1946, it has attained an influence comparable to that of the Confederación de Trabajadores de Colombia.[37]

Christian unionism had its greatest and most rapid development in Costa Rica. A very modern archbishop, Monsignor Víctor Sanabria (1895–1952), trained several priests and Catholic young people in sociological study. The union federation Rerum Novarum, founded in 1920, played an important role in the 1948 revolution under the leadership of Father Benjamín Núñez (born 1918). Núñez was labor minister in José Figueres's revolutionary government, and proclaimed a series of social laws. He said: "We consider the human person and his sense of dignity fundamental. We [Catholics] have not worried enough about reaching any conclusions concerning Christ's social doctrine, and many have tried to combat any attempt at modifying the status quo."[38] The Rerum Novarum lost its impetus when it began dividing into factions, particularly when Monsignor Sanabria died in 1952 and was replaced by a conservative prelate.

In Mexico the Catholic social movement has been more important for its organizational than for its theoretical efforts. Catholic congresses were held to study social and agricultural problems; the necessity of combating rural poverty was emphasized, and means of stimulating the ownership of small holdings were discussed. The movement was not persecuted, but simply met with cold hostility by the government.

In 1896 the bishop of Querétaro, Don Francisco Banegas Galván, had written: "There is certainly no contract of slavery between the rich and the poor. But the fact of slavery exists more horribly than in the past, because it is veiled in an appearance of freedom. . . . Rich gentleman, there is no way out: either open thy heart to charity or be stripped of the wealth as Catholicism orders, and consider thy servants as thy brothers and sons of God, lightening their suffering, reducing their hours of work, and increasing their wages according to the charitable thinking of Leo XIII, or thou art agglomerating hatreds and animosity, and when the socialistic wind blows through Mexico, and perhaps it will soon blow, it will stir those waves which thou hast prepared and under their swift and powerful impact thy wealth and thy life shall be buried."[39]

Trinidad Sánchez Santos, a journalist and lecturer, was the most outstanding representative of Christian-democrat thinking in Mexico. He tried in his speeches and articles to apply the papal encyclicals to Mexican realities. In regard to the moral elevation of the peasant, he said: "I do not know how it is possible to attend school before or after fourteen hours of work and sun, and how it is possible to attend school on an empty stomach. I do not understand how it is possible to think of grammar without thinking first of a tortilla. There were no schools in the world before there were homes." In his speeches published as *La Iglesia y los indios* (1902) he defended the Church's attitude toward the Indians during the early colonial period, and fought for new and similar protective legislation for the Indian. In the newspaper he founded and edited, *El País,* he maintained that progress, work, and industry had failed to give Mexico well-being, because justice, "the real objective of the state," was lacking; and this lack was what had incited the Revolution. But political maneuverings had frustrated this revolutionary aim, and so he felt it necessary for Catholics to adopt a concrete social position, which should be supported by the church hierarchy: "The great fight of Christian democracy against Masonic socialism; of the workers' clubs against the tavern and exploitation; of the savings bank against poverty and prostitution; of marriage against the brothel."[40]

In 1903 the first Congreso Católico Mexicano agreed to organize workers' federations, asking parish priests to manage them and owners to protect them. It recommended that owners of rural lands, besides encouraging the religious education of their workers, abolish Sunday work, establish schools and charity groups, provide help for workers injured on the job, and establish savings institutions for workers. It also recommended that Church lawyers be appointed to look after "the protection of the interests of the Indians and the division among them of communal lands in a prudent and adequate manner." Catholic workers' associations with pawn shops, workers' mutual-aid societies, and study centers were founded; these generally requested a six-hour working day, a Sunday day of rest, the establishment of wage rates, and the prohibition of child labor.

In 1905 the association of Operarios Guadalupanos was founded; it brought together all the Catholic workers' societies and published *Restauración* and *Democracia Cristiana.* In 1908 its 20,000 members formed the Unión Catolíca Obrera, which in 1911 supported the Partido Católico. In 1912 the Confederación de Círculos Obreros Católicos was established, and around it were created many pawn shops, savings institutions, and social-service organizations. In January 1913 the Dieta Obrera de Zamora, summoned by the Confederación, stated a general objective: "to unite all our efforts to promote a fundamental reform in the present economic regime, in accordance with the principles stated in the Rerum Novarum encyclical."

In 1923 the first Jornada Social Obrera urged the foundation of agricultural unions and a savings and loan system. Small property-holders, sharecroppers, tenants, and day workers were all to form part of the agricultural unions. Each union was to arrange its mutual aid society, and if possible its cooperative. It was also recommended that "all social classes, in view of the distressing growth of socialism, must pursue prudent and energetic activities in the Catholic social organization, the only force capable of saving present-day society."

The Secretariado Social Mexicano was established in October 1920 at a meeting of Mexican bishops, and organized under the leadership of Alfredo Méndez Medina, S. J. The secretariat, according to Monsignor Mora y del Río, coordinated many kinds of activities carried out by the Church, not all of them strictly religious, in such a fashion that "under a common technical leadership and a uniform social orientation, the current of social anarchy can be counteracted." Immediately after the meeting the secretariat organized conferences "to decidedly affirm the right of the Church to intervene in the social organization of the working class." It also organized a campaign "in favor of the good and dignified bourgeoisie," as it called the middle class.

In 1922 the National Catholic Congress of Workers founded the Confederación Nacional Católica del Trabajo (CNCT); its motto was "Justice and Charity." The congress of the CNCT, the Liga Nacional Católica de la Clase Media, and the Liga Nacional Católica Campesina were created in 1925, only to lose influence during the religious conflicts of 1926 to 1929. In a pastoral letter of May 15, 1951, the Mexican episcopate insisted upon the usefulness of the Rerum Novarum organization as an agent for solving the social and economic problems of the country.[41]

In 1962 and 1963 the Christian-democratic labor movement adopted new tactics. Christian unions began organizing in areas where existing unions seemed impermeable to their influence. At times they formed trade or company unions, or regional unions, and in some cases national federations; or they rejuvenated old organizations. The real strength of these organizations is difficult to estimate. The Christian-democrat movement has become more radical in its union sector, especially in the sense of taking anti-U.S. positions; on the other hand, the movement supports the Peronist faction of the Argentinian CGT.[42] Its concepts are still vague, but its tactic seems concrete: it tries to keep to the left of all possible competitors.

THE COOPERATIVE MOVEMENT

The union movement was born, in many parts of Latin America, out of the mutual-aid societies. Later, in certain countries, the socialist parties or the unions themselves stimulated the organization of labor cooperatives. But the cooperative movement has not managed to acquire significant weight in the economy of any Latin American country, and it has almost never participated in Latin American social struggles.

The first Latin American cooperative—in the modern, technical sense of the word—was founded in Mexico on September 16, 1873, by tailors, members of the mutualist society Círculo Obrero de México. Argentina followed in 1899 when a few colonists in Pigüe, most of them French, established El Progreso Agrario, a cooperative to insure members against crop losses from hail. A consumers' cooperative, El Hogar Obrero, was also founded in Argentina in 1905; it is still in existence. In Brazil a strong movement to form cooperatives began early in the century in the states of Rio de Janeiro and Rio Grande do Sul. Credit cooperatives were founded in those states in 1908 and 1909, and were particularly strong in Rio Grande do Sul.

In the three countries mentioned, which to a certain extent could be considered pioneers of the Latin American cooperative movement, organization proceeded slowly during the first decade of the century. Beginning with the 1910 Revolution, Mexican cooperativism grew rapidly. The growth of unionism left its mark on Mexican cooperativism, at least in the laws governing it. According to these laws, cooperatives could draw members only from the working class; production cooperatives were forbidden to have salaried employees, and workers could form union consumers' cooperatives only if a cooperative's general assembly was the same as that of the union itself.

The consumer cooperatives of Chile and Uruguay, which admitted only members of a specific guild, also had mutualist antecedents. In several countries cooperativism spread in response to the economic effects of the depression, which suggested to governments the convenience of adopting legislative measures for the creation of institutions designed to improve living conditions. The Ley de Cooperativas de la República Argentina was proclaimed in December 1926; cooperative federations were founded in Argentina, Mexico, and Brazil in the 1920's; the Departamento de Cooperativas de Colombia was established in 1929; and in 1941 and 1943, laws were passed authorizing the creation of cooperative banks in Mexico and Brazil, respectively. (These two countries have the only cooperative banks in Latin America.)

Agricultural and cattle cooperatives have developed rapidly in Argentina, Brazil, and Mexico. In 1960 there were 1,748 such cooperatives in Argentina, with 482,944 members. The steady growth of Argentine agrarian cooperatives has come about largely through the efforts of federations. Outstanding among these is the Asociación de Cooperativas Argentinas, founded in 1926, which promoted construction of the first network of grain elevators in the country.

Brazil has the most extensive agrarian cooperative movement in Latin America, although it has fewer federations and a weaker industrial program than Argentina. In 1960 there were 1,555 agricultural cooperatives registered in the country; these were served by eight wholesale warehouses and nine federations with a total of 389,949 members. The movement is most diverse and vigorous in the state of Rio Grande do Sul, where the affluence of foreign immigrants (most of them German or Italian) and the number of small holdings have greatly favored it. In Rio Grande do Sul in 1960, cooperatives produced 46 per cent of the meat, 42 per cent of the wine, 25 per cent of the wool and rice, 18 per cent of the dairy products, and 10 per cent of the wheat, tobacco, and silk.

In Mexico in 1960 there were 1,040 agricultural cooperatives with 67,131 members. The development of these cooperatives in Mexico ran parallel to the agrarian reform movement. An interesting example of Mexico's agrarian-industrial cooperativism is its sugar-plantation cooperatives, which combine in their membership peasants, workers, and refinery employees.

Latin American agrarian cooperatives generally began by solving the peasants' most urgent problems, which often had to do with merchandizing their products, and later diversified to offer services of consumption and credit. In Argentina, as in the majority of Latin American countries, the movement toward personal credit cooperatives has been weak. Greater importance has been given to agricultural credit cooperatives, the Casas Regionales de Préstamos y Ahorro, financed by the Banco de la Nación Argentina. Brazil has made great efforts to provide agricultural credit through authentic cooperatives, financed exclusively by the efforts of their own members. It has managed to create a sturdy system, mainly in Rio Grande do Sul. In Cuba, after the foundation of the Banco de Fomento Agrícola e Industrial in 1950, rural credit associations began to be established; now, of course, the system has disappeared. Personal-credit cooperatives were formed in Chile and the Dominican Republic on the initiative of Catholic priests.

Consumer cooperativism has some special features. In countries like Chile and Uruguay, consumer cooperatives, owing to their mutualist antecedents, were organized on the basis of specific labor unions. Several years ago in Costa Rica the Junta Nacional de la Habitación initiated government housing projects which provided buildings for local consumer cooperatives.

Finally, it bears mentioning that in Latin America in 1961, for the first time anywhere, workers' production cooperatives (in Uruguay) obtained loans from an international banking organization (the Inter-American Development Bank) within the framework of the Alliance for Progress, which has also promoted and financed the first workers' bank, in Venezuela. In 1962, ORIT began a campaign to promote workers' cooperatives. This continental federation believes that there are vast underdeveloped segments of the Latin American economy in which cooperatives could usefully serve, without seriously competing with private enterprise. It believes, for instance, that no agrarian reform can be successful without the support of well-organized cooperatives. In the same fashion, the field of public housing welcomes cooperativist initiative in solving the housing problem, which becomes increasingly serious with the rapid urbanization of many Latin American countries. ORIT believes that consumer cooperativism cannot attain its objectives without simultaneously developing production cooperatives tied to union organizations.[43]

PART III

The Labor Movements

8. Latin America Unionism

OF THE MANY IDEOLOGIES that have influenced the Latin American labor movement, only populism has been a moving force in political and social life—but although the populist movement often had a hand in shaping workers' activities, it was not strictly proletarian in character. The Communist movement, by contrast, today has little appeal for the proletariat; and its support, drawn chiefly from intellectuals, students, and middle-class elements, is often only indirect.

The Latin American union movement, until now the chief avenue of expression for the working class, differs markedly from the union movements of Europe and the United States, as well as from those of the new nations of Africa and Asia. In some nations the union movement was an outgrowth of workers' cooperatives; in others it was the creation of the socialists, the anarcho-syndicalists, or the populists. But today, with few exceptions, the union movement is independent of the traditional labor ideologies, and seeks its own forms of organization and its own ideological concepts.[1]

EVOLUTION OF THE WORKINGMAN:
FROM ARTISAN TO PROLETARIAN

A century ago, the union movement had already begun to take form. But though the worker had in fact become a salaried employee, he retained the outlook of the artisan, a sense of personal initiative and social obligation, as well as certain empirical knowledge. Trades remained closed, accessible only to those who had fulfilled an apprenticeship. And though workingmen had surrendered the economic independence of their artisan fathers or grandfathers, they continued to nurture a sense of individualism, a sort of Jacobin spirit sustained by the concepts of the early theoreticians of the modern labor movement.

Unions emerged, in fact, as the product of two essential factors: the need to defend certain rights, rights that in many cases were simply vestiges of a social order already left behind; and the desire to preserve the integrity of the individual, within the unions but also in society as a whole. Thus, in its early years, Latin American unionism drew its impetus from ethical motives as well as from personal interests. And in effect, the unions spoke not only for the worker but for vast levels of society—for intellectuals, for the proletarized middle classes, and for many more. And to the extent the union movement demanded a better living standard, it spoke for all but a few. For two, perhaps three, generations this legacy of revolutionary spirit was transmitted intact from father to son. Thus, until World War I, unionism was infused with ideology. And although it varied from one country to the next, labor ideology bore a certain common thread, characterized as much by its negative aspects as by its positive features: dreams of a classless society, rooted in labor communities, were matched by congenital distrust of the parliamentary system and hostility toward the state. The tactical variations of the labor struggle were simply responses to differences in national psychology and revolutionary heritage.[2]

Moreover, industrialization itself was a kind of movement. Seen in historical perspective, its dynamism is exceptional—a constant self-transformation affecting the structure of every preexisting economic system. Because it has been an incomparable technical innovator, industrialism has also been history's greatest social innovator.

Early industry, preserving as it did the milieu of the artisan, was uncomplicated in its administration. And the artisan turned employee needed no special preparation for union leadership; he was qualified by his own professional tradition. At the same time, the messianic quality of the unions tended to bring forth the best elements of the working class—men who perceived themselves committed to a struggle that went beyond their companions in trade, to the cause of all workers, and even of all humanity.

But as its volume increased, industry began to attract a human mass lacking social traditions. The unskilled worker—cheap manpower without social roots—had no love for his trade. Nor did he share with the artisans the sense of personal independence deriving from the possession of professional knowledge and tools. The miserable living conditions that were the lot of the unskilled worker simply emphasized this distinction, and in an efficiently organized industrial system the unskilled laborer came gradually to predominate over the artisan, then finally, by the end of World War I, to replace him completely.

The worker trained in the barrenness of the new mass-production plants was socially and psychologically distinct from the worker of the early days of the labor movement. Understandably, the tendency of this new unskilled worker was to ask state protection, and, failing that, to seek help elsewhere, but to avoid, in any case, taking up his own cause. In Latin America, state protection was perhaps less likely than state harassment. Because the political parties were generally prepared to promise deliverance, the worker would turn to them when they seemed to have demonstrated sufficient strength to press for benefits or social reform. On other occasions, help was found in the union movement; the workers flocked to the unions en masse during periods of effective agitation, but abandoned them quite as quickly in the interims of state oppression.[3]

With the change in its human constituency, the union movement lost its messianic tone but increased its membership; and it also began to encounter problems only indirectly concerned with politics. The change had important consequences. For one thing, it established organized labor (after 1935 in the U.S., Europe, and Latin America, and after World War II throughout the rest of the world) as an integral element of economic and social life, a force to be reckoned with by governments and employers alike. For another thing, it demanded a new breed of union leaders, men vastly different in talents and training from the early union figures.

In the course of this transformation, the wage-earning middle class emerged—clerks, bureaucrats, lower-echelon technicians, and others who receive a salary for their work but whose labor is not directly involved with the production of goods. The new class drew upon elements of the working and peasant classes, and upon fragments of the middle class content to trade relative economic independence for the security of steady wages. But wages in the white-collar middle class were low compared with those of skilled workers, in marked contrast to the higher cultural aspirations of the white-collar workers. The reaction of this class to its plight was generally that of the unskilled worker—turning first to the state, then to other sources of protection.

Faced with the presence of these two burgeoning groups, the skilled workers—spiritual descendants of artisans and of the founders of the labor movement—gradually yielded their seats in the leadership of the union movement, and, finally, even their identity as a union faction. But until about 1935, when labor and industry began to recover from the 1929 economic crisis, only the skilled workers were capable of directing the affairs of unions, and coalescing groups of union militants into viable protest functions.

Throughout this period, important changes occurred in union organization. As their membership increased, the unions became organically less stable; the proportion of unskilled and white-collar workers shifted in response to external political, economic, and moral pressures. These were, in fact, no longer trade unions, but *industrial* unions. Negotiations with the state and with management began to entail administrative problems beyond the knowledge and training of union leaders. To be a competent worker, with a feeling for the duties and problems of other workers, and to have social aspirations and idealistic hopes were no longer sufficient qualifications for union leadership. Special prerequisites had evolved—not talents, but a certain broad awareness fed by careful study. Experience could no longer serve for documentation, nor could enthusiasm replace preparation. A new occupation had emerged, just as it already had in labor's participation in politics, a specialized occupation that for the moment would make do without apprenticeships or teachers.

To assure themselves of an adequate voice in local and national arbitration, the unions might have chosen to be represented by legal and social experts. But such men would have had scant knowledge of the working-man's life and little feeling for his problems and aspirations. The better choice was to draft from the ranks of the workingmen a man of broad interests, an economic and social turn of mind, and a talent for articulate and forcible expression—a rare bird, to be sure, with qualifications quite different from those of the early union leader, whose mandate had been to oppose, in principle, the entire social order. This new leader would be prepared not only to seek accommodations protecting the interests of the rank and file, but often to press actively for the socioeconomic integration of the working class into capitalistic society.

The unions were of course no longer espousing idealism. Their purpose now was not so much to reshape society as to improve the immediate lot of the worker; and their attainments emerged no longer from dramatic victories but from quiet, incessant pressure. The messianic role had been discarded, to be taken on by the political parties and other nonunionistic organizations.

SOME STATISTICS ON THE LATIN AMERICAN LABORING CLASS

In seeking to characterize the structure of industrial manpower in Latin America, some statistics, from among the few available, are useful. Tables 8.1 through 8.5, which present these statistics, need no comment.

SOME DISTINCTIVE FEATURES OF THE LABORING CLASS

It might also be useful, at this point, to single out the more distinctive features of Latin American unionism.

Perhaps most significant is the high rate of illiteracy among Latin American workers. More dangerous, in its connotations, is the fact that many even of the literates have had no instruction beyond primary reading. Thus, workers are indifferent to cultural tastes and pursuits, impervious to complex explanation, and suspicious of authority. Moreover, this abysmal educational level promotes dissent among the rank and file, encourages the creation of castes of more educated workers, broadens the range of salaries, and undermines the solidarity of the unions.

Most industrial workers are of peasant origin, and in periods of mass unemployment or forced walkouts, many return to their villages, where they are assured at least of a roof and food, wretched as these may be. In not a few areas the unskilled worker walks off the job to attend prolonged fiestas in his village, or to help with the harvest. These random absences produce random fluctuations in manpower—as well as in union funds and membership—and seriously erode all efforts toward worker education and technical training.

The peasant mentality—isolation, suspicion, indifference to social questions and to culture—persists in the urban worker. Alcoholism, drug addiction, and family instability are brought on principally by the peasant's profound inability to adapt to urban life and work. The worker commonly finds himself relinquishing the satisfactions of the small workshop for the sake of industrialized mass production, a transition likely to erode his personal integrity and to impair his attitude toward the union and his behavior in general.

There are few women in industry, but many children work, generally

TABLE 8.1. GROWTH OF THE AGRICULTURAL AND NONAGRICULTURAL SEGMENTS OF THE LABOR FORCE IN LATIN AMERICA

Segment of Population	Labor Force by Years (Thousands of Workers and Percentages)				
	1925	1945	1950	1955	1975 (predicted)
Economically Active Population	32,800	46,800	53,100	59,900	97,400
Agricultural Workers:					
Total	20,800	26,300	28,200	30,400	35,500
Percentage	63.4	56.2	53.0	50.7	36.4
Nonagricultural Workers:					
Total	12,000	20,500	24,900	29,500	61,900
Percentage	36.6	43.8	47.0	49.3	53.6

Source: *Situação Social da América Latina,* Rio de Janeiro, 1965.

TABLE 8.2. LABOR FORCE, BY FIELDS OF ACTIVITY, IN 18 LATIN AMERICAN COUNTRIES

			Distribution of Workers by Field of Activity (Per Cent)								
Country	Reference Year	Total Workers (Thousands)	Agriculture and Forestry	Mining and Quarrying	Manufacturing Industries	Construction	Public Utilities	Commerce	Transportation and Communication	Services	Unclassified
Mexico	1960	11,332	53.3	1.2	13.7	3.6	0.4	9.5	3.2	13.5	0.7
Costa Rica	1963	400	48.9	0.3	11.3	5.5	1.1	10.1	3.5	17.2	2.2
El Salvador	1961	807	60.2	—	12.5	4.2	0.2	6.2	2.1	13.5	1.0
Honduras	1961	568	66.7	0.3	7.7	2.0	0.1	4.8	1.4	12.2	4.6
Nicaragua	1963	477	59.4	0.9	11.7	3.6	0.3	7.5	2.4	14.2	0.2
Panama	1960	337	46.2	0.2	7.6	4.3	0.5	9.1	3.0	20.1	9.2
Cuba	1953	1,972	41.5	0.5	16.5	3.3	0.4	11.8	5.3	20.1	0.5
Dominican Republic	1950	826	56.5	—	10.3	2.4	0.2	5.0	1.5	8.3	19.2
Haiti	1950	1,747	83.2	—	4.9	0.6	—	3.5	0.4	4.6	2.7
Argentina	1960	7,599	19.3	0.6	25.2	5.6	1.1	11.9	6.3	20.0	6.2
Bolivia	1950	1,361	71.6	3.2	8.1	1.9	3.1	4.2	1.6	5.1	—
Brazil	1950	17,117	57.8	2.8	13.0	*	*	6.3	4.1	15.8	0.3
Chile	1960	2,389	27.7	3.8	18.0	5.6	0.8	10.1	—	4.9	6.2
Ecuador	1962	1,484	56.6	0.2	14.1	3.2	0.2	6.2	2.8	13.2	3.4
Paraguay	1950	437	53.8	—	15.6	2.9	0.1	6.9	2.2	15.5	2.8
Peru	1961	3,125	49.8	2.1	13.2	3.4	0.3	9.0	3.0	15.3	3.2
Uruguay	1963	1,016	17.9	0.2	20.7	4.8	1.7	13.0	6.1	27.4	8.0
Venezuela	1961	2,407	32.1	1.9	12.3	5.3	1.1	12.6	4.4	23.8	6.4

Source: UN, *Demographic Yearbook 1964*, Table 9; UN, *Demographic Yearbook 1956*, Table 12. Table here is an abridgment of Table 36 of *Statistical Abstract of Latin America, 1965*, Norris B. Lyle and Richard A. Calman, Eds. (Latin American Center, University of California, Los Angeles), pp. 56–57.

* Included in preceding column.

TABLE 8.3. LABOR FORCE, BY PRINCIPAL SECTORS OF THE ECONOMY, AND GROSS PRODUCT PER INHABITANT, IN 21 LATIN AMERICAN NATIONS, 1960

Country	Gross Product per Inhabitant, 1960 (U.S. Dollars)	Distribution of Workers by Field of Activity (Per Cent)*								Employment Ratio: Services to Industry
		Primary Production			Industry			Services	Unclassified	
		Total	Agriculture	Mining	Total	Manufacturing	Construction			
Latin America	±250	54.1	53.1	1.1	18.2	14.5	3.7	25.3	2.4	1.39
Venezuela	400	43.8	41.2	2.6	15.5	10.1	5.4	32.3	8.4	2.08
Argentina	400	25.2	24.7	0.5	29.0	22.9	6.1	43.7	2.3	1.51
Uruguay	400	21.8	21.7	0.1	28.1	23.8	4.3	46.4	3.7	1.65
Cuba	300–400	44.2	43.8	0.4	18.3	15.6	2.7	36.6	0.9	2.00
Chile	300–400	34.6	29.8	4.8	24.0	18.5	5.5	37.6	3.8	1.56
Costa Rica	250–300	56.7	56.4	0.3	14.7	10.6	4.1	25.7	2.9	1.75
Panama	250–300	55.0	54.9	0.1	9.7	7.1	2.6	25.7	9.6	2.65
Mexico	200–250	59.0	57.8	1.2	14.8	12.0	2.8	21.8	4.4	1.48
Colombia	200–250	57.9	56.4	1.5	17.5	14.4	3.1	21.1	3.5	1.21
Brazil	200–250	61.8	61.1	0.7	16.7	12.8	3.9	21.2	0.3	1.27
Guatemala	150–200	74.9	74.8	0.1	10.3	8.3	2.0	11.6	3.2	1.12
Dominican Republic	150–200	69.7	69.7	0.0	10.8	8.1	2.7	17.5	2.0	1.62
Honduras	150–200	76.4	75.7	0.7	9.3	7.4	1.9	11.0	3.3	1.17
El Salvador	150–200	64.4	64.2	0.2	13.9	11.1	2.8	18.5	3.2	1.34
Nicaragua	100–150	70.6	69.7	0.9	13.2	10.7	2.5	16.2	—	1.23
Peru	100–150	60.2	59.8	1.4	18.4	15.5	2.9	19.6	1.8	1.06
Ecuador	100–150	51.3	50.9	0.4	25.3	23.1	2.2	19.1	4.3	0.76
Paraguay	Less than 100	59.1	58.3	0.8	17.5	14.8	2.7	20.8	2.6	1.18
Bolivia	Less than 100	67.5	63.3	4.2	13.2	10.7	2.5	18.4	0.9	1.40
Haiti	Less than 100	77.4	77.4	0.0	7.4	6.6	0.8	11.5	3.7	1.56

Source: *Situação Social da América Latina*, Rio de Janeiro, 1965, p. 391.
* In many cases, percentages do not total 100; source gives no explanation for discrepancies.

TABLE 8.4. TOTAL WAGES VS. NATIONAL INCOME IN TEN LATIN AMERICAN COUNTRIES

Country	Year	National Income (Local Currency) (Millions)	Total Wages Value in National Currency	Total Wages Per Cent of National Income
Argentina	1960	626,006 pesos	317,333	50.7
Brazil	1959	1,403,900 cruzeiros	665,100	47.4
Colombia	1960	21,882 pesos	9,133	41.9
Costa Rica	1960	2,245 colones	1,358	60.5
Cuba	1958	2,219 pesos	1,408	63.5
Ecuador	1960	11,697 sucres	6,290	53.8
Honduras	1958	615.5 lempiras	299.2	48.6
Panama	1960	366.5 balboas	253.6	69.2
Peru	1959	32,749 soles	13,050	39.8
Puerto Rico	1960	1,464.7 dollars	988.6	67.5
United States	1962	450,339 dollars	324,531	72.1

Source: *Situação Social da América Latina,* Rio de Janeiro, 1965.

TABLE 8.5. DISPOSITION OF INCOME BY WAGE EARNERS IN NINE
LATIN AMERICAN COUNTRIES

Country	Food	Clothing	Housing	Fuel	Habitation & Services	Others
Brazil	54.12	10.56	15.33	4.41	19.74	15.58
Colombia	65.70	5.40	16.20	5.80	22.00	6.90
Costa Rica	49.63	10.69	25.38	8.25	33.63	6.05
Chile	45.00	15.00	20.00	7.50	27.50	12.50
Guatemala	57.30	9.10	15.20	6.20	21.40	12.20
Mexico	76.02	11.38	—		12.60	12.60
Peru	55.00	12.00	18.00	—	18.00	15.00
Dominican Republic	39.02	16.19	26.44	2.37	28.81	15.98
Uruguay	59.68	6.10	12.00	—	12.00	22.22

Where "Component Items in Cost-of-Living Index (Per Cent)" spans Food, Clothing, Housing, Fuel, Habitation & Services, Others.

Source: *Situação Social da América Latina,* Rio de Janeiro, 1965, p. 341.

in violation of child-labor laws; such children emerge as workers lacking even a minimal education.

There is a general lack of interest in social problems, and in any case a paucity of reference sources on these problems (journals, libraries, books, conferences, workers' centers), in almost all Latin American countries.

These features of the Latin American union movement set it clearly apart from the movements of the United States and Europe. The experience of foreign labor movements is of course a ripe harvest for study, but any programmatic application would have to be adapted to the Latin American reality. A more slavish rendering would prove sterile, even disruptive.

STAGES IN THE HISTORY OF LATIN AMERICAN UNIONISM

In Latin America, there have been three great periods of labor agitation, with demarcations roughly at the 1929 economic crisis and the outbreak of World War II. The first period was brought on not only by miserable living conditions but also by the tradition of political *caciquismo,* which led, in practice, to suppression of the right to vote. (In Brazil, for example, in 1926, when the population of the country was 26 million, the winning candidate in the presidential election drew 290,000 votes.) With traditional means of protest driven to cover, only violence and direct action remained. This was the heyday of anarcho-syndicalism, the time of the massive general strike.

The second wave of agitation, following the 1929 economic crisis, was felt throughout Latin America as prices of raw materials plummeted and exports declined. Workers who had seen some small improvement in living standards—thanks in part to union action and in part to alliances with the middle classes—now found themselves, almost universally, under dictatorships, the avenues to political action once again sealed off. The period saw widespread strikes, revolutions (e.g., the emergence of a socialist republic in Chile), repressions (e.g., the slaughter of peasants in El Salvador), and great mass movements.

The third period, from World War II down to the present, has been a time of both disillusionments and rising hopes. Industrialization was to have provided for the increase in manpower brought on by increasing rates of population growth. But the facts have often proved otherwise: in many countries, the workers have been left in the backwash of dramatic expansions in industrialization. Where the middle classes have taken an interest in political life and in the progress of the labor movement, democratic reforms have begun to come about; where they have not, demagoguery has taken the place of protest.[4]

Social unrest persisted during World War II. In spite of CTAL (Confederatión de Trabajadores de América Latina) admonishments to labor to stay on the job, strikes broke out frequently—especially against cost-of-living increases, the most inciteful of which were increases in urban transportation rates. More and more frequently, governments resorted to the militia for breaking strikes and scattering demonstrations. This practice, "justified" by the exigencies of war, continued after war's end, and in many countries became habitual. Strikes were of course more frequent in countries suffering inflation; but it is a curious fact that in those countries the unions had no program for solving national problems and curbing inflation, but on the contrary demanded increases each time the purchasing power of the monetary unit suffered a decline.

The labor movement emerged from World War II weakened, divided, and disillusioned, its idealism and its role as social reformer largely dissipated. In several countries, management took upon itself the task of pressing for such measures as social security and workmen's compensation, by way of averting the threat of strikes and heading off incipient revolutions. In many cases, governments affirmed civil rights by proclamation. The unions, in the meantime, simply failed to keep pace with the advance of industrialization into new processes and new technologies—to the inevitable detriment of effective union action.

In the years following the war, the unions looked for the establishment of continental industrial federations, but the federations failed to materialize. Not until the professional secretariats of ICFTU (International Confederation of Free Trade Unions) dispatched organizers to Latin America were international contacts established between counterpart unions in comparable industries. And when ORIT (Organización Regional Interamericana de Trabajadores, of ICFTU) entered a period of crisis, in 1959–60, many of these contacts were maintained only via international secretariats.[5] In 1961, roughly half of the extant union organizations still remained unaffiliated with international or continental union federations, either because they found themselves in the hands of dictatorships or because their members were unwilling.[6]

The union movement in fact took little part in the economic and social transformations occurring after the war. In 1946, a labor expert could write: "The union movement is well aware it will not be asked to participate in the reshaping of hemispheric economic relations. Plans for this process are of course still tentative, but it is already apparent that countless programs—such as those for investments and for the use of agricultural surpluses—will have been drawn up *for* the union movement but not *with the cooperation* of the union movement. In the structure gradually taking form, there is not a single representative of the Latin American labor movement. Unless labor is given a suitable share in the planning, the future of democracy in Latin America would appear to be bleak."[7]

The socialist parties of Latin America have divided over the issue of Castroism—some favoring Castro, others critical of the Cuban Revolution's acquiescence to Communism, though most agree that the revolution was justified. Castroism has provoked schisms in the populist parties, and has even made inroads into anarcho-syndicalist groups; but pro-Castro feeling in the unions is minimal. Only in Venezuela has Communism been active; there the CTV (Confederación de Trabajadores de Venezuela) even signed a pact of friendship with the CTC (its Cuban counterpart), which was, however, broken in 1960 after Castroites and Venezuelan Communists began a campaign of terror against the democratic governments and attempted to seize CTV leadership. Though the Latin American union movement is sympathetic with Cuba's right to rebellion, it does not consider Fidel Castro's regime to be either a natural or defensible expression of that right.[8]

It would be interesting to know the numerical strength of the union movement, but neither governments nor unions have concerned themselves with gathering the relevant statistics. Such figures as are available are given in Table 8.6, for the years 1946 and 1960.[9]

TABLE 8.6. UNION MEMBERSHIP IN 20 LATIN AMERICAN COUNTRIES, 1946 AND 1960

Country	Number of Members (Thousands)	
	1946	1960
Latin America	3,765	6,640
Argentina	500	2,500
Bolivia	70	100
Brazil	500	1,000
Colombia	150	150
Costa Rica	30	25
Cuba*	300	800
Chile	350	300
Ecuador	75	75
El Salvador	—	25
Guatemala	50	15
Haiti*	15	10
Honduras	—	25
Mexico	1,000	1,000
Nicaragua	25	25
Panama	25	15
Paraguay*	25	25
Peru	350	200
Dominican Republic	25	25
Uruguay	75	75
Venezuela	200	250

Sources: Robert J. Alexander: *Labour Movements in Latin America* (material for 1946); "Algunas características generales del movimiento obrero latinoamericano," from *Política*, Caracas, June–July 1961 (material for 1960).
* Unions are appendages of dictatorial regimes.

SOCIAL LEGISLATION

Social legislation in Latin America was the product not of the labor movement but of revolutionary and democratic processes, and occasionally even of demagogic dictatorships. But without the labor movement, without its protest and heroics, its struggles and triumphs and failures, social legislation would not have emerged, or would have taken a different form.[10]

Let us review briefly the history of social legislation in Latin America, inasmuch as it bears heavily on the history of the union movement.

Civil rights were first constitutionally guaranteed in Mexico, in 1917; then in Chile, 1925; Peru, 1933; Honduras, 1936; Brazil, 1937; Paraguay and Cuba, 1940; Dominican Republic and Uruguay, 1942; Bolivia, Colombia, and Guatemala, 1945; Panama, Ecuador, and Haiti, 1946; Venezuela, 1947; Nicaragua, 1948; Argentina and Costa Rica, 1949; and El Salvador, 1950. In some cases, these guarantees emerged in consequence of revolutionary processes; in others, from the desire of dictators to appear democratic; and occasionally even from normal legislative evolution.

Acceptance of the idea of social security often begins with the passage of laws concerning occupational hazards. Workmen's compensation is now assured by law in every Latin American nation—in Guatemala, since 1906; El Salvador and Peru, 1911; Argentina, Colombia, and Venezuela, 1915; Chile, Cuba, and Panama, 1916; Mexico, 1917; Brazil, 1919; Uruguay, 1920; Bolivia, 1924; Costa Rica, 1925; Paraguay, 1927; Ecuador, 1928; Nicaragua, 1930; Dominican Republic, 1932; Honduras, 1936, and Haiti, 1938.

Argentina, Brazil, Cuba, and Uruguay, early in this century, began to assemble programs for social security, grouping together the risks of incapacitation, old age, and death, first for public officials and later for workers in the various trades. Later, the tendency was toward broader programs, toward incorporation into a single law of all, or most, of the protection measures. Unified social security, in Latin America, began in Chile in 1924 (though each Chilean trade was assigned its own system), followed by Ecuador, in 1935; Peru, 1936; Venezuela, 1940; Panama and Costa Rica, 1941; Mexico, 1942; Paraguay, 1943; Colombia and Guatemala, 1946; Dominican Republic, 1947; Bolivia, El Salvador, and Haiti, 1949; Honduras, 1954; and Nicaragua, 1955. The governments of Argentina, in 1953, and Brazil, in 1954, took steps toward unified social security legislation.

Several contingencies are covered by unified social security in every Latin America nation; these include illness, childbirth, incapacitation, old-age retirement, and death. On the other hand, only a few systems (those of Costa Rica, Ecuador, El Salvador, Honduras, Mexico, Nicaragua, and Venezuela) furnish unemployment insurance, and family subsidies are almost nonexistent. Where occupational hazards are concerned, the laws vary. Some laws (those of Bolivia, Colombia, Ecuador, El Salvador, Haiti, Honduras, Mexico, Nicaragua, Paraguay, and Venezuela) have subsumed workmen's compensation within the provisions of social security. In other countries (Costa Rica, Chile, Peru, Panama, and the Dominican Republic), benefits for on-the-job accidents and work-incurred illnesses are not included in the general system. In Mexico, social security has recently begun to extend to the peasantry.[11]

In several countries, the law accords workers a share in corporate profits, but the law is almost never enforced. In Mexico, as of 1964, the constitutional precept approved in 1917 had only begun to be practiced. In Bolivia, Colombia, Peru, and Venezuela, gratuities and premiums are issued in place of profit shares. In Chile, an annual percentage is paid in place of regular shares. In Ecuador and Brazil, profit sharing is established by law but has never been applied. In Argentina, certain firms voluntarily concede a sort of employee participation.[12]

Tables 8.7 through 8.9 reflect the volume of Latin American social security systems.

TABLE 8.7. CONTRIBUTORS TO SOCIAL SECURITY COMPARED WITH ECONOMICALLY ACTIVE POPULATION IN 17 LATIN AMERICAN COUNTRIES, 1959

| | | Contributors to Social Security | |
Country	Economically Active Population (Thousands)	Persons Contributing (Thousands)	Per Cent of Economically Active Population
Mexico	10,151	1,293	12.0
Costa Rica	379	86	22.7
Guatemala	1,208	258	21.4
Nicaragua	450	25	5.6
Panama	340	70	20.6
El Salvador	880	32	3.6
Dominican Republic	1,117	200	17.9
Argentina	8,314	3,831	46.1
Bolivia	1,498	119	7.9
Brazil	21,453	4,934	23.0
Chile	2,519	1,540	61.1
Colombia*	4,476	380	8.5
Ecuador*	1,511	145	9.7
Paraguay*	501	66	13.2
Peru*	3,810	559	14.7
Uruguay†	1,083	793	73.2
Venezuela	2,233	328	14.7

Source: *Situação Social da América Latina,* Rio de Janeiro, 1965.
* 1958 figures.
† Figures for six social security institutions.

TABLE 8.8. SOURCES OF SOCIAL SECURITY FUNDS IN 17 LATIN AMERICAN
COUNTRIES, 1959

| | Contributions (Per Cent) | | | |
Country	From Insured	From Employers	From State	From Other Sources
Mexico	24.9	49.7	17.7	7.6
Costa Rica	33.8	35.9	18.2	12.1
Guatemala	30.3	68.0	—	1.7
Nicaragua	16.0	50.0	31.8	2.2
Panama	35.4	33.6	6.9	24.1
El Salvador	25.0	48.9	24.9	1.2
Dominican Republic	24.7	49.7	11.8	14.1
Argentina	39.8	49.8	0.1	10.3
Bolivia	16.7	56.9	23.4	3.0
Brazil	27.8	26.0	25.2	21.0
Chile*	24.1	47.4	12.6	15.9
Colombia†	28.1	58.7	7.4	5.8
Ecuador†	29.7	35.8	1.7	32.8
Paraguay†	29.3	53.5	7.4	9.8
Peru†	28.5	54.9	14.4	2.2
Uruguay‡	27.6	34.2	0.8	37.4
Venezuela§	29.3	48.4	18.2	4.1

Source: *Situação Social da América Latina,* Rio de Janeiro, 1965.
* Funds from Social Security Service for 1950 plus other Social Security Institution funds for 1956.
† 1958 figures.
‡ Figures from Retirement and Pension Fund for University Professors; Retirement and Pension Fund for Citizens and Students; Montevideo Jockey Club Fund for Retirement, Pension and Subsidy; Industry and Commerce Retirement and Pension Fund; and Notarial Fund for Retirement and Pensions.
§ Figures from Venezuelan Institute of Social Security and Institute for Aid and Social Welfare of the Ministry of Education.

LABOR LEGISLATION

In 1961, the majority of Latin American countries had not signed ILO (International Labor Organization) conventions 87 and 98, which guarantee to labor the right to organize. Most countries, in fact, still prohibited unionizing of officials, and several countries prohibited the unionizing of peasants. In 1961, ILO reported that of the 116 international labor agreements then current, Cuba had approved of 64; Uruguay, 57; Argentina, 56; Mexico, 47; Chile, 36; Guatemala, 34; Nicaragua, 30; Brazil, 29; Peru, 26; Colombia, 25; Dominican Republic, 22; Venezuela, 19; Costa Rica, 17; Panama and Honduras, 11; Bolivia and Ecuador, 6; El Salvador, 4; and the others, none.

TABLE 8.9. DISPOSITION OF SOCIAL SECURITY FUNDS IN 19 LATIN AMERICAN
COUNTRIES, 1959

Country*	Disposition of Funds (Per Cent)				
		Benefits		Administra-tive Expen-ditures	Other Expendi-tures
	Total	In Services	In Cash		
Mexico	75.6	57.6	18.0	23.0	1.4
Costa Rica	74.7	54.3	20.4	19.6	5.6
Guatemala	80.6	49.0	31.6	19.4	—
Nicaragua	80.7	70.1	10.6	19.3	—
Panama	86.5	49.2	37.3	11.6	1.9
El Salvador	72.9	59.1	13.8	14.3	12.8
Cuba	92.9	—	—	6.6	0.6
Haiti	70.9	35.2	35.7	29.0	0.1
Dominican Republic	52.2	48.8	3.4	21.8	26.1
Argentina	95.6	—	95.6	3.8	0.6
Bolivia	59.5	32.0	27.5	8.7	31.9
Brazil	79.0	13.8	65.2	15.3	5.8
Chile	86.5	10.6	75.9	12.6	0.9
Colombia	88.3	61.6	26.7	8.4	3.3
Ecuador	65.4	—	—	—	34.6
Paraguay	81.7	67.3	14.4	18.3	—
Peru	90.6	—	—	7.8	1.7
Uruguay	93.1	1.2	91.9	5.8	1.2
Venezuela	85.6	70.0	15.6	12.7	1.7

Source: *Situação Social da América Latina*, Rio de Janeiro, 1965.
* Because detailed information is lacking for some countries, some percentages are not strictly comparative: figures are for 1959, except those of Colombia (1958), Cuba (1954–55), Chile (1957), Ecuador (1960), and Haiti (1953–54). Moreover, some figures have been rounded off.

But labor codes have been enacted in almost every Latin American nation. These codes have two purposes where the unions are concerned: to guarantee to labor the right to organize; and to government certain controls, both over procedures for contracting labor and over labor organizations themselves.

In almost every Latin American country, the structure and activities of the unions are subject to government supervision. Unions must be recognized by the government if they are to take part in official mediation and conciliation proceedings and sign collective contracts. In some cases, labor and management must submit to arbitration before government-appointed conciliation boards; in others, arbitration is optional. Union constitutions must be approved by the government. All union meetings in which officials are elected or a strike vote is taken must be attended by a government labor inspector. In some countries, the government reserves the right to veto the election of union officials if the winning ticket fails to satisfy the perceived provisions of the labor code. Generally, certain restrictions are put on the use of union funds; political contributions, for example, are usually prohibited. Strikes are sanctioned by the state only when they have been declared in the manner required by law. In Mexico, when a strike is sanctioned, management must shut down all affected facilities until the dispute is settled.

But the actual exercise of these measures depends to a considerable extent on the party in power: a government sympathetic to labor executes the code more heavily against employers than against unions; when a conservative regime comes to power, the effect is reversed.[18]

9. Argentina

THE LABOR MOVEMENT in Argentina has had a complex history. The anarcho-syndicalist unions, which predominated initially, were succeeded by socialist unions, and in turn by apolitical organizations that paved the way for Peronist influence. Generally, labor federations with differing ideologies existed simultaneously, often as a result of divisions that produced rival federations with identical names. Because it would be tedious and probably not very useful to recount the details of these internal struggles, we shall examine only the major trends of Argentine unionism, dwelling only on the more significant moments in the workers' struggle.

In 1840 there were no factories of any kind in Buenos Aires. By 1845, however, steam machinery had been introduced, and by 1853 there were already 746 workshops, 106 factories, and 3,008 business concerns in the city. In 1857 the first railroad began operation with about seven miles of track. In the same year the country was opened to immigration, and by 1900 more than 1.5 million people had entered Argentina. During that period, the capital acquired a refrigeration industry, department stores, breweries, tobacco processing plants, furniture factories, and in 1897, its first electric trolley.

Industry increased in size and concentration, as well as in diversity. The 852 factories and workshops in Buenos Aires in 1853 employed only 1,500 workers, an average of 1.77 per establishment. By 1895 there were 8,439 establishments and 72,761 workers, an average of 8.06 employees per establishment. In 1913 these figures were 10,275 establishments, 149,289 workers, and an average of 14.5; and in 1932 there were 11,323 establishments and 255,000 workers, for an average of 22.8.

Wages were relatively high during this period of growth—although in 1890, during a serious economic crisis, the purchasing power of wages dropped considerably. At the turn of the century the working day was ten hours, but 30 per cent of the labor force worked 11, even 14, hours a day, and only 4 per cent enjoyed an eight-hour day.[1]

The *conchabo* practice was widespread in mid-century, especially in the countryside. Under this system the worker signed a practically unbreakable contract; his employer, on the other hand, could fire him at any time, without compensation. At the time of signing, the worker received a "conchabo booklet" that noted purchases made through the employer; until he liquidated these debts with his salary he was not permitted to leave the job. Workers' groups, and even the bourgeois press, condemned this practice so energetically that by the end of the nineteenth century it had been abolished.[2]

EARLY EFFORTS TO ORGANIZE

In 1857, Argentina's first mutual-aid associations appeared; the shoemakers' in San Crispín and the printers' in Buenos Aires. In 1864, workers' and artisans' societies were founded. And in 1871 the printers' mutual-aid society became the first to concern itself with defending the trade's interests, opening relations with Barcelona unions. In that year the society's president, Juan M. P. Méndez, closed his annual report with the comment, "We persevere in order that through economic equality, integrated education, and the universal free federation of workers', agricultural, and industrial associations, the motto 'Liberty, Equality, and Fraternity' can come to stand as truth in any country."[3]

The printers' union (Unión Tipográfica), founded in 1878, was absorbed the following year by the Tipográfica Bonaerense. By then it was already a true union. The same could be said of many others: the Internacional de Carpinteros, Ebanistas, y Anexos, founded in 1885; the bakers' union, founded in 1880; the masons', hatters', and German printers' unions, all founded in 1890. The organization in 1887 of La Fraternidad, a union of railroad engineers and firemen, was stimulated by the visits of a delegation of U.S. railroad workers in 1885 and 1886.[4]

In 1878 the first strike occurred in Buenos Aires, when the printers demanded a ten-hour working day in summer and a twelve-hour day in winter. The strike, which failed, was described by *El Nacional* as "an extraordinary and indefensible protest by the workers.... To comply with their demands would have been to abandon all rules governing labor." The shoemakers struck in 1887, and the railroad workers of Tucumán, Córdoba, Panamá, Tolosa, and Sola in 1891. There were nine strikes in 1894, 19 in 1895, and 26 in 1896.[5]

In all these strikes, wage increases were demanded. But beginning in

1894 the demand for a shorter working day became widespread.[6] Moreover, Argentine industry remained hostile toward unions. One factory's internal regulations called for a fine of four pesos to be levied on anyone caught speaking of union organization.[7]

THE FIRST FEDERATIONS

On May Day, 1890, several socialist groups and workingmen's societies founded an International Labor Committee (Comité Internacional Obrero), which in turn created the first Argentine labor federation. The statutes approved by the Committee and the member groups referred to the new organization as the Federación de Trabajadores de la Región Argentina, but it was later known by various other names—Federación Obrera Argentina, Federación de Obreros de la República Argentina, and Federación de Trabajadores de la República Argentina.[8] The Federation journal, *El Obrero,* was edited by the German geologist Germán Ave Lallement, who tried to analyze Argentine conditions by means of a rather schematic Marxism.

In June 1890 the International Labor Committee delivered to the Secretariat of the Chamber of Deputies a petition with 7,432 signatures, containing the following demands: a maximum working day of eight hours for adults; prohibition of child labor under 14 years of age, and a reduction of the working day to six hours for boys and girls 14 to 18 years old; abolition of night work for women and children under 18; an uninterrupted weekly rest period of 36 hours; an end to piecework pay, and of jobs obtained through bids; thorough inspection of shops and factories by government officials; strict control of the manufacture and sale of food and beverages, with penalties for manufacturers who adulterated their products; obligatory accident insurance for workers, at the expense of the state and the employers; the creation of special courts for the arbitration of labor disputes, costs to be borne by the government. Two years later the petition was filed in the Chamber; it was never so much as studied.[9]

Later in 1890, in a petition to the President of the Republic, appealing for protective legislation for labor and the nullification of consumers' taxes, the Federación asked for "a system of progressive, free-exchange, direct taxes, full universal suffrage, naturalization of the foreign-born so that all citizens might benefit from the legislation, and broader 'self-government' for municipalities."

In 1891, *El Obrero* pointed to the injustice of the fiscal system: "On gin, for example, the workingman's drink, a tax of 30 centavos per liter is levied. Since a case of gin usually sells for 5.5 pesos, of which 3.6 pesos is the tax, the taxation rate is 190 per cent. Champagne, on the other hand, pays only 25 centavos' tax per liter; a case sells for 63 pesos, of which 3 pesos is the tax—only 5 per cent."

The federation's first congress met in 1891, but no program was approved until the second congress in 1892. The program stated that "the aims of the Federación Obrera Argentina are the following: (1) exercise of political power by the working classes; (2) transfer of private or corporate ownership of production facilities to collective, social, or common ownership (that is, the socialization of industry); (3) organization of society as an economic federation; (4) international standardization and regulation of production; (5) equality of the vote; and (6) equal welfare for all."[10] Opposition and circumstance forced a quick end—the anarchists launched an intense propaganda campaign against the Federación, several member societies quit payment of dues, and an economic crisis forced the emigration of many workers—with the result that the Federación disbanded.

In July 1894, delegates from various workers' societies met to create a new federation. A program very much like that of the earlier federation was drafted, but was never adopted; the workers found it more appropriate for a political party than for a union organization. Nevertheless, in August, the new Federación Obrera Argentina was created; but the working class responded with apathy and the anarchists with invective, and by the end of 1895 the second attempt had failed.

In 1896, several unions managed to reestablish the Federación for a third try. During the winter of 1897 the country suffered a serious economic crisis brought on by droughts, falling prices on cattle and agricultural products, monetary instability, and black-marketing of gold. Unemployment and poverty were widespread. Faced with this situation the new Federación called the jobless to a rally "to protest government policy and demand that the government provide jobs." This proved to be the final act of the third federation.

The fourth attempt was effectively stillborn. Early in 1900 a rally on behalf of labor legislation called for the merger of all workers' societies in a common organization. A commission was designated, and a plan of action was drafted; but many societies chose not to join the proposed association, and it was abandoned.

The weekly La Organización, edited by the socialist painter Alfredo Pasqualetti, appeared on the initiative of the carpenters' society, in January 1901. The strong positions taken by the paper stimulated a new attempt to unify labor, and a meeting of delegates from 14 societies agreed to hold a congress. In May 1901, the congress took place; from the outset it was rent by disputes between socialist and anarchist factions, the anarchists seeking to goad the congress toward direct action and the general strike. The congress agreed to commit itself neither to socialism nor to anarchism, nor, for that matter, to any other political orientation. But nothing came of these efforts.

STRIKES AND OPPRESSION

Several major strikes were called in 1902. The first, initiated by workers of the central fruit market in Buenos Aires, spread to the interior of the country. To halt the movement, the government declared a state of siege, broke into workers' locals, jailed workers, and seized their newspapers. From that moment, the government declared a state of siege each time a social protest movement gained momentum. This was to happen five times in the next eight years.

Labor protest reached a peak in March 1902: jointing-plane workers gained their demands in a minor strike; the bakers of Chivilcoy lost a strike that lasted 24 days; copper workers and mechanics in Buenos Aires won a nine-hour working day; and a strike by Rosario dockworkers became a citywide general strike. In November the Buenos Aires dockworkers, whose organization counted more than 3,000 members, won a salary increase and an improvement in working conditions without resorting to strikes. In 1903 and 1904 there were two general strikes and several industrial strikes. A new wave of walkouts began in 1905 and continued until May 1910.

Many of the strikes were against particular industrial firms; the general strikes were in protest against the high cost of living, especially the excessive rental fees, and were frequently political in nature, directed against government repression.[11]

In November 1902 the National Congress approved the so-called residence law, which granted broad executive power for the deportation of aliens who had been convicted of crimes by foreign courts, or whose conduct compromised national security or disturbed public order. An alien thus notified was given three days to leave the country, and the government was even empowered to detain him until the moment he embarked. The law was intensely and brutally applied; from its inception, strikes were classed as crimes; strikers were arrested, and their homes were broken into. Workers' locals were closed down, and union assemblies were harassed by police agents.

On one occasion, the Buenos Aires police chief ordered the arrest of jobless workers on grounds that jobs were available for all who would work. In retaliation, the unions published an announcement calling for workers who wished jobs to apply at the police chief's home. Suddenly overwhelmed by throngs of applicants, the police chief dispersed the crowd in disgust and withdrew his order.[12]

During this period, the commemoration of May Day had become a custom, with the socialists and anarchists holding a joint demonstration. But differences between the two factions grew deeper, and after 1900 each celebrated the holiday in its own way.

In 1902 the Federación Obrera Regional Argentina (FORA), an anarchist group, was created; and in 1903 the socialists founded the Unión General de Trabajadores (UGT). Workers' action, though divided, made clear the need for labor legislation. In 1904 the Minister of the Interior, Joaquín González, commissioned the jurist Juan Bialet Massé to study the condition of the Argentine workers. This study served as the basis for a projected National Labor Law, which González presented to congress. The socialist José Ingenieros described the bill, perhaps with exaggerated optimism, as "a serious and far-reaching essay in state socialism." But as Ingenieros himself observed, the bill contained certain articles that made of it a repression of anarchism. Employers' organizations considered the bill "advanced, socialistic, and revolutionary." Anarchist organizations attacked it on principle and because it bore the means of their suppression. The socialists supported the bill, since key people educated in socialism— Bunge, Ugarte, del Valle Iberlucea—had helped to frame it. But when they saw that anarchist denunciations were attracting a following, they opposed the bill, even though the Socialist leader Juan B. Justo insisted that it reflected many of the demands of the Socialist Party.*

González's bill became law, but failed to stem the unrest: in November 1904, thousands of Rosario strikers were trampled by mounted police, and the government sent naval seamen from Buenos Aires to replace the striking workers. The Federación Obrera declared a general strike. When an attempted military revolt by the Radical (moderate) Party broke out in February 1905, the government declared a state of siege. The labor movement, which had condemned the military mutiny, nevertheless became joint victims of its suppression. The police closed socialist and anarchist

* This party was the most prolific source of protective labor legislation. By 1939, when socialism's legislative influence had almost completely waned, the list of the principal legislative projects presented by socialists was impressive: in 1904, a weekly day of rest; in 1907, regulations governing the labor of women and children; in 1912, inspection of working conditions in industrial and commercial establishments; in 1915, workmen's compensation and prohibition of liens on small salaries; in 1933, maternity insurance; and in 1938, medical assistance for students, prohibition of liens on working tools and the home, and reshaping of legislation along lines of international labor conventions.[13]

centers, confiscated copies of *La Vanguardia,* and jailed many workers. In September 1905 a strike in the port of Buenos Aires extended to railroad workers. Congress decreed a new state of siege, and UGT declared a general strike.

Two demonstrations were scheduled for May Day 1909, one by the Socialist Party, the other by FORA. Soldiers attacked the anarchists, leaving 80 people seriously wounded and 14 dead. A general strike, later called "the general strike of the week of May," was declared, paralyzing all activity for eight days. Both FORA and UGT participated, as well as the autonomous unions. The strike committee, after exacting government promises to release prisoners and to reopen the workers' locals, finally ended the walkout.[14]

In 1910, on the centennial of the May (Argentinian) Revolution, the anarchists declared a general strike, without the backing of the socialists; the strike demanded the repeal of the residence law, freedom for prisoners arrested for social issues, and amnesty for violators of the draft law. The government once again declared a state of siege. Workers' locals were attacked, hundreds of members were jailed, and the shops of *La Vanguardia* and the anarchist press were destroyed.

On June 26, 1910, a bomb exploded under the only unoccupied orchestra seat in Buenos Aires' Teatro Colón. One person was slightly hurt. Within a few hours, Law No. 7029 was proposed; called the Social Defense Law, it aroused indignation in the working class. The law empowered the government to deny anarchists admission to the country and to deport anarchists born outside Argentina. It also hampered union activities; in effect, its Article 25 threatened anyone attempting to provoke strikes or boycotts with prison sentences of from one to three years. "Provocation" included even an insult hurled at a strikebreaker.

The election in 1910 of Roque Sáenz Peña to the presidency began a period of greater freedom and less electoral fraud. Political leaders had finally come to view the labor movement as something besides a police matter. A simple statistic reflects the change of attitude: in 1906, the year of greater repression, there were 170 strikes in Buenos Aires, with some 70,000 strikers, whereas in 1912 there were 99 strikes, with 9,000 strikers.[15]

In 1911 the National Labor Department estimated that the minimum monthly income necessary to maintain a workers' family of four was 125 pesos. Because of union action, the average daily salary had risen from three to five pesos during the preceding decade. Thus, by working 25 days a month, a worker received precisely the amount needed to provide for his family. Without the unions his situation would have been intolerable.[16]

The period before and during World War I was one of relative social calm. Strikes were frequent, but were borne gracefully and incurred no violence. After the war, however, the country's economy deteriorated, and serious labor disturbances were brought on. In December 1918, 2,500 metallurgical workers declared a strike in support of fellow workers who had been fired. After 14 days of strike, a strikebreaker fired at and wounded a striker. The resulting exchange of gunfire left several dead. The following day the fighting continued, and the police resorted to open brutality. On January 9, another exchange of fire took place; the squadron of soldiers involved was commanded by Lieutenant Juan Domingo Perón, the man who later, as President, saw himself as the "savior of the working class." (Later, on May 1, 1947, when metalworkers held services in memory of the victims of this skirmish, Perón denied having directed the slaughter, saying he had reached the scene the following day.) The strike over, the police "uncovered" the purported plan of a Russian worker who sought to "replace the government with a maximalist soviet." On the pretext of jailing the guilty, the police and the "White Guard" (private terrorist reactionary group) began the "Russian hunt," and persecuted Jewish workers in order to force their confession of a nonexistent plan.

During the week of July 7, 1919, violence broke out when workers struck a British-owned iron works. Four workers were killed and twenty wounded, and a general strike spread throughout the country. Antilabor elements replied by organizing terrorist groups that sacked and closed labor headquarters and brutally beat workers. Within a week there were 700 dead and 4,000 wounded; the police made more than 55,000 arrests. This period later came to be known as "The Tragic Week."

In 1921 several violent strikes developed at La Forestal, the major source of quebracho bark in the Argentine Chaco, where working conditions approximated serfdom. A shepherds' strike in Patagonia in 1921 lasted a full year, and was suppressed only after considerable bloodshed. A dockworkers' strike in Buenos Aires the same year also occasioned many acts of violence.[17]

These were the conditions into which the first stable Argentine union federations emerged.

FORA

The Federación Obrera Regional Argentina (FORA) was formed in 1901; initially, its membership had been drawn from both anarchists and socialists. But dispute soon arose over conflicting tactical concepts. The socialists finally left the organization when the anarchist majority in the Second Congress approved, among others, the following resolutions:

"The Second Labor Congress, believing that militarism is contrary to the interests of humanity, favors powerful public protest against this barbaric system, so as to induce the greatest possible number of potential re-cruits to leave the country before they don the odious livery of authorized murder.

"The Second Labor Congress, recognizing the general strike as the su-preme instrument of economic struggle, believes that the organization and education of workers is necessary to achieve success. Moreover, it considers that boycott and sabotage produce effective results for the cause of labor, and proposes to employ all means within its power to minimize casualties among those who pursue this course of opposition. (The first cause of boy-cott, in 1906, was against the cigarette factory "La Popular," whose machine operators sustained a long strike.)

"The Second Congress feels that production cooperatives should be con-sidered only an incidental means of defense, and recommends that con-sumers create their own cooperatives so as to break free from the inter-mediaries who poison and exploit the worker."

In June 1903, FORA'S Third Congress was held, with 80 delegates at-tending. It pronounced itself in opposition to the residence law and po-litical action, and in favor of free schools, the eight-hour working day, and women's suffrage. The Fourth Congress simply reiterated previous pro-nouncements.

The Fifth Congress rejected almost unanimously the socialist UGT's proposal to establish a pact of solidarity, advocating, rather, communistic anarchy: "The Fifth Congress, mindful of the principles that have given the workers' federations their raison d'être, declares its approval of the broadest campaign of propaganda, to inculcate in the workers a sense of the economic-philosophic basis of communistic anarchy. Such an education will forestall their becoming contented with the simple achievement of the eight-hour day; it will carry them to social revolution and complete emancipation."

The Sixth Congress was held in Rosario in September 1906. The pact of solidarity proposed by the UGT and rejected by the previous congress was presented once again; the result this time was a decision to organize a unification congress in which all Argentine labor organizations would participate. The congress was held in March 1907 and involved 78 unions from the capital and 93 from the interior. Two positions were taken: one was by the socialist Jacinto Oddone; the other, by the anarchist Francisco Jaquét, captured the majority. The delegates opposing communistic an-archy then withdrew from the congress.

In February 1909, the autonomous labor societies organized a new con-gress to unify the country's unions, but the sessions were put off until September because few unions were represented at the initial meetings. The

September congress proposed to found a Confederación Obrera Regional Argentina (CORA); but when it was agreed that this organization would concern itself only with the economic struggle, the unions with anarchist leanings chose not to join. The congress did manage to dissolve the UGT, which, together with some autonomous unions, formed CORA.

During the next five years, the syndicalists became antiparliamentarians, foes of all political action. Many anarchists joined them, and the emerging anarcho-syndicalists began a long feud with the pure anarchists on one flank and the socialists on the other.

In 1912 the Second Congress of the Federación Sudamericana de Pica-pedreros (Stonecutters) under the leadership of syndicalists, decided to attempt again the unification of the Argentine proletariat. The new unifying congress, held on November 20, 1912, was attended by delegates from 30 unions from the capital and 31 from the interior. The platform, with syndicalist influence, stated that the new federation "pursues a better life for the working class.... It seeks, in fact, the total emancipation of the working class, which can be achieved only by expropriating capitalist industry." The platform proposed the general strike as a means of action and stated that the union, "today a resistance group, will in the future be the production and distribution group, the basis of social reorganization, since the union is the first and foremost instrument of the working class." This project was approved only after long discussions and against the opposition of the nonsyndicalist delegates. Unity, then, was never achieved.

In 1914, a congress called together by FORA's council, and given the name Concentración Obrera, led finally to all the organizations' joining FORA.[18] Unity of a sort lasted a year, with internal differences continuing as before. FORA's Ninth Congress, in April 1915, approved a declaration disavowing communistic anarchy as the Federación's ideology: "FORA is preeminently a labor institution, organized by groups of trades. Its component elements, however, belong to diverse ideological and doctrinal movements, and as such must exercise the broadest freedom of thought, if they are to maintain a solid union. Though it is imperative that their actions be guided by the revolutionary orientation of class struggle, i.e., by direct action, we must exclude groups and parties operating outside the organization of true workers. Thus FORA makes no official pronouncements in favor of, nor does it advise the adoption of, any philosophic system or determined ideology...."

Delegates from the fifteen unions favoring communistic anarchy withdrew from the congress and decided to reconstruct the old federation on the principles that had guided FORA prior to the convening of the Ninth Congress. Once the old federation had been recreated, its members renounced the resolutions of FORA's Ninth Congress and reaffirmed the espousal of communistic anarchy voted on in the Fifth Congress. Thus there were now two FORA's: the Ninth Congress FORA, as it came to be called, was syndicalist, and the Fifth Congress FORA was anarchist.

Frequent strikes motivated the formation of new unions, which were in turn incorporated into the Ninth Congress FORA; by the eve of the Tenth Congress, the affiliated organizations numbered 199, with 143,928 members. A new doctrinal dissent arose, at the instigation of the International Socialists, who had separated from the Socialist Party as a result of the Russian Revolution. During FORA's Tenth Congress, held in December 1918 and attended by 120 unions, a resolution was passed against the vote of many delegates, "expressing the broadest solidarity with the workers of the USSR and Germany for their heroic efforts toward fulfillment of the deepest yearnings of the universal proletariat: freedom of labor and suppression of the odious exploitation of man by man."

When the International Labor Conference was held in Washington in 1919, the Argentine government selected, as representative of the country's workers, a delegate from the railroad workers' union, La Fraternidad, an organization of no small prestige that seldom resorted to the strike. Many labor delegates to the Conference in Washington voted against accrediting the Argentine delegate, feeling that the Argentine workers could be suitably represented only by a FORA delegate. Nevertheless, the delegation was approved by a majority vote.[19] FORA, with its anti-state position, would no doubt have refused to let the government appoint a representative from its ranks.

The Fifth Congress FORA held its first congress in September 1920. The many supporters of the Russian Revolution among its participants provoked long discussions, but it was finally agreed that there would be no affiliation with internationalist organizations.

The Eleventh Congress of the Ninth Congress FORA was held in February 1921. A syndicalist delegate asked that socialist Congressman Agustín S. Muzio be barred from the meetings, on grounds that he was a "defender of the bourgeoisie." After six sessions a vote was taken: for rejection, 107 votes, by anarchists, syndicalists, and Communists; for admission, 60 votes, all by socialists. Another matter deepened the rift: those favoring FORA's affiliation with the Profintern withdrew from the congress after failing to achieve their objective.

In March 1922 a unification congress was held, organized by a committee of five Ninth Congress FORA members, five Fifth Congress FORA members, and five members from independent groups. By telegram, the Profintern invited the Argentine workers to join "in forming a great world revolutionary force." But by this time the congress had agreed, after long debate, to deny the credentials of Communist alderman José F. Penelón. Ultimately, the congress created a new federation (the Unión Sindical Argentina, or USA), recommended maintaining relations with revolutionary and anti-state labor organizations, but left undecided the matter of which international the new federation would join. The new Unión was established on the following principles: the refusal to recognize the right of intervention by organized political factions into the affairs of USA; the use of direct action as the most effective weapon in the anti-capitalist struggle, including the strike, the boycott, sabotage, and even insurrectional movements and revolution itself; and reliance upon USA's veteran unions as the revolutionary vanguard of the Argentine proletariat. The statutes of the new federation established, moreover, that "the Secretary General and all members of the Central Council, electees and replacements alike, may hold no political office; acceptance of candidacy for such office implies immediate resignation from the post held."

The desire for unity persisted. Thus, the Federación Obrera Poligráfica (FOP), an autonomous union, met with the boards of directors of USA, the Confederación Obrera Argentina (COA) (previously founded by the socialists and the railroad workers' unions), and the other autonomous unions, and proposed unification in a new federation. USA and COA agreed to the proposal, establishing a "labor federation independent of all political parties and ideological groups." The merging of the two federations (and their absorption of the FOP) saw the founding of the Confederación General del Trabajo (CGT) on September 27, 1930, during a meeting of both councils. The Fifth Congress FORA remained outside the CGT, aligned with some of the old autonomous unions. And in 1957, groups from the old USA reconstructed their federation, but managed to sustain it through only a brief and listless existence.

UGT

Socialist elements had withdrawn from the early FORA in 1903 to form the Unión General de Trabajadores (UGT). Its organ was the *Unión Obrera*. During the first UGT congress the following positions were adopted. (1) The general strike can be useful as an act of protest in matters directly affecting the working class, but the strike is to be eschewed when its ends are those of violence and social disruption—since, rather than favoring the proletariat, such action tends to be met by violent reaction from the capitalist class, which serves only to weaken the position of organized labor. (2) The barbaric and unconstitutional Residence Law is to be condemned; organized labor must spare no effort in effecting its total repeal, through legal means. (3) The working class must be concerned with politics, independently of the union struggle; labor votes must go to the parties whose programs include concrete proposals for labor and social reform legislation, such as the eight-hour work day, regulation of women's and children's labor, creation of a pension fund, workmen's compensation for on-the-job accidents, and the Sunday day of rest. (4) Finally—and perhaps of less consequence—the obligatory shaving of the mustache "is to be deplored" (a regulation then in effect required private chauffeurs and hotel waiters to be clean-shaven).[20]

The National Council of the UGT sought constantly to broaden the field of labor action. For example, it planned the establishment of a cigarette factory to raise funds for sustaining a Labor Chamber (club for studying labor problems) it had founded. In a few months the Council had collected 3,920 pesos, and in August 1904 began the manufacture of "Alba" and "Proletarios" cigarettes. But syndicalist elements quickly spoke out against the firm; sales dropped, and the factory had to be closed.[21]

By its third congress, in 1905, the UGT was giving evidence of syndicalist influence. The congress, in approving a resolution recognizing the value of political action, defined such action as "revolutionary class action undertaken by the organized proletariat to morally and materially reduce capitalist domination," though acknowledging that socialist parliamentary representation can be a useful complement to direct action by the proletariat.[22] And in December 1906, the fourth UGT congress turned its leadership over to the syndicalists.

Syndicalist thinking had also been taking hold in the Socialist Party for some time. But when the syndicalists took the position, at the party congress of 1906, that the party should consider itself no more than an appendage of the union structure, they were invited to withdraw. The syndicalists later declared themselves opposed in principle to all political parties, repudiating parliamentary action and any other democratic processes not purely unionist.

In 1903 the UGT comprised some 41 unions with 41,164 members; in 1906, 95 unions with 102,586 members; but in 1909, 26 unions with 22,453 members.[23] The dialogue between socialists and syndicalists continued to weaken the federation; and in 1909, as we have seen, the UGT joined with other groups to form the CORA. The socialists turned then to the ninth congress FORA and to the USA, achieving, finally, a limited influence in the Confederación Obrera Argentina (COA), founded in 1926 at the initiative of the two autonomous railroad workers' unions and some socialists.

Although the Argentine Communists had founded the Comité Nacional de Unidad Sindical Clasista,[24] a separate group within the COA, they failed to prevent COA's affiliation with the International Labor Federation of Amsterdam, in 1928. In 1930 they joined ranks with USA, just before its merger with COA formed the CGT.[25]

While organization of the industrial proletariat proceeded apace, FORA and other union organizations, as well as the Socialist Party, were engaged in sporadic but determined efforts to organize the agricultural workers and small tenant farmers.[26]

Though landowners opposed the agrarian movement, their tenants, who worked the land with the help of their families and a few peasants, encouraged the movement. Regardless of how poorly they lived, these tenant farmers continued exploiting the peasants, whose lot was even worse. But according to the official position of the Agrarian Congress of Pergamino,* there was no doubt that owing to the "rapacity of the owners," the tenants could offer the *peones* no better. In any case, the national labor federations felt compelled to concern themselves with the agricultural workers, while tacitly accepting the support of the tenant farmers.

FORA, in its Second, Sixth, and Ninth Congresses, agreed and reagreed to organize the field workers, who had previously been unable to achieve this goal because of the precarious nature of leases, which deprived the tenant farmers of even month-to-month security. The Ninth Congress, on the occasion of the application for membership of a tenant farmers' cooperative, stated: "The congress resolves that FORA, made up as it is exclusively of workers, cannot accept the membership of peasants until such time as they have become wage-earners; rather, the efforts of the Federación should tend to the formation of unions in all those rural centers in which the existence of a proletariat permits its own development."

By the close of 1919, the Sociedad Obrera de Oficios Varios de Carhué had joined FORA, demanding "a ten-hour working day in the *chacras* (small, isolated farms), an increase in daily wages, and better and more abundant food." And in June 1920, FORA signed a pact of solidarity with the Federación Agraria Argentina, the tenants' organization, recognizing in this pact that a common end existed in freeing the land and all other sources of production and marketing.

The first attempt at legislation for the betterment of agricultural workers was presented in the Chamber of Deputies in 1906, by the socialist Al-

---

* In 1902 the Sociedad Cosmopolita de Peyrano, founded by socialist unions, invited workers' federations from the north of Buenos Aires province and south of Santa Fe to a congress in the city of Pergamino, "toward the end of organizing the agricultural workers and improving working conditions during reaping and threshing."

fredo Palacios. It proposed that work be suspended in the fields between eleven in the morning and two in the afternoon, during November, December, January, and February (the Southern Hemisphere's summer months) and that during the rest of the year no work begin before five in the morning or continue later than eight at night.

During an assembly held in June 1912, small tenants agreed to demand certain benefits from the landowners. The Grito de Alcorta (as this assembly was called) encouraged *chacreros* from Buenos Aires, Santa Fe, and Córdoba provinces to declare a strike of several months' duration. The employers simply nullified contracts and confiscated machinery, and the police jailed and expelled many tenants. In 1921, socialist congressmen achieved the approval of a law assuring the *chacreros* a minimum of four years' tenancy in farms up to 750 acres, compensation for improvements left in the fields, and immunity from liens on working tools and food needed by the tenants' families. The *chacreros* obtained increased benefits when the Federación Agraria Argentina was formed.

CGT

The CGT was created in 1930, coincident with a coup that brought the military to power. The new federation, which resulted from a merger of the USA (Unión Sindical Argentina, founded 1922) and the COA (Confederación Obrera Argentina, founded 1926), progressed rapidly, gaining 262,630 members by 1936, and 311,076 by 1940. But doctrinal differences emerged early, and antipolitical tendencies again came to predominate, as they had in the UGT. Congressman Francisco Pérez Leirós, a committee member of the Unión de Obreros Municipales, was denied admittance to the CGT council in 1932 because he was not currently an active worker.

Time passed, and the CGT's National Committee took no action to institute a constitutional congress. The more important unions—who jointly formed the CGT majority, and who opposed the policies of the National Committee—alleged their right to be heard in matters of national policy. In December 1935 a group of delegates called together by the president of the Unión Ferroviaria deposed the CGT officers. The group then installed themselves as a provisional executive board, and called for a constitutional congress. Though the members of the deposed council protested, and several unions rejected the authority of the new executive board, the congress was held, in April 1936. The constitution approved read, in part: "To maintain organic unity, as well as harmony among its members, the CGT shall be independent of all political parties or ideological groups. In particular, the workers comprising its membership shall have the most complete freedom, consonant with their union duties, to develop, outside the confederated organizations, the activities that most effectively realize their hopes for social reform."

The unions backing the deposed National Council remained within the CGT, but took the additional tag "Catamarca 577" (their address) to distinguish themselves from those following the new leadership, who added the tag "Independencia 2880."

The CGT had by now become powerful enough to paralyze the economic life of the country if it chose to do so. Several leaders approached the Casa Rosada (Argentina's White House) to negotiate, with this influence as a lever. Some of these "leaders," with the mentality of "caudillos" of the labor movement, defended General José Felix Uriburu, concealing from the workers the dictatorial nature of his government. When several union leaders had been approached some time before and asked to join a movement against the dictatorship, they had refused. And in 1937, during General Agustín Justo's presidency, a CGT commission met with the General and indicated its firm support because of his "decisive intention to remain within the law—resisting, for the common good, any attempt to subvert order." At the same time the CGT conducted anti-Hitler and anti-Mussolini demonstrations throughout the country. The masses found these attitudes both contradictory and puzzling.

Thus the old concept of the class struggle began to lose its appeal. Why continue a strike if means could be accomplished simply by a visit to some influential person? In 1939, unions of metallurgists, textile workers, and construction workers, led by Communists, appealed to Monsignor Miguel de Andrea to intervene in their behalf in disputes with their employers. In so doing, they flattered Catholics and conservatives, in keeping with the Popular Front tactic.

When World War II broke out, the Communists, by then quite active in the CGT, described the conflict as a struggle between imperialist countries. And though the CGT Central Committee condemned the aggression in Poland, it was not reconvened for 29 months—to forestall discussion among its members, according to its secretary's statement. Thus the fiction of unity in the CGT was maintained.[27]

Little by little the CGT came to be a conservative body, bent only on achieving quick victories by any available means. But it could not entirely ignore the situation in the country; as its Second Congress approached, the federation was deeply divided. The congress, in 1942, decided that the CGT ought to support a democratic front against the dictatorship. This proposal was formulated by Angel Borlenghi, later a Peronist minister.[28]

A new schism, between the opportunist group and the old union tradition, divided the federation into "CGT No. 1," composed of a few socialists and union "caudillos," and "CGT No. 2," which included the majority of the socialists and Communists; CGT No. 2 favored a limited participation in the resistance to the dictatorship. The rift was aggravated by the military's new climb to power, and by the appearance of Colonel Juan Domingo Perón in the Ministry of Labor.

In June 1943 a representative of this Ministry called union spokesmen together to inform them that in future they would have to "unfailingly formulate their demands with the utmost respect, and with considered opinions and sound reasoning, as circumstances demand." If this was done, the government would, "through appropriate channels, try to satisfy just union claims, and undertake studies of living costs and possible cuts in the prices of basic commodities." It would, on the other hand, "keep in mind the public stance of labor associations, to ensure that their stated position is worthy of the permanent attention of public authorities." Meanwhile, the government began to restrict political freedom and to intervene in union operations. In July 1943 it shut down the headquarters of CGT No. 2, and soon dissolved this federation. On August 24, the government decreed the necessity for intervention in La Fraternidad and the Unión Ferroviaria, dismissed their leaders, and named two frigate captains as comptrollers (at the end of October, these captains were replaced by Lt. Col. Domingo A. Mercante). La Fraternidad and Unión Ferroviaria belonged to CGT No. 1; their delegates constituted the majority of the Central Committee, and the Secretary General and Associate Secretary of the CGT also belonged to these two organizations. Thus the intervention effectively decapitated the CGT. However, the unions not directly affected by the intervention resolved to keep the remnants of the CGT together and to name new leaders. What thus remained of the CGT formed a "Comisión Pro Unidad Sindical," which visited unions, gave conferences, toured the provinces, and tried to convince leaders of the necessity of reforming the CGT.

But there were other union leaders who saw the new situation as an occasion to reassess personal goals. The style of the union press changed. Speeches were made extolling the personal, professional, and laborite virtues of governing officials; the Army and the leaders of the Army "revolution" were praised. In Rosario the ex-Secretary of CGT No. 1 bestowed the title of "Primer Trabajador Argentino" on Colonel Perón. The government pledged friendship to these "leaders" and was generous to their unions, donating money and installing health centers, gymnasia, etc.

On May 16, 1944, the CGT Administrative Commission met to consider an invitation from the Labor Minister to take part in a government-sponsored Independence Day celebration. The invitation was turned down;

it was felt that participation would have been regarded as support for the government. Lieutenant Colonel Mercante, now ensconced as comptroller to the two major unions, admonished Commission delegates from these unions to vote for participation in the official celebration. The delegates refused, and resigned; but they were replaced by others more favorable to the government. Mercante was thus assured of a majority in the CGT's Administrative Commission, and hence of CGT attendance at the holiday function. From that moment on, the CGT was effectively controlled by the government.

THE PERONIST CGT

Under Peronism the CGT took on a new face and a new form. General Perón's demagogic regime accorded privilege to unions offering their support, and persecution to the more intransigent.[29]

After the events of May 1944, the CGT was in Perón's pocket. Dramatic proof of this strength was seen on October 9, 1945, when the military itself, seeking to oust Perón, jailed him; organized labor was the decisive element in forcing his release and return to power, by declaring a general strike, under the leadership of Cipriano Reyes (later discharged by Perón). The unions also supported Perón's candidacy in the elections that brought him to the presidency in 1946. To give this support a politically legal form, the Partido Laborista was organized, under the leadership of union elements.[30]

Thus Peronist domination of the CGT was absolute. When several Peronists, among them José Espejo, appeared to be leaning toward independence, in October 1952, they were eliminated. Espejo—whose merits for leadership consisted in his having served as doorman in the building in which Perón and Eva lived—was succeeded by his secretary, Vuletich, in the CGT General Secretariat.

But FORA remained impervious to the General's influence. When longshoremen, members of this federation, declared themselves on strike in 1951, they were supported by their trade's international federation. Ships under the Argentine flag, in ports all over the world, were unable to receive or discharge cargo. (The strike was finally broken, owing principally to the workers' lack of economic means; the official press stated that the movement was led from foreign shores, and placed at the service of "foreign interests.") In August 1952, FORA refused to pay "voluntary" contributions of two days' salary for a monument to Eva Perón, even though its leaders were jailed and tortured.

Perón's perversion of the labor movement sometimes proved embarrassing. Peronist unions were rich because all workers had been forced to join them and to pay heavy dues; on several occasions, the scramble for the union presidency, an especially lucrative post, produced gunfights. There were even struggles between moderate and radical Peronists, the latter supported by the Communists.[31]

In early 1951, union demands (presented, no doubt, by order of the Casa Rosada) provided the pretext for the legal attachment of the conservative newspaper *La Prensa*. With no free press, the democratic leaders of the unions were, for practical purposes, silenced, and workers now saw only the official version of union policy. This was left in the hands of Eva Perón, who from 1948 to 1951 carried out a complete purge of union administrations, substituting new Peronists for old leaders, and removing even the leaders who had supported Perón in 1943-45. Collective bargaining became more and more infrequent, to be replaced by decisions handed down from the Labor Ministry. Strikes were strictly prohibited, unless declared with political ends of interest to the Casa Rosada. This control was rounded out with the Eva Duarte de Perón Foundation, headed by the dictator's wife, which absorbed all of the country's charitable institutions, thus placing another powerful means of coercion in the government's hands. After Eva's death, in 1952, Perón himself took over control of the unions.

The cult of personality developed to a point comparable, in the same era, only to that of Stalin. Eva herself, during one rally, said: "What would have become of the country and the workers without Perón? We give thanks to God for having bestowed on us the privilege of having Perón, knowing Perón, understanding him, loving him, and following him." To such phrases, the Peronists in attendance would respond with an anthem:

> "Perón! Perón! How great you are!
> My general, how great is your worth!
> Perón! Perón! Great leader,
> You are the First Worker!"

But Perón's work in the unions did have certain positive aspects. For example, he obliged landowners to accept the unionization of their workers, who had formed the Federación Argentina de Seccionales Agrarias. As labor minister he promoted the Peasant Statute, which decreed an eight-hour work day and other benefits to agricultural workers, and in 1955 extended social security to the rural areas. At the same time, by establishing a state monopoly on the foreign sale of agricultural products, Perón considerably weakened the political and economic power of the landholding oligarchy, though to destroy it had not been his purpose.[32]

A declaration on workers' rights, in Article 37 of the Constitution written under Perón, illustrates the social concepts of Peronism. The worker was rightfully entitled to work, to a fair remuneration, to professional training, to decent working conditions, to the preservation of health, to well-being, to social security, to the protection of his family, to his own economic improvement, and to the defense of his professional interests. But the constitution offered no guarantee for these elemental rights. There is no reference to a "right to strike"[33] and no mention of the social institutions established by labor legislation prior to 1943.[34]

In 1950, Perón created the post of Labor Attaché in his embassies. He appointed Peronist union leaders of the second rank to fill these posts, and supplied them with ample funds. These offices managed to create Peronist union movements in Nicaragua, Uruguay, Colombia, and Panama; to establish organizing committees in Haiti, Chile, Peru, Cuba, Brazil, Paraguay, and Bolivia; and to obtain the support of the weakened Mexican CROM, and of Venezuelan unions led by Communists under Pérez Jiménez.

But in reality, the labor movement had become Peronist only in Argentina. This was made clear in February 1952, when delegates from a series of phantom unions met in Asunción, Paraguay, to constitute a new Latin American federation—financed by the Argentine CGT—which then pretended to oppose "Communist and capitalist imperialism." This new federation, called Agrupación de Trabajadores Latinoamericanos Sindicalistas (ATLAS), and formally established in a congress held in Mexico City in 1952, did nothing constructive and exerted no influence over the labor movement.

The CGT, and Perón, on occasion publicly admitted that the real condition of the worker had not been bettered by the government. On December 30, 1951, Perón acknowledged the lack of balance between rising prices and static salaries. At the time, he had been claiming to have rid the country of capitalism, and to have created a new economic system, based on his "Justicialista" doctrine (a simple rehash of "neutralist" slogans, without theoristic depth). Another "confession" came in February, 1952, when Perón found it necessary to request that no meat be consumed during two days of each week—in a country that had been the largest meat exporter in the world![35]

Perón liked to brag of his relationship with the CGT: "When the Confederation feels that something should be done in this or that fashion, it comes to me—President of the Nation—and tells me, and I do it that way. On the other hand, if I need something from the Confederation, I call the boys together and tell them, 'Look, boys, it seems to me such-and-such should be done this way,' and they do it. This understanding is no more than the result of our political and social orientation."[36]

Shortly afterward, he stated in print that he would have to return to his earlier practice of having always some bailing wire in his pocket. The reference here was to the time when, during a speech, he had offered bailing wire and rope to anyone wanting to hang an enemy of the regime. When a fanatic in the audience shouted "Give 'em hell!" the leader of Justicialismo incited the masses with these words: "You so kindly advise the giving of hell: why don't you begin to give some yourselves?" That night the Centro Radical, the Jockey Club, and the Casa del Pueblo (with Dr. Justo's prized library of socialist and historical literature) were burned. The only non-Peronist political offices left intact were those of the Communists.

The socialists were, in fact, often jailed during Perón's regime, and publication of their daily, *La Vanguardia,* was suspended on the pretext that the showers in the print shop were inadequate. Working through Minister of the Interior Angel Borlenghi, a socialist turncoat, Perón encouraged a split in the party, creating a "Peronist socialist movement," which, however, made no impression on party regulars.

In Perón's view, the union should be an organ of the state, and should be counted upon to come to the government's defense when danger threatened. For the Peronist regime, strikes were "legal" or "illegal." The distinction was not inherent in the circumstances of the strike, but was made at the convenience of the government. If workers walked out and their action was not considered "illegal," it was because they first offered fifteen minutes of inactivity in homage to the First Lady, or five minutes of silence signifying their allegiance to the regime. On other occasions the walkout was in obedience to a general order, so that they could hear a public statement by the Chief of State. In short, walkouts to obtain benefits for the working class itself were not permitted in Argentina; workers left the job only to pay homage to the powerful, to applaud their speeches, or to scream hysterically against victims of the regime's oppression.

In spite of all this, workers often struck "illegally" in defense of their interests; there were at least fourteen major illegal strikes in 1948 and perhaps another dozen in 1949. In September 1948 some 5,000 workers of the Frigorífico Municipal (Buenos Aires) launched a strike in protest against the arrest of some of their number. Police brutality injured more than thirty. Still more violent was the official response to a printers' strike in April 1949, when a thousand workers were jailed. In October 1949, more than 180,000 workers from the sugar plantations of Tucumán, Salta, and Jujuy declared themselves on strike only after having exhausted every other possible means of appealing for wage increases. There were many arrests, and one worker died while being tortured by the police in the cellar of the government building in Tucumán. The captive CGT condemned all acts designed to repudiate the torturers and, following its lead, Peronist justice let them off lightly. In April 1949, twenty-one telephone company employees, ten women and eleven men, were arrested and tortured. Gunfire caused four deaths in Salto on April 18, 1949, when ranks of workers demonstrated against the high cost of living.

These events of 1948 and 1949 were only a prelude to worse ills for the labor movement. The years 1950 and 1951 saw an increase in strikes; it was no coincidence that during these years the dictatorship approved new repressive measures against the free labor movement.

In November and December, 1950, railroad workers twice struck to demand wage increases. The government jailed hundreds of workers and closed down many unions. Work was resumed after a promise that the workers' wishes would soon be taken into account. The failure to keep this promise, and the subsequent abrogation of the right of meeting, caused a new and more vocal protest, which broke out on January 24, 1951. Thousands of workers were thrown in police dungeons, and thousands more were discharged. Only a military mobilization enabled Perón to force a return to work.

In May 1951, one event stood out: the attack on La Fraternidad's local, an institution that comprised railroad firemen and mechanics. The CGT had launched an imperious campaign of pressure for public union support of Perón's reelection. Faithful to its tradition of political neutrality, La Fraternidad refused to give its support. On May 9, Peronist groups took over the society's local, and on the following day proceeded to remove the legitimate union authorities.

On August 1, 1951, the fourth railroad strike broke out. Once again, workers were jailed or fired, and dozens left the country to escape torture by the police. And once again, by using the army, Perón was able to break the strike.

Perón employed a pseudo-labor vernacular that could easily confuse and coerce unwitting workers. Like all modern dictators, he took possession of the political and social vocabulary of the progressive movements and perverted it to the service of his own aims. He spoke of imperialism, plutocracy, the class struggle, and social justice, but such verbal pyrotechnics had no purpose other than gaining the firm support of workers for the dictatorship. Perón did give the workers, however—especially those in the provinces —a feeling of having a voice in government, of having acquired a new dignity and of sharing power; the feeling did not correspond to the reality, but it was important and it lasted long after the fall of Perón.

AFTER PERÓN

On September 17, 1955, the Army and Navy revolted. Military men not in favor took command of the rebel forces, and the people stood behind them. After 48 hours of uncertain struggle, Perón vanished from the Casa Rosada and took refuge aboard a Paraguayan gunboat in Buenos Aires harbor.

In exile, the free unionists had formed the COASI (Comité Organizador de Asociaciones Sindicales Independientes), under the leadership of Alfredo Fidanza and Cándido Gregorio. But when Perón fell, the COASI did not take over CGT leadership; hence many Peronists remained in union locals, though in others leadership was recovered by democratic elements acting on their own authority.

The new government of General Lonardi was soft on the Peronists. Although Hugo de Pietri, last Secretary General of the Peronist CGT, was removed from his post, many Peronist union leaders held on to their jobs. The government anticipated that the workers would see in the union elections the opportunity to shed themselves of the Peronists, but the elections were scheduled for 120 days hence, and the interval allowed the Peronists to strengthen their positions and to keep the CGT from reverting to genuinely democratic leadership. Aramburu's government, which followed Lonardi's, fully understood these processes, especially when a general strike ordered by the CGT against his administration failed to materialize. In November 1955, Aramburu issued an intervention order, and placed a government representative in the executive group of every union in the CGT. But his efforts were not supported by genuine backing for democratic leaders, and the CGT continued to drift, while working-class discontent increased. The intervention persisted for a year, and during this time the mood of the workers was generally one of helplessness.[37]

In 1957, labor elections began at the local level, and were eventually on a national scale. Strikes, frequent and sometimes violent, were brought on for the most part by inflation or by Peronists and Communists seeking to weaken the government.

Arturo Frondizi set out to return the CGT to some sort of normalcy during his presidency. But it seemed to him essential that one of the objectives of his overall policy be the assimilation of two million Peronists into the democratic regime, and he therefore had no wish to incur their hostility by removing them from their key union posts which they kept with the help and tacit alliance of the Communists. Frondizi had said: "The country needs powerful and responsible unions, with a single labor federation to represent them, not only to defend the workers' interests, but also to allow workers to participate actively and effectively in the formulation and execution of plans for national development. A powerful labor federation is a guarantee of stability and peace, the basic conditions for progress and prosperity in the Republic."[38]

Though nominally united by the CGT, the union movement has since

1957 been divided into three broad tendencies, called No. 19, No. 32, and No. 62 (because of the number of unions espousing each) : No. 32 is democratic; No. 62, Peronist; and No. 19, Communist. In 1961, unions from these three groups formed "The Slate of the Twenty" in an attempt to strengthen the CGT, but with little success, even though the government legislated a take-over of the CGT by the Twenty, through a Provisional Directive Commission that would include leaders from all tendencies.[39] The Peronists, in fact, had again gained control of the CGT. After 1963, their forces divided into two main tendencies: Peronists with Perón and Peronists without him, the second being more inclined to cooperation with other groups. When Lieutenant General Juan Carlos Onganía took power in 1966, the CGT opposed him for several days but finally came to terms with the military regime.

Corruption and dissension, provoked by demagoguery, are still present in the Argentine labor movement. The ineptitude of successive governments and of the democratic left-wing movements has permitted Peronism to sustain its influnce. Non-Peronist elements have been unable to seize upon either the program or the sounding board that might yield them influence over the masses and excite the workers to new enthusiasms.

10. Uruguay and Paraguay

URUGUAY

Argentine influence has always been strong in Uruguay. And the anarchist and socialist expatriates that arrived periodically from Europe generally settled on both sides of the River Plate. Yet Uruguay's labor movement invariably trailed Argentina's, for in Uruguay, a country dominated even more than Argentina by agriculture, the industrial proletariat was small. On the other hand, Uruguay was one of the first Latin American countries with a government that promoted modern social legislation—during the administration of José Batlle y Ordóñez, 1903–07 and 1911–15.

In 1884, the noodle makers of Montevideo struck for higher wages, the first Uruguayan strike on record. In 1888, the miners went on strike, led by French immigrant workers. And in 1895 another important strike led Batlle to remark: "The labor movement should be viewed as the participation of the working class in public affairs; seen in this way, the movement acquires national importance."

The first National Labor Congress, held in Montevideo in 1896, placed an eight-hour working day among its principal demands. That same year, a strike of seamen, rivermen, and longshoremen broke out. The liberal newspapers, which in Uruquay are quite unlike those in other countries, threw their support to the unions. The strike was so effective that the government resorted to severe repressions. In 1900 and 1901, the export crisis and Buenos Aires' example produced a new wave of strikes, touched off by another violent strike by the longshoremen, who seem always to have been in the vanguard of social struggle.

The proletariat increased in number with the mechanization of industry. Shortly after the turn of the century, there were 28 organized unions in the capital and 11 in the provinces, and seven labor newspapers were being published. The Federación Obrera Regional Uruguaya (FORU), led by anarchists, was founded in August 1905; and in the same year the Unión General de Trabajadores (UGT) was also established, under socialist leadership. In 1906, several important strikes took place, two by railroad workers and others by longshoremen and municipal workers in the capital. Montevideo was the natural meeting ground for Buenos Aires workers exiled by the Argentine residence law, and their presence helped strengthen and unite the Uruguayan labor movement.

In 1908, thirteen strikes were registered, with 3, 716 strikers; in 1911 there were 41, with 19,568 strikers.[1] In 1918, the anarchists led a general strike in support of streetcar conductors. But the failure of the seamen's and longshoremen's strike in 1919 dealt a blow to the anarchist unions, and to the preeminence of FORU, in particular. FORU in 1919 had some 25,000 members; in 1924 and 1928, it could offer only 4,000 to the International Workers Association, with which it was affiliated; and by 1929 its membership had fallen off to 1,500.[2]

In 1918, the Federación Obrera Marítima was created. A powerful group, it was from the beginning free of anarchist influence, though often dominated by the Communists. The Federación was organized by the Socialist Party, and its Secretary General, Eugenio Gómez, later served for many years as Secretary General of the Communist Party.

Batlle, during his two terms in office, encouraged the union movement. Earlier he had maintained that the workers found themselves confronted by conditions hardly advantageous to negotiation; and that if they took to aggressive behavior it was because employers, in defense of their own interests, refused to yield concessions. In 1904, Batlle began his instructions to the police by affirming the right of workers to declare themselves on strike. Before the end of his first term he created a Ministry of Labor and Industry, the first in Latin America. And a series of social laws that failed narrowly of congressional approval during his second term were written gradually into law in the years to come. He proposed, for example, a plan for workmen's compensation, a weekly day of rest, protection of working mothers, and the famous "law of the chair," which ordered that all women workers be afforded a place to sit where they worked. He established a system of social security that was later imitated by most of the Latin American countries—even to its most deficient provision, the establishment of different fixed pay scales for the various working groups (white-collar workers, laborers, industrial workers, etc.), a provision that led usually to galloping bureaucracy.

Legislation instituted by Batlle was designed to subjugate labor neither to government control nor to obligatory registration (the latter has been a common vice elsewhere in Latin America, even under democratic regimes). While serving his second term, he took particular care to assure striking FORU workers that they acted with his sanction, and that government authorities would protect them in the exercise of their rights so long as they proceeded legally.

Anarcho-syndicalist leaders indeed often expressed their respect and sympathy for Batlle.[3] But as time passed, the strength of his reforms came more and more to depend on social harmony, and to achieve it he was forced to seek a balance between labor and management. Thus, after establishing state control over a sizeable portion of the country's economy, he refused to allow civil servants the right to strike.

Uruguay was one of the first countries to ratify the international labor conventions. The basic labor law was passed in 1914, and supplementary laws enacted later assured the various trades—the miners and the industrial workers, for example—of the protection decreed by the 1914 legislation.

But in 1932, with the government shed of Batllism, reaction set in against the labor movement. On the pretext that a plot had been uncovered (none, in fact, had been laid), workers' sports and cultural centers were closed down, as well as the offices of all labor publications. In fact, and by design, this process eliminated all means of democratic recourse, to pave the way for dictatorship. By 1933, President Gabriel Terra and certain elements of the Army had instituted their dictatorship. Confronted by a worldwide economic crisis, Terra's government forced a reduction of working days to five per week, as well as a general reduction in wages. But it was helpless to prevent the outbreak of major strikes in 1934, culminating with a general strike in support of the printers—even though organized labor was at the time split into two rival federations.[4]

In 1942, after extended negotiations, the Unión General de Trabajadores (UGT) was reestablished, with a membership chiefly of socialists and Communists.* A meatpackers' strike in 1944 led to a Communist takeover of the UGT, and the socialists withdrew. Several socialist organizations then formed the Comité de Relaciones Sindicales, an amalgamation of extant federations representing several trades. The Communists found their principal support among Montevideo urban transit workers and in the woollen-cloth industry. Another federation, the Comité de Enlace de Sindicatos Autónomos, was made up of unions led by Trotskyite and anarcho-syndicalist elements. The Peronist Confederación General de Trabajos (CGT), founded in 1950, lasted only briefly.

In 1951, a group of free unionists formed the Confederación Sindical de

---

* In 1920, a Unión Sindical Uruguaya had been founded; for some time the socialists and syndicalists had vied for control of the Unión, and in later years Communist elements had begun to gather strength.[5]

Uruguay (CSU) to compete with the Communist-controlled UGT for labor support. The group succeeded in attracting many unions—so many, in fact, that in 1953 the UGT expired. Since 1953, the CSU has worked hard for agrarian reform (a conference on the subject was held in 1959) and for the creation of agricultural cooperatives. In 1957, the CSU rejected a Communist proposal for a united front and, in the face of national economic crisis, proposed a tax reform and the establishment of a minimum wage. The following year, the CSU began to work closely with the autonomous unions—rubber workers, rice planters, and oil workers. The CSU also lent its assistance to exiled Paraguayan unionists,[6] but has been losing influence lately in the face of renewed Communist strength. In 1961 the Communists established the Central de Trabajadores del Uruguary (CTU). There are also several important unions that remain autonomous.

PARAGUAY

In Paraguay, in 1906, a number of labor unions, principally of rivermen, artisans, bakers, and printers, formed the Federación Regional Obrera and began publishing a journal, *El Despertar*.[7] Following World War I, there was considerable union activity; but owing to scant local economic development the movement failed to gather new support, and by 1930 the Federation had collapsed.[8]

The country's first modern social legislation appeared in the aftermath of the revolution of February 1936: an agrarian reform law was enacted, an eight-hour working day and 48-hour work week were established, and wages were henceforth to be paid in cash, rather than in the customary *plata blanca* (vouchers). The government also created a department of labor. All but the agrarian reform law survived the social depredations of the counterrevolutionary government, during the following year.[9]

During this period the Confederación Nacional de Trabajadores del Paraguay (CNTP) was founded. When Higinio Moriñigo's dictatorship came to power, the Confederación came under constant harassment, and in 1944 Moriñigo established a "labor section" (the Organización Republicana Obrera, ORO) in his own party. The CNT lost ground quickly, and was forced to drop the word "Nacional" from its title (becoming the CTP) by a law prohibiting the use of the term for anything other than an official government body. The Communists, meanwhile, founded the Consejo Obrera Paraguayo (COP). In 1945, President Moriñigo proposed a law establishing rigid government control over the unions and a deduction of 3 per cent from all salaries for social security. (He also authorized the Communists to reestablish the CTP for a short time). Union leaders immediately took issue; convinced that the salary deductions would be turned to political profit, they ordered a general strike. But because of pervasive weaknesses in the union organization, the strike was fragmentary, and Moriñigo dissolved the unions and arrested labor leaders and their families.[10]

With Moriñigo's resignation in 1948, the labor movement began to revive—though under the considerable influence of remnants of the dictator's unions (integrated into the CTP), and in the face of Communist infiltration. Though the CTP had been rent by government intervention, it was, during those years in which various dictators succeeded each other, the workers' only avenue of defense. At its core were *Febreristas* and liberals. When Peronists attempted to seize the CTP, they were expelled from the federation. Through membership pressure, several strikes were declared in 1959, and the government arrested and exiled the CTP's leaders, then replaced them with elements of the official Colorado party—elements the police could trust. The exiled leaders formed a reorganizing committee in Uruguay, with the support of the CSU.[11] There is also a small Confederación Cristiana de Trabajadores (CCT), founded in 1963.

11. Chile

LABOR PROTEST movements began in Chile somewhat earlier than in the neighboring countries. Santiago tailors went out on strike in 1849, and during the fifteen years that followed, the press reported strikes by cigarette makers, shoemakers, day laborers, coal miners, copper and silver miners, seamen, printers, longshoremen, and construction workers. In 1855 a bill was drawn up that would have prohibited gatherings held for the purpose of organizing strikes, but the bill failed to pass congress. The government calculated that persuasion was more effective than repression, and many liberal economists lectured to workers' groups on the purported disadvantages of the strike.[1]

Women and children worked in the mines during this period. At times, women were also employed in the cities, as strikebreakers—during a Santiago cigarette workers' strike in 1888, for example. Wages—especially in the mines—were frequently paid in vouchers rather than in cash. And the owners of enterprises employing the voucher system in turn accepted the vouchers from the workers at a discount.

Fluctuating ore prices periodically led to mine shutdowns. At such times, the miners scratched out a miserable existence by such illegal practices as the removal of *cangalla* (remaining traces of silver) from the mines—though according to Sarmiento the removal of *cangalla* should be regarded as "a bonus, a professional fee, not as robbery." Attempts at preventing the scavenging of *cangalla* led to miners' rebellions—one of them, at Chañarcillo, as early as 1834.

Mutual-aid societies, or *mancomunales,* abounded. And there were also larger, national, mutualist bodies: we have already mentioned (in Chapter 5) the Sociedad de la Igualdad, which asked for the establishment of pawnshops throughout the country, a workers' aid bank, popular theaters, public baths, free schools, and an adequate election law.

In 1847 the Sociedad de Artesanos was formed in Santiago. Cooperatives also appeared in Santiago, Valparaiso, and Serena, among other cities; by 1860 there were 70 of them, throughout the country. Fermín Vivaceta, a friend of Bilbao and a student of socialist literature, was the guiding spirit of the mutualist movement, which he saw as a means of "assuring the triumph of labor over poverty." The first mutualities had no sense of class distinction; the Sociedad Tipográfica, for example, in 1853, included, as well as the typesetters and printers of Santiago's seven print shops, the owners of the shops.[2]

In 1873 a Workers' Club was opened in the capital, to serve primarily as a meeting place. Workers' glee clubs and the like, associated with this club, performed an important function, that of attracting the most respected elements of the working class, thus laying the foundations for the subsequent organization of unions. The Federación Santiago Watt, made up of railroad trainmen and engineers, was organized in 1886 after a visit by the group of American railroad workers who had earlier helped organize the railroad workers' union in Argentina.[3]

A number of conditions—the economic crisis brought on by fluctuating mineral prices, working days of ten, twelve, even sixteen hours, socialist and anarchist propaganda, and the activities of the first mutualist societies—led to a period of intense unrest and agitation. For the years 1884 through 1888, one investigator lists 70 strikes. Although conservative elements demanded immediate repression, the government chose, for the most part, to do no more than look on. In July 1890, the unrest came to a head in a series of major strikes—strikes that can, in fact, be said to have marked the beginning of the Chilean union movement. The first was a boatmen's strike in Iquique; the boatmen, facing what was in effect a salary cut resulting from currency devaluation, demanded to be paid in silver.* Other unions took up the demands, and the strike spread throughout the city, to become the country's first general strike. A workers' demonstration was broken up by the police, leaving a hundred wounded in the street. The government pressed for negotiations, but the strike spread to several northern provinces, and after four or five days the demand for wages in silver was accepted. When employers later ignored the agreements, the strikes were resumed, though less aggressively. At the same time, strikes broke out in Arica and Antofagasta, and the movement spread to the South. In Valparaiso, when women attacked stores which had been dabbling in stocks and speculating on prices, 50 were killed and 500 wounded, and hundreds of arrests were made. In most places, the demands for wages in silver were agreed to, but the pacts were repudiated when order returned.

The strikes aggravated the differences between the progressive, reform-

* In Argentina there had been demands, some years before, for wages paid in gold.

ist President, José María Balmaceda, and the congress, a disagreement that exploded the following year in an attempted civil war and in the suicide of the President. To Iquique employers who had demanded the repression of strikers, Balmaceda had said, "I admonish you first to outline the strikers' demands and the steps you have taken toward a reasonable and equitable agreement with the workers."

The determination of the strikers did not diminish, even though the crisis lowered their living standards considerably. Between 1891 and 1900 there were some 300 labor protests, many of them put down by violence. In 1892 the government proposed an antistrike law. The liberals opposed the measure, insisting that the strike was a basic manifestation of the worker's right to protect his livelihood. The proposal was finally rejected.

By the turn of the century there were 150 workers' societies in Chile, among them several women's organizations. Many of these societies—such as the Unión es Fuerza of Negreiros, which in 1890 led a strike by nitrate miners—were more than mere cooperatives; they were true resistance organizations. No national federations had yet been formed, but the occurrence of strikes on the national level indicated the need, at least in some fields or trades, for a close relationship among all societies.

In 1890, elements from the various socialist and democratic parties and from anarchist groups took up the task of organizing unions. One of the most effective organizers was Carlos Jorquera, who had become a socialist after a visit to Europe. He founded the Gran Unión Marítima—which enlisted 300 members in its first month—and the painters' and tailors' unions. In a newspaper advertisement he offered to all labor unions "to explain in detail how unions function in Europe and the United States." By the end of the century there were 30 societies openly declaring themselves, in Jorquera's words, "resistance groups committed to the defense of labor."

The first labor federation was created in Valparaiso in 1892, in response to the government's threat to prohibit strikes. Called the Federación de Uniones de Protección al Trabajo de Sudamérica (its organizers, many of them anarchists, clearly thought to give their group a continental character), it failed by 1893. The same fate befell other efforts to organize nationally: the Confederación Obrera de Sociedades Unidas, mutualist in character, in 1894; and the Confederación Obrera de Chile in 1896. On the other hand, federations of local or provincial *mancomunales* managed to survive.

In 1900, Santiago streetcar workers declared a strike that lasted two weeks and yielded salary increases and better working conditions. The seamen of Valparaiso struck in 1903. And in 1905 there were frequent strikes in the capital, often with violent demonstrations that forced the government to call out the Army. The strikers' objective was duty-free importation of Argentine cattle, to bring down the price of meat. Northern strikes in 1906 and 1907 were suppressed with great violence.[4] In April 1908 a strike among nitrate miners in Iquique was put down finally by the Army. A thousand peasants were killed or wounded while trying to join the townspeople.

The first Combinación Mancomunal de Obreros was formed in Iquique, in 1900; a Mutualist Party was even formed, again in Iquique, and began publication of a newspaper, *El Obrero Mancomunal*.[5] These organizations were influential in the unification of the labor movement. In 1902 the Congreso Social Obrero was created, from 192 societies totaling some 20,000 members. The societies of Valparaiso, toward the same end, formed the Federación General de Obreros, later renamed the Confederación General de Trabajadores de Chile.

Bills for labor legislation, introduced by congressmen of the Partido Democrático at the beginning of the century and still under consideration in 1910, were finally buried by the Chamber of Deputies. The first social legislation to be signed into law, in 1906, concerned workers' housing. A law passed in 1907 granted the Sunday day of rest—but only for women and children. Until 1917 there were no national holidays for all workers. In 1907 the Office of Labor Statistics was created in the Ministry of Industries.[6] In 1910 there were 433 workers' societies, with 55,136 members, in a total population of 3.2 million.

In September 1909, conservative labor elements founded the Gran Federación Obrera de Chile, to bring together the mutualities. They drew up, as principal demands, workmen's compensation, the establishment of large-scale cooperatives, a minimum wage, and an eight-hour working day; in 1916 the federation achieved passage of a law dealing with workmen's compensation. In the Gran Federación's congress of 1917, two clear factions emerged, one democratic and the other revolutionary, the latter made up mostly of northern workers. When the revolutionary elements carried the day in the congress of 1919, the federation shortened its name to Federación Obrera de Chile (FOCH) and adopted a red flag as its official emblem. It stated as its ultimate goal the abolishment of the capitalist system and its replacement by FOCH, which would control industrial production. The congress was followed by an intense organizational campaign. FOCH soon included 40,000 members in the nitrate-mining North and 10,000 in the coal-mining region. The FOCH Congress of 1921 agreed to join the Profintern.

FOCH continued to expand its influence. It acquired a print shop for its newspaper, promoted resistance funds, and used these funds to support strikes often of considerable proportions—such as the coalminers' strike in

1920, which lasted 60 days and finally achieved a working day of eight hours in the pits or nine hours on the surface. The miners also exacted, against the will of the companies, a prohibition on the sale of alcoholic beverages in the mining area. By 1921, FOCH's daily paper, *La Federación Obrera,* was being edited by Luis Emilio Recabarren. It survived for three more years, to be succeeded by the daily *Justicia,* an organ, as well, of the Communist Party.

But during this period FOCH's affiliation with the Profintern began to alienate the unions led by socialists, syndicalists, anarchists, or democrats. The railroad workers were the first to withdraw. With its strength drained, FOCH was unable to resist the oppressions brought down by the dictator General Carlos Ibáñez del Campo, in 1927.

For years, FOCH had been opposed by the anarcho-syndicalists, who in 1919 founded the IWW of Chile, a federation of industrial unions. The IWW espoused, as its tactic, direct action, and as its objective, the abolishment of wages and the control of production by the workers. Its journal *Acción Directa* appeared from 1920 to 1926. The IWW was influential among students, who contributed jointly to the editing of the weekly *Claridad,* and it was particularly active among seamen. IWW also boasted socialist leaders of some prestige, including Schnake and Piña. But it never approached the membership or the influence of FOCH; and in 1925 some of its stronger unions pulled out to form the Federación Obrera Regional Chilena. When General Ibáñez set himself up as dictator in 1927, the IWW disbanded and its leaders were deported.

Arturo Alessandri, President of Chile 1920–1925, was the second president in Latin America to propose broader social legislation (Batlle, in Uruguay, had been the first). But his proposals, especially the Labor Code prepared in 1921 by Moisés Poblete Troncoso, failed to find approval in the Chamber until 1924, the same year in which social security was established. In 1931 a new code was proposed, which recognized the existence of industrial and trade unions.[7]

The military coup of 1924 was regarded in a different light by each of the various labor groups. The IWW was the only labor group to openly oppose the new regime. The Communist-dominated FOCH was at first evasive, but then listed certain demands of the new regime, and ended finally by opposing the dictatorship.[8]

In Chile the labor movement was more closely bound to politics than in other Latin American countries. Many times the unions even presented their own candidates. For example, in 1931 the officeworkers' union of Valparaiso ran a candidate who received 7,500 votes (against 9,400 won by his conservative opponent). As a result of this participation in politics, the unions had frequently to involve themselves in issues that apparently did not concern them. In 1925, when a series of strikes in the North was put down with considerable brutality, many of the workers who lost their jobs came to the cities. Sensing the demand, tenement owners raised their rents, and the tenants responded by forming Ligas de Arrendatarios, which declared a rent strike. Ultimately, the strike forced the goverment to enact two new laws, one dealing with rentals, the other with workers' housing.

During Ibáñez's regime (1927–1931), FOCH almost totally disappeared. In its place, hundreds of "legal" unions were created, in compliance with the legislation pushed through by the dictatorship, and two new federations were formed: the Confederación de Sindicatos Legales Profesionales and the Confederación de Sindicatos Legales Industriales. The two organizations were later combined to form the Confederación Nacional de Sindicatos Legales. The majority of the members of the Confederación Republicana de Acción Cívica (Ibáñez' "labor party" in Parliament) were union officials. Following Ibáñez' fall, the Federación Nacional de Sindicatos y de Organizaciones del Trabajo de Chile was formed, in April 1932, from both legal and free unions. Resistance unions opposed the new federation and its dwindling element of "legal" unionism.

The fall of Ibáñez in 1931 encouraged a revival of anarcho-syndicalist efforts, which resulted in the formation of the Confederación General de Trabajo (CGT). Closer in structure to the Argentine FORA than to the old IWW, the CGT adopted the regional federation as the basis of its organization. oSme of its member unions were drawn from the better-paid workers of Chile—the painters, carpenters, electricians, and printers.[9]

When Alessandri returned to power, in 1932, the unions renewed their efforts to organize. But when go-slow strikes broke out in 1933, Alessandri sent in troops. Hundreds of persons died in the ensuing clashes, and strike leaders were deported.

FOCH continued weak after Ibáñez's fall, now under Communist influence. Its uncertain leanings led in turn to rifts in the member trade federations. Recabarren's old comrades withdrew from FOCH, some to organize various socialist groups, others to establish the Nueva Acción Pública (NAP), a political movement with a union basis. These groups participated in the Socialist Republic of 1932, in which the Communists were in no way involved.[10]

In 1934 the Confederación Nacional de Sindicatos (CNS) was formed by merging several groups with a total membership of 60,000. A year later a unification congress produced the Frente de Unidad Sindical, and in December 1936 this group joined the old FOCH, the CNS, and other groups (but not the CGT) to form the Confederación de Trabajadores de Chile (CTCH). At its first congress, in 1939, the CTCH agreed to join the CTAL (the Latin American labor confederation created one year before) and the International Labor Federation in Amsterdam. The Communists, moreover, having adopted the Popular Front tactic, refrained from their customary divisiveness, and unity—at least among groups not committed to anarcho-syndicalism—was achieved.

Meanwhile, the Liga Nacional de Defensa de los Campesinos had been formed, in 1935, and in 1939 the Confederación Nacional Campesina was created; but the government—the Popular Front notwithstanding—opposed attempts at agrarian unionization, and strikes in the countryside were prohibited during the harvest season.[11]

From 1938 to 1941 the CTCH found itself committed to Popular Front governments and their policies. Many of its leaders were elected to the Chamber of Deputies. Union life became trammeled in bureaucracy, and union democracy began to crumble. For example, the CTCH failed to throw its support behind a printers' strike organized by the anarcho-syndicalist CGT in 1939.

This drift away from the primary needs of labor led to internal repercussions in the labor movement. During the Second Congress of the CTCH, in 1943, socialists and Communists contested the federation's leadership, and came to terms only after several months of negotiations: Bernardo Ibáñez, a socialist, was elected Secretary General, and Salvador Ocampo, a Communist, Undersecretary.

By 1940 there were 629 industrial unions with 91,000 members and 1,259 trade unions with 80,000 members. The most powerful industrial union had 6,000 members.[12] The labor movement had finally amassed sufficient strength to command just application of the labor laws.

In 1946 the government withdrew the registration of two CTCH unions. A protest rally resulted, and the police opened fire, hitting seven demonstrators. CTCH retaliated by organizing a general strike that paralyzed the country. When demands were not met, the Communist-led unions sought to prolong the general strike, but the socialist faction felt the CTCH lacked the strength necessary to confront the Army, which opposed all attempts at revolution. The CTCH split: the Communists, backed by the mining and transport unions and by Christian-democrat and radical leaders, installed themselves in CTCH headquarters and deposed the socialist Secretary General. The CTCH, from that moment on, was divided into two rival federations, both with the same name and the two of roughly equal strength.

After President Gabriel González Videla removed the Communists in his government, during mid-1947, the Communist-controlled federation suffered crippling setbacks. The Communist Party was outlawed in 1948, and many Communist leaders were incarcerated in the fort of Pisagua. The other CTCH faction, meanwhile, was instrumental in creating the Confederación Interamericana de Trabajadores (CIT), with Bernardo Ibáñez, Secretary of the non-Communist CTCH, as its first president.[18]

In 1953 the Comisión de Unidad Sindical was formed and immediately called for a unification congress. The delegates attending the congress agreed to form the Central Unica de Trabajadores de Chile (CUTCH). Several of Chile's more powerful unions—notably the Confederación Obrera Maritima, the Confederación de la Química y Farmacia, the Federación Ferroviaria, and the Federación Petrolera—were affiliated with ORIT (which had succeeded CIT), while other unions were affiliated with CTAL. CUTCH statutes were made to provide that the international affiliations of each union would be respected. After another protracted struggle, the non-Communist members put down a proposal that CUTCH join CTAL.

Although the Communists in CUTCH were a minority, their rigid discipline gave them a powerful voice in the new federation—so much so that CUTCH joined every electoral front sanctioned by the Communists. CUTCH appeared at first to favor Ibáñez del Campo's second regime (1952–1958), but thought better of it when Ibáñez, in 1953, tried unsuccessfully to stimulate incipient Peronism with a Confederación de Trabajadores Independientes de Chile.

The Chilean labor movement, even today, is oriented heavily toward politics. Each political party has its union faction, and more CUTCH decisions are made in negotiations between parties than in the official leadership of the unions. CUTCH has lost considerable strength in recent years (it had 160,000 members in 1961, but only 60,000 were dues payers); its helm and its course are contested bitterly by Communists, Christian-democrats, radicals, and socialists. The syndicalists, in view of this situation, formed the Confederación Nacional del Trabajo (CNT) in 1960, but its development has been slow. (The CNT and the powerful Confederación Maritima de Chile are both ORIT affiliates.)[14]

The "Christian" (but not Christian-democrat) President of CUTCH, Clotario Blest, was forced to resign in 1961 after having courted the Communists for many years; the Communists opposed Blest's pro-Castro position.

After the Christian-democrat victory in the elections of September 1964, Christian-democrat union elements in CUTCH disclosed their intention to take it over or, failing that, to create their own federation. In fact, they failed on both counts, and CUTCH (which has since dropped "Unica" from its title) remains controlled by socialists and Communists and is one of their most powerful instruments in their opposition to the Frei government. When Frei closed an agreement with the copper-mining companies in 1965, which gave the government the control of the majority of stocks, the miners' union, under socialist leadership, struck for three months. The profits from the copper agreement were to have been used in financing land reform; the strike cost the government 30 million dollars, for political reasons; thus the miners effectively sabotaged the chances of agrarian reform.

12. Brazil

CORPORATIVE TENDENCIES have been evident at various times in various Latin American countries, but only in Brazil have they taken on constitutional form. This fact has in large measure determined the character of the Brazilian labor movement.

Brazil has a long history of attempts to organize labor. In the eighteenth century, slaves formed ostensibly religious brotherhoods for the purpose of obtaining funds to rescue their fellows; and a certain Chico Rei managed to buy a gold mine at Villa Rica, then used the profits for freeing slaves. A *Companhia de pretos* (company of blacks) established at Pernambuco in 1812 was in fact a union monopolizing the labor of loading and unloading ships in port. The guild tradition was also strong in Brazil; in the nineteenth century it led to the establishment of cooperatives and mutual-aid societies. But the small scale of Brazilian industry offered little basis for the formation of unions as such.

The Constitution of 1891 guaranteed the workers freedom of association, and the Supreme Court established that association for the purpose of inciting strikes could not be considered punishable under the Penal Code. A 1903 law authorized the formation of agricultural unions, and another law, in 1907, extended the right of unionization to all professions.[1]

Strikes broke out in 1891 among the cigarette makers and railroad workers of São Paulo, and again in 1906 among the railroad workers. But the most crucial strike in this city, already a burgeoning industrial center, took place in 1917 and provoked a government campaign to deport foreign-born labor agitators.[2]

Among the earliest trades to organize their own unions were the longshoremen and the railroad workers, in 1903; the merchant seamen and the fishermen, both before World War I; the textile workers, in 1917; and the printers, in 1919. The most powerful of these was the longshoremen's union. Yet even before this period, in 1892, the first union congress had been held, in Rio, and representatives from a dozen labor societies had attended. In Santos the unions had published *União dos operários* in 1905 and *Tribuna operária* in 1907; and in Rio, in 1907, *Semana operária* began publication. In 1906, at another national labor congress, the Federação Operária Regional Brasileira was created. During its second congress, held in Rio in 1913, the anarchists captured its majority, and in 1915 it scattered as a result of ideological differences. The very moderate Unión dos Agricultores appeared in 1914.

Throughout 1917–19, important strikes broke out in the large cities. The most effective was that on the Leopoldina Railroad in 1919, following which the anarchists found themselves the object of intense police persecution. But the police notwithstanding, the anarchists continued to dispute union leadership with the Communists; in 1923, anarchists succeeded in reorganizing the unions of the Federal District into a new federation, which the Communists later managed to destroy.[3]

In 1923 a law prescribing workmen's compensation was approved. And in 1925 a National Labor Council—made up of five workers, five employers, five officials, and five economists—was created in the Labor Department to set the Department's policy. But the next four years saw no progress toward the refederation of labor unions.

In 1929 the Confederação General do Trabalho (CGT) and the Confederação Nacional do Trabalho (CNT) appeared, the former a member of the Profintern, the latter syndicalist. Although the CGT was founded by Communist-dominated unions, the socialists had by early 1930 gained control. The Communists then withdrew to form the Confederação Sindical Unitaria, but their federation failed to achieve the strength of its parent organization. The CGT remained the most powerful labor federation in the country—until the suppression of all labor organizations by the Vargas government in 1937.

A "revolution" in October 1930 brought Getulio Vargas to power. At that time there were some 270,000 recognized union members, plus 4,000 in illegal Communist unions and 2,000 in illegal anarcho-syndicalist unions. These figures included the 30,000-member Associação dos Empregados no Comércio, made up of white-collar workers in Rio de Janeiro. The "revolution" was initially supported by a few elements from organized labor and produced a considerable upswing in union activity.

From 1930 to 1937, Vargas consolidated his power. The balance of labor relationships was shaken, and strikes were frequent, particularly in 1931 and 1932. Soon Vargas's government began to suppress organized labor—declaring strikes illegal, prohibiting meetings and demonstrations, and closing down labor publications. More than a hundred union leaders were arrested.[4]

But at the same time Vargas began a policy of instituting social laws that recognized certain labor aspirations while establishing tight controls over the union movement. In March 1931 and again in the 1934 Constitution, he set forth national codes for union organization and for workers' rights and obligations. One of his first acts was the creation of a Ministry of Industry, Commerce, and Labor, and shortly afterward he decreed that all unions must be registered with the government. Unions led by syndicalists, Communists, and socialists opposed the decree; but the majority of the unions had no recourse but to register, and from the moment of registration their militancy went into decline. By 1935 almost all unions had registered, many of them because employers could not legally refuse to negotiate with a registered union.[5] Workers seeking to unionize had first to organize into professional associations and then petition the government for the registration of their associations. Once official recognition was granted, a union was considered to represent all workers employed in its particular trade, whether or not they had been listed as members of the union; and each category of workers could be represented by only one union.

Observing that the workers were disposed to favor him on most counts, Vargas began to seek ways to bring them into the fold. He instituted measures for social welfare, and for restrictions on management; and in so doing he pursued "the art of obtaining money from the rich and support from the poor, on the pretext of protecting the one from the other."[6] This policy led to the establishment of a corporate state, the Estado Novo, in keeping with the fashions of the time, when fascism was on the rise.

The Constitution of 1934 gave management and labor equal representation in the Chamber of Deputies, and the Constitution of 1937 accorded the two forces equal representation in the Council for National Economy, in labor tribunals, and in the social security system.[7] But this Constitution denied workers, as a class, all rights. It prohibited them from striking, calling strikes "anti-social, prejudicial to labor and capital, and incompatible with the supreme interest of national production." It recognized freedom of organization, but unions were nevertheless required to register with the Labor Ministry to be considered legal representatives of the workers, and union dues were automatically withheld from wages.

Vargas and his historians advanced the theory that before the "revolution" of 1930 no true unions had existed, that labor had been in complete chaos. The Constitution of 1937 (formalizing Vargas's earlier decree that a given trade would be represented by a single union) pretended "to protect workers from unscrupulous politicians," who had prospered from union plurality. Vargas in fact ended plurality and established the single union. Using corporativist phraseology, he argued that the virtue of the single union was its capacity "for collaboration, rather than destruction or the class struggle." However that may be, the number of unions increased rapidly: in 1940 there were 1,149 labor unions, with 351,574 members, and 999 management unions, with 24,423 members: but there were only 22 labor federations and 12 management-union federations, and there were no national labor federations.

Although the 1937 Constitution established a minimum wage, the guarantee was frequently ignored, and in any case did not hold in rural areas. On the other hand, the regime offered paid vacations, a 48-hour work week, time off for maternity, workmen's compensation, and guaranteed severance pay; and in 1938 it established a system of obligatory insurance and another system of labor tribunals. In short, this was corporate paternalism, which gave Vargas absolute control of the working class. Nevertheless, the workers seemed content with him for some years, for improvements in working-class conditions, however small, did come through these laws.[8]

All workers had to pay one day's wage per year to the union system as an *imposto sindical,* or union tax. With these funds the system set up a network of charity institutions, with medical and educational services for union members. Collective bargaining was replaced by a hierarchy of labor tribunals: conciliation councils at the corporate level, regional tribunals, and superior courts. This system is still in effect, though since 1945 some unions have managed to bargain directly with their employers.

Toward the end of Vargas's rule, officials of the Ministry of Labor organized the Partido Trabalhista, impressing many leaders of registered unions into its high posts. Although the party's program was vague and the party itself was built around nothing more than a few strong personalities, many workers—lacking organizations of their own—soon regarded it as their representative. Vargas used the new party not only to support his own policy, but also to counteract the inroads of the Communist Party. The Communists had attracted workers disenchanted with Vargas and had gained influence at the lower levels of the union structure, especially after 1944, when Vargas permitted the unions to hold elections for the first time since 1937. All this led to greater union activity and the first wave of strikes in eight years. Attempts were made to establish a national federation, and the Movimiento de Unificação Trabalhista, led by both Communists and Vargaists, was created. But the movement was abandoned when Vargas fell.

A military coup in October 1945 ended Vargas's regime, and the new administration decreed union freedom, with resumed union plurality; but shortly afterward this decision was revoked, union elections were suspended, and many leaders were dismissed, chiefly because the unions continued to be controlled by Vargaist elements who could use them to block the reestablishment of political democracy.[9]

A national congress of workers, held in September 1946, reestablished the Confederação dos Trabalhadores do Brasil (CTB), which joined CTAL. But in 1947 the government outlawed the CTB and the Communist Party,[10] and in 1951 the elections returned Vargas to power. This time he ruled democratically, and unions were not obliged to fit into the corporative mold. Labor was for a time denied the right to international affiliation, but international pressure led Vargas finally to authorize affiliation with the ICFTU and its regional organization, ORIT. Under Vargas's successors (he committed suicide in August 1954), Filho, Kubitschek, Quadros, and Goulart, government control of the unions was relaxed. At the same time, many employers' unions were founded, affording the opportunity for more direct bargaining.

In no other Latin American country does the state control unions so completely as in Brazil. A law establishes their organization and the procedure for their elections. Agencies exist to register them and to guide them: the Technical Commission for Union Organization, the Recreation and Cultural Assistance Service, the Commission for Union Structurization. There is a union tax, and a Union Social Fund allocates the distribution of funds collected.[11] The government retains 20 per cent of union dues for "recreational and educational activities," and with these funds offers sinecures to union leaders. At a National Labor Congress, held in August 1960, the Communists, taking advantage of popular discontent with this system, were on the point of taking over control of the congress and forcing approval of their plan for a third Latin American union federation; but democratic delegates withdrew, and the congress was unable to reach agreement.[12]

Today, more than half of the labor unions are concentrated in six states: São Paulo, Río Grande do Sul, Minas Gerais, Guanabara (previously the Federal District), Paraná, and Santa Catarina. Most unions are affiliated with federations of workers in a specific trade. In 1958, there were an estimated 2,558 unions of all types, of which 1,489 were workers' unions, 957 were employers' unions, and 112 were unions of the professions, such as law and medicine.

Federations usually have a state as jurisdictional area. Legally, they must comprise no fewer than five unions, and must include workers in identical or closely related trades. For example, workers in the milling, baking, and meatpacking industries are united in a State Federation of Food Workers. There were 141 labor federations of all types reported in 1964; 80 of these were classified as representing industrial workers' interests, half of them in Guanabara and São Paulo states.

Confederations must be organized from no fewer than three federations, but may combine diverse elements within a broad classification, such as commercial workers or industrial workers. A confederation is national in scope, and must maintain headquarters in the national capital. The Confederação Nacional dos Trabalhadores na Industria (CNTI) is the largest of the present confederations; its affiliates comprise some 2 million workers in 50 federations, 15 regional councils, and about 700 local unions. The Confederação Nacional dos Trabalhadores no Comercio (CNTC), formed in 1947, is the country's second largest confederation; approximately 18 federations, including 340 local unions with a total estimated membership of 1.5 million, are reported as affiliates. The Confederação Nacional dos Trabalhadores no Transporte Terrestre (CNTTT), formed in 1952, has three national federations and one state federation as affiliates, with an estimated total membership of 500,000. The Confederação Nacional dos Trabalhadores nas Empresas de Crédito (CONTEX) formed in 1959, comprises six federations representing about 100 local unions, with a total potential membership of 130,000 (actual dues-paying membership is probably one-fourth of the potential membership). The Confederação Nacional dos Trabalhadores nos Transportes Marítimos, Fluviais e Aéreos, recognized in 1960, began operation with four affiliated federations. The two remaining legally authorized confederations have not yet been established; they are for workers in the communications media and public relations, and for workers in educational and cultural establishments.

A sizable, though unknown, number of workers remain unaffiliated with any of the national confederations, but most are members of independent unions or federations. Among the more prominent of the independent federations are the Federação Nacional dos Estivadores (FNE), with claims of membership reaching 35,000, and the Federação Nacional dos Trabalhadores Marítimos (FNTM), with an estimated membership of some 15,000. Airline employees, telephone workers, communications workers, journalists, and private-school teachers are also organized in independent national unions or federations. Teachers in public schools are not yet permitted to join unions.

The three major national confederations, CNTI, CNTC, and CNTTT, are members of ORIT. The National Federation of Maritime Workers is an affiliate of ICFTU. Brazilian labor laws prohibit labor unions from affiliating with international organizations without specific legislation. Legislation permitting affiliation with ORIT and the ICFTU was passed in 1952, as we have seen.

Other workers' groups, not to be confused with unions, though they are not without influence, include some 300 Catholic Workers' Circles, and the Associations of Public Employees. Civil servants are not allowed to belong to unions, and have therefore formed these Associations, which receive no funds from the union tax.

The law allows the Labor Minister to "intervene"—i.e., assume union control—if disputes or political activities hamper the union in carrying out its function. The Ministry may also appoint a deputy to administer the union and to supervise elections of new officers, if the laws governing trade unions have been violated. Irregularities may also be punished by fines, suspension of the union, or abrogation of the union charter. Furthermore, the Labor Ministry may appoint the chairman at union election meetings, draft model trade-union constitutions and bylaws, and interpret constitutions and bylaws.

The vast bureaucracy created by Vargas's corporativism, which survived his regime, has encountered difficulties since 1960. Two movements aspired to succeed it: one of these, the movement of union democratization led by groups of Catholic workers, attempted to coalesce and reorient existing unions; the other, the "union reform movement," was led by former syndicalists and by Communists who had broken with the Party.

When the Aliança Libertadora Nacional emerged, in 1935, the unions remained faithful to Vargas. The working class, dazzled by the dictator's demagoguery, did not protest the imprisonment of Communists and fellow travelers. Since then, in one way or another, the unions have chosen to be faithful to those in power, whatever the ideological bent of the man at the top: they ceased actively supporting Vargas when he was in trouble during his second term as President, which ended in his suicide in 1954; they did not back Janio Quadros in the days before he resigned; nor did they support João Goulart when the Army rose against him in April 1964, even though he had favored the entrenching of Communist leaders in many unions, especially in the powerful Confederação dos Trabalhadores na Industria. Goulart called on union leaders for support; but the workers stayed home without so much as attempting a general strike. Since then, the union movement has been in critical condition, with one part of its leadership opposing the military government and another supporting it.

After the 1964 coup, any union group suspected of Communist or pro-Goulart leanings was brought under military intervention. The government took full control of these organizations, replacing their elected officers with appointed officials who became responsible for all union activities until the membership could elect new officers. However, some of the organizations subjected to intervention have already been returned to the full control of the membership.

A new law passed in 1967 provides for collective contracts between individual unions and individual employers; this tends to weaken the previously accepted custom of drawing contracts on an industry or region basis. But any agreement that conflicts with the government's economic policies is void. The vote in unions becomes mandatory and persons deprived of their political rights by the government cannot be elected.

13. The Andean Countries

THE PERUVIAN LABOR MOVEMENT began earlier than the movements of Bolivia and Ecuador; but on the strength of a populist revolution the Bolivian movement has recently gained considerable ground. In these three Andean countries the unions have had constantly to bear in mind the existence of a massive Indian population, mostly non-Spanish-speaking and prohibited for years from taking part in national political life.

BOLIVIA

Working conditions have always been poor in Bolivia. In 1826 the State found it necessary to dictate a regulation providing for "an improved procedure for mine owners, lessors, or their *mayordomos,* regarding their day laborers." The provisions of the regulation constituted the first precepts of Bolivian social legislation, and gave notice of the State's intention of arbitrating relationships between capital and labor.[1]

The first Bolivian union, the Centro Social de Obreros, appeared in 1906. In 1912 the Federación Obrera Internacional was created; this group, which became the Federación Obrera del Trabajo in 1918, was Communist-dominated since 1925. On many occasions, this federation formed a united front with the anarcho-syndicalist Federación Obrera Local de La Paz; and in 1927 the two called together the first Bolivian labor congress. The Federación Obrera Local de La Paz remained the principal labor organization until shortly after the Chaco War, when a body of moderate labor legislation was enacted. The Confederación Sindical de Trabajadores de Bolivia (CSTB), established in 1936 and made up mostly of artisans, then took its place.[2]

In December 1942 the Army visited a terrible slaughter on striking miners in Catavi.* The oligarchic government attempted to justify this repression by claiming that the country would otherwise have been unable to fulfill its commitments to the Allied war effort. Indeed, even the Communists, under orders to desist from agitation prejudicial to the Soviet Union's conduct of the war, had failed to support the miners. In 1943, the miners and various middle-class groups led a successful revolution and established a government supported by the MNR (Movimiento Nacionalista Revolucionario, of populist inspiration). In 1946, Colonel Gualberto Villarroel, its head, was overthrown by the *rosca* (agents of the oligarchy), and his body was hung from a lamppost.

Villarroel's government had offered union freedom, and in 1944 the Confederación Boliviana de Mineros had been organized, with some 35,000 members. Juan Lechín, its Secretary General, later became Vice-President of the country. Some of the unions affiliated with this confederation had existed before—notably the Unión Minera Central of Potosí, created in 1933. Also of considerable power was the railroad workers' union, formed in 1938 with some 10,000 members, which had brought off the longest and most determined strikes in Bolivia's history.

For the first time, in Bolivia, negotiations for collective contracts had taken place. Under Villarroel, the miners' unions asked for a wage increase, the establishment of schools, ceiling prices on foods, improved housing, and the eradication of tuberculosis among mine workers. Villarroel created a Labor Ministry, prohibited the discharging of union leaders without just cause, and suppressed company stores. Groups seeking to form unions received economic aid from the government for the purpose. Villarroel's fall meant the resumption of black lists, reprisals, and harassment of union activities.

Following the 1952 revolution, the unions became a decisive element in national life. They came to hold four Ministries in all the MNR governments, and after 1956 enjoyed a majority in the Chamber of Deputies. The Ministry of Mining and Petroleum was proposed by the Federación Minera; Transport by the Confederación Sindical de Trabajadores Ferroviarios; Peasant Affairs, by the peasants' unions; and Labor, by the industrial unions.

The various federations and local unions finally joined forces in 1952, forming the Confederación Obrera Boliviana (COB), which was led by

---

* The wave of protests following the Catavi slaughter led the ILO to send a mixed U.S.-Bolivian investigating commission to Bolivia; the commission's report,[3] though drafted in a very circumspect manner, was unable to conceal the condition of Bolivian workers.

MNR elements, but also greatly influenced by declining POR (Trotskyist) and Communist groups. The CSTB, for years the nation's principal labor body, had by 1948 become dominated by PIR (Communist) elements, and dispersed in 1952. Only the Federación Obrera Local and the Federación Agraria Local (of La Paz), both anarcho-syndicalist, still opposed the COB, and both were absorbed in due course.

Internal dissension became critical in October 1952, when *Rebelión* (the COB journal, edited by the Trotskyist José Zegada) demanded that the revolution take a socialistic turn. At the First and Second COB Congresses (in 1954 and 1957), the nature of the revolution became the topic of heated debates. Communists and Trotskyists felt COB's proper course was to pull out of its alliance with MNR, but Juan Lechín and a group of ex-POR members affiliated with MNR won majorities in both congresses. Internationally, COB has had an eclectic position and has remained unaffiliated; it has sent delegates to CTAL, ORIT, and even Peronist meetings.

In the meantime, local unions and militants in Bolivia were gradually acquiring an awareness of the social realities of the country, and a sense of the power of their own decisions. To take one example, local organizers were responsible for the failure of the general strike against President Siles's stabilization plan, decreed by COB's Second Congress in June 1957.[4]

In 1961 the USSR dumped a surplus of tin and tungsten on the international market, placing Communist union leaders in Bolivia in a difficult position. The Communists seized upon the resulting near-bankruptcy of the Bolivian mines as an opportunity to stir up the miners. But the miners were not to be taken in; their awareness that the situation was the clear result of a Soviet decision left the Communists without a case.[5]

In 1963, violence broke out once again in the mining regions; the miners had refused to accept layoffs of personnel, but they had ultimately to relinquish their position when they found their protests bringing no response in public opinion. The following year, Lechín took advantage of the miners' discontent to form an alliance with military factions, who then brought off a coup against Paz Estenssoro's government. Later, the military imposed harsh conditions on the miners, crushed protest strikes, and, in fact, exiled Lechín.

PERU

In Peru the anarchists were the prime movers of the union movement, by virtue of their having assumed leadership of the Confederación de Artesanos Unión Universal (founded in 1884). The Unión created several artisans' communes, which later drifted away from their idealistic basis to become simple businesses—receiving, even, the support of the government.

The anarchists also led the first strike declared in Lima, in 1904. Haya de la Torre's early interests in the labor movement (see p. 168) were aroused by his readings in the library of the Peruvian anarchist headquarters.[6]

Strikes were frequent in the early years of the century: in 1906, and again in 1913, Callao stevedores' strikes were violently suppressed; in 1912 a strike by sugar-refinery workers in Chicama Valley was put down after 500 were killed. Organizing the agricultural workers, however, was a difficult process, since most of them lived in conditions bordering on serfdom —haciendas on the coast, for example, still used whips and chains on their Negro, mulatto, and Chinese-immigrant workers.

In December 1918 a strike was declared by workers in the El Inca textile factory in Lima, to demand an eight-hour working day. Haya de la Torre, then a student, talked with the strikers and urged them to seek the support of the students, who responded enthusiastically. (This collaboration between workers and university students in fact lasted many years, and left its mark on the labor and populist movements in Peru.) The strike soon became a general strike in Lima and spread to other cities. Employers accused the strikers of being "moved by the hand of the enemy"—i.e., Chile, then in conflict with Peru over border disputes. Ultimately, the workers asked a students' commission to negotiate with the government. Minister of the Economy Manuel R. Vinelli, at Haya's prompting, proposed the establishment of an eight-hour working day, and the government approved it. The day after the measure was approved, Haya suggested to delegates of the textile factories that they organize a Federación Textil, and the federation—today the most powerful in Peru—was formed. The first step had been taken toward a national labor federation.

At a labor assembly in April 1919, workers from most of the Lima unions and from the Centro de Estudios Sociales Manuel González Prada* created the Comité Pro-Abaratamiento de las Subsistencias, under the leadership of Nicolás Gutarra. The first women's assembly in the country met at the local of the Federación de Estudiantes, to contribute their support to workers' demands. And in July an assembly presided over by Adalberto Funken formed the Federación Obrera Regional Peruana (FORP). The Federación advocated the "destruction of capitalism," the creation of a society of "free producers," and the repudiation of all political parties, labor as well as bourgeois. It sought to effect "by means of collective action, all possible improvements within the existing order; relief from repressive policies; and

---

* González Prada (1848–1918) was one of the most important figures in the emergence of anarchist thought in Latin America. See pp. 49–50, in Chapter 4.

reduction of the judicial organs of the bourgeois state to a purely administrative function."[7] Though there were few unions or local federations outside Lima, the role of the Federación was important. It opposed, for example, President Leguía's attempt to consecrate Peru to the Sacred Heart of Jesus (see p. 168), a violation of the Constitutional right to freedom of religion.

In 1920, anarcho-syndicalist leaders supported Haya in his efforts to organize the Popular Universities (called "González Prada"), whose objective was the training of union leaders who could eventually organize and instruct the masses. Young men who were themselves then university students were to become the professors of the Universities. The first centers began operation in 1921; during their inauguration the crowd shouted a "Viva!" never before heard in the streets, "Viva la cultura!"[8]

When Haya de la Torre was jailed in October 1923, the unions and students went on strike. Many labor leaders were arrested, but the walkout ended only after Haya was released and the Popular Universities reopened (they had been shut down by the dictator Leguía, who in 1924 deported Haya).[9]

The large Indian population in Peru was a major concern of the Peruvian labor movement. Though they had been more or less in rebellion since the conquest, the Indian peasants entered a new period of restlessness at the beginning of the century. At times, Indians who had come to the capital allowed themselves to be used as strikebreakers—unaware, of course, of the implications of the ongoing struggle, or that they had entered the struggle on the wrong side. At other times, they accepted organization and participated in protest movements. Some of these movements came to have a distinctly Indian character: for example, several of the miners' strikes in Cerro de Pasco included among their unwritten objectives the establishment of a separate Indian state. During a period of 12 months in 1921–22, 33 Indian uprisings took place, concurrent with attempts to break up the haciendas.

The period from 1920 to 1930 was one of intense agitation. Students, organized around Haya de la Torre and the Popular Universities, continued their support of the union movement. During this period, FORP languished and was finally abandoned. In 1926 there were many workers' strikes, generally supported by students' strikes. And in that year also, students' and workers' groups began to take an active interest in the plight of the Indians, and tried to organize them. APRA later achieved some success in this. Workers' groups supported the APRA movement of Trujillo in 1932. The year 1934 saw an unsuccessful general strike in Lima and a general walkout of railroad workers in the South.[10]

The Communists, meanwhile, became active in the unions, hoping to gain control. In this they differed from Mariátegui,* for whom the union "ought to ask of its members only an acceptance of the classicist principle, and not political support."[11] Mariátegui's followers collaborated with apristas and anarcho-syndicalists to found the Confederación General de Trabajo (CGT) in 1926. Leguía, hoping to counter the growing influence of aprismo, supported the Communists, and the dictator Sánchez Cerro later accorded the Communist-led unions a degree of freedom denied to unions led by apristas. As a result, the CGT was divided and eventually disappeared. The succeeding dictator, Benavides, at first persecuted all unions, but in 1936 (the year he arranged the election of the Communist union leader Juan P. Luna to a congressional seat) he established a tacit alliance with the Communists in order that the latter might contest the apristas for control of the union movement. This alliance continued under the government of Manuel Prado, whom Lombardo Toledano characterized in 1941 as "the *criollo* Stalin." With Prado's approval the Communists established the Confederación de Trabajadores del Perú (CTP) in 1944, with Luna as Secretary General. But when Bustamante Rivero was elected in 1946 and APRA was reaccorded its legal status, the apristas replaced the Communists in union leadership.[12]

Throughout this period the labor struggle continued, in spite of divisions and persecutions. In 1930 the Federación de Choferes de Lima, with great popular support, gained working improvements in urban transport. Strikes in the mines of Oyolo and Mal Paso, in 1931, and a 1934 strike in Tamboraque, met bloody repression.[13] In 1944 a bakers' strike, touched off by a drop in the weight of bread, achieved not only improved working conditions but also stability in bread prices at a lower rate. Bus drivers obtained a wage increase in the same year, but a 50 per cent fare increase followed. The Federación Textil (which had itself been on strike earlier in the year) struck to protest the raised fares, and won nullification of the increase after violent fighting in the streets. In September 1944 a general strike was called, to support a number of small strikes that had been in stalemate for some time. It lasted three days, and its pressure forced favorable solutions to the minor disputes.[14]

Under the dictatorship of General Manuel Odría (1948–56), aprista leaders were once again persecuted, and the CTP was effectively dismantled. With the support of the dictator, who had placed Luna in the Senate, the Communists gained control of several unions. In 1949, Luis

---

* José Carlos Mariátegui (1895–1930) was perhaps Latin America's only Marxist theoretician. He founded the Peruvian Socialist Party in 1928, a member of the Communist International, but his ideas were later repudiated by Moscow.

Negreiros, a major figure in the labor movement, was killed, and the principal union leaders were jailed. Odría suppressed all attempts to reestablish the CTP; each time the CTP reorganization committee petitioned for its return, the government moved to place Communists in leadership posts, and when the old leaders refused to accept them, the government prohibited the reopening of union headquarters.[15]

After Odría resigned in 1956, the CTP resumed operation; for the most part its leaders were drawn from democratic elements, especially the apristas, though the Communists did for a time retain control of several unions in Arequipa and Cuzco. Arturo Sabroso, an old militant of anarcho-syndicalist origin with a long history of persecution, again became Secretary General of the CTP.

The CTP's success in affording its members ideological training is noteworthy. There are several union schools, and membership campaigns undertaken since 1957 have created some 900 new unions and, in 1959, a peasants' federation, which in 1961 included 300 union locals.[16]

In 1962, when a military revolt preempted the national elections, the CTP declared a general strike—which, however, failed to topple the new dictatorship. Nor was the labor picture in Peru effectively altered by the elections of 1963.

ECUADOR

Between 1890 and 1895 the artisans of Guayaquil and Quito organized mutual-aid societies; but the union movement in Ecuador actually began in 1920 with the formation of a railroad workers' union.[17] In 1922 the Confederación de Sindicatos Obreros was formed; though of little consequence, it did manage, in 1928, to encourage the enactment of Ecuador's first labor law.

The 1929 Constitution introduced the concept of "functional senators," selected by trades or social groups. Union representatives formed an electoral college, which elected a "functional" Labor Senator every four years in each of two electoral districts—one comprising the coast, and the other the interior.[18]

In 1937, two rival federations were formed, the Unión Sindical de Trabajadores de Pichincha and the Confederación de Trabajadores de Guayas; and in 1939, the Confederación General de Trabajadores and the Confederación de Trabajadores Católicos were added to this list. The last operated from Quito, whereas the other three maintained headquarters in Guayaquil.

But in 1941 a new law stunned the labor movement by authorizing the police to close down the union halls and presses.

In 1943, after long negotiations, a workers' congress was called, with government approval. The government hoped that the congress would back official policy, especially a new labor code then under consideration. But when it became evident during the first session that the congress was about to form a workers' federation and adopt an intransigent position, the government forcibly dissolved it, and attempted to organize its own labor congress. By 1944 the political climate had changed again, and the Confederación de Guayas and the Unión de Pichincha, both led by socialists and Communists, created the Confederación de Trabajadores del Ecuador (CTE), which joined CTAL.[19] Its first President was Pedro Saad, a Communist congressman.

Though the CTE has been, since 1955, the only Latin American federation affiliated with CTAL, it has not monopolized the Ecuadorian labor movement. In 1960 the Confederación Obrera del Guayas (COG) joined ORIT. Together with various autonomous unions, it formed a Coordinating Committee for Free Union Organizations, which founded the Confederación Regional de Organizaciones Clasistas del Litoral Ecuatoriano (CROCLE), also affiliated with ORIT.[20]

In various periods the CTE has formed political alliances for electoral purposes: one with the Popular Forces, initiated by a reactionary movement in Guayaquil, and several that brought Velasco Ibarra to power in 1952 and 1960. Velasco seems to have made a pact with the CTE that would guarantee him the Confederación's support within the country in exchange for his diplomatic support of Fidel Castro. The rising cost of living and new tax proposals in 1961 obliged CTE leaders to give way to pressure from below and oppose Velasco; but their opposition was decidedly half-hearted.[21]

The Confederación Ecuatoriana de Obreros Católicos (CEDOC), though not very powerful, has been active since 1938. And in 1962 a Comité Pro Unidad Sindical began working for the unification of non-Communist unions in a single federation and established the Confederación Ecuatoriana de Organizaciones Sindicales Libres (CEOSL), which affiliated with ORIT.[22]

When the military established a new dictatorship, in 1963, the union movement was weakened but not paralyzed. Labor rights were restored after the Junta was overthrown in 1966.

14. Colombia and Venezuela

THE UNION MOVEMENT in Colombia and Venezuela was late getting under way—owing, in Colombia, to the lack of an industrial proletariat, and in Venezuela, to the long dictatorship of Juan Vicente Gómez.

COLOMBIA

Before 1900, no unions existed in Colombia, though anarchist thought had by then attracted some following. And while the conservatives held power, possibilities for union development were slight: between 1909 and 1919 only 37 legally sanctioned unions were active; and between 1919 and 1930, only 107. When anarchists demonstrated in Bogotá on May 15, 1916, many workers were killed and 500 were jailed. The anarchists also inspired a longshoremen's strike in Cartagena, in February 1920.[1]

By the decade 1920–30, various small labor organizations had formed and a few important strikes had been declared—among them that of the Santa Marta banana workers in 1928, which attained revolutionary proportions. In October, official reaction produced the Social Defense Law, which prohibited meetings or organizing, under any label, for the customary purposes of the labor movement.[2]

In 1936 the Confederación de Trabajadores de Colombia (CTC) was created. It was supported by the government and included three powerful federations—the railroad workers, the rivermen on the Magdalena River, and the oilworkers—as well as a considerable number of industrial and professional unions. For some time it also had the backing of workers from the province of Antioquía, but they withdrew after 1940. Though it had been agreed at the outset that leadership of the CTC would be shared by Communists, socialists, and anarcho-syndicalists, the Communist Party came to dominate it.

In 1946 the CTC comprised 472 union locals and 109,477 members,[3] and was controlled by a coalition of liberals and Communists. When a conservative candidate was victorious in the 1946 Presidential election, the CTC's fortunes waned. A rival was born: the Unión de Trabajadores de Colombia (UTC), which derived its support from Antioquía workers and was led by Acción Católica and a group of Jesuits headed by Father Vicente Andrade. By the end of 1949 the UTC claimed as many members as the CTC.

Under the guise of mediator between the people and the oligarchs, the dictator Gustavo Rojas Pinilla (1953–57) attempted to stimulate his own union movement. To this end, he created in 1954 the Confederación Nacional de Trabajadores (CNT), and engineered its affiliation with the Peronist ATLAS. The CNT, together with the Movimiento de Acción Nacional, then proposed the constitution of a third force, of a *justicialista* type. The Army Chief of Staff, General Rafael Calderón Reyes, coordinated this effort. To lend Rojas' regime a democratic flavor, a Gran Central Obrera was improvised. When this maneuver failed, Rojas turned to wooing the Catholic UTC, which over the years had greatly liberalized its concepts.[4] But rather than fall in behind Rojas, the UTC supported the general strike (of laborers, industrial workers, tradesmen, and even bankers) that overthrew Rojas in March 1957. Meanwhile, the Communists had lost the leadership of the CTC.

In 1961 the two major union federations—the UTC and the CTC, both now affiliated with ORIT—renewed negotiations toward unification, initiated two years previously, but without success. Both federations began to turn some of their attention to agrarian issues.[5] Since 1963, several CTC unions have fallen again into Communist hands and have been expelled. The UTC has become the principal, most dynamic Federation of a rather weak and passive labor movement.

VENEZUELA

In Venezuela, until well into the twentieth century, workers were prevented from organizing by the succession of dictatorships that controlled the country. A Confederación de Obreros y Artesanos del Distrito Federal (COADF) was so thoroughly subjugated by the government that in August 1922 the "dean of Caracas workers" was prevailed upon to place a Confederación medal around the neck of General Juan Vicente Gómez.

During a conference of the American Federation of Labor, the Puerto Rican delegate Louis Muñoz Marín proposed that the Pan American Labor Federation be requested to conduct an investigation in Venezuela, in view of reports from Venezuelan exiles that human and union rights were being violated. The request was granted. The COADF immediately published a pamphlet in English accusing the AFL of attempted intervention in Venezuela's internal affairs. The pamphlet protested that Venezuelan workers had no reason to complain about Gómez's government—that, indeed, he had improved living conditions—and that "Our legislation includes no special legislation for the protection of the worker simply because of the equity of our civil law, and above all because of the safeguard afforded by our national traits." Photographs in the pamphlet show labor leaders visiting the "hero of peace and work," as the document characterized Gómez. It added that "almost all of us enjoy an eight-hour working day."

Nevertheless, workers began to take action on their own. In 1922 a strike of streetcar drivers took place. The public, despite bearing the brunt of the inconvenience occasioned by the strike, supported the workers' stand; and the government, finding itself helpless to break the strike, pressed for acceptance of workers' demands.[6] Gómez went on to decide that Venezuela should join ILO, and permitted the formation of a few unions (with police informers in the key posts). These unions, which made up the Federación Obrera, finally served as the pretext for the creation of authentic unions, which managed an opposition of sorts and declared several strikes. (A group of Spanish anarcho-syndicalists and socialists, exiled from Spain when General Miguel Primo de Rivera established his dictatorship, were an important element of the opposition.) Under Gómez's persecutions, many genuine unionists died in La Rotunda jail, or as a result of torture. But the repressions failed to prevent Valmore Rodríguez from creating unions in the provinces, or the old Asociación de Linotipistas from being reborn in Caracas.[7]

The oil workers were the first to organize after Gómez's death in 1935. For a time they took reprisals against the employers' goons and foremen, but soon they formed unions and settled down to a struggle on less brutal ground. To protest their miserable living conditions, they declared a strike, but the oil companies refused to heed their requests. For 43 days the strikers sustained the walkout, housed and fed all the while by industrial workers, tradesmen, and intellectuals. The government then decreed an obligatory return to work, at a slight increase in pay.

By now it had become apparent that the Federación Obrera would have to change hands. Leaders who had supported the dictatorship gave way to elements favoring nonpolitical unions, and the new elements rechristened the federation the Confederación Sindical Obrera de Venezuela (CSOV). But in 1936 the democratic parties had acquired enough support from the working classes to sponsor a Venezuelan Labor Congress, which put an end to the CSO.[8]

In 1937 the government blocked an effort to form a Confederación Nacional del Trabajo. But after 1941 the unions began to establish a firm footing, owing chiefly to the activities of elements from the Partido Democrático Nacional, from which Acción Democrática (AD) later emerged. Under President Medina Angarita, AD managed to place its members in the ranking elective offices of many existing unions; the Communists, nonetheless, competing with the support of the government, won considerable influence in the union movement.

Early in 1944 a congress was held to create a labor federation. But when a member of Acción Democrática proposed that Executive Committee posts be divided equally between Communist Party and AD representatives, the Communists refused. Medina Angarita adjourned the congress, on the pretext that the law forbade political activities in the unions. In the union elections held a short time later, Acción Democrática captured most of the directive posts, though a federation was still not on the horizon.

When Acción Democrática overthrew Medina Angarita in 1945 and came to power, the unions were able to take action. For the first time, workers and peasants were democratically elected to the National Congress. And in November 1947 the Confederación de Trabajadores de Venezuela (CTV) was formed. Later, CTV joined the CIT.

The victory of Acción Democrática was particularly beneficial to the oilworkers. In 1946 the first collective contract between the oil industry and the oilworkers' union was signed, with important gains for the workers. Communist groups opposed the agreement, and instigated local strikes wherever they could exert sufficient influence. The government declared these strikes illegal, and the federation expelled the Communists, who then created their own Confederación de Trabajadores del Petróleo. (In 1959, when Venezuela emerged from another dictatorship, history repeated itself, and the Communists were again expelled from the oilworkers' union.)[9]

The revolutionary government also adopted measures to fight unemployment. The average income of the worker increased 175 per cent in two years, without bringing on inflation. In 1936 there had been 113 unions; in 1948, when the military led a coup against President Rómulo Gallegos, there were 1,014. There were few strikes and many collective contracts, frequently achieved through the mediation of the government. The military coup interrupted negotiations with employers' organizations, initiated at the suggestion of the CTV, toward "safeguarding civic order and defending the nation's industry and human resources."[10]

"During the brief period of its first administration, Acción Democrática created the forces necessary to sustain itself, in order to effect reforms; this it did with unionism. Add to this the building of schools, the training of teachers and the drafting of an economic development program, and we have seen what is humanly possible to achieve in just over 24 months."[11]

One of the first tactics undertaken by the military, after the coup in November 1948, was the sacking and closing down of union locals. The tracking down of labor and peasant leaders became a vicious, brutal hunt; more than a few employers and hacienda owners took advantage of it to fire workers, lower salaries, and unilaterally nullify collective labor contracts. The workers responded with a series of strikes. Then, in February 1949, the dictatorship ordered the dissolution of the CTV and all its affiliate federations, including those of the peasants and oilworkers. The decree did permit individual unions to continue operation, though subject to police control. Moreover, the Communist-led union organizations were spared the government's attacks.*

During this period the Fourth Conference of the American States Members of the ILO was held in Montevideo. Several delegates—chiefly labor members of various delegations, but also governmental members from some countries—raised the question of current violations of union rights in Venezuela and Peru. Their allegations led the assembly to instruct the ILO Administrative Board to investigate labor conditions in these two countries. In its report, the ILO mission states that "During the course of this investigation the mission found not one person, neither among public authorities nor within industrial circles, who denied the repressions directed against union leaders." After confirming that "in Venezuela labor enjoys no freedom of action or organization," the mission added: "The labor movement in Venezuela has become indispensable to the normal functioning of industrial relationships; the elimination or subjugation of union organizations means the elimination or weakening of a regulatory element essential to the social life of the country."[13]

In 1948 there had been 1,014 unions operating in Venezuela, but by 1950 the number had fallen to 387. In 1950 a major strike broke out in the oil fields, paralyzing production. Meanwhile, 95 delegates to the Thirty-Third International Labor Conference, held in Geneva in June 1950, rejected the Venezuelan "labor" delegation as "usurpers."

In March 1952 the Minister of Interior Relations instructed local governors to recruit and send to Caracas, at government expense, a number of delegates chosen by labor inspectors. They were to attend the First National Convention of Independent Unions, which created a Confederación Nacional de Trabajadores, affiliated with the Peronist ATLAS, for which

---

* Betancourt had this to say of the Communists: "The position taken during this period by the lawyer Vicente Lombardo Toledano is significant: addressing a forum of the United Nations and speaking for the WFTU (a militantly Communist body), he concentrated his attacks on the Cuban government of Carlos Prío Socarrás and the Chilean [administration] of Gabriel González Videla—not a word did he devote to Venezuela. At that time only the [Venezuelan] labor organizations whose leaders were politically affiliated with Acción Democrática had been suppressed; the Confederación de Trabajadores del Petróleo and other groups under Communist leadership stood outside the hostility of the military junta."[12]

the government then constructed a luxurious headquarters in Caracas.[14]

The dictatorship, seeking international ties, had invited the ILO to hold the fifth meeting of its Oil Industry Commission in Caracas. The ICFTU and ORIT, as well as important national member federations from all parts of the world, objected to the proposal. The matter was heatedly discussed in the ILO Council. Disregarding the opposition of the labor group, the Administrative Board decided to accept the invitation. The International Federation of Oil Workers, the AFL and CIO, Great Britain's TUC, and other national union federations from all countries of the free world, directed their protests to the ILO General Director, and announced their decision to send no prominent representatives to the conference of the Oil Industry Commission. In a charged atmosphere the Caracas meeting finally got under way, in April 1955. During the inaugural session and in the presence of the dictator, and speaking for the labor group in the ILO Administrative Board, the Dutch oilworkers' leader, C. Vermeulen, stated: "For the past six years the Administrative Board has been receiving continuous complaints regarding the violation of free union principles in Venezuela. Even today, union leaders are still in jail. And in most cases the charges against them have never been given due legal consideration . . . it is clear that in Venezuela union freedom . . . remains an unrealized goal." The government ordered Vermeulen's immediate exile from the country. Faced with these conditions, the Oil Industry Commission had no recourse but to suspend its Caracas meeting. The following day the ILO General Director received a message from the Venezuelan Foreign Minister protesting the suspension and notifying him of Venezuela's withdrawal from the ILO.[15]

A strike committee, organized in January 1958 after Pérez Jiménez's fall, constituted itself as a Comité Sindical Unificado in order to reorganize the CTV, and submitted a report to the CTV's third congress, in 1959. More than a million urban and rural workers were represented at this congress, from nine national federations, 685 unions, and 1,250 peasants' organizations. The congress declared that although the CTV was not apolitical, it was nevertheless independent of the state and the political parties; that it was governed by the principles of union democracy; and that among its principal concerns were lasting peace, the defense of democracy, the struggle to achieve [for Venezuela] economic independence, industrialization, and agrarian reform, and the integration of Latin America.[16] At this congress the CTV also signed a pact of friendship with the Cuban CTC.

In July 1958 and again in September, the military attempted to overthrow the provisional regime that followed the dictatorship. On both occasions, labor promptly declared a general strike, and the attempts were quelled.

Although all the non-Communist elements in the CTV Congress of 1959 supported the new coalition government of Betancourt, two separate wings began to form: the majority continued to support the government, while the minority aligned itself with the Communist Party. The minority acquired a certain amount of strength when Acción Democrática elements led by José Domingo Rangel separated from AD and formed the MIR (Movimiento de Izquierda Revolucionaria). In October 1960, Castroite and Communist elements organized a sedition movement against the democratic government—it was not to Castro's advantage to allow Venezuela to demonstrate that a revolution can be successful without firing squads, totalitarianism, or Soviet help. The October movement coincided, certainly by no accident, with an attempted military insurrection. Castroite and Communist elements in the unions tried, unsuccessfully, to proclaim a general strike. Of the 14 members of the CTV Executive Committee, five supported the attempt and were suspended by the Committee's majority. The CTV also broke its pact with the Cuban CTC.

During its Fourth Congress, in November 1961, the CTV agreed to join the ICFTU and the International Federation of Christian Trade Unions, as well as their regional organizations, ORIT and CLASC. This decision, which led to increasing coordination difficulties, came about as a product of the tacit alliance between union militants of Acción Democrática and of the Christian-democratic party (COPEI), an alliance that consistently defeated Communist attempts to claim posts in the Federation's directive committees. The Congress condemned dictatorships, especially those of Castro and Franco, and offered its active support of the agrarian reform proposed by the Government. It finally rejected a proposal to support the creation of a Latin American union federation, on grounds that such a federation would tend to weaken the union movement of the hemisphere.[17] The Communists, in 1964, created their own Confederación Unificada de Trabajadores (CUT), but it proved to be of very limited influence.

In the fight against Castroite terrorism and reactionary coups, the CTV effectively backed Rómulo Betancourt's government. This support gave Acción Democrática leaders sufficient authority to insist on Raúl Leoni as AD's 1964 candidate. Several CTV leaders have held seats in the National Congress, and have supported the Leoni government. More important, however, has been its participation in non-labor-oriented activities: it has, for example, organized the peasants in a Federación Campesina, and has created a Workers' Bank and several housing cooperatives. But because of its growth, the CTV has become more moderate and has begun to suffer to some degree from bureaucratization.

15. Central America

In Central America, dictatorships and oligarchies delayed the onset of unionism for decades; its emergence there has in fact been quite recent.

Just as there have been various attempts to establish a Central American Union on a political and economic level, so the labor movement has often tried to create a Central American Federation. In 1911 the First Central American Labor Congress was held in San Salvador. In the late 1920's, labor groups representing Guatemala, El Salvador, Honduras, Nicaragua, and Costa Rica formed the Confederación Obrera Centroamericana, with headquarters rotating among the five nations, which joined PAFL for some time. The federation held several congresses, but was finally disbanded as a result of changing political conditions. In December 1961 the Third Union Conference of the Central American countries took place in San Salvador (only Nicaragua was absent), with ORIT sanction; a Consejo Sindical Coordinador Centroamericano was established by the Conference.[1]

PANAMA

Until 1920 there were no unions in Panama, though a strike broke out among canal workers in 1917. U.S. workers in the Canal Zone were organized within the AFL, but had no active relations with Panamanian workers. In 1926, labor groups in Panama created a Federación Obrera de la República and a Unión de Trabajadores Panameños de la Zona del Canal. These unions were heterogeneous groups: the workers mingled with intellectuals, who saw in the workers a means of political expression. Heavy immigration from the Caribbean, and marked differences in wages for equivalent jobs within and outside the Canal Zone, contributed to the weakness of Panamanian unionism.

Legislation did not favor union activity, and the few liberal elements who sought to win approval for a labor code failed. The dedicated urgings of two socialist congressmen led to the recognition of union freedom in the 1946 Constitution. It was, again, socialists who made the most effectual efforts in organizing unions, and in binding them together in a Federación Sindical de Trabajadores (FST). The new federation's leaders drifted away from the Socialist Party after 1948, and the union movement began to crumble, chiefly as a result of rivalry between socialists and Communists.[2]

In 1949, several rival organizations were competing for labor support: the Unión Nacional de Sindicatos Obreros (UNSO); the Confederación de Obreros y Campesinos (COC), which in 1956 merged with the Confederación Agraria Nacional; the Federación Sindical de Trabajadores (FST); and the Unión General de Trabajadores (UGT). Finally, in 1955, some 20 unions formed the Confederación de Trabajadores y Campesinos de Panamá (CTCP), which then absorbed most of these federations. The CTCP, affiliated with ORIT, backed the banana workers in their successful strikes of 1960, and has waged a strong campaign for wage equality in the Canal Zone.[3] It has never been possible to unionize the plantation workers and the seamen in ships flying the Panamanian flag; both groups have extremely poor working conditions.

COSTA RICA

Costa Rica's scant industrial development explains why its labor organizations have been mostly small-trade, almost artisan, unions. The most important labor group has been the banana workers, who, for example, called several important strikes against the plantations in 1934.

Two still-extant rival federations were created during World War II: the Confederación de Trabajadores de Costa Rica (CTCR), under Communist leadership; and the Confederación Costarricense del Trabajo "Rerum Novarum" (CCT), of Catholic leanings. The formation of the CCT was inspired by the Archbishop Víctor Sanabria, though one of his disciples, Father Benjamín Núñez, was its actual organizer. In August 1943 Núñez opened his campaign with a speech in Cartago; shortly afterward he had 15 unions operating. The CCT member unions never questioned the religious affiliations of their members. "The unions," said Núñez, "include among other humanitarian aims the inculcation [in workers] of ethical and moral standards that are common to all religions and are the exclusive property of none. What we consider fundamental are the individual human being and his sense of dignity. As a result, we are neither Communists nor socialists, but, if I may be allowed to coin the term, 'personists.'" A year later, plantation operators opened negotiations with the Communist unions, and the CTCR demands were mild in the extreme.

Rerum Novarum, on the other hand, was less easily put off, and the plantation workers began to switch their allegiance.[4]

In 1955, Rerum Novarum (the CCT) managed to effect a few contracts with coffee and sugar producers in which the workers were awarded a share of the profits. At about the same time, the CTCR was reorganized—after a period in which the Communist Party had been outlawed—under the name Confederación General de Trabajadores Costarricenses (CGTC). The rivalry between the two federations was most pronounced in the banana-growing regions. In 1961 the CCT, by then affiliated with ORIT, began efforts to penetrate these regions, which until then had been dominated by the Communist unions.[5] In 1966, the CCT changed its title and became the Confederación Costarricense de Trabajadores Democráticos (CCTD).

During the period 1943-51, 372 unions were formed in Costa Rica; but of these, 163 soon dissolved, most through the apathy of their members. This came about, so say the sociologists, because the Costa Rican is averse to social organization, owing partly to his country's history as an isolated nation and partly to his preference for scattered small agrarian holdings. These penchants have robbed the Costa Rican union movement of most of its strength.[6] The banana plantation workers are organized in the Federación de Trabajadores Bananeros, which since 1949 has remained independent, alternately under Communist and democratic leadership.

NICARAGUA

In 1924 the Obrerismo Organizado de Nicaragua (OON), a labor federation, was formed; it hoped to emancipate workers "by means of organization, education, and regular savings." Its founder, Sofonías Salvatierra, became Minister of Labor and attempted to promote a labor code. But the murder of César A. Sandino, Salvatierra's friend and colleague, caused Salvatierra to leave the Ministry. The OON, though politically moderate, had spoken out in Sandino's defense when he had led guerrillas against the U.S. Marines (1928-30). The OON later subjugated itself completely to the dictator Anastasio Somoza, and became, finally, nothing more than a letterhead.

In 1943, CTAL, on the pretext of requesting the freedom of several prisoners, established contact with General Anastasio Somoza.[7] The dictator permitted the formation, two years later, of the Confederación de Trabajadores de Nicaragua (CTN), a labor federation led by elements from the recently created Socialist Party, though in reality a Communist organization.[8] But in 1947 both the unions and the Party were abolished by the Government. In 1949 again Somoza permitted the organization of unions, though all were led by elements loyal to the dictator (except for a few union locals where Communists had infiltrated). For a short time there was a Peronist federation, the CGT. Also active have been the Communist-controlled UGT, the Federación Nacional de Sindicatos Democráticos (FNSD), the Comité Organizador de Sindicatos Libres (COSL), and the Federación de Obreros y Campesinos (FOC). Only after Somoza's death in 1956 was it possible for opposition parties (conservative and independent liberal) to exert influence in the unions; but the unions have never given evidence of favoring genuine independence.[9]

EL SALVADOR

In El Salvador, a country without industry, artisans' guilds were for years the sole extent of organization among the working classes. The guilds banded together in 1914 as the Confederación de Obreros. Eleven years later, Communist sympathizers organized the Federación Regional de Trabajadores de Oriente.

Around 1931 a peasant movement began to develop, headed, apparently, by Communists. In January 1932, the Communists (notably Farabundo Martí and Octavio Rodríguez) incited the peasants to a takeover of coffee plantations and military barracks. The theosophist dictator Maximiliano Hernández Martínez ordered a massacre, which produced, according to reports, 10,000 dead.[10] Martí, a law student and the scion of a prominent family, had been Sandino's secretary in the Segovia Mountains of Nicaragua, during the guerrilla resistance to the intervention of the U.S. Marines. A moment before being shot by order of Hernández Martínez, he stated: "My break with Sandino was not brought on, as has been said, by differences on moral points, or by different standards of conduct. I refused to join him again in the Segovias because he wanted no part of the Communist program I had been defending. His only interest was independence. A step away from execution, I solemnly maintain that General Sandino is the world's foremost patriot."[11] Martí's statement later became a serious blow to Communist propaganda.

A general strike—without organized unions—overthrew Hernández Martínez in May 1944.[12] After his fall, workers' groups organized the Unión de Trabajadores. The Unión exercised considerable influence on electoral politics, but was crushed when Chief of Police Osmín Aguirre came to power.

In 1948, when President Salvador Casteñeda Castro instituted measures to prolong his term of office, he was overthrown by the Army.[13] A Comité Nacional de Coordinación de Sindicatos was immediately created to reorganize the labor movement, but was soon suppressed because of its alleged Communist leadership. The Federación de Trabajadores Ferroviarios, which had, since its formation in 1945, become the most powerful union in the country, achieved a collective contract with the rail companies in a 1949 strike.

Under the governments of Colonels Oscar Osorio and José Lemus, several social laws favorable to labor were passed, but the peasants were completely ignored. The first to concern themselves with the peasants' plight were members of the Government Junta established by the Army in 1961. The Junta decreed that the landowners were to supply the peasants a certain minimum diet, but the coffee-growing oligarchy protested the decision and achieved its nullification.

The Confederación General Sindical (CGT), established in 1958, joined ORIT.[14] The Communists succeeded, in 1960, in forming the Federación Unitaria Sindical (FUS). Both groups are small and ineffectual.

HONDURAS

Labor unions made their first appearance perhaps later in Honduras than anywhere else in Latin America. The Federación Obrera Hondureña (FOH), formed in 1929, managed to be neither activist nor influential. It was not until 1948, when President Juan Manuel Gálvez permitted independent unions to organize, that the first social legislation was approved. With the help of ILO a statement of workers' rights was drafted and enacted into law in 1955.

In May 1954 the banana workers declared a strike. Employers seemed prepared to allow the strike to run on indefinitely, in the meantime promising bonuses in hard cash to anyone willing to abandon it, though to no avail. Communists tried to take over the movement; but democratic leaders exposed them, the workers themselves forced them out, and the strike finally gained its ends. Losses in wages, exports, and production were about 18 million dollars, after "a blind effort to resist petitions worth only a fraction of this amount, which were finally accepted anyway."[15] The strike led to unionization, which until that time had been as good as prohibited on the banana plantations;[16] the new union, SITRATERCO (Sindicato de Trabajadores de la Tela Railroad Company), promoted the formation of the Federación Sindical de Trabajadores Norteños de Honduras, which joined ORIT in 1960. The following year the Federación de Sindicatos de Trabajadores Libres del Centro also joined ORIT.[17] And in September 1964 the two groups united as the Confederación de Trabajadores de Honduras (CTH), retaining the ORIT affiliation. Meanwhile, in 1959, the liberal government of Dr. Ramón Villeda Morales had enacted a Labor Code and established a social security system.

The military take-over in 1963 placed the unions in a difficult position, but could not destroy them. Today, Honduras has the strongest labor movement in Central America.

GUATEMALA

El Porvenir de los Obreros was the hopeful title adopted by the first workers' society in Guatemala, when it was established in 1894. Other groups arose later, and in 1912 the various societies united as the Federación de Sociedades Obreras, later the Federación Obrera de Guatemala para la Protección Legal del Trabajo, which soon vanished.

Around 1920 there were a number of artisans' mutual-aid societies which at times allied with conservative leaders. In 1928, during a period of brief freedom, a new Federación Obrera was formed. Small Communist groups, more disciplined than the unaligned workers' groups, soon gathered strength in the Federación. But from 1931 to 1944, under the harsh dictatorship of General Jorge Ubico, all attempts to organize labor were punished with imprisonment or death. Finally, in June 1944, students organized a general strike; after six days, Ubico resigned, and unions immediately began to organize, meeting in the Federación Obrera's locals, which the dictator had kept shut down. Printers were the first to organize, followed by the railroad workers. The latter had formed the Unión Ferrocarrilera before Ubico; in 1941 they had attempted a reorganization, but had been prevented by the dictator.

Soon the first strikes broke out, and General Federico Ponce's government reacted by obstructing union activities. The situation was such that a hastily organized businessmen's party could seriously call itself the Partido Social Democrático. In September 1944 a group called Claridad was founded, whose members, indoctrinated by Communists, worked actively within the unions. The group also created a school to train workers for union membership.

In October 1944, ten unions founded the Confederación Guatemalteca de Trabajadores (CGT), with the slogan "For the unification of the proletariat and its social vindication." Various groups struggled for power within the CGT: anarchists, Claridad (Communists), and a group supporting Juan José Arévalo, who was then a presidential candidate.

On October 20, 1944, elements of the Army overthrew Ponce. Workers and students received arms from the soldiers. The CGT ran several congressional candidates in the ensuing election, but their man attracted only a few votes; this, and the Revolutionary Junta's expulsion of some CGT advisers accused of intrigue with General Ponce, considerably weakened the federation. Claridad, without revealing its true ideology, began to take over key posts. Many of the men thus established were Salvadorian exiles, and their opponents in the unions invoked superpatriotism in their objections—with the effect of jeopardizing, rather than enhancing, the anti-Communist position.[18] The CGT thereafter suffered several schisms, from which other organizations emerged—the Federación Sindical de Guatemala, the Federación Obrera Regional de Trabajadores, and the Confederación de Trabajadores de Guatemala (Communist), each linked to a different political party.

In 1945 a Congreso de Unidad Sindical was held, which stated its support of Arévalo's government but failed to unite the different federations. There followed a period in which the Arévalo regime opposed the unions: it banned the unionization of peasants and, until a labor code was enacted in May 1947, prohibited strikes. Meanwhile, the Comité Nacional de Unidad Sindical was created. On May 1, 1951 (when Communist influence was already strong in many parties), the Comité formed the Confederación de Trabajadores de Guatemala (CGTG), which affiliated with CTAL and united the earlier federations. The new federation grew rapidly and had official backing. When it held its Second Congress, the CGTG included 500 unions and 104,000 members—and the Communists had already assumed its leadership. Communists also controlled the Confederación Nacional Campesina, which years before had broken with the CGT and had since joined the CGTG. As of 1952 there were no independent unions, and labor spokesmen trying to oppose Communist domination of the CGTG were persecuted, beaten, or exiled.[19]

The CGTG became a tool of Jacobo Arbenz's regime (1951–54), and of the Partido Guatemalteco del Trabajo (Communist), and participated in the succession of fronts mounted to assure Communist control of Guatemalan politics. Arbenz's fall in 1954 led to the dissolution of the CGTG, which had made no attempt at all to defend Arbenz's regime. Labor, for a time, was without union representation.

Under the regime of Colonel Carlos Castillo Armas (1954–57), the unions began to reorganize, but have still to achieve any real influence. The working class was disenchanted and apathetic, and lacked well-trained leaders. Little by little, however, the unions grew in strength, and eventually created a Consejo Sindical de Guatemala (CSG), which, though not actually a union federation, coordinated the activities of the affiliated unions and organized seminars and training courses. A Federación Autónoma Sindical (FAS), established in 1956 by Christian-democratic elements, soon fell under Communist control. Leadership posts in the Consejo were contested by the Christian-democrats and elements of the Partido Revolucionario. The Consejo Sindical joined ORIT. Its first congress, held in

October 1961, was attended by delegates from ten unions; the congress resolved to press for true agrarian reform and for government ratification of ILO agreements.[20] The railroad and plantation workers' unions remained independent.

The military coup mounted against President General Miguel Ydígoras, undertaken to prevent the 1963 elections, apparently failed to affect the unions, some of them even collaborating with the new dictatorship. The government of Julio César Méndez Montenegro, elected in 1966, has respected the unions, but has not enacted new social legislation.

16. The Caribbean Countries

DICTATORSHIPS HAVE BEEN CHRONIC in the independent nations of the Caribbean; and the union movement has in consequence been almost nonexistent, except in Cuba. We shall pass over Puerto Rico and the recent island colonies of European powers, since the labor movements there are markedly different from those elsewhere in Latin America, more nearly resembling the labor movements in the countries of their colonizers, even where colonization has given way to independence or autonomy. Here we shall deal only with Haiti, the Dominican Republic, and Cuba.

HAITI

Haiti's Dessalines Constitution of 1805 called agriculture "the most noble of the arts," and also specified that "every citizen ought to master a mechanical art." But since 1814, when Petion distributed lands, the country has remained essentially agricultural. The working class is very small.[1]

Although a few (generally mutualistic) artisans' organizations existed during the period 1920–30, the labor movement began to emerge only after the 1946 revolution. Several federations were created in subsequent years. The first was the Fédération des Travailleurs Haitiens, founded immediately after the revolution. A schism in 1948 created the Fédération Haitienne du Travail, which by 1949 had become the stronger group. The Union Nationale des Travailleurs, created by the Mouvement Ouvrier et Paysan, was also established.[2] The dictatorship of Paul Magloire (1950–56) dissolved the first two groups.

Although strikes were invariably suppressed with considerable brutality, a general strike in 1956 nonetheless managed to end Magloire's rule. Yet the lesson of Magloire notwithstanding, the new President took no interest in promoting legislation that would guarantee union freedom.

In 1961, leaders of the disbanded Union Nationale des Travailleurs formed a committee in exile, and affiliated with ORIT.[3] The dictatorship of François Duvalier has, since 1957, suppressed all independent unionism.

DOMINICAN REPUBLIC

The first attempt to organize unions in the Dominican Republic took place in the years following World War I. A few strikes were also declared, especially among the longshoremen. Unions were rudimentary, and membership was confined to the artisans of the capital. With the onset of worldwide depression, union activities were intensified, and several major strikes were declared by the Confederación Dominicana del Trabajo (CDT). The CDT, organized in 1929, soon surpassed in importance the Federación de Sindicatos, which had been established in 1928.[4] Rafael Leonidas Trujillo, who rose to power in 1930, organized employers' unions and ordered every known or suspected labor leader liquidated. Two of these—Mauricio Báez, in 1951, and Hernando Hernández, in 1952—were murdered in Cuba, during a time when Trujillo began to be unnerved by his opponents. The opposition had been making the most of the reaction against him on the continent and in the United States.

As part of his entrenchment process, Trujillo completely subordinated the CDT, rendering it no more than an instrument of his policy.[5] In 1944, he sent delegates from the restyled CDT to the CTAL congress, hoping the CDT would join the Communist labor federation. Later, he sent Ramón Marrero Aristy to Cuba to organize the return of the Communist exiles to the Dominican Republic, with the help of the Communist-led CTC of Cuba.* In March 1945, *La Nación,* Trujillo's daily, invited the Communists to organize legally, and Communist exiles returned, forming the Partido Socialista Popular (PSP). Trujillo gave many of them posts in the CDT, but when he saw the PSP meetings becoming a staging area for elements promoting opposition to his regime, he dissolved the PSP. The return of the Communists coincided with preparations for a landing by democratic exiles. The moment thus seeming unpropitious for such a move, the landing had to be postponed and finally failed.

In August 1946, the Communists asserted in Trujillo's *La Nación* their determination to continue the struggle "in accordance with the rights and democratic freedoms [!] espoused in the present constitution [Trujillo's]." In the same journal the Generalissimo remarked: "What better answer, when the existence of a democratic government is questioned, than the very existence of the Partido Socialista Popular, and the freedom of its leaders

---

* Marrero was subsequently appointed Labor Minister in Trujillo's government; he was later killed in an accident, under somewhat doubtful circumstances.

to express themselves in these terms?" Years later, in 1960, Trujillo repeated the maneuver when the other Latin American nations broke off diplomatic relations with him in retaliation for his backing of an attempt on the life of Venezuela's President Betancourt. Trujillo responded by authorizing the formation of the Movimiento Popular Dominicano, led by the Communist Máximo López Molina, which claimed Castroite leanings.[6]

Delegates from Dominican unions appeared at the 1949 Constitutional Congress of the ICFTU, but were barred from the meeting. The congress voted condemnation of Trujilloism, a stand that would be taken time and again by the ICFTU (especially in 1956, when it denounced the regime before the ILO). In 1958 an ICFTU delegation made up of Daniel Benedict of the AFL-CIO and Raúl Valdivida of the Federación de Trabajadores Azucareros de Cuba visited the Dominican Republic and reported that independence in the union movement was a fallacy, and that collective bargaining was nonexistent.[7]

After Trujillo's death in 1961, union leadership began to fall to the opposition parties. Some 70 per cent of the workers had received their wages from the government or from Trujillo family enterprises, and had therefore belonged to the CTD; after Trujillo's death the CTD was left with little more than its officers. The first strikes were organized—by taxi drivers and bus drivers—with a warning to the students to cease their attempts to convert strikes into political movements.[8]

In July 1961 the Frente Obrero Unido pro Sindicatos Autónomos (FOUPSA) was organized; it was led by Augusto Rodríguez Guerrero (a carpenter arrested several times during the Trujillo regime), Miguel Soto, and Héctor Espinal Lucer. In order to counteract the Frente's success, Balaguer's government made contact with the U.S. Teamsters' Union and asked that it take over the reorganization of the CTD. The maneuver failed, and the CTD dissolved.[9]

Differences soon arose in the Frente Obrero. A group of Castroites and Communists, representing unions still not affiliated with any federation, opposed the Frente's joining ORIT. Notwithstanding, in December 1961 the Frente joined ORIT; but Communist and Castroite elements later managed to regain leadership and demanded subsidy from the government.

Democratic unionists created the Bloque de FOUPSA Libre. The Central Sindical de Trabajadores Dominicanos (CESITRADO) and the Confederación Autónoma de Sindicatos Cristianos had also been formed.[10]

All the unions, except for a small group of leaders belonging to the reactionary Unión Cívica Nacional, condemned the military take-over of September 1963, which had overthrown the democratic government of Juan Bosch seven months after it had come to power. The union movement divided on the question of U.S. intervention in April 1965; while Christian and other unions opposed it and supported the constitutionalists, some of ORIT's affiliates remained neutral.

CUBA

Social agitation is an old story in Cuba. By the eighteenth century the *vegueros*—tobacco growers, owners of small fields—had rebelled three times against the fiscal measures adopted by the colonial authorities.[11] And in the nineteenth century, labor struggles were almost periodic: in 1812, Juan Aponte led an uprising that was to have turned the island into a Negro republic; in 1823, when the *vegueros* refused to plant tobacco unless their salaries were raised, twelve of their leaders were hanged; in 1831 the copper miners rebelled; in 1868, when the first war of independence was barely under way, a group of Spanish anarchists led by Saturnino Martínez organized the Sociedad de Tabaqueros; in 1883 the guilds asked that their wages be paid in gold, but dared not strike to achieve their ends;[12] and in 1892 a Congreso Regional Obrero was held, to demand among other things the island's independence and a working day of eight hours.

At the height of the war for independence, Máximo Gómez, the rebel leader, wrote that "We have attracted the willing and steadfast support of the workers; but with very few exceptions, we have been unable to enlist the rich man, the hacendado, to come to our aid." It was, in fact, the hacendado who finally ruled in independent Cuba.

During the decade following independence the labor movement advanced fairly rapidly. By 1902 the longshoremen had already sustained a long and bloody strike, now generally considered the turning point of the Cuban union movement.[13] The strike was resumed in 1908 with, this time, the longshoremen, the masons, and the tobacco growers joining forces to demand that their wages be paid in dollars instead of devalued pesetas. The brotherhood of railroad workers and the seamen's union were formed during World War I, and the first steps were taken toward unionizing sugar-plantation laborers.[14] About this time also, and during the years that followed, the socialists and anarcho-syndicalists were engaged in a bitter, sweeping struggle. But this in no way diminished the effectiveness of pressure from labor, which soon led to important legislation.

In 1910 a proposed law limited the working day in stores and established an eight-hour day for government employees. Later, work was forbidden for minors under 14. The Arteaga Law prohibited the use of vouchers for payment of day wages, but was rarely respected. A 1916 law dealt with on-the-job accidents. Comisiones de Inteligencia were created in 1924 to mediate labor disputes on the docks; representation was drawn from employers and workers, and their meetings were presided over by local judges.[15]

There were many strikes in 1923. President Alfredo Zayas used the police against the strikers and deported several leaders.[16] In 1925 the Confederación Nacional Obrera (CNO) was organized during a congress held in Camagüey that had been called by the Federación Obrera de la Habana. The two organizations were closely allied until the Trotskyite–Stalinist rift emerged in the USSR. The CNO then found itself in the hands of the Stalinists, and the Federación de la Habana in the hands of the Trotskyites. The latter then withdrew from the Cuban Communist Party and founded a Partido Bolchevique Leninista. The Trotskyites felt there could be no revolution in Cuba so long as socialism remained a minor force in the United States, because of the island's economic dependence on the U.S. The Stalinists, on the other hand, sought an immediate revolution, believing that U.S. capitalism could be placated by economic concessions.

The tobacco workers, strongly influenced by the anarcho-syndicalists, were for many years the avant-garde of the Cuban labor movement. But when many of them emigrated to the United States, they lost considerable ground. After 1901 the railroad network began to expand, especially with the development of the sugar industry, and by 1923 the Hermandad Ferroviaria had come to be the most influential Cuban labor union. In 1925 the Federación Marítima was formed, and (a rare thing) the physicians also formed a union.[17]

When Gerardo Machado came to power in 1925, he suppressed strikes and announced that he would deport foreign-born union leaders (most especially, the Spanish anarcho-syndicalists). Leaders were murdered, and the offices of the CNO and the Federación de la Habana were closed down by the government. The only federation to enjoy a certain leniency was the Federación Cubana del Trabajo (FCT), which had been established some years before and had later affiliated with COPA, the Pan-American Labor Organization. The events of 1933 did away with the FCT.[18]

Under Machado—who as a candidate had made countless promises to the workers—the unions dispersed under the pressure of government persecution. Those of a group called La Fabril disappeared; the Hermandad Ferroviaria was neutralized; the Centro Obrero de la Habana (consisting of 50 unions) was dissolved; and the Federación de Torcedores, which boasted 50 tobacco workers' unions and a building worth a quarter of a million pesos, was forced to cease its activities. The situation was not totally attributable to the dictatorship: the bulk of the Cuban proletariat was scattered and seasonally employed (largely in the cane and tobacco fields); and Spanish immigrants, who could have helped to revive the labor movement, found themselves attracted to Spanish regional clubs, which opposed interference in the island's social structure. Furthermore, the workers, because of their scant political training, failed to exert control over their own leaders; corrupt governments took advantage of their laxity by attempting to woo their leaders, sometimes successfully. The situation was aggravated by the importation of workers from Jamaica and Haiti, who offered their labor for a pittance and thus made effective protest almost impossible.[19]

Suppression of the labor movement became so harsh that the AFL sent an investigative mission to Cuba, in answer to an epidemic of "suicides" among cane workers, who were found hanging from trees in many parts of the island. As a result of the AFL report, New York longshoremen refused to unload Cuban sugar. During a visit to the United States in 1927, Machado sought to arrange a meeting with William Green, president of the AFL, in the hope that he might see the report retracted, but Green refused the meeting. Yet the report prompted the FCT and the Hermandad Ferroviaria to dispatch reports of their own confirming Machado as "the worker's friend."

Until 1927 the Cuban delegation at the ILO Conference had a university professor as labor representative. In 1927 the unions intervened and chose Dr. Felipe Correoso del Risco, who had headed a movement to restore a law granting railroad workers' pensions, enacted years before. Judging by protests voiced at the conference, the voting was anything but honest.

In August 1933, revolutionary groups ordered a general strike against Machado. The Communist-led but almost defunct CNO attempted to undermine the strike effort but the Federación Obrera de La Habana refused to obey the CNO's order. The strike began with a bus workers' walkout in the capital—the bus workers demanding wage increases. The strike spread quickly and took on a political character. Businessmen joined the strike, paralyzing the economy of the entire island, although the Communists, who had just come to terms with Machado in return for legal recognition, did everything in their power to bring about the movement's failure. So widespread was the movement that on August 11, the Army, fearing that the masses would take over completely, overthrew Machado.[20]

New unions immediately began to organize, and two months later a wave of strikes began. Almost a third of the sugar mills and some of the mines were taken over by workers. The eight-hour working day continued to be a principal demand during this period.

By 1934 there were 800 unions in Cuba grouped in several federations, most of them heavily influenced by anarcho-syndicalism and Communism. The most militant among the working class were the sugar workers, organized since 1933 in the Sindicato Nacional de Obreros de la Industria Azucarera, the most powerful labor group on the island. The most important moderate union was the Hermandad Ferroviaria, with some 20,000 members. Aligned with it were the powerful artisans', longshoremen's, and tobacco workers' unions. The cigar makers (*torcedores*) had developed one of the more powerful unions—aggressive and almost impervious to Communist influence—largely under the leadership of anarcho-syndicalists. While the cigar makers worked, one of their number read newspapers, books, and magazines aloud, so that they might acquire broader social understanding.[21]

In 1934 these unions took measures to form a Unión General de Trabajadores (UGT), which was to be free of "foreign influences." The UGT asked for socialization of land, nationalization of public services, and profit sharing. Meanwhile the Confederación Nacional Obrera (CNO) had, by 1934, come to number more than 200 affiliate unions and 300,000 members, among them 100,000 from the sugar industry. The CNO was led by Communists (indeed, affiliated through the CSLA with the Profintern), but many of its unions did not share the views of the national leadership. A chief reason for the CNO's strength—apart from the absence of revolutionary rivals—was the position of many employers, who expected U.S. intervention and refused to yield to workers' demands. This induced workers to support the "all-or-nothing" position adopted during this period by the CNO's leaders.[22] After 1934 the CNO was weakened by the openly political nature of its activities.

The labor movement gained great impetus from the laws enacted by Ramón Grau San Martín's first government, especially a law of forced unionization and a law according state functionaries the role of arbiter in labor disputes. The government also decreed a minimum wage, the eight-hour working day, measures for the protection of women and children, and workmen's compensation. Above all, it enacted laws for collective contracts, and a "50-per-cent law," which obliged management to hire at least half its workers from the Cuban labor pool.[23] One of the most astonishing measures adopted during this period was the order to deport the foreign-born poor; the order was directed at the 100,000-odd Jamaican and Haitian workers who had been brought into the country in the preceding years to cut cane. When unemployment set in, the protests of the Cuban workers—they spoke even of the "Africanization" of the island—led to the deportation order.

Sergeant Fulgencio Batista's coming to power in 1935 brought on a general strike; but when the Communist-led CNO threw in its support only at the last minute, the strike was doomed. The union movement, for the moment paralyzed, began to recover in 1938. In January 1939 the Confederación de Trabajadores de Cuba (CTC) was organized; under its Secretary General, Lázaro Peña, the CTC joined CTAL. Four months earlier, Batista had legalized the Communist Party, which from the start controlled the CTC. The CTC frequently organized mass demonstrations in support of Batista, usually when the Communists had strengthened their collaboration with Batista's regime in return for some benefit—Radio Mil Diez, the newspaper *Hoy,* election victories, or cabinet posts.[24]

When Grau San Martín won the election of 1944, the Communists assumed, because they had supported Batista, and because their rivals were labor leaders from Grau's party (Partido Revolucionario Auténtico), that they would be removed from the CTC leadership. But when Grau set about to reform the labor movement, the Communists threatened him with a general strike. Grau, with a minority in Parliament and an Army inclined toward Batista, felt the time was inappropriate for a showdown with the Communists. To avoid it, he went so far as to make them a gift of $750,000 for the conversion of the jai alai *frontón* to a "Workers' Palace."

But during the three following years the militants of the Auténtico Party worked diligently in the unions, and leadership posts were gradually taken over by *auténticos* allied with independent groups and old syndicalists. Grau had meanwhile won a parliamentary majority and had purged the Army. During the spring of 1947 the Fifth CTC Congress met. The auténticos refused to accept the Communists' hold on the top posts. As a result, two CTC congresses were held; the government sanctioned that of the auténticos and independents, and by the end of 1947 the Communists had lost control of the unions.[25]

During Grau's administration, the unions enjoyed official favor. Indirect taxes on many products were established, in order to finance retirement funds in many professions: on toothpaste, for example, to provide a dentists' fund; and so forth.

Although it split in 1949 when its Secretary General, Angel Cofiño, withdrew with a small group, the CTC of the auténticos, led by Eusebio Mujal, united the vast majority of workers. It was strengthened still further during the administration of Carlos Prío Socarrás, in 1948, which generally favored the unions.

In March 1952, Batista, by this time a general, brought off a coup and returned to power. On the morning of the revolt, the CTC's leaders declared a general strike; but the military had taken over all means of communication, and the strike order never reached the workers. Nor was the CTC prepared for underground work. Furthermore, the Prío government abandoned the struggle before it had begun, and the strike was left without a cause to defend. Batista then prohibited all walkouts for a period of 45 days.[26] To ease this initial opposition, Mujal and his group saw no choice but to form a tacit alliance with Batista. CTC leaders concentrated their hostilities against the Communists, who had once again infiltrated, and the Peronists, who were soon vanquished. Inasmuch as Batista maintained, and even increased, workers' benefits, he faced no opposition from the urban proletariat.[27]

After Batista's coup, the Communists attempted to regain control of the CTC, and sought Batista's help in ousting Mujal, the ex-Communist who had routed them from the CTC leadership. The corruption of the regime penetrated the union movement: Mujal refused to openly oppose Batista, in spite of pressure from ORIT, to which the CTC belonged. And, within the CTC, several Castroite leaders tried unsuccessfully to mobilize the unions.[28]

On April 9, 1958, Fidel Castro gave the order for a general strike. The CTC immediately declared that "There is no general strike, and all workers will remain at their jobs." Indeed, there was not, thanks in part to the disruptive tactics of the Communists. The Communist La Carta Semanal, days after the thwarted strike, claimed that the walkout had failed because Castro refused to ally himself with the Communists.[29] Shortly before Batista's fall the Communists began an active campaign against CTC leaders sympathetic to Castro and against others who opposed Mujal's policies. They were aware that Mujal would be replaced if Batista fell from power, and they sought to forestall his replacement by a non-Communist.[30] This attitude changed when the Communist leader Carlos Rafael Rodríguez went to the Sierra Maestra and came to terms with Castro.

A Cuban labor leader described the evolution of the union movement during the months following Batista's fall: Shortly before Batista's defeat, Conrado Becquer, pro-Castro leader of the sugar workers, called a "workers' congress" in the mountains, to lay plans for the future. Four shifts of six hours each were proposed for the sugar mills, in place of the then-customary eight-hour shifts. This was the only promise, direct or indirect, made by Castro to the workers while he was in the Sierra. Castro's take-over coincided with the beginning of the 1959 sugar season. The workers greeted the proposal for four shifts with enthusiasm, for it would increase employment by 33 per cent. A national assembly of the Confederación de Trabajadores Azucareros was called for the end of January. Castro addressed the assembly personally, and asked that the workers abandon the idea of four shifts "because the revolution demands sacrifices on the part of every Cuban." The only "promise" he had made the workers was abandoned a month after his entrance into Havana.

The Communist Party (PSP), surprised by the sudden collapse of the Batista regime, was poorly prepared to assume the leadership of the unions. Its first attempt to gain control of the CTC was in fact frustrated by the auténticos, who had allied with elements of the July 26 Movement. Known Communists, such as Lázaro Peña, Ursinio Rojas, Juan Taquechel, Ricardo Rodríguez, and Faustino Calcines, withdrew from the scene, leaving secret members of the party to infiltrate the leadership of the unions and the CTC. In this fashion Jesús Soto Díaz, of the textile workers, and José María de la Aguilera, of the bank workers, got themselves appointed to the CTC Provisional Administrative Junta, established by law on January 3, 1959. The CTC also added the word "Revolutionary" to its name.[31]

David Salvador, leader of the Camagüey sugar workers, was named head of the Junta. Salvador had been a member of the Communist Party on one occasion, but had joined the auténticos in the early 1950's and had been with Castro in the Sierra. His aide, Octavio Louit Venzant (Cabrera), was an almost unknown figure in the union movement, but a member of the July 26 Movement who had been in charge of organizing the general strike in the spring of 1958. Other members of the Junta included José Pellón Jaén, of the brewery workers; Conrado Becquer, of the sugar workers; Antonio Torres, of the railroad workers; and two leaders of the Young Catholic Workers, Reinol González and José de Jesús Planas. At the first meeting, then, there were no known members of the PSP (Soto Díaz appearing as a member of the July 26 Movement).

In the spring of 1959, while Castro was on tour in the United States, the unions held their first elections. Elements from the July 26 Movement and the auténticos defeated the PSP candidates. At the end of May, the First Revolutionary Congress of the Confederación de Trabajadores Azucareros took place. Not a single Communist won a leadership post.

Encouraged by the victory of the sugar workers, other members of the CTC proposed plans for a Frente Sindical Humanista, with the backing of 28 unions. Unions of textile workers, bank workers, restaurant employees, and aviation and commercial employees were excluded from the plan because they were in the PSP's hands. The Frente's platform was based on the economic and political programs proposed by the revolutionaries who had toppled Machado's dictatorship in 1933; one of its slogans was "Neither Washington nor Moscow." The Communist daily *Hoy* maintained that this plan would "divide and weaken the revolution," and the plans for the Frente were finally abandoned.

Jesús Soto Díaz had by now become a strong candidate for the Secretary-Generalship of the CTC. To head off his growing strength, Salvador examined the police files on Soto. In military intelligence files he found material indicating that Soto had acted as an informer after the attack on the Presidential Palace in March 1957; no Cuban newspaper had dared mention this fact. Soto, meanwhile, tried to undermine Salvador's position by accusing him of involvement with the "Mujalists" remaining in the union movement.

During the preparations for the CTC's Tenth Congress a heated debate between Salvador and Soto developed. Salvador hoped to come to terms with the legally elected union officials, or wait until they were legally removed from office, rather than attempt a take-over of the unions by illegal means. But at Castro's direct order the debate was abruptly suspended.

A Salvador partisan[32] summed up the Tenth Congress and its outcome as follows:

> The Social-democrat Labor Minister Fernández García, who had been under attack from the Communists for some time, was discharged from his post just prior to the Congress. He was replaced by the lawyer Augusto Martínez Sánchez, a tool of Raúl Castro, who until then had been Defense Minister, and who had participated in the elections held by Batista in 1954. The Ministry quickly filled up with Communists, who immediately tried to exert pressure on the delegates to the Congress. In spite of efforts by the new Labor Minister and by Raúl Castro, it was obvious, when the union elections were over and the Congress convened, that democratic forces everywhere outnumbered those controlled by the Communists. Delegates from the July 26 Movement and the Auténticos numbered some 3,000, Communists and pro-Communists only 265. Moreover, six of the eight members of the CTC provisional board supported Salvador, and 27 out of 33 industrial Federations were anti-Communist.
>
> The Congress began on November 18, 1959, and lasted four days. During the first session a violent protest arose from the majority of delegates regarding the inclusion of three Communists among the 13 candidates for the new Executive Committee. Seeing themselves as an absolute majority, the anti-Communist delegates instituted a campaign to eliminate Soto and Aguilera from the new Executive Committee; they began to speak of them as "melons" (green on the outside, red inside). At that point Raúl and Fidel Castro used their influence to frustrate the intentions of the anti-Communists. "Unity of the working class" served as a pretext for preventing the expulsion of the pro-Communists and later imposing a "unity" committee.
>
> The Communists attempted to isolate Salvador by eliminating his principal collaborators, Octavio Louit and Reinol González, whose posts in the CTC were the most important after that of Secretary General. The Organization Secretariat, then in Louit's hands, was a key post, and was needed by the Communists; Reinol González was to be vetoed for having held that the CTC should maintain its affiliation with ORIT. A third victim was José Pellón, whose anti-Communist views were well known.
>
> In spite of Fidel's intervention, the Congress refused to accept the "unity" leadership. Raúl Castro worked the corridors, harassing the delegates with methods varying from persuasion to threat. When the opposi-

tion to the "unity" proposal was finally overcome, the number of members on the Executive Committee was reduced to six, with three assigned to each faction. Salvador, sworn in as Secretary General, would have the deciding vote. Louit was no longer to be Secretary of Organization, a post which passed over to Soto. The final Committee consisted of José Pellón, Octavio Louit, and Conrado Becquer for the democrats, and Jesús Soto, José María de la Aguilera, and Odón Alvarez de la Campa for the "melons."

For the Communists, the developments of the Tenth Congress were a victory. They managed to win two key positions: Organization Secretary and Secretary of International Relations. One post permitted the Communists to proceed with a take over of the unions now controlled by democratic elements, while the other led the CTC to the arena of international Communism. The Congress voted to withdraw from ORIT, and a new union federation was proposed for Latin America. The Communists, who at the outset of the Congress had had an 11-to-1 disadvantage, emerged with a "unity" Executive Committee, dividing representation equally with the July 26 group. Most significant, however, was not the "unified" Executive Committee but Fidel Castro's support of the Communists, which laid the foundations for the total conquest of the union movement by the Communists.

The elimination of democratic union leaders began immediately. During the first four months of 1960, more than 20 union leaders from the July 26 Movement, or others who had come to office in union elections, were purged, under the false accusation of "Mujalism." According to the Communists, a "Mujalist" was anyone who had worked in a union post while Mujal had controlled the CTC—that is, almost all the non-Communist leaders, many of whom had been staunch critics of Mujal and Batista. The instruments employed for the change were principally the Secretariat of Organization, in the hands of Jesús Soto, and the Labor Ministry, under Augusto Martínez.

In January 1960, Salvador met with Fidel Castro and complained of what had happened. In a meeting in the Presidential Palace, in the presence of many union leaders from the July 26 Movement, Castro openly criticized his brother Raúl and promised to dispose of the Communist problem by February. Reports of the meeting were leaked to the press in order to foster hope among non-Communist Castroites. In March 1960, while Salvador was out of the country, auténtico leader Luis Penelas, Secretary General of the Federación de Obreros de la Construcción, was deposed. On his return to Cuba, Salvador looked into the matter. Enraged at the proceedings, he described to Fidel what had taken place in the construction workers' meeting, accusing Jesús Soto and the Labor Ministry of official interference, with proof to back his statement. Castro sent for Minister Martínez and insulted him in front of Salvador. Martínez offered to resign from his post, and left the Palace visibly disturbed. Salvador, for his part, returned to his post convinced he had won a battle.

But shortly afterward Salvador realized that Jesús Soto and Augusto Martínez had acted at the instigation of Fidel Castro; that what had been done to Penelas was by order of Fidel himself; that the scene in the Presidential Palace was a farce designed to placate him, since he would continue to be useful in gaining complete control of the labor movement; and that to continue the farce the first meeting of the construction workers would be nullified, and Communist victory assured at a new assembly. In mid-March 1960, Salvador resigned from his post as CTC Secretary General. Visits and messages, including one from President Dorticós, failed to persuade him to reconsider. For the first time in the history of May Day parades—and they had been held even in the Batista days—the CCT Secretary General delivered no address to the workers. Neither the Secretary General nor any other labor leader addressed them, for in order to cover Salvador's absence, the only speaker at the event was Fidel Castro.

Salvador, meanwhile, was studying the situation. He conferred with many of his old companions in the fight against Batista and found that a large majority had come to the same conclusion as he had. In June he went underground. Finally, on November 5, 1960, two years after having been arrested by Batista's police, David Salvador was arrested by Castro's police. In the meantime, committees of various union factions had been formed in exile.

Even before Salvador's elimination, new laws contrary to the interests of the working class had been enacted: Law 696 (January 22, 1960), for example, reorganized the Labor Ministry and established the Labor Census, which required Cubans to register with the authorities, who then decided where to place workers. The right of strike had already been abolished, along with freedom of association and the right of workers to form new unions. Working conditions and wages were frozen, and revision of contracts was prohibited. Any pressure to change these decisions was denounced by the Communists as "counter-revolutionary." "Voluntary" contributions were demanded in the form of free labor. Social security taxes were raised from 3 to 5 per cent. A tax of 4 per cent was imposed on wages for "the industrialization of the country," as well as a "union tax" of 1 per cent. Furthermore, "contributions" were deducted for "arms and planes" or for "the agrarian reform," and many "voluntary" collections were made. Collective bargaining was done away with by decree, to be replaced by the decisions of the Labor Ministry.[33]

In November 1961 the ILO Committee on Union Freedom condemned the Castro regime for violating union liberty on the island. Only the USSR and Rumania voted in opposition. The condemnation stemmed from a complaint presented by the leaders of the Federación Sindical de Plantas Eléctricas de Cuba concerning execution by firing squad of three of its members in accordance with a law enacted 37 days after the arrest of the three workers. In reality, this federation had resisted the Communist intervention in its ranks decreed by the CTC Executive Committee, and had organized a protest demonstration in Havana. The three executions were a reprisal for this stand.[34]

That same November the CTC held a new congress. All the decisions were approved unanimously, and Lázaro Peña reappeared on the union staff. The congress decided to "voluntarily" renounce several benefits won by Cuban workers under democratic regimes: paid vacation for 30 days a year, sick leave of 9 days a year, extra wages for 26 days a year, a Christmas bonus, 26 days a year of supplementary summer weekend leave, 4 days a year for national holidays. In all, these renunciations meant a drop of 45 per cent in workers' annual earnings. The congress also accepted two extra hours on the job per day at no pay. Furthermore, it decided to continue the voluntary acceptance of taxes imposed by the Castro regime, which involved, in total, 17 per cent of net wages for state employees and 12 per cent for industrial workers.[35]

In 1963, Ernesto ("Che") Guevara declared that the unions should adopt a new function in "socialist Cuba"; and, in fact, they have become more and more an auxiliary of the police and a means of forcing workers to increase their productivity. The polemics of Castro with different factions of the Communist Party—now the only party in Cuba—have had no important repercussions in the CTC. The leadership is firmly in the hands of the old Communists, and there are no more congresses or elections in the unions. The workers, once very active in their unions, have become indifferent and passive; only among the young workers, formed politically under Castro, is some militancy to be found—and even this in lesser degree than that among students, peasants, and middle-class youth.

17. Mexico

THE MEXICAN LABOR MOVEMENT is notable for its anarcho-syndicalist origin, which led it to participate in the 1910–17 Revolution. Later the movement set aside its traditional principles and officially adopted the ideology of the nationalist revolution. It became, then, a unionism almost exclusively of negotiation.

The Mexican Revolution was the first agrarian revolution of the modern period, predating the Russian Revolution. Outside of the more recent events in Bolivia and Venezuela, the union movement in Mexico is the only such movement in Latin America to have engaged in a successful revolution and to have been confronted with the consequent problems.

The origins and nature of the Mexican Revolution have been much discussed. Its basis was clearly not in socialism—though socialism did influence the thinking of Mexican revolutionaries to a certain extent. It was a nationalist revolution, begun politically and continued as a social upheaval because of its inherent agrarian basis. It was, essentially, the first of the middle-class revolutions that have come to characterize the recent social history of Latin America.

THE BEGINNINGS

As Mexico industrialized—textile mills were installed, the mines were modernized, and the railroads were laid—many artisans and peasants found themselves drawn into industry. In 1823 there were 44,800 workers in the mines and 2,800 in the textile mills; salaries were 30 centavos per day, 12 centavos for women and children.[1] By 1854 there were already 50 textile mills with 12,000 workers, who were paid 37 centavos per day.

The first strikes broke out during the liberal regime that followed Maximilian's rule. One of these, in 1867, included among its demands a 14-hour day for women, "so that they can also attend to their household tasks."

In 1873 there were 43,000 industrial workers, 32,000 of them in the textile mills. The working day was 12½ hours in summer and 12 hours in winter. In 1880 there were 400 factories employing close to 80,000 workers; mining employed another 70,000.

For decades the labor movement amounted to no more than a defense of the artisan through formation of mutualities (workers' aid societies); there were no interventions in politics. The unions that were organized somewhat later were also nonpolitical. Eventually these unions tried to organize on a national level, and to concern themselves with the interests of society as a whole, as seen from the worker's point of view.

Luis Chávez Orozco characterized the objectives of the early Mexican labor movement: "The petty bourgeoisie, struggling in the van of the proletarian masses, pursue two objectives: first, to defend their own interests; second, to defend their allies, and in the process to weaken mutual adversaries." The first objective was to be gained by cooperativist organization; the second, by the "stimulation of a spirit of solidarity, by the regulation of work, by achieving the right to strike, and by threat of social revolution."[2]

Typical of the confusion attendant upon social concepts was the case of Guillermo Prieto (1818–1897); though a critic of socialism in his studies of economics at the University, he contributed impassioned harangues to one of Mexico's labor publications, *El Socialista*, which was published irregularly from 1871 until 1888.

La Comuna, a biweekly published briefly in 1874–75, defended the equality of Mexican and foreign-born workers, the right to strike, and (an almost unique position in those days) the dignity of womanhood. In 1875 *La Huelga* was published for a short time. But the most influential labor newspaper was *El Hijo del Trabajo*, edited by the tailor José María González. It enjoyed a relatively long life, from 1876 to 1886. González was no doctrinaire, though he did feel that in mutualism lay a solution to social ills. His editorial inclination was to denounce concrete cases of exploitation, generally contriving to show how mutualism could have provided an effective deterrent to such conditions. He drew particular attention to the Indian problem.

We know little about the programs and leaders of the first labor societies. Juan Cano, with the sculptor José María Miranda, founded the Gran Familia Artística, an institution that "dried many tears and awakened the spirit of association among artisans." The Fraternidad de Sastres, which had been formed in 1864, was followed by the Sociedad de Artesanos y Agricultores, in 1867, and by the Sociedad Artística Industrial, in 1867. All of these were of a mutualist nature; that is, their principal concern was to provide aid to the families of workers struck down by illness, injury, or death.

Mutualism, the artisan class's last attempt at survival, soon disappeared. The shoemaker Fortino Diosdado recognized in 1876 that "mutualist societies would sooner or later find it necessary to adopt the cooperative system," because, as Ricardo Velai pointed out, mutualism "may free them of their hospital expenses, but cooperativism frees them from misery—and, what is more, from the avarice of capital, which today more than ever is the greatest and most malicious enemy of labor."

But these cooperativist artisans had nothing of the revolutionary in them. It is revealing that in Mexico there were almost no utopians. The single noteworthy exception was Juan Nepomuceno Adorno (1807–1887), a tobacco revenue employee and inventor, who set forth his utopian principles in *Los males de México* (1858) and *La armonía del Universo* (1862).[3] In the former he presents a pseudo-Marxist theory: labor is the source of all wealth, of all worth. The solution to Mexico's evils, then, is found in labor; by working, anyone can become wealthy and contribute to the welfare of the nation; currency based on labor units would ensure just compensation to all citizens.

Fourierism, introduced by a few immigrants and promoted by the first socialists, considerably influenced the labor congresses, where Marxists were in the minority. Nationalism was also highly valued among artisans, as indicated by this comment from the newspaper *La Unión de los Obreros*: "We must seek the growth of our country through our own labor, under the protection of laws both wise and appropriate to our needs; we have no wish for the dominance of one class over others."

GRAN CÍRCULO AND GRAN CONFEDERACIÓN

Members of the Gran Círculo de Obreros, founded in 1870, were prohibited from joining political parties, although they could engage in politics as independents. The Círculo appealed for a protective labor law and advised the workers to fight in their own defense, turning to social revolution as a last resort. Dissensions between Marxists and Bakuninists erupted in Mexico, as elsewhere, but the Gran Círculo remained affiliated with the First International and considered itself socialistic.

The program of the Gran Círculo had the following objectives: the education of the workers, the establishment of workshops where jobs could be offered to the artisans, the defense of political guarantees and of equality in military conscription, free elections, the appointment of defense attorneys for workers, the establishment of artisans' industrial fairs, and pay increases "when the worker's need demands it."

Artisans had been ardent advocates of the strike. But the Gran Círculo remained more circumspect. *El Socialista* said of labor conflicts: "As inconvenient as the strike system may seem to some, it should be clear that it is the only system that can protect the working class from exploitation by the property-owners and from the despotism of the foremen." Shortly afterward the same newspaper said: "The strike is indeed a terrible weapon, one with which workers can destroy a business. Thus we, as your staunch allies, advise that it be turned to sparingly, just as a prudent man carries a weapon but uses it only in case of dire need." The revolutionary strike, though a frequent threat elsewhere in Latin America during this period, was scarcely discussed in Mexico. In fact, the general strike has never been seriously contemplated in Mexico, even during the most turbulent periods of the Revolution.

On November 20, 1874, the Gran Círculo formulated a plan for "general regulations governing work procedures in factories in the Valley of Mexico." Though never applied, it constituted the first aspiration in Mexico toward the collective work contract.

Also noteworthy was a certain influence from the U.S., especially among railroad workers. The success of the Knights of Labor in exacting benefits from their struggles induced their Mexican counterparts to organize. The influence of U.S. anarchists was also apparent, most notably in the constitution of the textile unions and in their affiliation in the Gran Círculo.[4]

The Gran Círculo, before it finally dispersed in 1880, gave rise to the Gran Círculo Reformista, led by José María González, editor of *El Hijo del Trabajo*. In 1874 the new Círculo proposed holding a Socialist International Congress in Mexico. Though nothing came of the proposal, the announcement of the congress contained a statement of faith worth quoting: "So long as the forces of the International are rooted in Europe, the emancipation of the working class will never become a practical reality, since the Americas are unaffected by socialism's positive efforts. Oppressions by the monarchies and oligarchies [in Latin America] hold the International behind its stage of development in republican countries where freedom is greater."

In March 1876 a labor congress was called together by various resistance societies. Its slogan was "My freedom and my rights"; and at its core were a mutualist-cooperativist majority and a Marxist-Bakuninist minority. González branded the leaders of the congress "traitors who have sold out" (they had accepted a building from the government for use as a headquarters). The congress nonetheless created the Gran Confederación de las Asociaciones de Obreros Mexicanos, which declared itself nonpolitical and "immune to the influences of public power," and fixed as its objectives "the promotion of liberty, the exaltation and progress of the working classes, unfailing respect for the rights of others, and the utilization of every possible means toward a solution to the problem of harmony between labor and capital."

This was a period in Mexico's history during which the labor movement acquired, if not greater strength, at least an enhanced ideological vitality. Strikes were frequent, polemics were constant, and the labor press was more active than at any previous time. The pressure of social problems was strong enough for General Porfirio Díaz, when he rose up against Lerdo in the coup of 1876, "to easily induce the peasants to revolt by promising them an agrarian law." Immediately after Díaz came to power, *El Socialista* began to appear daily, but it was soon afterward suppressed, along with the Gran Confederación and the rest of the labor organizations.[5]

In January 1880 the second Congreso Obrero met, presided over by Carmen Huerta (women, curiously enough, were more active in labor struggles than in liberal or conservative politics). The congress held intermittent sessions for four months and finally dispersed when several of its members sought to impose a political position favorable to certain candidates. The congress concluded that workers would resort to insurrection only if an attempt were made to wrest from them their natural rights.

General Díaz, who remained in power for 30 years, was unable to ease the pressure of the agrarian problem. As early as 1870 a manifesto had appeared in San Luis Potosí requesting equitable laws for land distribution. Its authors were jailed by the government. In August 1877 the first Congreso Campesino was held in Mexico City, and the Gran Comité Central Comunero was formed, with delegates from the agricultural communities. Later the Ligas Campesinas were formed, in several states, and peasants' movements (mostly attempts to establish rights to uncultivated land) were frequent. In La Barranca, on June 1, 1879, delegates from 15 towns signed a manifesto that proposed a military uprising and the creation of a "socialist or municipal" government, which would return land to local ownership. In 1880 General Tiburcio Montiel (died 1885), a former legal adviser for the Gran Comité Central Comunero, founded the Liga Agraria Mexicana. He was deported to Baja California, accused of being a communist.

A peasant from Chalco, Julio Chávez López, was the first to discuss the agrarian problem from the peasants' point of view. A disciple of the Rhodakanaty school, he called himself a socialist-communist. "I am a socialist," he said, "because I am an enemy of all government, and a communist because my brothers want to work the lands in common." In 1869 he wrote to Zalacosta: "There is great discontent among my brothers, because the generals seek to take over their lands. What would you think of our starting the Socialist Revolution?" In April an insurrection was organized and a manifesto was published: "We want land; we want work; we want freedom; we want to preserve law and order: in short, what we want is the establishment of a social pact among men, based on mutual respect." The rebellion spread through Puebla to Veracruz; but Chávez was captured after four months, and was shot in the courtyard of the Free and Modern School of Chalco, where he had studied.

Elements from the Partido Liberal of the Flores Magóns continued these movements, and sustained an active resistance during the period prior to the Revolution.[6] During the Revolution itself, the Casa del Obrero Mundial was created; it signed a pact with Venustiano Carranza, the Chief of the Constitutionalist Army, and organized "red battalions" to fight with him against the most radical peasants' groups. This permitted the Casa to exert a certain influence in obtaining broad social legislation.

SOCIAL LEGISLATION

The labor movement in Mexico has followed a path quite the reverse of Europe's. In Europe, intellectuals fashioned a doctrine, then organized an already literate working class behind it. In Mexico, "the movement was organized by the workers themselves; the basic program and doctrine were formed later, along lines of practical experience."[7]

Just as modern labor organization in the Mexican states is older than that in the capital, social legislation also appeared first in the provinces and later at the federal level. In 1904, a law regarding on-the-job accidents was proposed in the State of Mexico. In 1914, the first labor law in the country was enacted in Veracruz, and was followed by similar laws in Yucatan and Coahuila; these laws recognized, and regulated, the right to strike.

The social legislation of the Revolution can be summarized by the following: the Constitution of 1917, with its Article 123, was the basis for all subsequent laws; in 1931 the Federal Labor Law still in effect was promulgated; and in 1939 a juridical statute was approved for state employees.

The Federal Labor Law assures freedom of unionization and prohibits all coercion designed to force workers to register in unions. Nevertheless, it concedes certain advantages to unionized workers and upholds the principle of "exclusion by separation"—the union, for example, can ask the employer to fire a worker who has been expelled from the union or has left its ranks, provided the labor contract includes a clause to this effect. The genesis of the Federal Labor Law was expressed by President Emilio Portes Gil: "The juridical notion of ownership has changed; *jus fruendi, jus utendi,* and *jus abutendi* have been replaced by the concept of the social function of property. In the same implicit fashion, the law forbids revolutionary syndicalism." By recognizing this evolution, the Labor Law "tends to balance the factors of production." Establishment of the Labor Law was made possible by the development of strong unions—unions, moreover, that had formed into federations for the purpose of increasing their effectiveness.

CROM

In October 1917 a labor congress was held in Tampico. The congress, in admonishing doctrinaire groups to pursue their activities outside the union organizations, marked the end of anarchist influence in the Mexican labor movement. During the years immediately following the Revolution the IWW sent organizers into Mexico. Though they were largely unsuccessful, they did manage to found and lead several unions of oil workers in the Tampico area. But after many years of such struggle, and an unsuccessful attempt at an alliance with the Communists, the IWW organizers retired permanently, in 1922.

Nonetheless, the second clause in the declaration of the Tampico Congress (which represented a transition of power to the anarchists) asserted as a final goal the "communization of means of production." It also recommended the union organization as "the most effective means for achieving the aspirations of the proletariat."*

The third Congreso Nacional Obrero, held on May Day, 1918, voted to apply the terms of the Tampico Congress to the creation of a Confederación Regional Obrera Mexicana (CROM). An initial CROM statement protested that "inequality in our land originates in the concentration of land ownership and of all natural and social wealth; thus the disinherited class can find its emancipation only in the decentralization of land ownership and natural wealth, and in an equitable distribution of social wealth among those who participate in its creation, whether by effort or by intelligence." CROM also declared itself nonpolitical—but not antipolitical. Although the congress offered the government its collaboration, it asked that the decisions of the Conciliation and Arbitration Councils be unappealable, which would dissociate them from the government itself. It also offered to aid the government in enforcing the requested measures. If the government refused these proposals, the workers would solve their own problems through their own efforts. Thus direct action was openly superseded by a position that was then considered reformism in Europe.[8]

Throughout its early years, CROM demonstrated a certain militancy, a posture attributable to the many key members who had been part of the Casa del Obrero Mundial. Later, through circumstances of internal policy, the federation lost its initiative, and important groups broke away to form new federations—though most of them followed CROM's pattern in their relations with public authority. CROM felt that "the united world front of

---

* In a curious statement, the congress recognized the right of the worker to "avoid unlimited procreation, when this might aggravate his economic circumstances or imply a possible degeneration of the species."

the proletariat must operate exclusively on a basis of respect for the principles and practices of each region or country. Solidarity and international cooperation among groups of workers must not involve the subordination of any one group to the others, or of all to the tyranny of one or a few.... What unites the people against the world capitalist regime must not be, then, uniformity of tactics, but rather unanimity of purpose.... CROM is more a socialist movement than a merely syndicalist movement, at times allying itself with the Mexican Government, making the government program CROM's program; for the government has always been prepared to defend not only the so-called sovereignty of the nation but also the sources of public wealth, from which the people's economic liberation should derive, and upon which the forces of international capitalism direct their main assault. ... The labor movement is quite aware that national life, and therefore its own life, is not possible without the development of industry and agriculture or the growth of private enterprise; and it is aware that without this progress it is not possible to realize the ultimate aim, the socialization of wealth and a change in the organization of the State."

In 1918, CROM, in deliberations with the U.S. AFL, assisted in the creation of the Pan-American Federation of Labor (PAFL), which met in congress in Mexico in 1921 and 1924. CROM also, in 1919, joined the International Federation of Trade Unions. In reality, CROM was led by the Grupo Acción, which congregated around Luis Napoleón Morones (died 1963). The Grupo, which organized a publishing house and an Institute of Social Sciences,* exerted great influence because of its ability to formulate CROM policy for years, as well as its training of effective labor leaders. It created (and also destroyed) the Partido Laborista. But the Grupo was unable, years later, to prevent the diminution of CROM's strength.

CROM's orientation underwent a gradual shift. At the convention of the Federación de Sindicatos Obreros del Distrito Federal in 1924, Reynaldo Cervantes Torres announced a change in tactics: "It is no longer the destructive demonstrations, pursued without regard to national considerations, that assert the rights of workers. The actions of the Confederation are today geared to very broad principles of justice and tend to include workers' rights as part of a reasonable and highly advanced program. Our purpose is not the destruction of capital, but rather the harmonious consolidation of labor and capital, to the ultimate benefit of the workers."

At its sixth congress, in 1924, CROM named Plutarco Elías Calles (1877–1945) Honorary President of CROM and declared his government social-

---

* An important member of the Institute was Vicente Lombardo Toledano (1884–   ), about whom we shall hear considerably more.

istic. Later, in November 1929, a Labor-Management Convention was held to study the application of Article 123 of the Constitution. During this convention a lively debate was sustained between the Communist painter David Alfaro Siqueiros and Vicente Lombardo Toledano, of CROM. Compulsory arbitration was opposed by Alfaro Siqueiros, but favored by Lombardo, who argued that "workers have confidence in the government because it represents the interests of the Revolution. Compulsory arbitration is therefore necessary." At the 1928 convention of the Partido Laborista, Lombardo proposed the dissolution of the Party, toward the end of strengthening CROM. This stand became a bone of contention between Morones and Lombardo.[9] Lombardo finally disillusioned his own supporters by failing to appear at CROM's 1932 congress, despite their having nominated him for the post of Secretary General. His withdrawal marked the end of CROM's hegemony over the labor movement. Other, previous, divisions, which had led to the formation of other federations, had already undermined it considerably.

THE CGT

The most powerful of these other federations, for many years, was the CGT, an organization of anarcho-syndicalist leanings. In 1923 the CGT joined the AIT,* in spite of attempts by its Communist elements to affiliate it with the Profintern. The CGT did adopt as its slogan, "Communist anarchy and direct action." At its congress of September 1921 it set as a task for itself the assistance of peasants seeking to obtain "the communization of the land and of working tools, for we believe that the soil was meant to be shared by all human beings." The CGT also stated that neither social security nor profit sharing would solve the wage problem.

In a letter to President General Alvaro Obregón (1880–1928), dated November 30, 1922, the CGT Executive Committee made its position clear: "For us it is a fundamental truth that there are not, nor can there ever be, good governments. The very word 'government' connotes abuse.... The CGT is not a political organization: it is rebellious, anti-state, and anarchist. It does not preach peace and harmony between wolves and sheep." The third congress, in 1924, decided to occupy factories that had closed down, and also formed "technical labor councils," because it had come to the conclusion that "factories can be properly administered by the workers themselves, among whom an excellent technical training is evident." The move to attach factories, however, never became widespread. Finally, the congress of December 1938 affirmed the failure of all efforts to solve the agrarian problem. It asked that exploitation of the *ejido* (land owned collectively by

* See p. 58.

a peasants' community) be carried out on an individual basis, and that harmony be maintained between the *ejidatario* and the small rural farmer.

CGT action was energetic, at times violent. But though it was the only labor federation to show concern for the peasants, and the only one to create industrial unions or to study the possibility of labor administration in industry, its strength gradually slipped away—notwithstanding the fact that the principle of direct action was still apparent in some protest movements, especially in Veracruz. For a time, CGT and CROM were rivals, but the former came to predominate until its ouster by the new CTM.

THE CTM

Under Lázaro Cárdenas (1895–   ), President 1934–40, the Confederación de Trabajadores de México (CTM) was formed. In 1933 a Comité Nacional de Defensa Proletaria was created to support General Cárdenas's regime; this committee took the initiative in bringing together a National Unification Congress, from which the CTM emerged in February 1936. The CTM then came to dominate the Mexican union scene for many years.

In its declaration of principles, drawn up by Lombardo Toledano, CTM stated that bourgeois society, concerned as it is with its own survival, could be expected to resort to fascism to suppress the labor movement. Three factors were seen to be characteristic: private control of production sources by a minority; a working class earning starvation wages; and exclusion of the worker from the leadership of the economic process. Although the Mexican proletariat would at some time have to fight for the abandonment of the capitalist system, it had first to achieve the political and economic freedom of the country.

Among CTM's immediate demands was technical education for the workers, so that they might have "opportune possession of the means of economic production, as well as a revolutionary mentality, as prior conditions for social change." The declaration warned that dictatorial ambitions would be countered by the general strike; it also pronounced itself in favor of closer ties between the Army and the people, and opposed to all religious creeds.

Though the CTM might occasionally resort to cooperativism, its principal tactics would be those of revolutionary syndicalism. It would maintain its ideological and class independence, but might accept temporary alliances not in conflict with its fundamental principles. The declaration concluded: "The Mexican proletariat recognizes the international nature of the labor and peasant movements, and of the struggle to achieve socialism." This was the first open break with the nationalist principle that until then had inspired the Mexican labor movement.

The CTM's slogan was, "For a classless society." And its first concern was to oppose "the semi-feudal structure of the country and the intervention of imperialist forces in the economy ... thus guaranteeing the continued development of the revolution." Lombardo stated that without acting as a political party, the CTM had "oriented itself toward the broad principles of socialism as a basis for the solution of its problems," and as Secretary General he defined the position of the CTM with respect to the government: "The proletariat has no master but its own conscience. Today, and I hope always, we are in agreement with Cárdenas—but we shall not be subjugated by him. ... Hopefully, we can reach accord with other men as well. But the day will come when the proletariat of Mexico will need to seek accord only with its own conscience and its own efforts."

With the onset of World War II the labor movement entered a period of decline. One cause was the utilization of the union federations as strong-arm groups in the fight for political power. When, for example, Calles and Obregón were at odds, CROM suffered because of its alliance with Calles. In the same fashion, Cárdenas had promoted CTM's establishment in 1936 in order to oppose Calles. Thus, from its inception, the CTM was more or less bound over to Cárdenas, and Lombardo was not the man to gain independence for his federation, not even in the days before he showed himself receptive to Moscow's party line. Perhaps one of the most obvious manifestations of this double jeopardy—interference by the government and by Moscow—was the pact for labor unity signed June 4, 1942, by CTM, CROM, CGT, CPN, and COCM and directed toward the goals of increased quantity and quality of production, strengthened national industry, and national economic independence; the strike was to be employed only in extreme cases. Later came the labor-management pact of April 1945 between the CTM and the Cámara de la Industria de la Transformación. Commenting on this pact, Lombardo stated: "We intend to respect the vested interests because we respect private ownership, because—and note this carefully—we favor private ownership at this stage in Mexico's history. On this basis of respect for private ownership, which is guaranteed in the Constitution of the Republic and the laws deriving from it, the economy of our country can go forward."[10]

In January 1948 a group of leaders called "the five little wolves," led by Fernando Amilpa (1899–1953) and Fidel Velázquez (1901–   ), counting on the protection of President Miguel Alemán, expelled Lombardo Toledano from the CTM. Those who followed him formed the CUT (Confederación Unificada de Trabajadores), which was affiliated with CTAL but soon replaced by the UGOC (Unión General de Obreros y Campesinos). After Lombardo's expulsion the CTM revised its declaration of principles. Its aim now became "the elevation of the socioeconomic status of its members." This would in turn require improvement in the antiquated working conditions. "The CTM supports the democratic regime and the good-neighbor policy," recognizes "national unity" as a tactic, but by no means intends to renounce the class struggle or pressure for improved living conditions, but seeks rather "a guarantee of the concrete objectives of the working class." The slogan "For a classless society" was replaced by "For the emancipation of Mexico."

Fernando Amilpa stated in 1950 that "The Mexican labor movement is focused at last on demands that relate to the needs of the people in their struggle against oppression. It no longer seeks the survival of the anarchism of the days of Flores Magón or of a Communism shored up by the Third International in Moscow; rather, it is the product of a Revolution sustained with the intention, not of changing the world, but of abolishing the material and spiritual servitude imposed on the people." At the 1950 congress Fidel Velázquez proposed profit sharing as benefiting workers more effectively than salary increases. "By this system of profit sharing we hope to eliminate all motive, all pretext, for management to raise prices, and we seek thus to obtain greater moral authority for demanding of the State a check on inflation."

In 1954 the CTM adopted a more energetic and independent attitude, at least in theory. Velázquez explained this new posture before the 51st National Council in June of that year: "We have fallen into the same error as the governments of the Revolution, believing that by friendly, legal means and through brotherhood and peace we could obtain better economic conditions for workers from management." Nothing could be expected from the peasants, since they depend on the government. The working class thus had only its own resources to rely upon. But a few months later, in October 1954, the CTM made it clear that though it remains a class organization "it recognizes its obligation to participate in the solution of national problems." Toward this end it recognized increased state intervention in economic life, a production increase stimulated by wage increases, further technological progress, and State coordination of the economy.

Toward the end of 1955, several union organizations (CTM, CGT, CROM, the social security system employees, the railroad workers, the mine workers, the telephone employees, the actors' guild, etc.) formed the Bloque Nacional de Trabajadores, declaring that "the aims of the Mexican Revolution are rightfully sacred to the country's proletariat; with a basis in the Revolution's advanced principles of social justice, Mexicans have no reason to adopt imported doctrines."

The CTM affiliated in 1936 with the International Federation of Trade Unions, and in 1938 became the nucleus of the Confederación de Trabajadores de América Latina (CTAL), from which it withdrew in 1948. Since 1953 the CTM has been part of ORIT.[11]

OTHER FEDERATIONS

Small union federations appeared frequently in Mexico. In 1928 the Communists created a union federation affiliated with the Profintern, the Confederación Sindical Unitaria Mexicana (CSUM); it commanded little influence or support. On August 15, 1929, a Workers' Congress was called by the Alianza de Artes Gráficas in the hope of unifying the various union federations. Lombardo Toledano, replying to Siqueiros at the congress, remarked that: "So long as the Communist faction fails to demonstrate to the workers of Mexico that Communists are now prepared to replace the bourgeois regime and to assume the leadership of the government, the workers will regard them as a band of delinquents, and will recognize their calculated efforts to bring on the failure of labor organization as, in fact, a crime. So long as the Communist faction fails to demonstrate that conditions in Mexico permit the working masses to bring about a radical and abrupt change in the existing order, the Communists ought not to merit more from Mexican workers than recognition as perverse agitators, false leaders, and men of little honor." The proletarian struggle, he stated, was affected by geographic, historical, and other factors; though this struggle might have identical aims throughout the world, "the method of achieving these aims ought to vary from country to country, so as to reflect specific national conditions." Mexico still had no unifying ideology or purpose: "The majority of Mexican workers are ill-prepared to undertake an abrupt change of social regime because they do not yet comprehend the nature of the regime." Therefore, "It is not only utopian, but in fact absurd, to speak of a social revolution."

Lombardo later headed the Confederación General de Obreros y Campesinos de México (CGOCM), which was founded by dissident elements from CROM and CGT in October 1933. CGOCM prepared a manifesto that was reproduced almost verbatim five years later, in the CTM's declaration of principles; both documents were, in fact, drafted by Lombardo.

In 1942 two new federations were established: the Confederación Obrera y Campesina (COC), led by Ricardo Treviño, and the Confederación Nacional Prolataria (CNP), led by Enrique Rangel and Alfredo Navarrete.[12] In 1961 the Confederación Nacional de Trabajadores (CNT) was formed, from various autonomous unions, in the hope of capitalizing on CTM discontent with its bureaucratic leadership. In addition, there are currently many powerful autonomous unions, particularly among oil workers, railroad workers, mine workers, electrical workers, and telephone employees.

CHARACTERISTICS OF MEXICAN UNIONISM

The labor movement in Mexico was fundamentally a nationalist movement—and, as time went on, a movement that relinquished its own independence. That, at least, is how it is now regarded by its own militant founders.

The Mexican labor movement moreover evolved from anarchism to nationalism; this evolution began with the pact between Carranza's followers and the Casa del Obrero Mundial. Because the most fervent anarchists were concentrated in the capital, provincial labor leaders could evolve their own nationalist doctrine, at the same time diversifying the tactics of their struggle —often abandoning direct action in favor of other tactics. Nevertheless, in their first attempts at national organization they continued to rely upon principles typical of the European syndicalist movement: class struggle, socialization of the means of production as a basic objective, direct action as a major tactic, and the antipolitical stance.

A strong expression of nationalist sentiment in the Mexican labor movement appears in Treviño's attitude toward the AFL. In the Chamber of Deputies, Treviño voiced his preference for the IWW (AFL's rival), which had educated him, but conceded that the IWW was weak and the AFL powerful: "Therefore, in defense of our interests, our sovereignty, and our independence, we must recognize the AFL as the established labor movement in the United States, without regard to its characteristics." Contributing to this attitude was the AFL's defense of Mexican interests during the U.S. occupation of Veracruz and General Pershing's punitive expedition.

Another nationalistic aspect of the Mexican labor movement emerged from the discussion aimed at persuading management organizations to accept the exclusion clause allowed by the 1921 Federal Labor Law. During these debates, there arose "the concept of a responsibility shared by labor and management where the nation is concerned, a concept that has contributed considerably to their subsequent cooperation in the mutual interests of an improved national economy."[13]

At CROM's Guadalajara Convention, in 1923, it was stated that "the defense of national interests is inherent in the program of CROM's constituent labor groups." Because Communism is incompatible with "the nationalist sentiments of the workers," CROM unions were ordered to expel from their ranks any members of the Communist party "subordinated to the Soviet government." When we reflect that this took place in 1923, before the campaign for the "bolshevization" of the Communist parties got under way, it becomes apparent that Mexican labor was precocious in its knowledge (or intuition) of the nature of Communism, especially when we consider the leftist intellectuals of a decade later, whose ignorance of Communism was, by contrast, appalling.

CROM's 1923 convention also resolved "that the Mexican labor movement is at once nationalist and international in nature—our solidarity with the labor movements of the world does not preempt our right and obligation to attack the problems affecting Mexico and the Mexican people."

Whether or not the unions should interfere in the management of nationalized industries was seldom debated. After the railroad workers' union had managed the national railroads for some months in 1937, and the oil workers had managed the oil fields—though only for a matter of weeks, in 1938—the union movement, faced with the urgency of the situation, simply adopted the principle of union involvement without debate. According to a CTM theorist, the working class had already endorsed the principle.[14] He added that this endorsement could have evil results only if it encouraged the belief that such union control was the panacea that would lead the country to socialism. Administration of industries by labor should be seen as preparing the proletariat for future responsibilities, such as workers' participation in the municipal councils and in the parliaments; this would reduce the danger that labor leaders might want to become "good administrators" in the capitalist sense.

The Communists took the opposite stand. In the beginning they accepted labor administration; but by October 1938—after oil expropriation—they had risen up against it: "In broad terms, the direct administration of firms by the unions is not advisable, for it endangers the independence and freedom of action of the unions in the fulfillment of their true function. . . . The administration of the large nationalized firms ought to remain in the hands of the government, with cooperation from the unions and with a system of labor control." Shortly afterward, Hernán Laborde, then Secretary General of the Mexican Communist Party, said in his report to the Party's Seventh Congress, in 1939, that the administration of a firm by a union restricted the union's function and robbed it of its personality: "It comes to be a defender of worker and administrator alike, i.e., a defender of management. Inevitably, one function conflicts with the other, and the union must choose between the firm and the worker; and it will very likely abandon the interests of the worker, since it is bent on making the administration a successful one." Furthermore, "Labor administration decentralizes and muddles the economy, instead of concentrating and organizing it." No doubt this opinion was an attempt to justify the total absence of labor administration of firms in the USSR.

The oil worker B. M. Gutiérrez, in a study of the merits of the labor movement's administration of expropriated industries,[15] came to the following conclusions: A labor administration contributes to the technical and economic progress of such industries, as well as to their centralization; on the other hand, it leads to the fusion of union leaders and state machinery. The more backward the political conscience of the union masses, the greater the danger of the union becoming a capitalistic administrator of the industry under its control, thus converting itself into an oppressor of the working class. But if the union masses were given a certain amount of political training, the labor administration would help the union to fulfill its task, strengthen the anti-imperialist bourgeois-democratic revolution, and hasten the eventual socialist revolution. Thus to oppose labor administration is to be counterrevolutionary.

The decree signed by President Cárdenas on June 23, 1937, expropriating for reasons of public utility Mexico's national railroads (Ferrocarriles Nacionales de México, S.A.), advanced an interesting thesis: a public utility should orient its performance principally toward social benefit; if it is unwilling or unable to do so, the state should take over the utility for the benefit of society and assume responsibility for the utility's liabilities. The utility then becomes an instrument of the State (autonomous, but dependent on the executive power), whose administration should be turned over to an appropriate labor union.[16]

But since that time, nothing more has been said of the problem. The unions have never expressed a desire to administer the nationalized industries, nor have they asked for the nationalization of other industries—not even the public utilities.

Profit sharing, accepted in principle by the 1917 Constitution, has been the object of more discussion than labor control of industry. Participation in profits, it was argued, ought to complement the minimum wage in the sense intended by the constitution. When General Obregón, in June 1921, presented a bill for workmen's compensation to the Chamber, he stated as justification for the bill that "Until now it has been impossible to institute measures in support of profit-sharing . . . because it is difficult to determine actual profits. Furthermore, profit evaluation, if it were possible, would be a source of constant friction between capital and labor, which the law ought to try to avoid or, at least, to resolve equitably." The bill failed to find approval.[17] Finally, in 1962, Congress passed a law providing workers' participation in profits, acting on the initiative of President Adolfo López Mateos.

Without exception, the labor movement in Latin America is dependent on, and to a large extent controlled by, the national governments, through labor legislation. In Mexico this dependence is more pronounced. Most of the labor federations are members of the PRI (Partido Revolucionario Institucional), the party of the "revolutionary family" that controls the government and is the victor in practically all elections. The PRI has three branches: the peasant branch, formed by the Confederación Nacional Campesina; the popular branch, formed by several professional and middle-class organizations; and the worker's branch, formed by the CTM and nearly all other federations and autonomous unions. Thus the labor movement has a voice in the deliberations of the PRI, but it must also submit to the decisions of the PRI. By tradition, the labor branch has nominated the PRI candidate for the presidency, not of its own choice but as a result of negotiations with the various ideological tendencies within the PRI.

This lack of independence is due in part to the labor policies of Cárdenas, as we have seen, but it can be traced primarily to the desultory participation of labor in the revolution of 1910–17—it was not until 1916 that labor became active in the struggle. Before that year, the labor organizations, all of them ineffectual, were controlled by the anarchists, who considered the revolution a struggle among bourgeois factions. Because of this indifference, labor was not in a position, when the struggle concluded, to demand recompense for its support. If labor received solid protection from the constitution and the governments, it was because the ruling middle class understood the need for a strong labor movement and for the betterment of the working class as preconditions for continuing industrial developments (and as barriers to foreign economic influence), rather than as attainments of the labor movement itself.

The absence of labor in the decisive moments of the revolution allowed the revolution to become tutelar and paternalistic, and, of course, relegated the labor movement itself to the tutelage of the governments emerging from the revolution. But the present condition of Mexico's industrial development, 50 years after the close of the revolution, may well force the labor movement to seek more independence and a stronger voice. This appears likely to be the main task of the younger generation of labor leaders, now emerging from a disillusioned, indifferent, and rapidly expanding working class.

18. Continental Labor Organizations

In Latin America, where the labor movement has suffered from constant divisiveness, the establishment of international labor organizations has been difficult. Only in recent decades, as national federations have begun to stabilize, have lasting international affiliations been possible.

The Latin American union movement has debated for many years whether international organizations should be interhemispheric (that is, including unions in the U.S., Canada, and the newly independent Caribbean islands) or strictly continental (that is, confined to Latin America). The nationalists and Communists favored the latter stand; democratic elements, on the other hand, encouraged an interhemispheric alliance.

THE FIRST FRUSTRATED ATTEMPTS

The first attempts to create continental federations began early in this century. In 1909 the Federación Obrera Regional Argentina was the host at a conference of anarcho-syndicalist labor organizations that included groups from Chile, Paraguay, Uruguay, Brazil, and Peru. No practical results were achieved. It was not until 1929 that the perseverance of the anarchists finally bore fruit, with the establishment of the Asociación Continental Trabajadores, in Buenos Aires, a regional affiliate of the International Association of Workers;* but it accomplished little, and soon dissolved.

In 1926, Mexico's CROM (Confederación Regional Obrera Mexicana) invited all the major labor associations in Latin America to a conference in Mexico City. The Confederación Obrera Argentina instructed its delegates to propose a single continental federation, and the proposal was unanimously accepted. CROM, in spite of its membership in the Pan-American

* See p. 58.

Federation of Labor, pressed for the establishment of a continental movement affiliated with the Amsterdam International (IFTU). The resolutions adopted by the conference were never put into practice because of CROM's subsequent internal difficulties.

In 1929 the Federación Regional Obrera del Paraquay held a conference of Latin American labor organizations to protest the war then threatening between Paraguay and Bolivia. The Unión Sindical Argentina, which attended the conference, withdrew because of its disapproval of the participation of the Communist Comité Pro Confederación Sindical Latinoamericano. The meeting produced nothing.

In May 1932, in Santiago, Chile, a Centro Obrero Internacional de Solidaridad Latinoamericana was founded, with delegates from Bolivia, Chile, Guatemala, Paraguay, Colombia, Peru, Mexico, and Argentina. It accomplished nothing of consequence, and soon broke up.

Meanwhile, a few federations had affiliated themselves with international organizations: the Communist unions owed allegiance to the Profintern; Brazil's labor organization sent a delegate to the conference that reorganized the IFTU after World War I; and Argentina's CGT, Mexico's CTM, and Chile's CUTCH joined IFTU just prior to World War II.[1]

General Perón's government and the Peronist CGT attempted to organize an Asociación de Trabajadores Latinoamericanos Sindicalistas (ATLAS), with conferences held in Asunción (1951) and Mexico (1952), which was attended by more or less Peronista unions from various countries. But though the Communists offered an alliance, the ATLAS was never more than a letterhead.

One more attempt might be mentioned: the Confederación Latinoamericana de Sindicalistas Cristianos (CLASC), which was formed in 1954, with headquarters in Santiago.*

COPA (PAFL)

The impulse for the formation of the first interhemispheric federation of any permanence came from U.S. and Mexican unions. The AFL had, since its inception, cultivated an interest in Latin American affairs: in 1895 it endorsed the stand of the separatist Cubans; and the following year the AFL congress approved a resolution suggested by its president, Samuel Gompers, that freedom and truth, the foundations for the "reconstruction of the world," had to be attained before the Cuban proletariat could organize itself. Following the peace treaty with Spain, the AFL condemned the annexation of Puerto Rico and the Philippines by the United States. The

* See also pp. 188–89.

1907 AFL Congress protested the arrest of Mexican anarchists Ricardo Flores Magón and Librado Rivera by U.S. authorities, and asked the U.S. Congress to investigate the alleged prosecution of certain Latin American political refugees. The 1912 AFL Congress declared itself in favor of a "hands off" policy in Latin America and sent friendship greetings to the Mexican revolutionaries. In 1915 Gompers wrote to President Wilson, asking him to recognize Venustiano Carranza's revolutionary government in Mexico, and sent the greetings of the AFL to the Casa del Obrero Mundial. Ultimately, in 1916, Luis Morones and Salvador González, representing the Mexican unions, met with AFL leaders; and the AFL Congress of 1916 ordered the Executive Committee to explore the organization of a Pan-American Labor Federation (PAFL or, in Spanish, Confederación Obrera Panamericana, COPA).[2]

Late in 1917 Gompers went to Cuba, hoping to convince several U.S. workers who had been taken to the island as strikebreakers to return to the United States.

In 1918, a joint AFL and CROM conference opened in Laredo, Texas, two days after the signing of the armistice that ended World War I. Seventy-two delegates attended—46 from the United States, 21 from Mexico, and the others from Guatemala, El Salvador, Costa Rica, and Colombia. The result was the founding of the PAFL, with headquarters in Washington. It was resolved that PAFL request the freedom of political prisoners, and the AFL delegation promised to seek an improvement in the treatment of Mexican immigrants and political prisoners in the U.S. Gompers was elected President. The PAFL was quite obviously a Caribbean organization, from the time of its formation; important affiliations in South America were never established.

In its founding manifesto, PAFL declared that relationships among the Pan-American countries would remain tenuous until they were made to reflect the will of the masses and were in accord with concepts of justice; and that an essential step toward democracy and justice was to offer the masses a chance to make their voices heard and thus to contribute to the solution of international problems. Briefly, PAFL's aims were: "To establish better living conditions for workers emigrating from one country to another; to establish a better understanding and relationship between the peoples of the Pan-American republics; to draw upon every lawful and honorable means for the protection and promotion of the rights, interests, and welfare of the peoples of the Pan-American republics; to draw upon every lawful and honorable means for the cultivation of favorable and friendly relations between the labor movements and the peoples of the Pan-American republics."

PAFL's second congress took place in New York in 1920, with delegates attending from Peru, El Salvador, Nicaragua, the Dominican Republic, Mexico, and the U.S. Mexico City was the site of the third congress, in 1921, with delegations from the U.S., Puerto Rico, Mexico, the Dominican Republic, Guatemala, and El Salvador. When the Dominican delegate described the condition of the workers in his country, the AFL immediately dispatched a mission to the Dominican Republic, then under the control of U.S. military authorities. The mission condemned prevailing economic conditions and proposed a reform plan. At Gompers's suggestion the congress approved a resolution by which PAFL would commit itself to encouraging and abetting "the independence and autonomy of all the Pan-American countries."

The AFL congress of the same year asked the United States government to recognize the revolutionary Mexican government of General Alvaro Obregón; in 1923, recognition was effectively granted. Toward the end of 1923, when it was learned that a rebel group opposing the new Mexican government was receiving arms from abroad, the AFL enjoined the unions affiliated with the IFTU to block the shipment of the weapons. The measure was so effective that the rebel leader, Adolfo de la Huerta, attempted to make contact with AFL leaders to convince them that his movement was not anti-labor; but Gompers refused to see his messengers.

PAFL's fourth congress also met in Mexico City in 1924. Delegates attended from Mexico, Nicaragua, Panama, the Dominican Republic, the U.S., and Guatemala. The congress, supported by the AFL, asked that U.S. troops be withdrawn from Santo Domingo, and also requested an investigation of the Nicaraguan situation.[3] Gompers fell ill during the discussions and died shortly afterward. He was succeeded in the AFL by William Green. When PAFL began to decline in subsequent years, Gompers's leadership was sorely missed.

The fifth PAFL congress, held in Washington in 1927, "attracted the attention of the United States to the necessity of withdrawing its troops from Nicaragua." The sixth congress, in Havana in 1930, began the decline of PAFL: when the Cuban delegation withdrew, because the congress did not go along with Cuba's demand for its support against American interference in the affairs of Cuba, PAFL was effectively doomed. Though an attempt was made to revive it in 1940, no more congresses were held.

The Socialist Santiago Iglesias, Secretary of the Federación de Trabajadores Libres of Puerto Rico (affiliated with the AFL) was for many years the Secretary and leading figure in PAFL. Communists and other groups accused PAFL of having become an instrument of the AFL. PAFL's partisans alleged that it had held the principal union organizations of that period together; and that on several occasions it had protested so-called dollar diplomacy and local dictators, had furnished aid to persecuted Cuban union leaders, and had defended the Mexican government when it was attacked by U.S. rightists.

PAFL was the first major attempt to unite the principal Latin American labor organizations in a hemispheric federation. Its positions proved to be an important influence on U.S. policy in Latin America. It was neither radical nor reactionary.[4] Perhaps its greatest weakness was its refusal to accept unions of radical leanings, which at that time predominated in Latin America. In this sense, PAFL ran counter to the trends of the times.

Gompers, who had inspired and encouraged PAFL in its early years, hoped that its activities would serve as a permanent asset, not only to the progress of labor, but also in maintaining peace in the western hemisphere. The PAFL, he added, had never been associated with any effort to force economic concessions, nor with any struggle for the domination of world markets; therefore, it had never found it necessary to explain or defend its motives. All were aware, he went on, that PAFL's motive had always been the improvement of human welfare, and "what better principle could there be in laying the foundation for international trust?"[5]

CSLA

The Communists, in Latin America as elsewhere, at first made a maximum effort to take over existing unions, ousting socialists or anarchists from the leadership. Where they failed in this, they sought to divide the unions, using the factions that emerged to form new national federations. Later, during the "Bolshevization" of the Communist parties, the Communists established everywhere—even where they lacked strength and contented themselves with a simple letterhead—the so-called "unity" unions. These groups, for the most part skeletal, pretended to favor labor unity initiated from the bottom—i.e., achieved by bypassing the leadership of the non-Communist unions. This tactic invariably failed.

The Communists were concerned with following the precepts of the Comintern and the Profintern: to "debilitate the capitalist system" in countless limited struggles and to "unmask traitorous reformist leaders." The results were long lists of dead and injured, long prison terms for members acting in good faith, and not a single lasting victory. Principal Latin American strikes led by the Communists were by: the nitrate workers in Chile in 1925, 3,000 victims; workers in Guayaquil, Ecuador, in 1925, 500 victims; the Santa Marta banana workers in Colombia in 1928, 4,600 victims; Standard Oil Company workers in Peru in 1931, 160 victims; the peasants' movements in El Salvador in 1932, close to 10,000 victims.

At the same time, the Communists sought to create workers' and peasants' blocs, on instructions from Moscow. They were successful in this in Mexico, owing to the efforts of Ursulo Galván (died 1930), who for a time allowed the Communists to control him, and who came, finally, to be looked upon as a "traitor." Diego Rivera (1886-1959) was President of this utterly ineffective bloc. Similar blocs founded in Argentina and Brazil were as ephemeral and as sterile as the one in Mexico.

In May 1929 a Communist union congress was held in Montevideo. Delegates were sent by the United Mine Workers and the National Educational League of the United States (both Communist-controlled) and France's Communist CGTU. The Profintern was officially represented by Alberto Mayer, and by its Soviet leader, Anatol Losovsky, and the entire Buenos Aires office of the Third International was present. The congress resolved to form the Confederación Sindical Latinoamericano (CSLA) from the so-called "unity" unions; the CSLA affiliated with the Profintern.

The General Council elected by the CSLA included Mahecha (the Colombian responsible for the Santa Marta slaughter), David Alfaro Siqueiros and Valentín Campa from Mexico, and Ricardo Martínez from Venezuela. Chile, where the Communists had acquired considerable strength in the unions, was unable to send a delegation (because of police interference); a post was, however, set aside for Chile on the Council.

The congress approved several resolutions: supporting the anti-imperialist struggle; supporting the necessity of channeling a war (if it broke out) into a civil uprising; opposing PAFL and the IFTU; and affirming the efficacy of reorganizing the union movement on the basis of industrial unions.

The CSLA survived until 1936, when it disbanded on the pretext that such a move would favor the emergence of a broader union movement—the CSLA, obviously, had failed to create such a movement. The CSLA indeed was a wholly bureaucratic organization, and in fact led no continental movements; though some movements were either Communist-instigated or erroneously understood to be.

The CSLA had, on the whole, one accomplishment going for it: it contributed to forming the militants that Vicente Lombardo Toledano was to call upon for support in the formation of CTAL. Though CSLA claimed to have 11 million members affiliated with its unions, that figure was never attained, not even in the combined Latin American union movement.[6]

CTAL

The first Conferencia Americana del Trabajo was held in Chile in 1936, under the sponsorship of the ILO; it was attended by government, employers and labor representatives from most of the Latin American countries. A private meeting of the labor representatives decided that unity in the Latin American union movement was imperative, and drafted a document that read:

"Gathered in January 13, 1936, in Santiago, Chile, the undersigned union militants, attending as official delegates and observers at the Conferencia Americana del Trabajo, have noted that the Latin American proletariat lacks solid organization, owing to a widespread ignorance of its interests as an exploited class, and to the failure of its own labor organizations to pursue concerted action. We have therefore resolved to address all of the workers on the continent, in urging them to work toward the unity so essential to the realization of their aims.

"We also note that the Latin American proletariat has common problems; and that to reach an early solution to these problems, a solution that will satisfy the yearnings of the suffering and working masses, it is necessary to undertake the establishment of a vigorous continental workers' organization as soon as possible.... We propose also immediate agitation toward satisfaction of the following demands: (1) defense of the democratic freedoms of speech, of assembly, of association, of the press, of the right to strike, etc.; (2) a maximum work week of forty hours, without reduction in salary; (3) a raise in wages; (4) strict enforcement, as well as broadening, of national labor laws and international labor agreements, such as insurance against occupational hazards, sickness, incapacitation, old age, unemployment, and death; (5) freeing of all political and social prisoners; and (6) a policy against fascism and war."

This need for a Latin American organization was perceived by the CTM, and a congress of representatives from various federations met in September 1938 in Mexico City. Delegates were sent from Argentina, Bolivia, Chile, Colombia, Paraguay, Venezuela, Nicaragua, Costa Rica, Peru, Ecuador, Cuba, Mexico, and the United States. The congress approved by acclamation the creation of the Confederación de Trabajadores de América Latina (CTAL), whose statutes were accepted unanimously. Its declaration of principles stated: "The workers and intellectuals of Latin America insist that the social order prevailing in most of the world's countries should be replaced by an order founded on justice; based on abolition of the exploitation of man by man; upholding the democratic system as a means of governing the interests of the human community; respecting the economic and political autonomy of every nation and the solidarity of all the peoples of the world; ending, for all time, the use of armed aggression as an instrument for resolving international conflicts; and condemning the war of conquest as contrary to the interests of civilization.... They declare that if the ideal of social justice is to become possible, it is vital that the working class in each country be united. The permanent and inviolable alliance of workers in each region and each continent is likewise vital, as is a clear and firm understanding among the workers of the world, if true international unity is to be achieved.

"They declare that the principal task of the working class in Latin America is to obtain full economic and political autonomy of the Latin American nations and to eradicate the surviving vestiges of feudalism in these countries, with the goal of raising the economic, social, and moral conditions of the masses."[7]

Altogether 37 delegates from 13 countries were present at the Mexico conference, as well as Léon Jouhaux of the French CGT, Ramón González Peña of the Spanish UGT, John L. Lewis of the CIO, and union representatives from Sweden and India. William Green, president of the AFL, refused to attend, observing that in view of the political leanings of its organizers, the convention could be no more than an occasion for Communist propaganda.

The origin of the CTAL was partly the unforeseen result of a Communist maneuver. On March 7, 1935, the Profintern proposed to the IFTU a unification meeting, but the proposal was rejected. In August 1937 the Soviet unions agreed to negotiate directly with the IFTU. By the time World War II broke out, the negotiations had still failed to produce any agreements. But on the strength of the propaganda accompanying these proposals, the Communists of several countries managed to merge their unions with those led by socialists or syndicalists—in France with the CGT, and in Spain with the UGT, for example. The same phenomenon occurred in Latin America, where almost all union federations joined CTAL. Elements of diverse leanings were for a time included among CTAL's leadership, but gradually the Communists gained control, at the same pace as militant Communists or Communist sympathizers began replacing old leaders in the national unions. The process was, in different circumstances, identical to that in France and Spain.

The CTAL unified many unions and was especially successful in fusing Communists with independents. In countries where no union federation existed, one was created, always under the name Confederación de Trabajadores. In the early years the CTAL had considerable success and awakened many hopes. It has had but one President, Vicente Lombardo Toledano.

The CTAL congresses, after the constitutional meeting, were in Mexico City in 1941; Cali, Colombia, in 1944; again in Mexico City in 1948; and in Santiago, Chile, in 1953. The 1941 congress expressed CTAL's support for an alliance between capitalist democracies and the USSR, which had just been invaded by Germany. Previously, from the time of the signing of the

German-Soviet Pact, the CTAL had opposed the war, calling it imperialistic and placing the blame for it wholly on the democratic countries, following Moscow's line. But the CTAL, though conducting several strikes, never dared undertake sabotage; the membership of the unions and federations was heterogeneous, and anything beyond a verbal antiwar attitude would have led to the disintegration of CTAL.

At the Cali meeting, a "good neighbor" congress, Lombardo spoke of the friendship between the peoples of North and South America. However, the Mexican congress of 1948 was completely changed in tone—the cold war had begun. CTAL attacked the Clayton Plan and the "imperialism of the FBI," a position strengthened at the skeletal Santiago congress, where the closing session was attended by a bare 3,000—which was the last.

At the Cali congress it was affirmed that CTAL had over 8 million members. In 1950, according to the ILO, it had 6.8 million. Estimates for 1944, prepared by the Communist writer William Z. Foster, are shown in Table 18.1.

The CTAL performed an undeniable service: under the conditions imposed by the war, it accustomed Latin American management and governments to accepting the unions as a normal feature of society. On the other hand, it exerted a negative influence on the struggle for improved working conditions, better salaries, guarantees from employers, etc. For example, Lombardo stated at Cali: "We have abandoned the romantic and sterile attitudes that provoked our outcries against imperialism"; and, he

TABLE 18.1. MEMBERSHIP OF FEDERATIONS AFFILIATED WITH CTAL, 1944

Federation	Members
Confederación General del Trabajo, Argentina	250,000
Federación de Obreros Bolivianos	25,000
Confederación de Trabajadores de Colombia	200,000
Confederación de Trabajadores de Costa Rica	40,000
Confederación de Trabajadores de Cuba	500,000
Confederación de Trabajadores de Chile	400,000
Confederación de Trabajadores del Ecuador	150,000
Confederación de Trabajadores de México	1,300,000
Comité Organizador de la C. T. de Nicaragua	10,000
Federación de Sindicatos de Panamá	1,000
Consejo Obrero de Paraguay	50,000
Confederación de Trabajadores del Perú	300,000
Confederación de Trabajadores de la República Dominicana	10,000
Federación General de Trabajadores, Uruguay	40,000
Confederación de Trabajadores de Venezuela	40,000

Source: Foster, p. 522.

added, "During the war against the Nazi-Fascist Axis, the Latin American working class should not employ the strike as a normal instrument of struggle." The results of this Moscow-inspired position, which demanded every kind of sacrifice from workers all over the world in order to help the USSR, were the labor-management pacts (the most important was signed in Mexico at Lombardo's initiative), and the condemnation of strikes.

Furthermore the CTAL and Lombardo criticized attempts to overthrow dictatorships (in Venezuela, Guatemala, etc.), on the pretext that these were "progressive" regimes (they thus described Batista in Cuba, whose government included Communist ministers) and allies of the United Nations. In 1942 Lombardo toured Latin America and visited all the dictators of that period: Somoza, Ubico, Medina Angarita Peñaranda, and Moriñigo. He called Prado, of Peru, the "criollo Stalin." Somoza embraced him publicly in Managua's plaza—Lombardo, in turn, remarking that the dictator was "an intelligent, determined man, doing good for his people in his own way; he is, we might say, a paternal dictator to his people."

CTAL, then, unified the union movement at a time when it served the purposes of the USSR (when Hitlerism was threatening) and later divided the same movement when it was convenient for Moscow (during the Cold War). It attempted, without success, the destruction of all labor forces not ready to accept its slogans.[8]

Communist domination of CTAL was seen clearly at the Cali congress of December 1944. Resolutions asking for the liberation of the leader of the Brazilian Communist Party, Luiz Carlos Prestes, were approved, and a censure of "Trotskyist" activities received an ovation. The outstanding figures in this congress were Enrique Rodríguez (Uruguay), Juan Vargas Puebla (Chile), and Pedro Saad (Ecuador), all members of the Communist Parties of their respective countries. The nine members of the Executive Committee elected at this congress, with the exception of the Mexican Fidel Velázquez, were all Communists or Communist sympathizers. The congress announced a new program: to postpone socialism as a political objective and cooperate with "progressive capital" in a "broadly based united front."

Communist influence in CTAL was strengthened by the withdrawal of several non-Communist organizations. This occurred with the Peronist CGT in Argentina, with the Confederación de Trabajadores de Chile, and with the Confederación de Trabajadores del Perú, which broke relations with CTAL after the apristas took over its leadership. In 1948, the Confederación de Trabajadores de México withdrew from CTAL and expelled Lombardo Toledano from its membership.

Affiliated from its inception with the IFTU, CTAL participated in the negotiations that led, immediately after World War II, to the formation of the World Federation of Trade Unions (WFTU), to which CTAL remained affiliated even after the 1949 separation of the democratic unions (who thereafter constituted the ICFTU).[9]

In 1948 the CTAL leadership was made up of President Vicente Lombardo Toledano and his two aides, Salvador Ocampo, Communist ex-senator from Chile, and Roberto Moreno, leader of the Communist Party of Brazil. Five years later, at the congress held in Santiago in March 1953, there were only two public sessions. Most matters were dealt with behind closed doors.

At a WFTU Executive Committee meeting in December 1950, CTAL's work was reviewed. It was agreed that CTAL should have more direct contact with the workers of the Latin American countries. CTAL should, in fact, unify labor around "immediate and concrete objectives, capable of bringing together the greatest working masses—objectives such as salary increases, social security, improved working conditions, etc." Bonds with the WFTU should be strengthened by an exchange of delegations with unions of the Soviet Union and by affiliation of union federations with the corresponding WFTU departments. From that time on, WFTU's direct influence in CTAL increased. The WFTU had failed in Europe, and its Executive Committee shifted priority from "capitalist Europe" to the "colonial and semicolonial" areas.

WFTU and CTAL, and their respective Professional Departments, held two continental conferences in May 1951, an Agrarian Conference in Mexico City and a Transport Conference in Guatemala. The principal objective at these conferences was a more intimate affiliation of Latin American unions with WFTU's Professional Departments.[10]

CTAL, of course, supported all Communist campaigns, especially the so-called "Stockholm Manifesto," and collaborated in the Communist strategy established for Latin America. Significant was a wave of strikes that broke out in Chile and Brazil in 1951, in which Communist influence was carefully concealed. Deliberately excessive demands were made, demands that had no hope of being satisfied. Nevertheless, the Communists failed in their principal objective, which was to provoke serious industrial disorders in as many countries as possible.

Later, the dynamism of CTAL began to decline. It proposed an alliance with the Peronist ATLAS and devoted much of its activity to combating ORIT and backing those Communists who, in countries ruled by dictatorships, took advantage of that political situation to take over unions whose democratic leaders had been persecuted, jailed, or exiled. As would be supposed, CTAL did not condemn the Soviet intervention in Hungary, nor did they censure Soviet tin and tungsten dumping, which had important repercussions in the Bolivian labor movement.

At the beginning of 1964, Lombardo, still President of CTAL, announced: "CTAL's historical mission has ended." After 26 years the federation that had been founded with so many hopes had vanished, almost without anyone's realizing it. CTAL had actually been for many years only a simple letterhead and a small office in Mexico City; it published no newspapers and held no meetings.

The Communists have found themselves, in recent years, completely without allies in the union movement. To break out of this isolation they have tried to induce some federations to form a new Latin American union movement, which they present as neutralist, or as a "third position." The first such attempt took place in 1959, when the Cuban CTC, then led by Castroites, withdrew from ORIT and signed a pact with the Confederación de Trabajadores de Venezuela (CTV), which then had no international affiliation and whose leadership included Christian-democrats, Populists, and Communists. Through the CTV, the Castroites tried to organize a union movement to oppose the free unions of ORIT. But the proposal was ignored by the other national federations, and the maneuver failed. In 1961 Castro, unable to tolerate the success of a democratic revolution such as Venezuela's, initiated a campaign of terrorism calculated to bring on its failure. Venezuelan unions, whose interests lay in the success of the democratic regime, broke with the Cubans, the Communists were defeated in all union elections, and the CTV refused to continue pursuing the creation of a new Latin American union federation.

At the WFTU's Bucharest meeting in 1959 it was decided that CTAL should be abandoned. Later, the Chilean CUT called a "meeting of unification," and announced that ORIT, the Christian CLASC, CTAL, CTV, and the Cuban CTC would participate. But when the meeting was held, in Santiago in September 1962, only the CUT, the Cuban CTC, the CTAL, and a few union locals of little importance attended. The only resolution passed was the creation of a Secretariat. The delegates at Santiago represented a scant 2 million workers, of which 1.5 million were Cuban. The Secretariat then began to organize a new congress, in the hope of gaining greater membership—encouraged by the fact that the Communists had meanwhile managed to take over one of the three great Brazilian federations (the industrial workers). The congress, which was to have been held in October 1963, was postponed until January 1964, when it met in Belo Horizonte and Brasilia (the Rio and São Paulo authorities refused to allow it to take place within their boundaries).

But again, neither ORIT nor CLASC attended the congress. And among participating delegates, though they were all Communists, there were dissensions—between partisans of Moscow and partisans of Peking. Only a few vague declarations received unanimous approval. It was pointed out that the Secretariat could be installed neither in Brazil, owing to the "lack of maturity in Brazilian unions," nor in Mexico, owing to "the conservative nature" of the Mexican unions; thus it remained in Santiago.

Thus the intended formation of the Central Unica de Trabajadores de Iberoamérica (CUTAL) failed to come off. Ironically, it was with an eye toward the forming of this new organization that Lombardo Toledano decided to announce the official demise of CTAL.

CIT

The 1947 congress of the Confederación de Trabajadores del Perú discussed the necessity of creating an inter-American union federation that would effectively meet the needs of the workers of the American continent. The Confederación de Trabajadores de Chile, led by Bernardo Ibáñez, spoke in similar terms—as did the Cuban CTC, and other federations that opposed the Communist nature of CTAL. In 1947 the Peruvian and the Chilean federations began consultations on the subject. The Confederación Interamericana de Trabajadores (CIT) was finally established at a conference held in Lima in January 1948; the delegates in attendance represented labor organizations in Bolivia, Brazil, Colombia, Costa Rica, Chile, the United States (AFL), Dutch Guiana, Mexico, Peru, and Venezuela, and there were also observers from Argentina (COASI), Haiti, Panama, and Paraguay.

The congress established the following as some of the objectives of CIT: the organization and unification of the workers in each of the Latin American countries; the defense of interests and gains of the Latin American union movement; the application and promotion of international labor agreements and other agreements established by international or inter-American organizations; the incorporation into the political constitutions of all Latin American countries of clauses to guarantee union freedom, the right of coalition, the right to strike, the maximum working day, collective contracts, and so on; the cooperation of unions of the Western Hemisphere in raising workers' standards of living; and the study of economic and social problems and the adoption of adequate measures for the improvement of living conditions.

CIT was to have had its headquarters in Lima, but shortly after its foundation it was expelled by the new dictatorial Peruvian government, and its headquarters were moved to Santiago, and still later to Havana.

The second CIT congress, held in Havana in 1949, issued an appeal to all democratic labor organizations within the WFTU to leave that body. At the same time, CIT decided to participate in the establishment of a democratic world organization, the ICFTU.[11] Great emphasis was placed on the independence of unions from government—at that time the majority of Latin American countries were under dictatorships or semi-dictatorships that tried to dominate or control the unions. The congress rejected Luis Morones's request for affiliation on behalf of the Mexican CROM, which later allied itself with the Peronist CGT in creating the brief ATLAS.

The CIT's program, prepared in 1949, established, among others, the following objectives:

To defend the right of Latin American countries to regulate their own economies, even if this implies the nationalization or socialization of the economy;

To oppose all signs of imperialism, inasmuch as it has allowed Latin American resources to be exploited for the benefit of the more industrially developed countries;

To reject all capitalist overtures that would tend to industrialize the countries of the continent;

To enforce agrarian reform by dividing the latifundios, since this offers the best hope for emancipating the millions of workers now confined under a semi-feudal system;

To work for the right of agricultural workers to organize without restriction and with the same rights and guarantees that industrial workers enjoy;

To achieve respect for Indian communes and their collective-oriented labor organizations;

To seek the establishment of democratic universities, particularly technical institutes, whose doors will be open to young workers;

To defend the democratic rights of workers to assemble, to think freely, to elect their own governments, and to adopt any political or religious belief;

To reject any movements tending to establish dictatorships of any kind;

To reject discrimination by race, creed, color, or language, in the Latin American countries, in employment as well as in civic life;

To reject all intervention by governments, political parties, or management in the internal affairs of unions;

To enlist all Latin American workers affiliated with CIT in the struggle for world peace, and, in addition, to bring into CIT all workers of democratic leanings;

To oppose imperialist plans that aim at subjugating the governments of the Americas to the service of their political, economic, and military designs, and to condemn the Soviet expansionism and totalitarianism expressed in Latin America and throughout the world through the Communist parties;

To stimulate support of the international community represented by the United Nations;

To support world disarmament, in order to make future wars impossible, while recognizing at the same time the temporary need of the democratic nations to maintain their military defenses in the face of totalitarian aggression;

To support the free and democratic workers of countries where totalitarian governments exist—in Eastern Europe, Spain, and elsewhere—in their struggle for freedom.

CIT made one consistent mistake, more psychological than political—and the Communists made the most of it. Although CIT's key posts—President, Secretary General, etc.—were always held by eminent Latin American unionists, "its principal orientation was actually provided by Americans. This was, to a certain extent, to be expected, since the majority of Latin American unions were—and still are—organically and financially weak, with fewer experienced leaders than their companions to the north. It would be inexact to say that CIT's direction, as outlined by Americans, was always a sham. But in general this direction did not adjust to the psychology or the complex sociopolitical realities of the various Latin American countries in which CIT operated. This caused resentments and angers where Latin American unionism was involved; moreover, it contributed to the easy propagation, by Communist agents, of anti-U.S. slogans in which, with obvious injustice and in bad faith, the unions of the U.S. and their most notable figures were seen to be in league with the State Department and Wall Street in a combined expression of imperialism."[12]

But the mistake was later rectified in great part; as can be seen from the following recommendations, formulated by specialists at the University of Chicago and aimed at an effective collaboration between union organizations of the U.S. and Latin America: "Both parties should sincerely acknowledge and accept the diversity of labor organizations in the two zones of the Western Hemisphere. They should recognize that this diversity corresponds to basic differences in historical and cultural background, to diverse situations, tasks, and experiences. Any conscious or unconscious attempt to formulate a Latin American organization in accordance with a U.S. model, or vice versa, would be not only useless but disastrous to true democratic cooperation. Democratic labor organizations ought to differ fundamentally from those controlled by the Communists in their awareness of the diversity of outwardly similar international organizations, and in their total repudiation of the idea that there can be only one philosophy and one effective method of procedure for all labor organizations.

"To emphasize democratic cooperation it is recommended that the various labor organizations work toward carrying out mutual activities in which an equally shared [inter-American] cooperation would be feasible. Unions and educational activities with a minimum of ideological content would seem to offer the best opportunities for democratic cooperation of this sort. Above all, communication and the exchange of ideas are the first essentials for successful cooperation.

"Judging by historical experience, we shall do well to avoid encouraging suspicion that the action of U.S. unions is controlled by or subjected to the U.S. State Department or other official bureaus. This does not, of course, deny the possibility of U.S. unions bringing their influence to bear on the U.S. Government through normal democratic channels. More exactly: if the U.S. Government were to seem committed to backing reactionary or dictatorial governments or firms adverse to Latin American labor organizations, the U.S. unions would lose the bonds of respect that permit them to exert a friendly influence in Latin America should they fail to openly oppose the official U.S. attitude.

"This policy requires that representatives of the U.S. Government keep in mind, in labor matters, that they do not represent U.S. labor organizations, much less management. They should insist that Latin American union leaders understand the distinction between functions of U.S. Government representatives and the functions of U.S. labor leaders....

"Effective democratic cooperation requires, finally, the formation of a well-informed public opinion in the ranks of the U.S. labor organizations concerning the problems that affect the international labor movement."[18]

The experience that inspired these recommendations was used to advantage in ORIT.

ORIT

When the ICFTU was established in London in December 1949, the need for a Latin American regional organization arose. As a result of a meeting held in Mexico City in January 1951, the CIT became the regional branch of ICFTU for the Western Hemisphere. The new organization was fortified by the addition of groups that had not participated in CIT (the CIO and the United Mine Workers of the U.S., Mexico's CTM, and several organizations from Canada, West Indies, Uruguay, and elsewhere); it was called the Organización Regional Interamericana de Trabajadores

(ORIT). Its headquarters, originally in Havana, were moved to Mexico City in 1952.

In 1956, its brightest year, ORIT included 49 affiliated union organizations in 17 countries and 18 dependent territories. Its Latin American membership, as of 1959, is shown in Table 18.2.

ORIT believes that unions should foster a democratic system based on economic interdependence, founded on equality among all countries and solidarity among all peoples. It feels that the principal aim of the Latin American working class should be to rid the Latin American countries of the feudal systems still subsisting within them, and to elevate the present economic, social, and moral conditions of the masses. It declares that all forms of totalitarianism oppose the aspirations of workers, and it maintains a firm opposition to Communism. It seeks the elimination of the great economic burdens borne by the Latin American peoples: "The greatest guarantee for peace is a permanent improvement of all peoples' standard of living."[14] During its fifth congress, held in Rio in 1961, ORIT condemned

TABLE 18.2. MEMBERS OF ORIT AND PIS, 1959

Country	Total # ORIT Members	Members, Professional International Secretariats (PIS)					
		Total	Mail, Telephone & Telegraph	Agri- culture	Transpor- tation	Con- struc- tion	Technical & Commercial
Argentina	—	65,187	45,187	—	20,000	—	—
Bolivia	—	5,200	5,200	—	—	—	—
Brazil	2,680,000	230,600	38,600	—	192,000	—	—
Chile	211,000	41,627	7,127	—	10,500	—	—
Colombia	402,331	16,356	733	—	9,423	—	—
Costa Rica	12,000	3,460	960	1,500	1,000	—	—
Cuba	1,200,000	618,139	7,547	518,432	36,500	15,453	7,311
Ecuador	1,000	400	—	—	400	—	—
Guatemala	2,000	323	23	—	—	—	—
Haiti	3,500	—	—	—	—	—	—
Honduras	10,000	9,000	—	9,000	—	—	—
Mexico	1,000,000	80,189	7,500	—	55,050	—	—
Nicaragua	—	3,000	—	—	3,000	—	—
Panama	1,149	700	—	—	700	—	—
Paraguay	55,000	3,400	400	—	3,000	—	—
Peru	500,000	52,795	2,795	50,000	—	—	—
Uruguay	40,000	10,300	1,600	—	6,700	—	—
Venezuela	200,000	—	—	—	—	—	—

Source: *Boletín de Información de la CIOSL,* June 29–July 4, 1959. Latest available figures.

the Castro dictatorship "just as it formerly condemned the odious dictatorship of Batista."

This fifth ORIT congress was preceded by the first Economic Labor Conference, in São Paulo. The doctrinal resolutions of both the Labor Conference and the subsequent congress could be summed up as follows: "Financial aid [for development plans] must not be absorbed by the privileged classes; it must reach the social levels that have been forgotten and abandoned until now. The essential condition for the achievement of these objectives of development and economic integration is proper representation of the unions in the planning and execution of development programs, on both national and continental levels." Economic aid should be withheld from countries governed otherwise than by an impeccable system of representative democracy; likewise should it be withheld from countries whose plans for economic development are inspired by other than a desire for genuine social reform. . . . Economic aid must be placed at the disposal not only of governments, but also of nongovernmental bodies, cooperatives, and unions, for productive goals.

The Economic Labor Conference clearly stated: "In broad terms, each development program should give preference to the solution of the most urgent problems: the wiping out of illiteracy and substandard housing; the improving and broadening of social security, which should extend to all the population in need of it." Economic advancement and social progress are "vital to the principles of democracy and freedom contained in our national constitutions, and there can be no economic development without social progress." The first step for Latin America is "an urgent and radical transformation of its agrarian economy. . . . and ownership of land by those who work it and the recognition of their right to receive wholly the benefits of this work. . . . But those who work the land must receive broad financial and technical aid in order to make their efforts fruitful. Cooperative methods must be stimulated and promoted."

The conference stated that industrialization could not depend exclusively on foreign financial and technical aid: "Countries in the process of industrialization must derive the necessary capital from their own resources and must accelerate the training of specialized workers and technicians. They must balance the development of their industries in such a way that industrial products can be exported as well as satisfy the national needs."

Financing and development are a crucial problem: "We must somehow manage, without discouraging private investment in any way, to amass sufficient public capital for the financing of projects that do not attract private initiative or, for economic and social reasons, cannot be entrusted to [private enterprise]. . . . A fiscal reform that would provide public funds for investment in projects for education, health, housing, etc., becomes imperative. Governments must revise archaic systems of tax collection, and tax systems must be based on taxpayers' capacity."

The conference also studied the problem of economic integration in Latin America: "Projects for international trade cooperation now in progress or in the planning stages merit the full support of the free unions. Membership should be based on the principle of a complementary economy. Each country's prosperity rests to a large extent on the vigor of its own internal markets, which must be expanded by eliminating artificial economic barriers. The process of integration must be accelerated in any way possible and must be directed not to benefit special group interests but to raise the workers' standard of living."[15]

ORIT has had as Secretaries Francisco Aguirre of Cuba, Luis Alberto Monge of Costa Rica, Alfonso Sánchez Madariaga of Mexico, and Arturo Jáuregui of Peru. In recent years ORIT has emphasized activities in the field of labor education, and an Institute of Labor Studies has been established in Cuernavaca, Mexico. The rivalries between ORIT and ICFTU—due to the tendency of the latter to act on its own in Latin America, without going through ORIT—and between ORIT and the Professional International Secretariat (PIS) have been overcome, and at the present time there is fair cooperation between them.

19. Contradictions and Prospects

WE HAVE DEALT at length with labor movements and workers' movements. We shall undertake now to reflect on the contradictions and prospects of the movements. Of the two concepts, the labor movement is of course much the more limited. In Latin America, as in Europe, a workers' movement comprises not only a labor, or union, movement but also the political movements concerned with the interests of the working class—socialism, Communism, anarchism, revolutionary syndicalism, and in some measure populism and Christian democracy.

There is a tendency in the United States to forget that the U.S. "labor movement" had strongly political and ideological origins; and that during the initial stages of its development it was a movement of protest against the existing social order, a movement that hoped to transform the structure of American society. Only when workers found adequate living conditions and a place in society to their liking did the movement abandon its political character and ideological objectives to become what today we call "labor"—that is, "the unions" as simply one element of a democratic capitalist society, content with and accepted by that society, its members concerned with preserving group solidarity but at the same time generally diffused into society. But in Latin America, the labor movement preserves its political tone and its varying ideological objectives, confronted as it still is with conditions that no longer exist in the United States. In denying the working class a satisfactory station in life, the present Latin American social structure actually retards the development of industry, and thus of capitalism. The result is that the workers' movement falls chronically short of the growth needed to achieve even its immediate aims—the work force remains too small and too ineffectual to command the attention of society.

The society that thus confines the Latin American worker can be described only along general lines.[1] Neither a Marxist model nor a sociological model—the first a rigid division along class lines, the second wholly divorced from reality—can serve the purpose. Both approaches have helped to create an image of a Latin American that has no relation to reality.

It is usual to speak of "the working class," "the peasant," or "the middle class" in Latin America as if they were in fact classes in the European sense of the word. But this "working class" we have in mind is actually a minority of the industrial work force. This "peasantry" we refer to is no more than the leaders of peasant organizations or, at most, a limited stratum of rural dwellers who possess a certain consciousness of their own character. And this "middle class" represents no more than certain groups of professionals, intellectuals, students, civil servants, and businessmen—since the less prosperous members of what would otherwise be called the "middle class" have no awareness of belonging to it, and the more prosperous cooperate tacitly or ally themselves openly with the landowning oligarchy.

Latin American society is thus divided not into traditional classes, but into two great sectors: one representing public opinion, the other constituting the submerged and "forgotten" masses, referred to generally as *el pueblo,* the people. This division is no casual choice; it corresponds rather to the social and economic realities. Raúl Prebisch, an economist little given to sociological formulations, described these realities in this way: "While half the population accounts for approximately 20 per cent of total consumption, 5 per cent of the inhabitants at the other extreme of the scale enjoy almost 30 per cent of the total, according to estimates. This upper 5 per cent has an average consumption per family 15 times that of the 50 per cent who constitute the lower strata. If the upper-class consumption were reduced to 11 times the lower-class consumption, and if the wealth saved were channeled into increased investments, the annual growth rate of per capita income could rise as much as 3 per cent. And if the figure were reduced to nine times, the growth rate could rise to 4 per cent or even higher, depending on the political possibilities of this undertaking and the ability of each country to put it into practice."[2]

Public opinion, to put a form to it, consists of those who are regular readers of the press, or no more than 10 to 15 per cent of the population. These are the more or less informed, those with a certain awareness of national problems and with concrete personal aims: they are politically active; they discuss issues, and vote with an idea of what they are voting for; and they keep informed of world events. These are also the people whose economic condition has improved in recent decades, who feel most keenly the pull of nationalism, who are the most impatient for progress and the most anti-Yankee—and who, until lately, showed the greatest desire for social change. (There is of course a small sector of public opinion—the existing oligarchy and its political adherents, the old-line military men, and the old-style businessmen—that seeks to hold the line. This sector includes no more than 1 to 3 per cent of the population.)

In spite of differences over aims and methods, the various factions of public opinion are bound together by certain common features: they consider themselves representative of the nation as a whole; they are indifferent to the submerged masses; they live (often unconsciously) at the expense of the masses; and their high standard of living has been achieved, thus far, only through a lowering of the living standards of the masses, or at best by a retarding of improvement in the masses' condition.

Available statistics suffice to show that (except occasionally, in a few countries) population increase in Latin America is not matched by a corresponding rise in productivity. True, the public opinion group becomes more numerous, and its standard of living continues to improve; more and more people live better and better. But the failure to achieve increased productivity has a tragic implication: the source of the means that enable a growing segment of society to steadily improve its living standards is invariably the masses, whose condition grows ever more deplorable.

The populist political movements have been quick to adopt these submerged masses as their own—the peasants, small merchants, Indians, unskilled labor, and floating urban populations who together form the 85 to 90 per cent of the population that reads no newspapers, has no concept of its own interests and scarcely any aspirations, is unconsciously resigned to its condition, and is unaware of its own exploitation by the privileged public-opinion sector. But since social realities allow supporters of the populist parties to emerge only from the public-opinon sector, and since this sector views the masses with indifference, if not with an almost racist contempt, the populist parties have found themselves effectively cut off from the masses. Except in Mexico, Bolivia (from 1952 to 1964), and Venezuela, where special circumstances have obtained, the submerged masses remain submerged, even where the populist movements have gained control of the government. Thus the middle sectors of society have lost their power (or desire) to produce social change.

What perpetuates the submergence of the masses is not their cultural level or their ethnic composition; it is rather the existence of the oligarchy, which in order to govern creates (not, to be sure, by conscious effort, but by a sort of spontaneous evolution) a society in which the opportunity to influence decision-making is restricted to a small group.

Latin American society is not strictly a feudal society, since there is no sovereign or other superior authority, and the lower authorities do not exercise local sovereignty. Nevertheless, the operative systems of land tenure are much the same as those of feudalism, especially where the social status and living conditions of the peasants are concerned. We might thus call the society an enlightened despotism, much like that of the typical state in eighteenth-century Europe, except that there is no single sovereign from whom all power emanates. But the masses today, like those of the eighteenth century, support a minority group that does not consider them as having any meaningful rights.

One might also compare Latin American society with that of Soviet Russia in the sense that a single group (in the USSR, the bureaucrats; in Latin America, the landholders) exercises control over the entire nation. But whereas in the USSR the dominant class controls all means of production collectively, in Latin America it controls the basis of production—the land. Perhaps the Latin American condition may best be described as government by landholding oligarchy—in some countries, by a banking-land-holding oligarchy.

The urban population in Latin America, which has tripled and in some cases quintupled over the last few decades, continues to have its roots in the country. In spite of material differences between city and country, especially in the comforts of life, the two worlds are much closer in Latin America than in the industrial nations. Their closeness explains certain aspects of the Latin American economy, such as the instability of the labor force and its consequent lack of skills, despite the marked adaptability of the Latin American worker to adjust himself to new tasks. It explains the parasitism of the metropolitan areas, where only a small part of the population contributes actively to the economy: the peasant, accustomed as he is to the lowest standard of living, can survive in the city despite the discouraging conditions that confront him. It explains, also, the persistence of personalism in political movements and trade unions. Finally, it explains why economic crises, galloping inflation, unemployment, and other financial disasters have less serious repercussions than they would have elsewhere: the unemployed worker simply returns to his village; and the merchant or small businessman views the fortunes of his enterprise with detachment, safe in the knowledge of a haven in the country, where there are family resources and where he has invested the first profits of his business venture in the city.

On the other hand, more than half the Latin American population is under eighteen years of age—and if the proportion is less in the public-opinion groups, which enjoy greater longevity, it is greater in the submerged classes, where death is frequently easier than life.

What, then, is the class composition of the work force? If its membership still must be counted largely among the submerged classes (nonspecialized workers, agricultural workers, etc.), though some to be sure are among the higher strata of the poor (specialized workers, craftsmen), the smaller portion organized in unions or in labor, populist, or Christian-democrat parties is to be found in the lower strata of the public-opinion sector. The workers' movement, then, is in conflict with respect to change in the social structure: on the one hand it must press for change, so as to increase in strength; but on the other hand, where it forms an element of public opinion it must seek to preserve the status quo, or at least to avoid losing its privileged station. The interests of the workers' movement coincide, in the first case, with those of the submerged masses; in the second case, with oligarchic society.

The contradiction is a serious one, and if it is to be resolved the workers' movement must choose between two widely divergent courses: it could become a revolutionary force, dedicated to awakening the downtrodden masses, to guiding them, organizing them, and joining with them in the struggle for social change; or it could as easily become a simple pressure mechanism for obtaining better working conditions, for achieving limited, immediate improvements, i.e., a union movement of the U.S. type, for negotiating labor disputes, and nothing more. Predicting the outcome from the present vantage point would be a sketchy proposition.

Moreover, in a society based, with a few rare exceptions, on a system of large landholdings and its attendant oligarchy, industry is denied rapid growth simply by the lack of domestic markets. Without industrial growth there is no marked increase in the labor class and, therefore, no progress in the union movement or in the living standards of the workers and peasants. The advancements achieved, generally at a cost in effort out of all proportion to the results, are reaching their limit. If a change in social structure fails to be forthcoming, the union movement will find itself denied the chance for further advancements, at which point it will cease simply seeking means of enhancing its prospects and be reduced to fighting for survival.

Again, in this society, much of the stimulus for industrial development comes from abroad, in the form of foreign capital, public or private. At the same time, however, both in Latin American society and at the core of its worker movement, nationalist feelings are evoked that look with distrust upon these stimuli—though to be sure the sources evoking these sentiments have failed entirely to suggest means of substituting stimuli of national origin, for such stimuli are nonexistent or grossly ineffectual in societies with a semifeudal agrarian basis. The labor movement should welcome new foreign investments, so as to stimulate industry and, in turn, its own prospects; but since the movement is at the same time made up of Latin Americans, it must oppose an imbalance between foreign and national capital.

The solution to these contradictions has been offered by neither socialist, Communist, nor anarcho-syndicalist movements, and therein lies their failure and their progressive loss of influence. It could in fact be said that the ideologically oriented labor movement, as a political and social force, has all but disappeared. But this is not to say that ideology has vanished while the union movement has remained. On the contrary, the Latin American union movement remains heavily ideological, not in the sense of adhering to some specific ideology, but in a pervasive sense, of desiring a fundamental change in social structure, of aspiring toward a society in which the economic, political, and social components of democracy might function. This is indeed a source for the appeal of the populist parties (and, in some countries, of the Christian-democrats) in the labor movement. These parties offer the union movement an interpretation of reality, a program for the future, and even a mechanism for social pressure. But the U.S. labor movement, the natural ally of its Latin American counterpart, has never been able to understand these ideological impulses, in spite of the fact that it has consistently collaborated with Latin American unions and has helped them to organize continentally. In thus collaborating, the U.S. labor movement has been at its most energetic when its aim has been to awaken in them a distrust of Communism, but it has failed to understand that this aim could be achieved only by orienting the Latin American unions toward the transformation of society. The U.S. unions at times came to accept this pragmatically (if not really to understand it), during periods when populism was the only active force against Communism; on the other hand, U.S. unionists (like U.S. diplomats) have persistently failed to comprehend that what they call the "Latin American revolution" is no more than a ground swell of desire among forces on the continent to achieve a democratic capitalist society. It would seem that the fear of disorder in the streets is stronger, in this case, than the hope that these disorders might lead to the destruction of a semi-feudal society and its replacement by a capitalist society—to the replacement of oligarchy by democracy.

At a more profound level, this fear reveals grave doubt that the union movement—and the Latin American democratic movements in general—has the capacity to awaken and lead the masses and to avoid, in the process, being taken over by Communists or by nationalist demagogues. Overlooked, as well, would seem to be the thought that the best hope for assuring this capacity would be to foster within the union movement a strong ideological foundation, a foundation that would tend to be forgotten when it ceased to be of value, i.e., when the working class had secured a place in a Latin American society free of oligarchic bonds, free from preoccupation with substandard living conditions.

Precisely because it has had neither the foundation nor the encouragement to construct one, and because the present oligarchic structure tends simply to ideologic anomie, the Latin American union movement has remained indifferent to national problems that do not immediately affect the unions, but that are of importance to the future of society. The abandonment of the basic plight of the workers, or perhaps indifference to it, that has been displayed by the workers' movement in the past has had a crucial effect on delaying the social evolution of Latin America. Only time and dedicated effort can repair the evils brought on by this indifference. The fact that in Venezuela, for example, and to a lesser degree in Colombia and Peru, a beginning has been made along this path is, sad to say, no guarantee that the same course will be followed by other countries. Bolivia's case demonstrates the pitfalls that attend this indifference: the unions, after triumphing in the 1952 revolution, soon saw themselves as among the aristocracy of the revolution, and in order to hold this privileged position against the pressure of the peasantry, they allied themselves with the army to overthrow the same revolutionary regime.

To say that the unions have been indifferent to national problems is no exaggeration; nor is it an exaggeration to say that this indifference and the growing bureaucracy of the unions have proceeded apace. But, in fact, no Latin American union is sufficiently large or powerful to justify this bureaucratization: the Latin American unions of today could serve their interests quite as well by assembling their leadership, as in years past, from the rank and file, and by pursuing union interests after working hours. They have no need for salaried leaders or paid experts, nor for elegant facilities. It would suffice to display the concern and the vitality necessary for attracting intellectual and student elements—as, for example, the Peruvian unions did with the Popular Universities, during the 1920's. The unions are remiss in not offering to the intellectuals and students, as well as to their own militants, an opportunity for purposeful commitment. Bureaucratization can follow in due course, as it inevitably does, when society, free of oligarchic bonds, has taken finally the form of a democratic, capitalistic society. Union militancy, to be sure, implies sacrifices and risks; notwithstanding, the unions should reject bureaucratization and resume being what they logically must be in oligarchic societies—an instrument of protest and of change, beginning with a redirection in the lives of the militants themselves.

The comments of Latin American unionists themselves are enlightening:[3] "Union leadership is constantly shuffled about among a handful of members, for lack of a labor education program." Thus a militant Mexican printer describes his union's plight, in an article the union organ refused to publish. And, though made with Mexico in mind, his observations are valid, in general, for all of Latin America. He goes on to say: "This is the daily reality of our unions: ignorant of their origins, oblivious of their doctrines.

But be that as it may, when May Day approaches and when the collective contract is due for renewal, the old banners are dusted off and the old repertoire of slogans is trotted out: solidarity, social struggle, proletariat. We go through the motions, pay suitable lip service, then return to life as before. And what of that life? Bourgeois self-indulgence. The more powerful unions, those of the railroad, oil, and electrical workers, constitute a privileged sector, with interests virtually those of the middle class. The differences that periodically arise between these large unions and the bourgeoisie come to nothing more than a haggling." To confirm this isolation of the unions he adds: "What do we, the great unions, do to alleviate the misery of the Indians, the women who do piecework at home, the beggar children, the many laboring in small workshops? Have we ever dared strike to demand that public institutions come to the aid of these forsaken millions who, like ourselves, make up el pueblo? Quite the contrary, we make our small gains at the expense of the defenseless, for we present our demands so irresolutely as to lead only to price increases. El pueblo, therefore, look with indifference on our May Day posters and our calls to renew contracts...."

In some regions or countries union leaders are so entrenched in their posts that they can do as they please, because of the indifference of members who are obliged to pay dues (including automatic withholding of dues from wages, in some industries and countries) but who are given no voice in union affairs. Some union leaders indeed sell strikes, while others use the threat of them to extract substantial payoffs from employers. Not infrequently, the indifference of the rank and file has become so great, its disillusionment so deep, that their leaders make no secret of owning several homes or businesses, and can arrive at union assemblies ensconced in expensive automobiles without arousing a single hoot.

Conditions vary, of course, from place to place. There are many honest leaders who resist the temptations of extortion and bribery, but most of them, in most countries, are in any case subject to state jurisdiction. The unions enjoy no real independence. Capricious enforcement of the labor laws often causes unions to trust not in their own militancy but in support of public power, in pursuing demands. And the union leader is both cause and effect of bureaucratization, a product of the imbalance provoked by an industrialization which, being unplanned, has left orphaned the peasant turned industrial worker.

The unions have evolved. Many of them are no longer trade unions, as in years past, but industrial unions, with consequent problems—of organization, of administration, of relations with the state and with management organizations—that go beyond the knowledge and training of the present leaders. Unless they are represented by labor experts (who, by definition, cannot know or feel the life of the workingman, or reflect it in union negotiations), the unions need leaders who not only live the life of the union man, but possess intelligence, a breadth of knowledge, a certain economic and social vision, and diplomacy—and such men are of course rare. More often, union leaders exhibit neither the Messianic fervor and collective mission that in years past raised them above background and training, nor the skills, the knowledge, and the training demanded by the realities confronting them. With leaders such as these, the rank and file look upon their unions with a sense of inferiority.

The fact that the working class is of peasant origin, that it has no urban tradition, explains the existence of this type of leader. The uprooted peasant, no longer a laborer, though not yet a city-dweller, needs guidance. The union leader, with all his defects, does provide him a certain guidance. But the leader, himself a product of this transitory condition, tends to the perpetuation of it. Because of personal interests, more frequently because he lacks an ethical sense, he tends simply to establish and entrench his privileged circumstances. He therefore does nothing to accelerate the "urbanization" of the worker, i.e., to develop in him a sense of responsibility, an awareness of social role, a desire to look to himself, and to join actively in the life of his union.

Society, then, in seeking to eliminate the peasant-born union leader, must eliminate the conditions that create him. But if union chaos is not to result, the elimination of the old-line union leader must coincide with the emergence of a leader of a new sort, one also drawn from the union ranks. The transition could be fostered, though not guided or provoked, by diverse means, such as special worker education undertaken by the unions themselves; measures by state and private initiative tending to facilitate the adaptation of the peasant to urban life; creation, in rural areas, of elements to prepare future emigrants for life in the city; establishment, in the city, of a system of fundamental urban education.

Such undertakings would of course be sterile if forces to favor and demand them failed to emerge from the union movement itself. For this, certain conditions must be met, conditions that are developing very slowly in the union field: first, the formulation of a union ideology, broadly speaking, that would tend to forge the unions into fundamental instruments of social change; second, greater interest on the part of the middle class and the liberal professions in union activity.

Latin American unions had achieved legal recognition generally under oligarchic governments. These governments denied, and many continue to deny, to peasants and agricultural workers the right to organize, and where they have withdrawn from this position with the industrial workers, it has been because the advantages thus ceded to labor presented no fundamental danger to the oligarchic system. But the oligarchy is cautious. To be sure, it capitulated to the labor movement, but in the process created the conditions for subjugating labor. In most countries, though the legality of the unions was accepted—and seen as a triumph for labor—regulations were quickly established linking the unions to the government, and further rules had the effect of creating rivalries at the heart of the working class. Union-government ment links were achieved in some cases by imposing registration of the union as a precondition for labor-management negotiations. In other cases, obligatory mediation was established, and even arbitration by government labor officials. At other times a government labor ministry was entrusted with the duty of channeling withheld union dues from employer to union, often with a "service fee" skimmed off the top. Rivalries were created, meanwhile, through the almost general prohibition of peasant organization, an expedient that separated the industrial working class from the rural masses. Moreover, most of the social security systems that came to be established shared a structure in which separate funds and standards were established for each trade or industry, a structure calculated to foment envy and hamper the development of labor solidarity. Thus the union movement, once in a position to stand its ground against the oligarchic state, and thus to effect social change, found itself, on the contrary, linked to the state through legislation. The operative mechanism one recognizes in all this is the old shell game at the county fair.

The nationalization of industries frequently undertaken in Latin America has not usually represented an effort at socialization, but rather a passage from private hands into state control, without benefit to society. Nationalization generally places the unions in another delicate situation, at such times as they feel called upon to defend the interests of workers in the nationalized firms, against the state or the state management agency. And legislation, which often prohibits strikes, and even organization, of civil servants, tends to look upon workers in nationalized firms as government employees, leaving them virtually defenseless. (Much of this fails to hold true in Mexico, where more firms have been nationalized than anywhere else in Latin America: there, civil servants are organized, but are denied the right to strike; whereas the workers in nationalized firms may strike.)

Perhaps these contradictions are logical and inevitable, given the origins of organized labor and the late development of industrialization and of the labor movement, as well as the peculiar direction that capitalism has taken in Latin America. These are circumstances without parallel or precedent, for Latin America is more backward than Europe or North America, but more advanced than the other continents—and its circumstances are reflected in the mentality of the workingman.

The Latin American worker in general (though not the Argentinian, for local reasons) lacks two essential elements of social personality, elements found to a marked degree in the European and the U.S. worker: he gives no evidence of having been influenced by the ideologies and history of nineteenth-century social struggle; nor has he any recollection of mass unemployment.

Among Old World union militants, one generally observes a certain nostalgia for the old days (those that came to an end sometime after World War I) when social struggles were picturesque and heroic, and when ideologies were the backbone of resistance. Though circumstances have tended to neutralize the influence of ideology and of the noble tradition of the early labor movements, the memory remains, to serve as a stimulus and to act on occasion as a deterrent to incipient bureaucratization.

And within the labor masses in Europe, still more alive is the memory of widespread unemployment, which all workers over fifty years of age have experienced. The fear of unemployment steels the resolve to fight, should need be. Such fears have perhaps fostered in the European worker a sense of responsibility toward society, of participation in a community larger than that encompassed by the unions and the working class.

In Latin America these two elements are largely lacking. The continent's tradition of labor struggle is generally an unimpressive one, and the imported traditions, a shaky foundation at the outset, tended quickly to be forgotten. Moreover, unemployment and economic crises were never as serious in Latin America as in the U.S. and Europe. And in any case there was always the option of returning to the villages, a process that led naturally to alleviating the harshness of such a period. There is, therefore, among the masses no sense of heritage in organized labor, and no notion of the individual worker as a responsible participant in society. Their ignorance of both notions has led both worker and union to an indifference to the general interests of society. Society, for its part, has reacted to labor's problems with a monumental indifference of its own. At a time when in the Old World and in the United States the condition of labor is the subject of countless studies, debates, legislation, and propaganda, there is almost no one in Latin America sufficiently moved to concern himself with the subject, unless for political motives.[4]

Most Latin American countries are in a stage of economic and social evolution that could be termed the prolegomenon of industrial capitalism. Nascent Latin American capitalism must be permitted to develop without the more evil aspects of the capitalism born in the eighteenth and nineteenth centuries. Labor ought, therefore, to prepare itself for urging this revolution along appropriate paths, by such means as its influence can provide. For labor, of course, this implies an emphasis on bringing appropriate pressure to bear, an awareness of its own capacity to exert pressure, and a resolve among its leaders to consider this their mission and to make the most of the possibilities afforded them by the special circumstances of their continent.

In the Latin American countries there are certain activities, once pursued but now all but forgotten, that the unions could recultivate, activities peculiar to certain of these countries. The more important of these might be mentioned.

An activity of enormous potential benefit to society can be taken up wherever Indians make up a sizeable part of the population: in Mexico, the Central American countries, and the Andean countries. Many of the inhabitants of these countries still live, of course, in conditions of natural economy. But the developing national economy more and more impels the Indian masses to seek jobs in industry—in the mines, for example, or in small local workshops or public works. For these Indians, being thus uprooted from their small agrarian world frequently constitutes a tragedy.

The shock can be eased if the Indians find not only acceptance and human concern among the workers, but also work companions who are disposed to help them and trained to do so. Goodwill and simple common sense, of course, are not enough; an understanding of the Indian mentality, a knowledge of his customs, and respect for his ways are also important. Without this knowledge and this understanding, no one can really help the Indians to integrate themselves into modern life, or to soften the shock this represents for them.

No one is in a better position to offer this help than the Indians' own coworkers. But training of a sort is imperative, and the unions should provide the training. It is, after all, in their own best interests to do so. If the Indians are not given union membership when they are drawn into industry, and if they fail to understand the union's mission, they can easily be converted—in all innocence and with no notion of the consequences—into strikebreakers or cheap labor, thereby posing a deadly threat to the attainments of organized labor. Arousing its members to a concern with the problem and training them to deal with it (through conferences, classes, pamphlets, field trips to Indian areas, etc.) is, then, a mission of great social virtue and one of immediate importance to the union movement itself.

In these same countries, and elsewhere in Latin America, a corresponding effort should be mounted by labor to acclimate newly arrived peasants to industry and to urban life. Though the Indians pose a more difficult problem, the acculturation of the peasants is no less important. And whether Indian, or peasant, or city dweller, continuing industrialization demands attention to worker education. Though the state must be given principal responsibility for elementary education and for vocational and industrial training, the unions can contribute a great deal by pursuing permanent literacy campaigns and by urging employers to establish professional training for their members.

In order to intervene effectively in all these aspects of social life, the unions should of course participate actively in national economic and social planning. But no Latin American government, not even those of the democratic left, has invited the unions to take part in planning. At best, they have accepted union opinion. In Latin America, where public opinion is weak and pressure groups are few, national planning implies important advantages, but also serious pitfalls, for labor as well as for society. The advantages are perhaps obvious; the most serious pitfall is the tendency of experts and technicians toward totalitarianism, toward technocracy, at times toward autarchy. In any event, labor participation in planning is decisive for the future course of society in Latin America, for labor is the only force in contemporary society able to defend both society and the working class, to say nothing of the Indians and peasants, against the potential dangers of planning. Moreover, labor would be in a position to head off the dehumanizing effect that has characterized massive industrialization elsewhere, and to have a hand in determining, for example, whether atomic energy should be nationalized, entrusted to private enterprise, or otherwise disposed.[5] But the participation of labor in national planning will be really effective only with the appearance of certain prerequisites: the emergence in the union movement of a new humanist concept of its mission and the establishment of a program for the future of society; the attraction of intellectuals and technicians to the cause of developing this new ideology and of restoring in labor a sense of idealism; and the de-bureaucratization, democratization, liberation from government control, and moralization of the union movement so that it may develop the capacity to apply the new concepts.

The eve of a second industrial revolution is approaching, a revolution based on expanded use of automated processes. The union movement must have a hand in determining whether it is to develop along the same antisocial lines as the first. Implicit in this second industrial revolution is a new concept of work that will lead, perhaps, to the birth of a new class of artisans. But the possibility also exists of the worker's becoming even more expendable, leaving him with less initiative than before, and less sense of personal identity. The psychological and social consequences, for the worker and for society in general, would be serious. The unions will do well to consider the prospects from this perspective, while there is still time.

In the forms of industrial organization evolving today, the worker often no longer knows his boss. He finds himself controlled by a series of decisions of uncertain origin, which he must attribute simply to entelechy: the company. The only human relationship between worker and company in these cases—daily more infrequent as industrialization advances—takes place through the union. This produces, for the union, new duties and the necessity to adapt its form and its purpose to the new circumstances. Latin American union forms, however, still correspond to the realities of half a century ago, even where these realities have been surpassed. The union member thus often feels unprotected; he fails to find in the union an effective means of establishing dialogue with the company, and tends inevitably to a lack of interest in the union, to a drifting away from participation in union activities. The drift will become critical if the unions fail to adapt to the times. The unions will become, not merely bureaucratized organisms—many are already beyond that point—but simple instruments of social legislation, and will continue to exist not because the workers wish them to, but because the law requires their existence for its application.

We would do well also to observe that although Latin American intellectuals and students have been, in general and as of many decades, non-conformist elements, and have defended social progress, they have not, in recent years, contributed to union activity. We have seen that the unions must seek the collaboration of technical experts; they must face problems for which workers have been given no training. The complexity of collective bargaining, for example, often demands knowledge that workers obviously lack. But this collaboration on the part of intellectuals was achieved only during one brief period: when the university-reform movement in certain countries opened the way for the creation of the Popular Universities. Whether the responsibility for this gulf falls to the intellectuals or to the union movement is problematical—causes can probably be found within both sectors—but in any case, the gulf must be spanned.

The lessons of the past, and the current experience of the Latin American labor movement, have been absorbed by some leaders. One of them has this to say concerning prospects and pitfalls:[6]

"Let us be frank about the failings of the Latin American union movement, past and present.

"With very encouraging exceptions, emotion has generally predominated over reason in the attitude of our union organizations. I cannot believe a union movement to be strong if it lacks passionate commitment, but allowing the emotions to predominate systematically over a conscientious and objective analysis of problems often leads to sterile sacrifices and errors that not only discourage the rank and file, but actually lead them to resist our efforts! Unions guided almost exclusively by emotion also have a careless disregard for the importance of administrative efficiency and technical skill. In the world today, with its complicated social and economic relationships, emotion and even noble ideals demand a minimum of efficiency and technical counsel, if their goals are to be approached.

"A second failing, perhaps not entirely confined to Latin America, is what we might call isolationism. This implies conceiving of the union and its activities and aspirations as a world apart from the larger world, from the community. The activities of the union can be invalidated if the other elements of the community are ignored. Its ambitions can be realized only to the extent that the aims of other elements of society are fulfilled. Isolationism not only clouds our vision of the world, but also seriously limits constructive action. It makes of the union a mechanism active only in situations of conflict. And, clearly, the union in a society such as ours, where injustices and contradictions abound, should act within criteria of justice and general interests—not simply for, or through, conflict. The union of our time must go beyond the walls of the factory and the workshop in pursuing constructive action: the union should develop constructive group action in company with the contiguous sectors of society, and with other sectors that see themselves as operating on the same cooperative and constructive level.

"Union leadership is everywhere insufficient, especially in terms of the number of leaders with adequate education, knowledge, and experience. We should admit to the world that union education has been carelessly discarded in many of our countries, entirely apart from causes removed from the union movement itself. Several union or political groups that have pretended to impart it, by using inappropriate methods or by instilling erroneous ideas, have, far from training union leaders, actually warped many men who might otherwise have contributed invaluable service. If it is to overcome this failing the union movement must, as a fundamental obligation, intensify its efforts toward training competent leaders. And these in turn, as one of their first responsibilities, must pursue constant study.

"Failings of an individual order can reflect negatively and in fact have so reflected in the union movement. A dishonest labor leader causes as much or more damage to the unions as an arbitrary or unjust employer. A union leader indifferent to, or lacking faith in, the struggle for the betterment of man is a parasite.

"The ideology of the Latin American union movement, save exceptions in certain groups, fails to correspond to an academic synthesis *a priori,* nor does it constitute an orthodox dogma. Without disdaining important contributions from the anarchists, the Marxist groups in general, and the Christian-democrats, the most characteristic ideas of Latin American labor thinking have been forged by degrees, from confrontation of the problems them-selves followed by successive approximations, each time finer, to our own economic, social, and political reality.

"The unions defend the democratic way of life; they affirm that only within a democracy is human betterment possible. Moreover, they pursue, as a common aim, social reform. Wanton injustices exist, to the detriment of the majority and the benefit of a privileged few. A change—more or less profound, according to each country's circumstances—is in order, to put an end to the exploitation of labor forces, to poverty, and to extreme ignorance, all so widespread in our countries.

"Another idea, less clearly formed but rapidly gaining strength in the union movement, involves the possibilities of successful social reform founded on economic growth, and the possibility of breaking the ties of economic dependency to more developed countries. Judicious plans must be drawn for economic growth, and foundations of fair interchange must be established.

"It is also a commonly accepted idea that every economic, social, or po-litical program must take fully into account the reality to which it must be applied. The Latin American countries have a great deal in common, but they also have many differences. As a result, solutions to problems in one country may appear similar to those in others, but they are by no means identical.

"The Latin American unions have taken three different positions where their relationships with political organizations are concerned. Some sectors have maintained that the unions should abstain from participating in party and electoral politics—their policy should remain aloof to party interests. Occasionally they have been able to accommodate to this rigid thesis, but all indications point to a reality quite apart from the thesis. It could almost be said that it has not been possible for organized labor to maintain an un-alterably apolitical position. Other union organizations, without acknowl-edging as much, have accepted total submission to the aims of political parties. This extreme thesis has brought on experience demonstrably con-trary to the interests of the worker: Communists, Peronists, and others have accepted the union as a simple instrument of their electoral party objectives. Of course, for labor, such a position nullifies partially or wholly the alter-native of action, in seeking their demands. The more realistic position is characterized by a marked interest in influencing the orientation of political parties and public institutions, as a means of counterbalancing the influence exerted by management sectors. The unions taking this position make no political commitment but tend predictably to aid the parties that offer the best prospects for progress in the affairs of labor and society.

"The attitude of public authorities, whether arising from indifference or hostility toward the unions, is almost always determined by the influence exerted over them by socially and economically privileged groups. It is logical, then, that the unions seek to eliminate this influence, or at least to counterbalance it."

To sum up, the Latin American union movement has followed a rather uncertain course. It began to take form in the nineteenth century, emerging first out of the influence of immigrants fleeing the repressions of 1848 and 1870 in Europe, and later, in certain countries, from the activities of U.S. IWW and Spanish anarcho-syndicalists. It was a movement with a positive ideological content. It sought to defend the immediate interests of the working class, then still in transition from artisanship to proletarianism, from peasant or rural artisan to urban worker, but it coveted also its own vision of what Latin American society ought to be. It tried, just as workers' parties and political groups tried, to advance society's evolution toward desired ends.

The period between the wars took the union movement on a different tack. Communist influence, exerted for the most part through fronts and alliances, sterilized the political effectiveness of the unions by placing them at the service of interests apart from the working class. By the time the USSR had entered World War II, the Communists, through CTAL, had achieved the unification of the union movement at the price of suppressing its every yearning toward change. They pursued its emasculation to "avoid jeopardizing the allies' war potential." As a result, when the war was over, the Latin American proletariat, numerically weak and ideologically debilitated, felt profoundly disillusioned and abandoned its political position, to take refuge in a sort of business unionism, only and exclusively in defense of its immediate interests.

The union movement thus played no essential part in the series of movements against dictatorships in 1944 and 1945, nor was it later in any position to defend the democratic regimes during the wave of military coups in 1948 and 1949, nor had it any notion of how to resist the seduction of the praetorian demagoguery of Peronism. Where there has been some measure of political stability, as there has been in Mexico, the union movement became a factor in uniting the working class, with the sanction and implied direction of the government.

Up to the outbreak of World War I, the union movement had failed to achieve a synthesis of European and U.S. ideological influences with the Latin American necessities. Communist sectarianism later vitiated attempts by Latin American Marxists to make this synthesis. The mission of forging a Latin American ideology of reform, of conceiving a program for continental unity, fell to a new social element that with industrialization had begun to grow in number: the middle class. It was the populist movements that began to fashion, through action, the new ideology, and it has been the populist movements that have carried the ideology to positive practical application.

After its first great push of activism, when it valued principles more highly than tactics, the union movement found its dynamism waning, and the successive continental union federations (CTAL, CIT, ORIT) were unable to arouse it from its lethargy. CIT and ORIT did protect the movement from becoming the outright instrument of CTAL (an organization of decidedly Communist influence), but they failed to instill in it an ideological content. The influence of U.S. labor, in the form of nonpolitical unionism, prevailed, in spite of the wholly disparate social contexts of the two continents. The result has been that the union movement has become, simply, a lever to be operated by others. When these others have been democratic political forces the result has been, if not ideal, at least not negative. But when the unions have been managed by demagogues like Perón or Vargas, or by dictators like Batista or Castro, the result has been wholly negative, both for the working class and for society as a whole.

The ensuing bureaucratization of the unions has brought with it corruption of union officials, subordination of the unions to public power, and indifference among the union masses. Far from becoming an active element in the adaptation of the peasant or artisan to industrial life, or in the acclimation of Indians lately emerged from the fields, union leadership has tended increasingly to constitute no more than a coterie of parasitic officials and militants. The working class, of course, is not, as a class, intrinsically parasitic, but it *is* so, in effect, to the extent that it allows its leaders, through concessions to demagogues, dictators, or their governments, to enjoy privileges paid for at the cost of continued despair among the masses.

The first consequence of this abandonment of ideology by the union movement has been that the middle class has found itself cut off from its natural ally, in its attempts to mold and transform society. Thus when the military has effected coups, the democratic regimes have failed to establish the means of their own defense—the union movement, more often than not, has simply deserted them. Failure to commit has cost the union movement, under subsequent dictatorships, the loss of its power to oppose, for in order to gain control of the union movement the dictators have systematically supported Communist elements and rejected democratic elements in the union leadership. And even the Communists, seeking ends of their own through breakdown of the democratic institutions, have been left with nothing. Later, upon reestablishment of democracy, union movements have found themselves divided, with democratic elements contested for control of the unions by Communist opportunists previously supported by the dictator. Elsewhere the Communist tactic has been to make of union corruption the pretext for organizing new movements, movements seen by enthusiastic militants as social crusades, but by the more perceptive simply as devices for Communist infiltration and agitation.

The ideal ideology for the Latin American union movement cannot now be prescribed; but it would not, in any case, be one fashioned from the ideologies that in Europe and the United States have already been left in the backwash of time. Through action itself, new aspirations will arise, to give Latin American unionism its own vision of the future, and to incite it to act toward the realization of this vision. The emergence of this ideology, from its gestation in the very immobility and conformity of the contemporary union movement, will transform the movement into an essential element in Latin America's development. One way or another, a change in Latin American society is inevitable.

The time is ripe for the appearance of this new ideology: its need is urgently felt; a continental solution to Latin American problems is becoming more and more the sensible approach; the need to coordinate economic planning throughout Latin America is increasingly more apparent; the conviction grows that nothing short of continental agrarian reform can provide industrialization with a sound economic basis; and many no longer doubt that national armies can be prevented from upsetting the social progress of the continent only by replacing them with a Latin American armed force.

All this would have seemed a fantasy twenty years ago, but today these are realities within reach. If they are to redound to the benefit of Latin American society as a whole, and not to that of privileged groups, a commitment from the union movement is imperative.

Notes

Notes

Complete authors' names, titles, and publication data are given in the Bibliography, pp. 373–89. There are no notes to Chapters 1–3.

CHAPTER 4

1. Nettlau.
2. Giménez, pp. 30–33; Dufey, p. 47.
3. Santillán, "El anarquismo en la vida intelectual argentina."
4. Santillán, *El movimiento anarquista en la Argentina,* pp. 34–38.
5. E. Dickmann, pp. 68–69, 76, 79, 95.
6. Cúneo, p. 125.
7. *Ibid.,* pp. 258–60.
8. Simon, pp. 57–59; E. Dickmann, pp. 138–40.
9. E. Dickmann, pp. 167–68.
10. For details on Radowitzky, see Alba, "Ha fallecido Radowitzky."
11. Dufey, pp. 14–15, 23–24.
12. Simon, p. 59.
13. *Ibid.*
14. *Un trentenio,* pp. 90–97.
15. Simon, p. 62.
16. Ghitor, p. 41.
17. *Ibid.,* p. 37.
18. Santillán, "Anarquismo," p. 184.
19. L'Itinerant.
20. Pintos, *Batlle,* p. 134.
21. Simon, p. 64; Giménez, pp. 33, 36.
22. Ghitor, p. 47.
23. L'Itinerant.
24. Ramírez Necochea, pp. 224, 239, 241.
25. Jobet, *Recabarren,* pp. 24, 95.
26. Simon, p. 65.
27. Lagos Valenzuela, pp. 60–61.

28. Ghitor, p. 48
29. L'Itinerant.
30. Simon, pp. 66–67; Woodcock.
31. Alexander, *Labor Parties,* p. 29; T. A. Bastos, pp. 103 *et seq.*
32. Costa, p. 137.
33. Ghitor, p. 48.
34. González Prada, *La anarquía,* p. 35.
35. Chang-Rodríguez, *La literatura política de González Prada, Mariátegui y Haya de la Torre,* one of the best studies of the thinking of González Prada.
36. González Prada, *La anarquía,* pp. 19, 20, 35–36, 41, 72.
37. Sánchez, Prologue to *Antología,* p. x.
38. *Antología del pensamiento democrático americano: Manuel González Prada,* pp. 60 *et seq.,* 81, 84, 91.
39. González Prada, *La anarquía,* pp. 24–25.
40. Simon, p. 68.
41. Ghitor, p. 48.
42. Araquistaín, p. 281.
43. Delegacíon General del Movimiento Libertario Cubano en el Exilio.
44. Alba, *Las ideas sociales,* pp. 100 *et seq.*
45. Literature on the Flores Magóns is abundant. See Alba, *Las ideas sociales,* pp. 120 *et seq.,* where sources are fully detailed.
46. Amezcua, p. 43.
47. Fuentes Díaz, I, p. 87.
48. Flores Magón and Flores Magón, pp. 122 *et seq.*
49. Cit. by Frank Tannenbaum, *La revolución agraria mexicana,* p. 60.
50. Flores Magón, *Sembrando ideas.*
51. Flores Magón, *Epistolario revolucionario e íntimo,* p. 39.
52. Agetro, p. 35.
53. Ghitor, p. 48; Montefilpo Carvallo.
54. Simon, p. 68.
55. Alexander, *The Bolivian National Revolution,* pp. 123–24.
56. Simon, pp. 68–69.
57. *Ibid.,* p. 69.
58. Alexander, *Labor Parties,* p. 37.
59. Simon, p. 69.
60. *Ibid.,* pp. 69–70.
61. Pérez Leirós, p. 52.
62. *Conferencia Anarquista Americana.*

CHAPTER 5

1. Máiztegui.
2. Fernández Artucio, Part II.
3. It is interesting to compare the true history of the Latin-American socialist movement with that outlined by U.S. Communist leader William Z. Foster in his *Outline of Political History of the Americas.*
4. Giménez, p. 14.

5. Echeverría, *passim*; see also Palacios, *Estevan Echeverría.*
6. Frugoni, II, p. 291.
7. Oddone, *Historia del socialismo argentino,* I, p. 117.
8. Giménez, p. 14.
9. Sarmiento, pp. 69 *et seq.*
10. Cúneo, p. 217.
11. Giménez, pp. 26–28.
12. Longuet, p. 619.
13. Pan, pp. 24–26, 52.
14. E. Dickmann, pp. 83–85.
15. Pan, pp. 39, 43, 45.
16. Cúneo, pp. 448–49.
17. Justo, *Internacionalismo y patria,* pp. 8, 26, 51, 130, 140.
18. Frugoni, II, p. 292.
19. Zea, pp. 286, 303–4.
20. Frugoni, II, pp. 285 *et seq.*
21. Justo, "Discurso en la Cámara de Diputados."
22. Pan, p. 58.
23. E. Dickmann, pp. 101–3.
24. Giménez, pp. 56 *et seq.*; E. Dickmann, p. 428.
25. E. Dickmann, pp. 99–100.
26. Cúneo, p. 189.
27. Longuet, p. 623.
28. Cúneo, pp. 243–47.
29. E. Dickmann, pp. 105, 118–21.
30. Cúneo, pp. 290–91.
31. E. Dickmann, pp. 86, 112–13.
32. *Ibid.,* pp. 153–55, 182, 192.
33. Longuet, pp. 622–23; on the legislative work of the Socialist Party, see Palacios, *Soberanía y socialización, La defensa del valor humano,* and *La justicia social.*
34. Cúneo, pp. 326–29.
35. Frugoni, II, p. 291; Valle Iberlucea.
36. Cúneo, pp. 346–48; during its 1948 congress the party eliminated from its statutes all references to dueling.
37. *Ibid.,* pp. 342, 365–69, 397, 401–6.
38. E. Dickmann, p. 282.
39. *Ibid.,* pp. 227, 290, 294–98; Coca.
40. Alexander, *Labor Parties,* p. 27.
41. *Ibid.,* p. 2.
42. E. Dickmann, pp. 318–24.
43. Szulc, *passim.*
44. *Afirmación,* May 31, 1961; *Diario de la Tarde,* December 12, 1961; and private communications with the author.
45. Giménez, pp. 8, 13.
46. Frugoni, II, pp. 319–20.
47. Pintos, *Batlle,* pp. 111–13, 138.
48. Frugoni, II, p. 321.
49. Durán Cano, *Emilio Frugoni,* pp. 17 *et seq.*; Frugoni, II, p. 335.
50. Alexander, *Labor Parties,* pp. 39–41.

51. Durán Cano, *Documentos y testimonios*; and private communications with the author.

52. Giménez, pp. 42 *et seq.*

53. Ramírez Necochea, pp. 145–46, 205.

54. Jobet, *Los precursores*, p. 56; Jobet, *Santiago Arcos Arlegui*, Chapter I, and p. 133.

55. Ramírez Necochea, pp. 80 *et seq.*, 90 *et seq.*

56. *Ibid.*, pp. 149, 161 *et seq.*, 252–53.

57. Jobet, *El socialismo en Chile*, pp. 3–4.

58. Ramírez Necochea, pp. 207, 214 *et seq.*

59. *Ibid.*, pp. 226, 246.

60. Alexander, *Labor Parties*, p. 7.

61. *Ibid.*, p. 9.

62. Jobet, *Recabarren*, pp. 15, 17, 45, and *passim.*

63. *Ibid.*, p. 70.

64. Lagos Valenzuela, p. 47.

65. Poblete Troncoso, *El movimiento de asociación profesional obrera*, pp. 39–40.

66. Alexander, *Labor Parties*, pp. 15–17; Alexander, *Prophets*, pp. 65–68; Donoso, II, p. 104; Lagos Valenzuela, p. 50; Jobet, *Ensayo crítico*, pp. 186 *et seq.*; Baeza Flores, pp. 72–73, 161.

67. Lagos Valenzuela, pp. 55–56.

68. Jobet, *El socialismo en Chile*, pp. 6, 10; Jobet, *Ensayo crítico*, p. 198.

69. Lagos Valenzuela, p. 54; Baeza Flores, p. 173.

70. Jobet, *El socialismo en Chile*, pp. 13–18.

71. Waiss, pp. 126 *et seq.*

72. Jobet, *El socialismo en Chile*, pp. 18–22.

73. Ampuero Díaz and Silva Ulloa; Máiztegui; Baeza Flores, p. 280.

74. Giménez, pp. 8, 40–41; Costa, pp. 37, 124.

75. Alexander, *Labor Parties*, pp. 29–33; Máiztegui.

76. Szulc, p. 90; Ferrari.

77. Francovich, pp. 85, 103; Fernández Artucio, pp. 196 *et seq.* See also the section in this book on the Movimiento Nacionalista Revolucionario.

78. Fellman Velarde, pp. 89, 90, 95 *et seq.*, 138; Alexander, *The Bolivian National Revolution*, pp. 61 *et seq.*, 223 *et seq.*; the Fourth International was that formed by the Trotskyist parties in 1932.

79. Sánchez, *El Perú*, p. 150.

80. Mariátegui, *Siete ensayos*, pp. 26, 118, 196.

81. Baeza Flores, pp. 27–29.

82. Mariátegui, *Pensadores de América*, pp. 17, 23, 53.

83. Secretariado Sudamericano de la Internacional Comunista, *El movimiento revolucionario latinoamericano*, p. 149.

84. Chang-Rodríguez, *La literatura política*, p. 167.

85. Máiztegui; Szulc, p. 187.

86. Máiztegui; Alexander, *Labor Parties*, pp. 41–42; Blanksten, pp. 24, 68, 70, 79.

87. Carrión.

88. Henríquez Ureña, p. 132.

89. Neale Silva, pp. 385–86.

90. Alexander, *Labor Parties*, pp. 36–38.

91. Máiztegui; Alexander and Porter, p. 103.

92. Valle, pp. 286 *et seq.*, 292.
93. López, pp. 58 *et seq.*; Masferrer, *En torno*; Masferrer, *Páginas escogidas*.
94. James, *Red Design,* pp. 66, 216.
95. Alexander and Porter, p. 175.
96. Pereira Burgos.
97. James, *Red Design,* p. 210.
98. *Revista Internacional,* p. 57.
99. Longuet, p. 615.
100. Baeza Flores, p. 81.
101. Lumen, pp. 149 *et seq.*; on Communist activities during the period in which Communist support was withdrawn from Batista and transferred to Grau, see II Asamblea Nacional del Partido Socialista Popular, *Los socialistas y la realidad cubana, passim.*
102. Alexander and Porter, pp. 33, 167–69; Larson, pp. 353–54.
103. Alba, *Las ideas sociales,* pp. 102 *et seq.*; Díaz Ramírez, p. 63.
104. Clark, pp. 71 *et seq.*
105. López Aparicio, p. 187; Clark, p. 201; Salazar, pp. 109, 306.
106. Alexander, *Prophets,* p. 110.
107. Pérez Leirós, pp. 53–54.
108. Alexander, *Labor Parties,* pp. 43, 46.
109. Máiztegui; Humberto Máiztegui headed the Latin-American Secretariat of the Socialist International from the time of its inception.
110. Alexander and Porter, p. 30; and private communications with the author.

CHAPTER 6

1. The history of Communism in Latin America is far more complex than that of other social movements. Bibliographies and reliable documentary sources are scarce, and I have frequently had to rely on personal experience and information from persons involved in some of the episodes of this history. My principal sources have been Alexander, *Communism,* and the third edition of Alba, *Esquema histórico del comunismo;* the present chapter is a synthesis of the latter work, and has been further reorganized and condensed for the purposes of this English-language edition. Where concrete sources are not cited in this chapter, the exact documentation may be found by consulting the analytic indexes of these two references.
2. A. Dickmann, pp. 72–73.
3. Jobet, *Recabarren,* p. 54 *et seq.*
4. García Treviño, *La ingerencia rusa,* pp. 25–44.
5. Mariátegui, *Siete ensayos,* p. 27 *et seq.*
6. Alba, *Las ideas sociales,* p. 234 *et seq.*
7. For more on Lombardo, see the sources mentioned in Alba, *Las ideas sociales,* pp. 451 and 464.
8. García Treviño, *La ingerencia rusa,* pp. 25–44; Roy, Part I.
9. Escobedo and Salazar, pp. 115–16.
10. Treviño, pp. 19–28.
11. Communist International, *El movimiento revolucionario en los países coloniales.*
12. Alba, *Historia del frente popular,* p. 136.
13. Claraval, *passim.*

14. Documents mentioned in García Treviño, *La ingerencia rusa,* p. 78.

15. On Stirner, see García Treviño, *La ingerencia rusa,* p. 66 *et seq.*

16. Alexander, *Communism,* p. 162 *et seq.*; Cuadro Caldas, p. 54.

17. Cuadro Caldas, p. 146 *et seq.*

18. Communist International, *El movimiento revolutionario latinoamericano.*

19. García Treviño, *La ingerencia rusa,* pp. 71–72.

20. On these congresses and the League Against Imperialism, see Cuadro Caldas, p. 99; Nehru, p. 151 *et seq.*; Alba, *Esquema histórico del comunismo,* pp. 78 *et seq.,* 88 *et seq.,* 92 *et seq.*

21. Haya de la Torre, *Sobre la historia del comunismo.*

22. Nehru, p. 154.

23. Communist International, *El movimiento revolucionario latinoamericano.*

24. Cuadro Caldas, pp. 52–85.

25. Jobet, *Ensayo crítico,* p. 186 *et seq.*; Lagos Valenzuela, p. 55 *et seq.*

26. Krehm, pp. 107–23; Alexander, *Communism,* p. 367 *et seq.*

27. Volman, "El general Batista y la revolucion 'comunista.'"

28. A. Bastos; Amado; Ravines (p. 54 *et seq.*); Henriques (Chapters 16 and 17); and Peralva.

29. For sources on this subject, see Alba, *Historia del frente popular,* especially Chapter 14.

30. Ravines, Chapter 6.

31. Volman *op. cit.,* Ravines, p. 285.

32. Communist International, *La Correspondencia Internacional* (March and August 1940).

33. *La Voz de México* (June 22, 1941).

34. Alexander, *Communism,* p. 194 *et seq.*

35. *Izquierda* (November 1958).

36. Alexander, *The Perón Era,* pp. 71–74 and 100 *et seq.* Page's article contains ample data on the policy of "critical support."

37. Ricaurte.

38. Volman.

39. *Acción Democrática,* "Mensaje a Venezuela"; Boersner.

40. *Mundo del trabajo libre,* October-November 1958, p. 25; *Est et Oest,* November 16–30, 1964, pp. 19–20.

41. Alba, "El caso de Costa Rica."

42. Mentioned in Alba, *Esquema histórico del comunismo,* p. 149 *et seq.*

43. On the case of Guatemala, see Alba, "Latin America, Tragedy and Prospect"; James, *Red Design*; and the works of Blanc, Schneider, Toriello, and Osegueda.

44. The bibliography is so abundant in the case of Cuba that, in addition to works mentioned, titles have been selected showing the best representations of the different points of view. It is noteworthy that few solid works in Spanish exist on the subject.

Of the works listed in the Bibliography, the most important are those by the following writers: Draper, Dubois, Goldenberg, Guilbert, James, Julien, Matthews, Mills, Phillips, San Martin, Smith, and Weyl.

In addition, naturally, are Fidel Castro's speeches and Cuban legislation beginning in 1959. As curiosities without documentary value, see the articles by Jean-Paul Sartre in *France-Soir* published later in book form under the title *Sarte on Cuba,* New York, Ballantine Books, 1961.

45. ORIT, *Datos y cifras,* July-August 1955.

46. *Ibid.,* November-December 1957.
47. Alba, "The Struggle Inside Cuba."
48. Mezerik, pp. 31–42. See also the press from this period.

CHAPTER 7

1. Crevena; Johnson, *Political Change*; Alba, "The Latin American Style."
2. Villanueva del Campo.
3. Castro Delgado.
4. Monteforte Toledo, pp. 31–34, 123–25; For immediate historical background, see Alexander and Porter; Szulc. The latter offers an excellent résumé of the economic thinking of populism.
5. Villanueva del Campo. The text of the Lima Declaration is in *Latinoamérica más allá de sus fronteras*, pp. 109 *et seq.*
6. In addition to the works of Haya de la Torre, see, on APRA: Cossío del Pomar: *Haya de la Torre*, and *Víctor Raúl*; Seoane: *Las seis dimensiones*; Orego; Kantor, *Ideología y programa del movimiento aprista*; and Chang-Rodríguez, *La literatura política*, which contains a complete bibliography of Haya's works.
7. Rodríguez Vildósola.
8. Alexander, *Labor Parties*, p. 35.
9. Pareja Diezcanseco.
10. Seoane, *Obras apristas.*
11. Villanueva del Campo.
12. Martínez de la Torre, p. 26. See also, Haya de la Torre: *Sobre la historia del comunismo, passim.*
13. Townsend Ezcurra.
14. *Mensaje a Venezuela.* On Acción Democrática there is no work more informative than that by Rómulo Betancourt: *Pensamiento y Acción*; *Posición y doctrina*; *Venezuela, política y petróleo; Trayectoria democrática*; and the volume *Rómulo Betancourt.*
15. Betancourt: *Venezuela*, pp. 314 *et seq.*
16. Monteforte Toledo, pp. 78–81.
17. Betancourt: *Trayectoria democrática,* pp. 245 *et seq.*
18. Betancourt: *Venezuela*, pp. 774 *et seq.*
19. Paz Estenssoro, *La revolución boliviana.*
20. Fellman Velarde, pp. 76, 95, 111, 118, 126, 137, 146, 173, 237, 263 *et seq.*
21. Paz Estenssoro, *La revolución boliviana.*
22. MNR: *Programa de Gobierno 1960–1964*; Monteforte Toledo, pp. 96–100.
23. Kantor, "También hay democracia en el Caribe."
24. Kantor, *Ibid.* On the subject of Liberación Nacional, see: Navarro Bolandi: *José Figueres,* and *La generación del 48.*
25. Alexander: *Prophets,* pp. 149–58.
26. Figueres, pp. 62 and 135.
27. Dion, *passim.* See also the discussion, in Chapter 6 of this book, on Guatemala.
28. Cibils, pp. 44–49.
29. Maspero.
30. Alexander, *Reseña del movimiento obrero,* p. 13.

31. Ramírez Necochea, pp. 142, 171, 253, 272 *et seq.*
32. Jarlot.
33. Blaya Allende, pp. 12 and 14.
34. Frei.
35. Alexander, *Reseña del movimiento obrero,* pp. 12, 13.
36. Maldonado Jarrín, p. 61.
37. Alexander, *Reseña del movimiento obrero,* p. 13.
38. Interview with the author, 1960.
39. López Aparicio, p. 143.
40. Islas García, *passim.*
41. Ledit, p. 131; Alba, *Las ideas sociales,* pp. 111 *et seq.*
42. *SOCI.* Santiago, December 15, 1964, p. 7.
43. Pan American Union, *Desarrollo del movimiento cooperativo*; ORIT, *"Las cooperativas."*

CHAPTER 8

1. The literature on national union movements is scanty. Moreover, there is no existing compilation of memoirs of the founders of these movements. Errors no doubt occur in the succeeding chapters of this part of the book; none, I trust, will seriously distort the basic impressions. I have tried—as I have in the preceding portions of this book—to limit the use of proper names, and I have included dates of birth and death, when they are known, of the persons mentioned. That these are furnished in only a few cases indicates the scarcity of documentary material on this subject.
2. Collinet, "Comunismo y asalariados."
3. *Ibid.*
4. Johnson, *Political Change,* pp. 155, 187.
5. Galarza, *Memorandum.*
6. Maspero.
7. Galarza, *Journey Behind the News.*
8. L'Itinerant.
9. Alexander, *Reseña del movimiento obrero,* p. 5.
10. Concerning Latin American social and labor legislation, see OIT: *Segunda Conferencia del Trabajo de los Estados de América miembros de la Organización Internacional de Trabajo,* and reports on: *Minimum Wages in Latin America; Labor Courts in Latin America; Indigenous Population;* and *Living Conditions of the Worker.* See also Secretaría General del Comité Permanente Interamericano de Seguridad Social, *Manual de instituciones de seguridad social en América Latina;* Poblete Troncoso: *Evolución del derecho social;* Despontin; Mendieta y Núñez; Tieffenberg.
11. Conferencia Interamericana de Seguridad Social.
12. "La experiencia de otros países," from *Visión,* Panama, December 25, 1964, p. 31.
13. Alexander: *Reseña del movimiento obrero,* pp. 18–19.

CHAPTER 9

1. Oddone, *Historia del socialismo argentino,* pp. 67, 80, 189.
2. Oddone, *Gremialismo proletario,* pp. 12–14.

3. Giménez, pp. 29–30.

4. Alexander, *Reseña del movimiento obrero,* p. 5.

5. Pan, pp. 19–20.

6. Palacios, *La justicia social,* pp. 114–15.

7. Pan, p. 52.

8. E. Dickmann, p. 70.

9. E. Dickmann, p. 83.

10. Oddone, *Gremialismo proletario,* p. 68.

11. Simon, p. 57.

12. E. Dickmann, pp. 91, 132.

13. Despontin, p. 116; Palacios, *La defensa del valor humano,* p. 5; Levene, p. 189; Ingenieros, pp. 268–71.

14. E. Dickmann, pp. 141–77.

15. Justo, *Teoria y práctica de la historia,* p. 393.

16. Oddone, *Historia del socialismo argentino,* II, 407, 192.

17. Simon, p. 61.

18. Oddone, *Gremialismo Proletario,* pp. 250–52.

19. Palacios, *El nuevo derecho,* pp. 245 *et seq.*

20. Oddone, *Gremialismo proletario,* pp. 126–30.

21. Oddone, *Historia del socialismo argentino,* II, 143.

22. Oddone, *Gremialismo proletario,* p. 169.

23. Oddone, *Historia del socialismo argentino,* p. 151.

24. Ghitor, p. 45.

25. Burnett and Poblete Troncoso, pp. 48–49.

26. On peasant and agricultural unionism, see Palacios: *El nuevo derecho,* Chapters VI, VIII, and IX; Grela.

27. Oddone, *Gremialismo proletario,* pp. 369–73.

28. *Ibid.,* pp. 383–93.

29. On Peronism, see Alexander: *The Peron Era,* especially pp. 84 *et seq.,* 187 *et seq.*; Arciniegas, *Entre la libertad y el miedo,* Chapters II–V; Magnet, Chapters III, V; Benedetti, Chapter IV; Santander; Lux-Würm.

30. Alexander, *Prophets,* pp. 250–51.

31. Magnet, pp. 87 *et seq.*

32. Alexander, *Prophets,* pp. 250–56.

33. Remorino, pp. 19 *et seq.*

34. Tieffenberg, p. 57.

35. Benedetti, Chapter IV.

36. *Ibid.,* p. 143.

37. Alexander and Porter, pp. 80–84.

38. Frondizi, p. 206.

39. ORIT, *Informe del V Congreso,* p. 39; Poblete Troncoso and Burnett, p. 57.

CHAPTER 10

1. Pintos, *Historia del Uruguay,* pp. 85, 104, 124, 133–35.

2. Simon, p. 36.

3. Alexander, *Prophets,* pp. 14–17.

4. Pintos, *Historia del Uruguay,* pp. 146 *et seq.*
5. Alexander, *Reseña del movimiento obrero,* pp. 20–21.
6. ORIT, *Noticiario Obrero Interamericano.*
7. Simon, p. 68.
8. Alexander, *Reseña del movimiento obrero,* p. 21.
9. Cibils, p. 49. See also the material on *Febrerismo* in Chapter VII of this book.
10. MacDonald, p. 519.
11. Alexander and Porter, *The Struggle for Democracy,* p. 164.

CHAPTER 11

1. Ramirez Necochea, pp. 132–38.
2. Lagos Valenzuela, pp. 7, 12.
3. Alexander, *Reseña del movimiento obrero,* p. 22.
4. Ramirez Necochea, pp. 255–95, 320; Lagos Valenzuela, pp. 24–26.
5. Jobet, *Recabarren,* pp. 13, 105–6.
6. Silva Cristi, p. 264.
7. Jerez Horta, p. 94.
8. Bowen, p. 75; Lagos Valenzuela, pp. 46–47; Alexander, *Labor Parties,* p. 11.
9. Alexander, *Reseña del movimiento obrero,* p. 23; Jobet, *Recabarren,* pp. 141–42; Simon, p. 66.
10. For additional material on the socialist movement in Chile, see Chapter 5 of this book.
11. Lagos Valenzuela, p. 65; Alexander, *Reseña del movimiento obrero,* p. 23; Jobet, *Recabarren,* pp. 150–64.
12. Lagos Valenzuela, pp. 60, 63.
13. Alexander, *Reseña del movimiento obrero,* p. 24; Galarza, *Memorandum,* p. 45.
14. L'Itinerant; ORIT, *Informe del V Congreso,* p. 41.

CHAPTER 12

1. S. Vianna, *O sindicato no Brasil,* pp. 16–20, 24.
2. Costa, p. 137.
3. Simon, pp. 66–67.
4. Alexander, Labor Parties, pp. 30–31.
5. Alexander, *Prophets,* p. 224.
6. Johnson, *Political Change,* pp. 167–68.
7. O. Vianna, *As novas directrizes,* p. 29.
8. Loewenstein, pp. 338 *et seq.*
9. S. Vianna, *O sindicato no Brasil,* pp. 25 et seq., 36, 43; Alexander, *Prophets,* pp. 227–29, 233–34.
10. Alexander, *Reseña del movimiento obrero,* p. 22.
11. S. Vianna, *O sindicato no Brasil,* p. 115 *et seq.,* 211.
12. Benton, pp. 65, 90.

CHAPTER 13

1. Paz Estenssoro, p. 39.
2. Alexander, *Reseña del movimiento obrero,* p. 24.
3. ILO, *Los problemas del trabajo en Bolivia.*
4. Alexander, *The Bolivian National Revolution,* pp. 122 *et seq.,* 130 *et seq.,* 140. For additional material on this period, see the discussion in this book on the MNR, in Chapter 7.
5. La Nación, *La Paz,* December 21, 1961.
6. Bolognesi, p. 68.
7. Chang-Rodríguez, *La literatura política,* pp. 135–36.
8. Cossío del Pomar, *Víctor Raúl,* pp. 53, 92, *et. seq.,* 138 *et seq.* See also the discussion in this book dealing with APRA, in Chapter 7.
9. Simon, p. 68.
10. Beals, *Fuego sobre los Andes,* pp. 101, 369.
11. Martínez de la Torre, pp. 47, 51.
12. Alexander, *Prophets,* pp. 93–99.
13. Alexander, *Reseña del movimiento obrero,* p. 26.
14. Bolognesi, pp. 55–68.
15. Alexander and Porter, pp. 94–95.
16. L'Itinerant; Pareja Diezcanseco.
17. Alexander, *Reseña del movimiento obrero,* p. 26.
18. Blanksten, pp. 106–7.
19. Maldonado Jarrín, *passim.*
20. ORIT, *Informe del V Congreso,* p. 46.
21. Carrión.
22. *Noticiero Obrero Interamericano,* Mexico, January 1962.

CHAPTER 14

1. Uribe.
2. *Ibid.*
3. Alexander, *Labor Parties,* p. 38.
4. Szulc, pp. 222–35.
5. ORIT, *Informe del V Congreso,* p. 43.
6. *Message of the Workmen's and Artisans' Confederation, passim.*
7. Pérez Salinas.
8. Paiva, pp. 119 *et seq.*
9. Betancourt, *Venezuela,* pp. 86 *et seq.,* 277 *et seq.,* 300 *et seq.*
10. Alexander, *Prophets,* pp. 127–28. See also material on Acción Democrática in Chapter 7 of this book.
11. Pareja Diezcanseco.
12. Betancourt, *Venezuela,* pp. 523 *et seq.*
13. ORIT, *Documentos.*
14. Betancourt, *Venezuela,* pp. 523–32.

15. ORIT, *Documentos.*
16. CTV: *III Congreso de Trabajadores de Venezuela, passim.*
17. *Noticiario Obrero Interamericano.*

CHAPTER 15

1. *Noticiario Obrero Interamericano.*
2. Pereira Burgos.
3. ORIT, *Informe del V Congreso,* p. 50.
4. Krehm, pp. 200–5. See also the portion of this book dealing with Liberación Nacional in Chapter 7.
5. Rodríguez Vega, pp. 49–50, 116.
6. ORIT, *Informe del V Congreso,* p. 43.
7. Pérez Leirós, p. 106.
8. Alexander and Porter, p. 175.
9. Alexander, *Reseña del movimiento obrero,* p. 30.
10. Valle, p. 291.
11. Briones Torres.
12. Sáenz, p. 227.
13. Krehm, p. 110.
14. *Noticiario Obrero Interamericano.*
15. James, *Red Design,* p. 222.
16. Valle, pp. 291–92.
17. ORIT, *Informe del V Congreso,* p. 49.
18. Ruiz Franco, pp. 48, 216 *et seq.,* 220 *et seq.*
19. Díaz Rozzotto, pp. 135 *et seq.* See also the material in this book on Guatemala in Chapter 6.
20. *Acción Democrática,* Caracas, November 11, 1961.

CHAPTER 16

1. Bellegarde, p. 158.
2. Alexander, *Reseña del movimiento obrero,* p. 29.
3. *Noticiario Obrero Interamericano,* Mexico, November 1961.
4. Alexander, *Reseña del movimiento obrero,* p. 29.
5. Bosch, *Trujillo,* pp. 164–65.
6. Baeza Flores, pp. 252–58.
7. Alexander and Porter, pp. 146, 149.
8. UPI cable, November 16, 1961.
9. *Noticiario Obrero Interamericano,* Mexico, November 1961.
10. *Washington Post,* Washington, December 22, 1961; *Noticiario Obrero Interamericano,* Mexico, March 1962.
11. Rivero Muñiz.
12. Justo, *Teoría y práctica de la historia,* p. 393.
13. Schwartz, p. 165.

14. Alexander, *Reseña del movimiento obrero,* p. 28.
15. Foreign Policy Association, pp. 221, 228 *et seq.*
16. Smith, pp. 101, 116.
17. Foreign Policy Association, pp. 205–6, 218.
18. Correoso del Risco, pp. 118 *et seq.*, 132 *et seq.*
19. Araquistain, pp. 277 *et seq.*
20. Baeza Flores, p. 87.
21. Foreign Policy Association, pp. 203 *et seq.*, 220 *et seq.*
22. Baeza Flores, p. 115.
23. Lumen, pp. 148 *et seq.*
24. Baeza Flores, pp. 211, 219.
25. Alexander, "Decline of Communist Parties." See also the material on Cuba in this book, in Chapter 6.
26. Phillips, *Cuba,* pp. 229, 239, 245, 262.
27. Alexander and Porter, p. 128.
28. Baeza Flores, p. 301.
29. Phillips, pp. 308–9, 352.
30. Baeza Flores, p. 351.
31. Barrero Díaz.
32. Rodríguez Quesada, pp. 14–20.
33. Barrero Díaz; Alexander and Porter, pp. 137 *et seq.*
34. *Siempre,* Mexico, January 24, 1962, p. 14.
35. *Noticiario Obrero Interamericano,* Mexico, February 1962. See also the material on Fidel Castro's regime in Chapter 6 of this book.

CHAPTER 17

1. For material pertinent to the entire chapter, see Alba, *Las ideas sociales,* Chapters IV and XIII.
2. Chávez Orozco, p. 4. This work is the source of many of the subsequent quotations here from the early labor press of Mexico.
3. González Casanova, pp. 31 *et seq.* See also the portion on Mexico in Chapter 5 of this book.
4. Clark, p. 5.
5. López Aparicio, p. 110.
6. Díaz Ramírez, pp. 35–37. See also the discussion on Mexico in Chapter 4 of this book.
7. Treviño, p. 91.
8. Salazar and Escobedo; Salazar, *passim.*
9. Salazar, pp. 138, 165, 316, 344.
10. López Aparicio, pp. 230, 234.
11. *Ibid.,* pp. 256 *et seq.*; Confederación de Trabajadores Mexicanos, pp. 7–8; Velázquez.
12. *Memoria del I Congreso Mexicano de Derecho Industrial,* p. 7.
13. Treviño, p. 114.
14. García Treviño, "Los sindicatos."

15. Gutiérrez. See also Trotsky's comments on his Mexican experiences, in Alba, *Le mouvement ouvrier en Amérique Latine,* p. 128.

16. Rodea, pp. 273–74.

17. Bremauntz, pp. 52, 98, 100, 140, 198; *Excélsior,* Mexico, December 30, 1961.

CHAPTER 18

1. Alexander, *Labor Parties,* pp. 42–43; Pérez Leirós, p. 48.

2. For more details on the AFL's position regarding the Latin American union movement, and for discussions in COPA's congresses, see Lorwin, Chapter XII; Snow, *passim.*

3. Taft, *passim.*

4. ORIT, *Esta es la ORIT*; Alexander, *Reseña del movimiento obrero,* p. 15.

5. Gompers, p. 501.

6. Confederación Sindical Latino America, *passim.*

7. Confederación de Trabajadores de América Latina, *Resoluciones, 1938–1948*; Confederación de Trabajadores de América Latina, *Congreso de Cali*; Confederación de Trabajadores de América Latina, *Tercer Congreso General de la CTAL,* Mexico, 1948; Lombardo Toledano, *La CTAL*; Confederación de Trabajadores de América Latina, *Congreso Obrero.* The last of these references contains the greetings of the delegates to the CTAL first congress, and the constituting act, but none of the resolutions and no references to the debates.

8. García Treviño, *La ingerencia rusa,* Chapter IV.

9. Alexander, *Reseña del movimiento obrero,* pp. 16–17.

10. World Federation of Trade Unions, *Boletín,* January and June, 1951.

11. ORIT, *Esta es la ORIT*; *Confederación Interamericana de Trabajadores.*

12. Vélez.

13. *Latinoamérica más allá de sus fronteras,* pp. 67–69.

14. ORIT, *Esta es la ORIT.*

15. *Mundo del Trabajo Libre,* Mexico, September 1961.

CHAPTER 19

1. This description follows the lines of Alba, *Alliance Without Allies,* pp. 7 *et seq.*

2. Prebisch, pp. 5–6.

3. Alba, *Esquema histórico del movimiento obrero,* pp. 137 *et seq.*

4. Dubreuil; Collinet, *Essai*; Bell.

5. On all these issues see also Alba, *El líder.*

6. Monge, *Interpretándonos,* pp. 14–20.

Bibliography

Bibliography

Titles are given in the language of the edition consulted by the author. Where English-language editions exist, they are given in parentheses.

Agetro, Leafar. Las luchas proletarias en Veracruz, historia y autocrítica. Veracruz, 1942.

Alba, Víctor. Alliance Without Allies. New York: Praeger, 1965.

———. América Latina, un continente ante su porvenir. Mexico: Instituto de Investigaciones Internacionales del Trabajo, 1958.

———. "El Caso de Costa Rica," Resaca, February 1955. Mexico.

———. Esquema histórico del comunismo en Iberoamérica. Mexico: Ediciones Occidentales, 1960. Third edition.

———. Esquema histórico del movimiento obrero en América Latina Mexico: B. Costa-Amic, editor. n.d.

———. "Ha fallecido Radowitzky," Excélsior, February 4, 1956. Mexico.

———. Historia del frente popular. Mexico: Libro Mex, 1959.

———. Las ideas sociales contemporáneas en México. Mexico: Fondo de Cultura Económica, 1960.

———. El industrialismo. Mexico: Secretaría de Educación Pública, 1950.

———. "Latin America, Tragedy and Prospect," Dissent, Fall 1954. New York.

———. "The Latin American Style and the New Social Forces," in Latin American Issues. New York: The Twentieth Century Fund, 1961.

———. El líder, ensayo sobre el dirigente sindical. Mexico: Instituto de Investigaciones Sociales, 1957.

———. El militarismo. Mexico: Instituto de Investigaciones Sociales, 1959.

———. Le Mouvement ouvrier en Amérique Latine. Paris: Editions Ouvrières, 1953.

———. "The Struggle Inside Cuba," The New Leader, November 23, 1959. New York.

———. The Bolivian National Revolution. New Brunswick: Rutgers University Press, 1958.

Alexander, Robert J. "The Decline of Communist Parties in Latin America," *Modern Review,* March-April 1948. New York.

———. Communism in Latin America. New Brunswick: Rutgers University Press, 1957.

———. Labor Parties in Latin America. New York: The League for Industrial Democracy, 1942. *Also,* Labour Parties in Latin America. London: Fabian Publications, Ltd., 1947.

———. Labor Relations in Argentina, Brazil, and Chile. New York: McGraw-Hill, 1962.

———. The Peron Era. New York: Columbia University Press, 1951.

———. Prophets of the Revolution. New York: Macmillan, 1962.

———. Reseña del movimiento obrero en la América Latina. Washington, D.C.: Pan American Union, 1948.

———, and Charles O. Porter. The Struggle for Democracy in Latin America. New York: Macmillan, 1961.

Altamira, Rafael. Diccionario castellano de palabras jurídicas y técnicas tomadas de la legislación indiana. Mexico: Instituto Panamericano de Geografía e Historia. Mexico, 1951.

Amado, Jorge. Vida de Luiz Carlos Prestes. Sao Paulo: Martins, 1946.

Amezcua, Genaro. ¿Quién es Flores Magón y cuál es su obra? Mexico: Avance, 1943.

Ampuero Díaz, Raúl, and Ramón Silva Ulloa. Una política nacionalista para el cobre. Santiago: Prensa Latinoamericana, 1955.

Araquistain, Luis. La agonía antillana. Madrid: Espasa Calpe, 1928.

Arciniegas, Germán. Los comuneros. Santiago: Zig Zag, 1940.

———. Entre la libertad y el miedo. Mexico: Cuadernos Americanos, 1952.

———. Este pueblo de América. Mexico: Fondo de Cultura Económica, 1945.

Arcos, Juan. El sindicalismo en América Latina. Santiago: Feres, 1964.

Arrieta, Agustín de. "Enrique del Valle Iberlucea," *Afirmación,* August 30, 1961. Buenos Aires.

Baeza Flores, Alberto. Las cadenas vienen de lejos. Mexico: Letras, 1960.

Bagú, Sergio. Economía de la sociedad colonial. Buenos Aires: El Ateneo, 1949.

———. Estructura social de la colonia. Buenos Aires: El Ateneo, 1952.

Bargalló, Modesto. La minería y la metalurgia en la América española durante la época colonial. Mexico: Fondo de Cultura Económica, 1955.

Barrero Díaz, Mario. "Metamorfosis del obrerismo en Cuba," *Noticiario Obrero Interamericano,* August 1961. Mexico.

Bastos, A. Prestes e a revolução social. Rio de Janeiro: Calvino, 1946.

Bastos, Tocary Assis. O positivismo e a realidade brasileira. Belo Horizonte: Editorial Revista Brasileira de Estudios Políticos, 1965.

Baudin, Luis. El imperio socialista de los Incas. Santiago: Zig Zag, 1940. (Socialist Empire: The Incas of Peru. Princeton, Van Nostrand, 1961.)

Beals, Carleton. América ante América. Santiago: Zig Zag, 1940. (America South. Philadelphia: Lippincott, 1937.)

———. Fuego sobre los Andes. Santiago: Zig Zag, 1942. (Fire on the Andes. Philadelphia: Lippincott, 1934.)

Bell, Daniel. "Notes on Work," *Encounter,* June 1954. London.

Bellegarde, Dantès. Haiti et ses problèmes. Montreal: Valiquette, n.d.

Benedetti, Antonio. Perón y Eva, Trayectoria y fin de un régimen. Mexico: Editores Panamericanos Asociados, 1956.

Benton, William. The Voice of Latin America. New York: Harper, 1961.

Bermann, Gregorio. Juventud de América. Mexico: Cuadernos Americanos, 1946.

Betancourt, Rómulo. Pensamiento y Acción. Mexico, 1951.

————. Posición y doctrina. Caracas: Cordillera, 1958.

————. Trayectoria democrática de una revolución. Caracas: Imprenta Nacional, 1948.

————. Venezuela, política y petróleo. Mexico: Fondo de Cultura Económica, 1956.

Blanc, V. "Triunfo comunista en Guatemala," *Resaca,* November 1954. Mexico.

Blanksten, George I. Ecuador, Constitutions and Caudillos. Berkeley: The University of California Press, 1951.

Blaya Allende, Joaquín. Monseñor José M. Caro habla de los palpitantes problemas sociales que afligen al mundo de hoy. Santiago, 1940.

Boersner, Demetrio. Análisis del Partido Comunista en Latinoamerica y Venezuela. Caracas: Universidad Popular Alberto Carnevali, 1961.

Bolognesi E., Alberto. Sindicalismo. Lima: Tipografía Peruana, 1945.

Bosch, Juan. Trujillo, causas de una tiranía sin ejemplo. Caracas, 1961.

————. The Unfinished Experiment, Democracy in the Dominican Republic. New York: Praeger, 1965.

Bowen, J. Ensayo sobre el movimiento sindical y el sindicalismo agrícola. Santiago: La Fama, 1934.

Boxer, C. R. Os holandeses no Brasil. Sao Paulo: Cia. Editora Nacional, 1961. (The Dutch in Brazil, 1624–1654. New York: Oxford University Press, 1957.)

Braunthal, Julius, ed. Yearbook of the International Socialist Labour Movement, 1865–1957. London: Lincolns-Praeger International, 1956.

Bremauntz, Alberto. La participación en las utilidades y el salario en México. Mexico, 1935.

Briones Torres, Ignacio. "Actualidad de Augusto César Sandino," *Combate,* October-November 1961, San Jose de Costa Rica.

Brooks, Tom. "Neutralism Splits Latin American Labor," *The New Leader,* March 28, 1960. New York.

Burnett, Ben G., and Moisés Poblete Troncoso. The Rise of the Latin American Labor Movement. New York: Bookman Associates, 1960.

Capitán, L., and H. Lorin. El trabajo en América. Buenos Aires: Argos, 1948.

Caravaca, Francisco. Esclavos. Barcelona: Joaquín Gil, 1933.

Carneiro, Edison. Guerra de los Palmares. Mexico: Fondo de Cultura Económica, 1946.

Carrancá y Trujillo, Raúl. Panorama crítico de nuestra América. Mexico: Imprenta Universitaria, 1950.

Carrión, Alejandro. "La revolución constitucionalista ecuatoriana," *Servicio de Prensa,* November 1961. Paris.

Castro, Américo. La realidad historica de España. Mexico: Porrua, 1954. (The Structure of Spanish History. Princeton: Princeton University Press, 1954.)

Castro Delgado, Enrique. "Los comunistas y la pequeña burguesía," *Examen,* September-October 1961. Mexico.

Chang-Rodríguez, Eugenio. La literatura política de González Prada, Mariátegui y Haya de la Torre. Mexico: Andrea, 1957.

———, and Harry Kantor. La América Latina de hoy. New York: Ronald Press, 1961.

Chávez Orozco, Luis. Prehistoria del socialismo en México. Mexico: Secretaría de Educación Pública, 1936.

Cibils, Manuel J. Anarquía y revolución en el Paraguay. Buenos Aires: Americalee, 1957.

Claraval, Bernardo. Cuando fui communista. Mexico, 1944.

Clark, Marjorie Ruth. Organized Labor in Mexico. Chapel Hill: University of North Carolina Press, 1934.

Coca, Joaquín. El contubernio, Memorias de un diputado obrero. Buenos Aires: Claridad, n.d.

Collier, John. The Indians of the Americas. New York: Norton, 1947.

Collinet, Michel. "Comunismo y asalariados en Francia," *Cuadernos,* March-April 1954. Paris.

———. Esprit du syndicalisme. Paris: Editions Ouvrières, 1951.

———. Essai sur la condition ouvrière. Paris: Editions Ouvrières, 1951.

Comité Permanente Interamericano de Seguridad Social. Manual de Instituciones de Seguridad Social en América Latina. Mexico, 1956.

Commission on Cuban Affairs. Problemas de la nueva Cuba. New York, 1935.

Communist International. El movimiento revolucionario en los países coloniales y semicoloniales. Brussels: Adelante, n.d.

———, South American Secretariat. El movimiento revolucionario latinoamericano. Buenos Aires: Correspondencia Sudamericana, n.d.

Confederación Interamericana de Trabajadores. Programa de labor. Santiago, 1949.

Confederación Sindical Latino Americana. Bajo la bandera de la CSLA, Resoluciones y documentos del congreso constituyente de la CSLA. Montevideo. La Linotipia, 1929.

Confederación de Trabajadores de América Latina. Congreso de Cali, Diciembre 1944. Mexico, n.d.

———. Congreso Obrero Latinoamericano, México, Septiembre 5–8, 1938. Mexico, n.d.

———. Resoluciones de sus asambleas, 1938–1948. Mexico, 1948.

———. Tercer Congreso General de la CTAL. Mexico, 1948.

Confederación de Trabajadores Mexicanos. Informe al XI Congreso Nacional Ordinario. Mexico: Editorial Cuauhtémoc, 1954.

Confederación de Trabajadores de Venezuela. III Congreso de Trabajadores de Venezuela. Caracas: Imprenta Nacional, 1960.

Conferencia Interamericana de Seguridad Social. Legislación comparada de los seguros sociales en América Latina. Mexico, 1956.

Correoso del Risco, Felipe. La décima reunión de la Conferencia Internacional del Trabajo. Havana: Maza, Caso y Cia., 1927.

Cossío del Pomar, Felipe. Haya de la Torre, el indoamericano. Mexico: Editorial América, 1939.

————. Víctor Raúl. Mexico: Cultura, 1961.

Costa, Cruz. Esbozo de una historia de las ideas en el Brasil. Mexico: Fondo de Cultura Económica, 1957.

Crevenna, Theodore B., ed. Datos para el estudio de la clase media en América Latina. Washington, D.C.: Pan American Union, 1950–51. Six vols., mimeographed.

Cuadro Caldas, Julio. Las trágicas payasadas de los comunistas criollos. Puebla: S. Loyo, 1934.

Cué Cánovas, Agustín. Historia social y económica de México, 1810–1854. Mexico: Editorial América, 1947.

Cúneo, Dardo. Juan B. Justo y las luchas sociales en la Argentina. Buenos Aires: Alpe, 1956. Second edition.

Cunha, Euclydes da. Os Sertoes. Rio de Janeiro: Paulo de Azevedo, 1940. (Rebellion in the Backlands. Chicago: University of Chicago Press, 1957.)

Delegación General del Movimiento Libertario Cubano en el Exilio. Declaración. Miami, December 9, 1961. Mimeographed document.

Despontin, Luis A. Derecho del Trabajo. Cordoba: Universidad Nacional de Córdoba, 1957.

Díaz Ramírez, Manuel. Apuntes históricos del movimiento obrero y campesino de México, 1844–1880. Mexico: Fondo de Cultura Popular, 1954.

Díaz Rozzotto, Jaime. El carácter de la revolución guatemalteca. Mexico: Horizonte, 1958.

Dickmann, Adolfo. Los congresos socialistas. Buenos Aires: Vanguardia, 1936.

Dickmann, Enrique. Recuerdos de un militante socialista. Buenos Aires: Vanguardia, 1949.

Dion, Marie Berthe. Las ideas sociales y políticas de Arévalo. Mexico: América Nueva, 1958.

Donoso, Ricardo. Alessandri, agitador y demoledor. Mexico: Fondo de Cultura Económica, 1952. Two vols.

Dozer, Donald M. Are We Good Neighbors? Gainesville: University of Florida Press, 1959.

Draper, Theodore. Castroism, Theory and Practice. New York: Praeger, 1965.

————. "Cuba y la política norteamericana," *Cuadernos,* August 1961. Paris.

————. "Las teorías del castrismo," *Cuadernos,* June 1961. Paris. (Material from the two articles in *Cuadernos* appears in book form under the English title Castro's Revolution, Myths and Realities. New York: Praeger, 1962.)

Dubois, Jules. Fidel Castro. New York: Bobbs-Merrill, 1959.

Dubreuil, Hyacinthe. Le travail et la civilisation. Paris: Plon, 1951.

Dufey, Enrique T. La defensa social, Medios preventivos y reprisivos. Buenos Aires, 1913.

Durán Cano, Ricardo. Documentos y testimonios. Montevideo, 1961.

―――. Pensamiento y acción de Emilio Frugoni. Montevideo, 1950.

Echeverría, Esteban. Dogma socialista de la Revolución de Mayo. Barcelona: Maucci, 1905.

Economic Commission on Latin America. Estudio sobre la mano de obra en América Latina. Santiago, 1957.

Elizondo, Juan Manuel, and Rafael López Malo. La derrota de la clase obrera mexicana. Mexico, 1954.

Encina, Dionisio. Unidad nacional para la defensa de la patria y la derrota del hitlerismo. Mexico, 1942.

Escobedo, José G. La propriedad inmueble de los trabajadores y otros tópicos históricos de crítica. Mexico, 1954.

―――, and Rosendo Salazar. Las pugnas de la gleba. Mexico: Avante, 1923.

Faria, Otavio. "Sindicalismo novo," Sintese, April-June 1964. Rio de Janeiro.

Fellmann Velarde, José. Víctor Paz Estenssoro, el hombre y la Revolución. La Paz, 1955.

Fernández Artucio, Hugo. La organización secreta nazi en Sudamérica. Mexico: Minerva, 1942.

Ferrari, Fernando. Minha companha. Rio de Janeiro: Globo, 1961.

Ferreira Reis, Arthur Cezar. A Amazonia e a cobiça internacional. Sao Paulo: Editora Nacional, 1960.

Figueres, José. Cartas a un ciudadano. San Jose de Costa Rica: Imprenta Nacional, 1956.

Flores Magón, Ricardo. Epistolario revolucionario e íntimo. Mexico: Grupo Cultural Ricardo Flores Magón, 1925.

―――. Sembrando ideas. Mexico: Grupo Cultural Ricardo Flores Magón, 1923.

―――, and Jesús Flores Magón. Batalla a la dictadura. Mexico: Empresas Editoriales, 1948.

Foreign Policy Association. Problemas de la nueva Cuba. New York: Commission on Cuban Affairs, 1935.

Foster, William Z. Outline of Political History of the Americas. New York: International Publishers, 1951.

Francovich, Guillermo. El pensamiento boliviano en el siglo XX. Mexico: Fondo de Cultura Económica, 1956.

Frei, Eduardo. La verdad tiene su hora. Santiago: Editorial del Pacífico, 1958. Sixth edition.

Freyre, Gilberto. Interpretación del Brasil. Mexico: Fondo de Cultura Económica, 1945. (New World in the Tropics, The Culture of Modern Brazil. New York: Knopf, 1959.)

Frondizi, Arturo. "Mensaje para veinte millones de argentinos," in La América Latina de Hoy. New York: Ronald Press, 1961.

Frugoni, Emilio. Génesis, esencia y fundamentos del socialismo. Buenos Aires: Americalee, 1947. Two vols.

Fuentes Díaz, Vicente. Los partidos políticos en México. Mexico, 1954. Two vols.

Furtado, Celso. Formação económica do Brasil. Rio de Janeiro: Fondo de Cultura, 1959. (Economic Growth of Brazil, A Survey from Colonial to Modern Times. Berkeley: University of California Press, 1963.)

Galarza, Ernesto. Journey Behind the News. Washington, D.C.: Pan American Union, 1946.

———. Memorandum. Washington, D.C.: Pan American Union, 1946. Mimeographed document.

García Treviño, Rodrigo. La ingerencia rusa en México y Sudamérica. Mexico: Editorial América, 1959.

———. "Los sindicatos en la administración de las industrias," *Revista de Economía*, Vol. III, No. 1–2. Mexico, 1939.

Ghitor, Eduardo. La bancarrota del anarcosindicalismo. Montevideo, Ministerio de Educacion. 1932.

Gil Fortul, José. Historia constitucional de Venezuela. Caracas, Ministerio de Educacion. n.d.

Giménez, Angel M. Páginas de historia del movimiento social en la República Argentina. Buenos Aires: Vanguardia, 1927.

Goldenberg, Boris. The Cuban Revolution and Latin America. New York: Praeger, 1965.

Gompers, Samuel. Setenta años de vida y trabajo. Mexico: Intercontinental, 1956. (Seventy Years of Life and Work. New York: Dutton, 1957.)

Gonnard, René. Essai sur l'histoire de l'émigration. Paris: Valois, 1928.

González Calzada, Manuel. Las Casas, el procurador de los indios. Mexico: Talleres Gráficos de la Nación, 1948.

González Casanova, Pablo. Una utopía en América. Mexico: El Colegio de México, 1953.

González Prada, Manuel. La anarquía. Santiago: Ercilla, 1936.

———. Antología del pensamiento democrático americano: Manuel González Prada. Mexico: Imprenta Universitaria, 1945.

Gorkín, Julián, and Marcel Pivert, Gustavo Regler, and Víctor Serge. La GPU prepara un nuevo crimen. Mexico, 1942.

Grela, Plácido. El grito de Alcorta. Buenos Aires: Tierra Nuestra, 1958.

Guilbert, Yves. Castro, l'infidèle. Paris: Table Ronde, 1961.

Gutiérrez, B. M. Las administraciones obreras en las industrias. Mexico, 1939.

Halperin, Ernst. Nationalism and Communism in Chile. Cambridge, Mass.: M.I.T. Press, 1965.

Harbison, Frederick H. Preface to A. A. Liveright, Union Leadership Training. New York, 1961.

Haya de la Torre, Víctor Raúl. El antiimperialismo y el Apra. Santiago: Ercilla, 1936. Second edition.
———. Pensamiento político de Haya de la Torre. Lima: Pueblo, 1961. Five vols.
———. Sobre la historia del comunismo en América Latina y una rectificación. Mexico: Cuadernos Americanos, 1955.
———. Treinta años de aprismo. Mexico: Fondo de Cultura Económica. 1956.
Henriques, Affonso. Vargas o maquiavélico. Sao Paulo: Palacio do Livro, 1961.
Henriquez Ureña, Pedro. Historia de la cultura en la América Hispana. Mexico: Fondo de Cultura Económica, 1949.
———. A Concise History of Latin American Culture. New York: Praeger, 1966.
Hering, Ernesto. Los Fúcar. Mexico: Fondo de Cultura Económica, 1944.
Heysen, Luis E. Las poblaciones indígenas como problema. Mexico: ORIT, 1957.
Hirschman, Albert O. "Ideologies of Economic Development in Latin America," in Latin American Issues. New York: Twentieth Century Fund, 1961.
Horowitz, I. L. Revolution in Brazil. New York: Dutton, 1964.
Ingenieros, José. Sociología argentina. Buenos Aires: Losada, 1946.
Instituto de Historia de la Academia de Ciencias de la URSS. Historia de los países coloniales y dependientes. Santiago: Nueva América, 1941.
ILO (International Labor Organization, or Organización Internacional del Trabajo.) Condiciones de vida y de trabajo de las poblaciones indígenas de América Latina. Geneva, 1949.
———. Informe sobre las Conferencias del Trabajo de los Estados de América miembros de la OIT. Geneva, 1950.
———. Labour Courts in Latin America. Geneva, 1949.
———. Legislación social de América Latina. Geneva, 1928.
———. Minimum Wages in Latin America. Geneva, 1954.
———. Poblaciones indígenas. Geneva, 1953.
———. Los problemas del trabajo en Bolivia. Montreal, 1943.
Islas García, Luis. Trinidad Sánchez Santos. Mexico: Jus, 1945.
L'Itinérant (pseud.). "Croquis de l'Amérique Latine," La Révolution Proletarienne, October 1961. Paris.
James, Daniel. Cuba, The First Soviet Satellite in the Americas. New York: Avon Books, 1961.
———. Red Design for the Americas. New York: John Day Co., 1954.
Jane, Cecil. Libertad y despotismo en la América Hispana. Madrid: Editorial España, 1930.
Jarlot, Georges. "El padre Alberto Hurtado, S.J., iniciador social en Chile," Política y Espíritu, No. 151 (February 1, 1956). Santiago.
Jerez Horta, Alberto. Libertad y unidad sindical. Santiago: Editorial Universitaria, 1956.
Jobet, Julio César. Ensayo crítico del desarrolla económico-social de Chile. Santiago: Editorial Universitaria, 1955.

———. Los precursores del pensamiento social de Chile. Santiago: Editorial Universitaria, 1955. Two vols.

———. Recabarren, Los orígines del movimiento obrero y del socialismo chileno. Santiago: Prensa Latinoamericana, 1955.

———. Santiago Arcos Arlegui y la Sociedad de la Igualdad. Santiago: Cultura, 1942.

———. El socialismo en Chile. Santiago: Asociación por la Libertad de la Cultura, 1956.

Johnson, John J. The Military and Society in Latin America. Stanford: Stanford University Press, 1964.

———. Political Change in Latin America, The Emergence of the Middle Sectors. Stanford: Stanford University Press, 1959.

Juan, Jorge, and Antonio Ulloa. Noticias secretas de América. London: R. Taylor, 1926.

Julien, Claude. La révolution cubaine. Paris: Julliard, 1961.

Justo, Juan B. "Discurso en la Cámara de Diputados del 19 de junio de 1913," *Afirmación,* May 31, 1961. Buenos Aires.

———. Internacionalismo y patria. Buenos Aires: Vanguardia, 1933.

———. Teoría y práctica de la historia. Buenos Aires: Vanguardia, 1932.

Kantor, Harry. Ideología y programa del movimiento aprista. Mexico: Humanismo, 1955. (Ideology and Program of the Peruvian Aprista Movement. New York: Octagon, 1966. Rev. ed.)

———. "También hay democracia en el Caribe," *Combate,* March-April 1960. San José de Costa Rica.

Kantor, Harry, and Chang-Rodríguez, Eugenio. La América Latina de hoy, New York: The Ronald Press, 1961.

Keller R., Carlos. "Chile," in El pensamiento económico latinoamericano. Mexico: Fondo de Cultura Económica, 1945.

Krehm, William. Democracia y tiranías en el Caribe. Mexico: Unión Democrática Centroamericana, 1949.

Krickeberg, Walter. Las antiguas culturas mexicanas. Mexico: Fondo de Cultura Económica, 1961. (First published as Altmexikanische Kulturen. Berlin: Safari-Verlag, 1956.)

Lagos Valenzuela, Tulio. Bosquejo histórico del movimiento obrero en Chile. Santiago: Esfuerzo, 1941.

Larsen, Einar. Rusia avanza. Mexico: Difusora del Libro, 1949.

Latinoamérica mas allá de sus fronteras. San Jose de Costa Rica: Editorial Combate, 1960.

Laurat, Lucien. Du Komintern au Kominform. Paris: Plon, 1951.

Ledit, Joseph. Le front des pauvres. Montreal: Fides, 1954.

Lenin, V. I. Imperialism, The Highest Stage of Capitalism. New York: International Publishers, 1940.

Levene, Ricardo. Historia de las ideas sociales argentinos. Buenos Aires: Espasa-Calpe, 1947.

Lieuwen, Edwin. Arms and Politics in Latin America. New York: Praeger, 1960.

———. Generals vs. Presidents, Neomilitarism in Latin America. New York: Praeger, 1964.

Lipschutz, Alejandro. El indoamericanismo y el problema racial en las Américas. Santiago: Nascimento, 1944.

Loewenstein, Karl. Brazil Under Vargas. New York: Macmillan, 1942.

Lombardo Toledano, Vicente. La CTAL ante la guerra y ante la postguerra. Mexico, 1945.

———. Teoría y práctica del movimiento sindical mexicano. Mexico: Ediciones del Magisterio, 1961.

———. "La tercera posición en el movimiento obrero latinoamericano," *Siempre,* July 12, 1961. Mexico.

Longuet, Jean. "Le mouvement socialiste international," in Encyclopédie Socialiste. Paris: Quillet, 1913.

López, Matilde Elena. Masferrer, alto pensador de Centro América. Guatemala: Ministerio de Educación Pública, 1954.

López Aparicio, Alfonso. El movimiento obrero en México. Mexico: Jus, 1952.

Lorwin, Lewis L. Historia del internacionalismo obrero. Santiago: Ercilla, 1937. (Labor and Internationalism. New York: Macmillan, 1929.)

Losovsky, A. El movimiento sindical latinoamericano, sus virtudes y sus defectos. Montevideo, 1929.

Lugon, C. La République communiste chrétienne des Guaranis. Paris: Editions Ouvrières, 1949.

Lumen, Enrique. La revolución cubana. Mexico: Botas, 1934.

Lux-Würm, Pierre. Le Péronisme. Paris: Librairie Générale de Droit et de Jurisprudence, 1965.

MacDonald, Austin F. Latin American Politics and Government. New York: Crowell, 1954.

Machado Ribas, Lincoln. Movimientos revolucionarios en las colonias de América. Buenos Aires: Claridad, 1940.

Magnet, Alejandro. Nuestros vecinos justicialistas. Santiago: Editorial del Pacífico, 1953.

Máiztegui, Humberto. "El socialismo en América Latina," *Combate,* September-October 1958. San Jose de Costa Rica.

Maldonado Jarrín, Gonzalo. El sindicalismo y el cooperativismo. Quito, 1943.

Mariátegui, José Carlos. Pensadores en América—Mariátegui. Mexico: Imprenta Universitaria, 1937.

———. Siete ensayos de interpretación de la realidad peruana. Santiago: Editorial Universitaria, 1955.

Martínez de la Torre, Ricardo. De la reforma universitaria al partido socialista. Lima: Frente, 1943.

Masferrer, Alberto. Páginas escogidas. San Salvador: Ministerio de Cultura, 1953.

———. En torno a Masferrer. San Salvador: Ministerio de Cultura, 1956.

Maspero, Emilio. "L'Amérique Latine entre dans une phase decisive," *Labor,* No. 3, 1961. Brussels.

Matthews, Herbert L. The Cuban Story. New York: Braziller, 1961.

Mejía Fernández, Miguel. El problema del trabajo forzado en América Latina. Mexico: Instituto de Investigaciones Sociales, n.d.

Memoria del I Congreso Mexicano de Derecho Industrial. Mexico: Talleres Gráficos de la Nación, 1934.

Mendieta y Núñez, Lucio. El derecho social. Mexico: Porrúa, 1960.

Message of the Workmen and Artisans' Confederation of the Federal District to the AFL and all the Labor Federations of America. Caracas: Tipografía Moderna, 1923.

Mezerick, A. F. "Cuba and the United States," *International Review Service,* VI, No. 60 (1960). New York.

Millon, Robert Paul. Mexican Marxist—Vicente Lombardo Toledano. Chapel Hill: University of North Carolina Press, 1966.

Mills, C. Wright. Listen, Yankee. New York: McGraw-Hill, 1960.

Monge, Luis Alberto. "¿Esperanza o frustración?," *Cuadernos,* September 1961. Paris.

———. Interpretándonos. Mexico: ORIT, 1957.

Montefilpo Carvallo, Reinaldo. "Rafael Barret y su genio evangélico," *Alcor,* November-December 1961. Asuncion.

Monteforte Toledo, Mario. Partidos políticos de Iberoamerica. Mexico: Instituto de Investigaciones Sociales, 1961.

Moulian, Tomás. Estudio sobre Chile. Santiago: Orbe, 1965.

Movimiento Nacionalista Revolucionario. Programa de gobierno 1960–1964. La Paz, 1960.

Navarro Bolandi, Hugo. La generación del 48. Mexico: Humanismo, 1957.

———. José Figueres en la evolución de Costa Rica. Mexico: Quirós, 1953.

Neale Silva, Eduardo. Horizonte humano. Mexico: Fondo de Cultura Económica, 1960.

Nehru, Jawaharlal. Ma vie et mes prisons. Paris: Donoël, 1952.

Nettlau, Max. "La internacional en Buenos Aires en 1872," *La Protesta,* November 15, 1926. Buenos Aires.

Oddone, Jacinto. La burguesía terrateniente argentina. Buenos Aires: Ediciones Populares Argentinas, 1956.

———. Gremialismo proletario. Buenos Aires: Vanguardia, 1949.

———. Historia del socialismo argentino. Buenos Aires: Vanguardia, 1934. Two vols.

Orego, Antenor. Pueblo-Continente. Lima, 1957.

ORIT (Organización Regional Interamericana de Trabajadores). "Las cooperativas y el movimiento sindical," *Mundo del Trabajo Libre,* January 1962. Mexico.

————. Las cooperativas y el movimiento sindical. Mexico, n.d.

————. Datos y cifras. July-August 1955, November-December 1957. Mexico.

————. Documentos para la historia—Venezuela. Mexico, 1955.

————. Esta es la ORIT. Mexico, 1956.

————. Informe del V Congreso Continental. Mexico, 1961.

————. *Noticiario Obrero Interamericano,* October 31, 1961. Mexico.

Ortega y Gasset, José. Historia como sistema. Madrid: Revista de Occidente, 1941.

Osegueda, Raúl. Operación Guatemala OK. Mexico: América Nueva, 1955.

Ots Capdequí, J. M. España en América. Mexico: Fondo de Cultura Económica, 1959.

————. El estado español en las Indias. Mexico: Fondo de Cultura Económica, 1957. Third edition.

Page, Charles A. "Communism and the Labor Movement in Latin America," *The Virginia Quarterly Review,* Summer 1955. Charlottesville, Va.

Paiva, Víctor H. Apuntaciones obreras. Caracas: Latorre, 1939.

Palacios, Alfredo L. La defensa del valor humano. Buenos Aires: Claridad, 1939.

————. Estevan Echevarría, albacea del pensamiento de Mayo. Buenos Aires: Claridad, 1951. Third edition.

————. La justicia social. Buenos Aires: Claridad, 1954.

————. El nuevo derecho. Buenos Aires: Claridad, 1952.

————. Soberanía y socialización de industrias. Buenos Aires: Vanguardia, 1946.

Pan, Luis. Juan B. Justo y la fundación del Partido Socialista. Buenos Aires: Vanguardia, 1956.

Pan American Union. Desarrollo del movimiento cooperativo en América. Washington, D.C., 1954.

————. La población económicamente activa en América. Washington, D.C., 1964.

Pan American Union and Inter-American Statistical Institute. América en cifras. Washington, D.C., 1961. Eight mimeographed pamphlets.

Pareja Diezcanseco, Alfredo. "Tres afirmaciones de consciencia latinoamericano," *Cuadernos,* November 1961. Paris.

Partido Comunista del Uruguay. Bajo la bandera de Artigas. Montevideo: Justicia, n.d.

Partido Revolucionario Institucional. La mujer ante los problemas de México. Mexico: PRI, 1952.

Partido Socialista Popular. Los socialistas y la realidad cubana. Havana: PSP, 1944.

Paz Estenssoro, Víctor. "Bolivia," in Pensamiento económico latinoamericano. Mexico: Fondo de Cultura Económica, 1945.

————. "La revolución boliviana," *Tribuna Universitaria,* June 1957. Montevideo.

Peralva, Osvaldo. O retrato. Belo Horizonte: Editorial Itatiaia, 1960.

Peramás, José Manuel. La República de Platón y los guaraníes. Buenos Aires: Emecé, 1946.

Pereira Burgos, César A. "Socialismo y sindicalismo en Panamá," *Política*, January 1961. Caracas.

Pérez Leirós, Francisco. El movimiento sindical de América Latina. Buenos Aires: Vanguardia, 1941.

Pérez Salinas, J. Bernardo. "El momento obrero en AD," *Acción Democrática*, September 13, 1961. Caracas.

Phillips, R. Hart. Cuba, Island of Paradox. New York: McDowell, Obolensky, 1959.

Picón Salas, Mariano. De la conquista a la independencia. Mexico: Fondo de Cultura Económica, 1945. (Cultural History of Spanish America, From Conquest to Independence. Berkeley: The University of California Press, 1962.)

Pike, Fred B., ed. Freedom and Reform in Latin America. Notre Dame, Ind.: University of Notre Dame Press, 1959.

Pinto, Luis. Tiradentes. Rio de Janeiro: Editora Panamericana, n.d.

Pintos, Francisco R. Batlle y el proceso histórico del Uruguay. Montevideo: Panorama, 1940.

——. Historia del Uruguay. Montevideo: Pueblos Unidos, 1946.

Poblete Troncoso, Moisés. La economía agraria de América Latina y el trabajador campesino. Santiago: Universidad de Chile, 1953.

——. Evolución del derecho social en América. Santiago: Nascimento, 1942.

——. El movimiento de asociación profesional obrera en Chile. Mexico: El Colegio de México, 1945.

——. El movimiento obrero latinoamericano. Mexico: Fondo de Cultura Económica, 1946.

Poppino, Rollie. International Communism in Latin America. Glencoe, Ill.: The Free Press, 1964.

Prado, Jr., Caio. Historia Económica do Brasil. Sao Paulo: Editora Brasiliense, 1945.

Prebisch, Raúl. Hacia una dinámica del desarrollo latinoamericano. Mexico City, 1963.

Ramírez Necochea, Hernán. Historia del movimiento obrero en Chile. Santiago, n.d.

Ramos, Arthur. Las culturas negras en el Nuevo Mundo. Mexico: Fondo de Cultura Económica, 1943.

Ravines, Eudocio. The Yenan Way. New York: Scribners, 1951.

Reinhard, Marcel R. Histoire de la population mondiale de 1700 à 1948. Paris: Domat-Montchrestien, 1949.

Reiser, Pedro. L'Organisation Régionale Interamericaine des Travailleurs. Geneva: Droz, 1962.

Remorino, Jerónimo. La nueva legislación social argentina. Buenos Aires: Ministerio de Relaciones Exteriores y Culturales, 1953.

Report of the Second Inter-American Conference for Democracy and Freedom. New York, 1961.

Revueltas, José. Letter to *Excelsior,* June 20, 1950. Mexico.

Ricardo, Cassiano. La marcha hacia el Oeste. Mexico: Fondo de Cultura Económica, 1956.

Ricaurte, Antonio. "Breve storia del comunismo colombiano," *Corrispondenza Socialista,* February 8, 1959. Rome.

Riera Hernández, Mario. Historial obrero cubano 1574–1965. Miami: Rema Press, 1965.

Rivera, Diego. Lo que opina Diego Rivera sobre la pintura revolucionaria. Mexico, 1935.

Rivero Muñiz, José. Las tres sediciones de los vegueros en el siglo XVIII. Havana: Academia de la Historia, 1951.

Rodea, Marcelo M. Historia del movimiento obrero ferrocarrilero, 1890–1943. Mexico, 1944.

Rodrigues, Nina. Os Africanos no Brasil. Rio de Janeiro: Cia. Editoria Nacional, 1932.

Rodríguez Quesada, Carlos. David Salvador, prisionero de Castro. New York, n.d.

Rodríguez Vega, Eugenio. Apuntes para una sociología costarricense. San Jose de Costa Rica, 1953.

Rodríguez Vildósola, J. Preface to Pensamiento político de Haya de la Torre. Lima: Pueblo, 1961.

Romero, Ramón. Somoza, asesino de Sandino. Mexico: Patria y Libertad, n.d.

Rómulo Betancourt—Interpretación de su doctrina popular y democrática. Caracas: Summa, 1958.

Roy, M. N. Memoirs. Bombay: Allied Publishers, Private, Ltd., 1965.

Ruiz Franco, Arcadio. Fermentos de lucha, hambre y misería. Guatemala, 1950.

Saco, J. A. Historia de la esclavitud de los indios en el Nuevo Mundo. Havana: Cultural, S.A., 1932. Two vols.

———. Historia de la esclavitud de la raza africana en el Nuevo Mundo y en especial en los países hispanoamericanos. Havana: Cultural, S.A., 1938.

———. Historia de los repartimientos y encomiendas. Havana: Cultural, S.A., 1932.

Sáenz, Vicente. Rompiendo Cadenas. Mexico: Unión Democrática Centroamericana, 1951.

Salazar, Rosendo. Historia de las luchas proletarias de México, de 1923 a 1936. Mexico: Avante, 1938.

Sánchez, Luis Alberto. Prologue to Antología del pensamiento democrático americano—Manuel González Prada. Mexico: Imprenta Universitaria, 1945.

———. Los fundamentos de la historia americana. Buenos Aires, 1940.

———. El Perú, retrato de un país adolescente. Buenos Aires: Continente, 1958.

———. "La universidad en América Latina," *Américas,* issues from December 1961 to March 1962. Washington, D.C.

San Martín, Jr., Rafael. El grito de Sierra Maestra. Buenos Aires: Gure, 1960.
———. Reforma agraria. Buenos Aires: Agroamérica, 1960.
Santander, Silvano. Técnica de una traición. Montevideo, 1953.
Santillán, Diego Abad de. "Anarquismo," Gran enciclopedia argentina, Vol. I. Buenos Aires: Ediar, S.A., 1956.
———. "El anarquismo en la vida intelectual argentina," *Solidaridad Obrera,* August 24, 1961. Paris.
———. El movimiento anarquista en la Argentina. Buenos Aires, 1930.
Sarmiento, Domingo F. Antología del pensamiento democrático americano— Domingo Faustino Sarmiento. Mexico: Imprenta Universitaria, 1944.
Sartre, Jean-Paul. Sartre on Cuba. New York: Ballantyne Books, 1961.
Schmitt, Karl M., Communism in Mexico. Austin, Texas: University of Texas Press, 1965.
Schneider, Ronald M. Communism in Guatemala, 1944–1954. New York: Praeger, 1959.
Schwartz, Ernest. "Some Observations on Labor Organization in the Caribbean," in The Caribbean—Its Economy. Gainesville: University of Florida Press, 1954.
Selser, Gregorio. Sandino, general de hombres libres. Buenos Aires: Triángulo, 1959.
Seoane, Manuel. Obras apristas. Lima: Continente, 1957.
———. Las seis dimensiones de la revolución mundial. Santiago: Zig Zag, 1960.
Shub, Daniel. Lenin. New York: Doubleday, 1948.
Sierra, Justo. Evolución política del pueblo mexicano. Mexico: Imprenta Universitaria, 1948.
Silva Cristi, Adriana. Estudio sobre el trabajo a través de la historia. Santiago, 1936.
Simon, S. Fanny. "Anarquismo y anarcosindicalismo en América del Sur," *Mundo Libre,* No. 54 (July 1946). Mexico.
Situação Social da América Latina. Rio de Janeiro: Centro Latino Americano de Pesquisas em Ciências Sociais, 1965.
Smith, Robert F. The United States and Cuba. New York: Bookman Associates, 1960.
Snow, Sinclair. The Pan-American Federation of Labor. Durham, N.C.: Duke University Press, 1964.
Soustelle, Jacques. La vida cotidiana de los aztecas. Mexico: Fondo de Cultura Económica, 1957. (The Daily Life of the Aztecs, on the Eve of the Spanish Conquest. London: Weidenfeld and Nicolson, 1961.)
Stalin, Josef. Le marxisme et la question nationale et coloniale. Paris: Editions Sociales Internationales, 1937.
Stark, Harry. Modern Latin America. Coral Gables, Fla.: University of Miami Press, 1957.
Szulc, Tad. Twilight of the Tyrants. New York: Holt, 1959.
Taft, Philip. The AFL in the Time of Gompers. New York: Harper, 1957.
Tannenbaum, Frank. "La revolución agraria mexicana," *Problemas agrícolas e*

industriales de México, Vol. 4, No. 2 (April-June 1952). Mexico. (The Mexican Agrarian Revolution. New York, Macmillan, 1929.)

Tejera, Humberto. Maestros indoibéricos. Mexico: Minerva, n.d.

Tella, Torcuato S. di. "Tensiones sociales en los países de la periferia," *Revista de la Universidad de Buenos Aires,* January-March 1961. Buenos Aires.

Tieffenberg, David. La legislación obrera en el régimen peronista. Buenos Aires: Ediciones Populares Argentinas, 1956.

Toledo, Domingo P. de. México en la obra de Marx y Engels. Mexico: Fondo de Cultura Económica, 1939.

Toriello, Guillermo. La batalla de Guatemala. Mexico: Cuadernos Americanos, 1955.

Tourret, F. "L'ère atomique, âge d'or ou apocalypse?," *Preuves,* July 1954. Paris.

Tovar, Antonio. Catálago de las lenguas de América del Sur. Buenos Aires: Sudamericana, 1961.

Townsend Ezcurra, Andrés. Prologue to Volume III of Pensamiento político de Haya de la Torre. Lima: Pueblo, 1961.

Un trentenio di attività anarchica. Casena (Forli): L'Antistato, 1953.

Treviño, Ricardo. El espionaje comunista y la evolución doctrinaria del movimiento obrero en México. Mexico, 1952.

UNESCO. La información en el mundo. Paris, 1956.

United Nations. Capital extranjero en América Latina. New York: United Nations, 1954.

Uribe, Antonio José. La defensa social. Bogota: Imprenta Nacional, 1929.

Urquidi, Víctor L. Viabilidad económica de América Latina. Mexico: Fondo de Cultura Económica, 1962. (The Challenge of Development in Latin America. New York: Praeger, 1964.)

Valcárcel, Daniel. La rebelión de Tupac Amaru. Mexico: Fondo de Cultura Económica, 1947.

Valle, Rafael Heliodoro. Historia de las ideas contemporáneas en Centro América. Mexico: Fondo de Cultura Económica, 1960.

Valle Iberlucea, Enrique del. Discursos parlamentarios. Valencia: Prometeo, n.d.

Velázquez, Fidel. Dos posturas ante el pueblo de México—la CTM lucha por el pan y la justicia, la clase patronal mantiene su egoísmo. Mexico: Editorial Cuauhtémoc, 1954.

Vélez, Antonio. "Las relaciones entre las dos Américas," *Examen,* August 1961. Mexico.

Vianna, Oliveira. As novas diretrizes de política social. Rio de Janeiro: Servicio de Estadística de Providência e Trabalho, 1939.

Vianna, Segadas. O sindicato no Brasil. Rio de Janeiro: Ministerio do Trabalho, Industria e Comercio, 1953.

Villanueva del Campo, Armando. "Partidos democráticos revolucionarios en indoamérica," *Combate,* September 1961 through February 1962. San José de Costa Rica.

Volman, Sacha. "El general Batista y la revolución 'comunista,'" *Combate,* July-August 1958. San Jose de Costa Rica.

Waiss, Oscar. Nacionalismo y socialismo en América Latina. Santiago: Prensa Latinoamericana, 1954.

Weyl, Nathaniel. Red Star Over Cuba. New York: Devin Adair Co., 1960.

Wolfe, Bertram D. Diego Rivera—His Life and Times. New York: Knopf, 1939.

Woodcock, George. Anarchism. London: Penguin Books, 1963.

World Federation of Trade Unions. Boletín. January and June 1951.

Zavala, Silvio. Filosofía de la conquista. Mexico: Fondo de Cultura Económica, 1946.

Zea, Leopoldo. Dos etapas del pensamiento en Hispanoamérica—Del romanticismo al positivismo. Mexico: El Colegio de México, 1949. (The Latin American Mind. Norman, Okla.: The University of Oklahoma Press, 1963.)

Index

Index